Fodor's

SOUTH
FLORIDA

Excerpted from *Fodor's Florida*

WELCOME TO SOUTH FLORIDA

From the resorts of Palm Beach to the humblest gingerbread cottages in the Keys, South Florida has something for everyone—romantic retreats for couples, fun activities for families, and hot spots for singles. Whether you're taking a thrilling airboat ride through the Everglades, visiting a world-class art museum, snorkeling off Key Largo, or dancing the night away in a glitzy Miami club, there is plenty to do. Beautiful beaches beckon, so when you're not dining in a great restaurant or playing a round of golf, grab a towel and relax in the tropical warmth.

TOP REASONS TO GO

★ **Miami:** A vibrant, multicultural metropolis that buzzes both day and night.

★ **Palm Beach:** Glamorous and sophisticated, the city offers great dining and shopping.

★ **Beaches:** Sceney in South Beach, buzzing in Fort Lauderdale, quieter in the Keys.

★ **The Everglades:** The "river of grass" is home to crocodiles, manatees, and panthers.

★ **Fort Lauderdale:** A glittering and revitalized downtown fronts a gorgeous beach.

★ **Key West:** Quirky, fun, and tacky, it's both family-friendly and decidedly not.

Fodor's SOUTH FLORIDA

Design: Tina Malaney, *Associate Art Director*

Photography: Jennifer Arnow, *Senior Photo Editor*

Maps: Rebecca Baer, *Senior Map Editor*; David Lindroth, Mark Stroud (Moon Street Cartography), *Cartographers*

Production: Angela L. McLean, *Senior Production Manager*; Jennifer DePrima, *Editorial Production Manager*

Sales: Jacqueline Lebow, *Sales Director*

Business & Operations: Chuck Hoover, *Chief Marketing Officer*; Joy Lai, *Vice President and General Manager*; Stephen Horowitz, *Head of Business Development and Partnerships*

Writers: Lynne Helm, Jill Martin, Galena Mosovich, Paul Rubio

Editor: Douglas Stallings

Production Editor: Elyse Rozelle

14th Edition

ISBN 978–1–101–88018–0

ISSN 1526–2219

All details in this book are based on information supplied to us at press time. Always confirm information when it matters, especially if you're making a detour to visit a specific place. Fodor's expressly disclaims any liability, loss, or risk, personal or otherwise, that is incurred as a consequence of the use of any of the contents of this book.

SPECIAL SALES

This book is available at special discounts for bulk purchases for sales promotions or premiums. For more information, e-mail specialmarkets@penguinrandomhouse.com.

PRINTED IN THE UNITED STATES OF AMERICA

10 9 8 7 6 5 4 3 2 1

CONTENTS

Fodor's Features

CONTENTS

MAPS

ABOUT THIS GUIDE

Fodor's Recommendations

Everything in this guide is worth doing—we don't cover what isn't—but exceptional sights, hotels, and restaurants are recognized with additional accolades. Fodor's Choice★ indicates our top recommendations. Care to nominate a new place? Visit Fodors.com/contact-us.

Trip Costs

We list prices wherever possible to help you budget well. Hotel and restaurant price categories from $ to $$$$ are noted alongside each recommendation. For hotels, we include the lowest cost of a standard double room in high season. For restaurants, we cite the average price of a main course at dinner or, if dinner isn't served, at lunch. For attractions, we always list adult admission fees; discounts are usually available for children, students, and senior citizens.

Hotels

Our local writers vet every hotel to recommend the best overnights in each price category, from budget to expensive. Unless otherwise specified, you can expect private bath, phone, and TV in your room. *For full hotel information, visit Fodors.com.*

Top Picks	Hotels &
★ Fodor's Choice	Restaurants

Listings

✉	Address	🏨	Hotel
✉	Branch address	↘	Number of rooms
☎	Telephone	¶◎¶	Meal plans
🖶	Fax	W	Restaurant
⊕	Website	⌛	Reservations
✎	E-mail	👔	Dress code
🎫	Admission fee	▭	No credit cards
⊙	Open/closed times	$	Price
Ⓜ	Subway		
⊕	Directions or Map coordinates		

Other

⇨	See also
☞	Take note
🏌	Golf facilities

Restaurants

Unless we state otherwise, restaurants are open for lunch and dinner daily. We mention dress code only when there's a specific requirement and reservations only when they're essential or not accepted. *For full restaurant information, visit Fodors.com.*

Credit Cards

The hotels and restaurants in this guide typically accept credit cards. If not, we'll say so.

EUGENE FODOR

Hungarian-born Eugene Fodor (1905–91) began his travel career as an interpreter on a French cruise ship. The experience inspired him to write *On the Continent* (1936), the first guidebook to receive annual updates and discuss a country's way of life as well as its sights. Fodor later joined the U.S. Army and worked for the OSS in World War II. After the war, he kept up his intelligence work while expanding his guidebook series. During the Cold War, many guides were written by fellow agents who understood the value of insider information. Today's guides continue Fodor's legacy by providing travelers with timely coverage, insider tips, and cultural context.

EXPERIENCE
SOUTH FLORIDA

WHAT'S WHERE

The following numbers refer to chapters.

2 Miami and Miami Beach. Greater Miami is hot—and we're not just talking about the weather. Art deco buildings and balmy beaches set the scene. Vacations here are as much about lifestyle as locale, so prepare for power shopping, club hopping, and decadent dining.

3 The Everglades. Covering more than 1.5 million acres, the fabled "River of Grass" is the state's greatest natural treasure. Biscayne National Park (95% of which is underwater) runs a close second. It's the largest marine park in the United States.

4 The Florida Keys. This slender necklace of landfalls, strung together by a 113-mile highway, marks the southern edge of the continental United States. It's nirvana for anglers, divers, literature lovers, and Jimmy Buffett wannabes.

5 Fort Lauderdale. The town *Where the Boys Are* has grown up. The beaches that first attracted college kids are now complemented by luxe lodgings and upscale entertainment options.

6 Palm Beach and the Treasure Coast. This area scores points for diversity. Palm Beach and environs are famous for their golden sand and glitzy residents, whereas the Treasure Coast has unspoiled natural delights.

GEORGIA

ATLANTIC OCEAN

Chattahoochee 19
Quincy
Osceola National Forest
Amelia Island
95
TALLAHASSEE
Jacksonville
65
319 98
Perry
Lake City
St. Mary's R.
St. Augustine
98
19
75
Gainesville
301
Ocala National Forest
Eastpoint
Apalachicola
41
Ocala
1
40
Daytona Beach
Cedar Keys
27
4
Titusville
Kennedy Space Center
Orlando 50
Cape Canaveral
528
Cocoa Beach
Walt Disney World
Kissimmee
Merritt Island
Tarpon Springs
75
Melbourne
Clearwater
4
Winter Haven
Florida's Turnpike
Sebastian Inlet Recreation Area
Tampa
95
St. Petersburg
Vero Beach
Tampa Bay
27
Fort Pierce
Bradenton
Kissimmee R.
Hutchinson Island
Sarasota
70
Venice
75
Lake Okeechobee
Singer Island
Peace R.
West Palm Beach
6
Caloosahatchee R.
80
Palm Beach
Cape Coral
Fort Myers
Big Cypress National Preserve
27
Boca Raton
Captiva Island
Sanibel Island
5
Fort Lauderdale
Naples
75
2
Miami Beach
Everglades City
41
Miami
Biscayne Bay
Everglades National Park
Florida City
Biscayne National Park
3
9336
Homestead
Cape Sable
Key Largo
Florida Bay
1 KEYS
Key West
4
FLORIDA

0   50 miles
0   75 kilometers

WHEN TO GO

South Florida is a year-round vacation venue, but it divides the calendar into regional tourism seasons. Holidays and school breaks are major factors. However, the clincher is weather, with the milder months being designated as peak periods.

High season starts with the run-up to Christmas and continues through Easter. Snowbirds migrate down then to escape frosty weather back home, and festival-goers flock in because major events are held this time of year to avoid summer's searing heat and high humidity. Winter is also the time to visit the Everglades, as temperatures, mosquito activity, and water levels are all lower (making wildlife easier to spot).

Climate
Florida is rightly called the Sunshine State, but it could also be dubbed the "Humid State." From June through September, 90% humidity levels aren't uncommon. Nor are accompanying afternoon thunderstorms; in fact, more than half of the state's rain falls during these months, although these afternoon showers usually pass as quickly as they arrive. Florida's two-sided coastline also makes it a target for tropical storms. Hurricane season officially begins June 1 and ends November 30.

MIAMI EVENTS

HOME RUN HOMETOWN
Marlins Park opened up during the 2012 baseball season. Catch baseball games and bask in the team's sparkling digs, which made a huge splash with a L.E.E.D.-certified retractable roof, air-conditioning, and glass walls showcasing panoramic views of the Miami skyline. ⊕ *miami.marlins.mlb.com*

LITTLE HAVANA
Each winter during **Carnaval Miami,** salsa tunes blare and the smell of spicy chorizo fills the air on Calle Ocho, the commercial thoroughfare and heart of Miami's Little Havana. The roaring street festival, which culminates in the world's longest conga line, is the last of 10 events comprising the Latin-spiked Carnaval.

QUINTESSENTIAL SOUTH FLORIDA

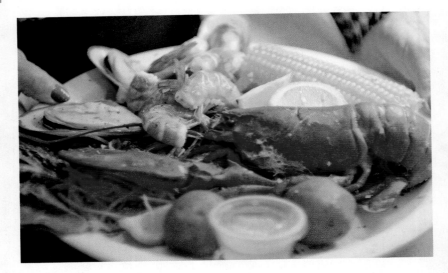

Food, Glorious Food

Geography and gastronomy go hand in hand in Florida. Seafood is a staple almost everywhere, yet the way it is prepared changes considerably as you maneuver around the state. In South Florida, menus highlight "Floribbean" cuisine, which marries Floridian, Caribbean, and Latin flavors (think mahimahi with mango salsa), while inland, expect catfish, gator tails, and frogs' legs, all of which are best enjoyed at a Cracker-style fish camp with a side order of hush puppies. A trip to the Miami area is not complete without a taste of Cuban food. The cuisine is heavy, with pork dishes like *lechon asado* (roast suckling pig) but also *arroz con frijoles* (the staple side dish of rice and black beans) and *arroz con pollo* (chicken in sticky yellow rice). Key West is a mecca for lovers of key lime pie and conch fritters. Stone-crab claws can be savored from October through May.

The Arts

Floridians celebrate the arts year-round. Miami Beach's annual Art Basel festival draws 40,000 art lovers to town in the first week of December. Meanwhile, every April the Palm Beach International Film Festival hosts documentaries, shorts, and feature films. It's easy to catch a bit of bluegrass, country, classical, jazz, blues, or Americana with such festivals as the weeklong SunFest in West Palm Beach, or hear some of the nation's best jazz performers at the annual Hollywood Jazz Fest. Miami's ArtCenter South Florida is dedicated to incubating Florida's cultural life with programs for emerging artists of all ages. The oral tradition remains vibrant with the South Florida Storytelling Project, where live readings, storytelling slams, and festivals are free and open to the public through Florida Atlantic University in Boca Raton.

Florida is synonymous with sunshine: every year, more than 80 million visitors revel in it. However, the people who live here — a diverse group that includes Mouseketeers, millionaires, and rocket scientists — know that the state's appeal rests on more than those reliable rays.

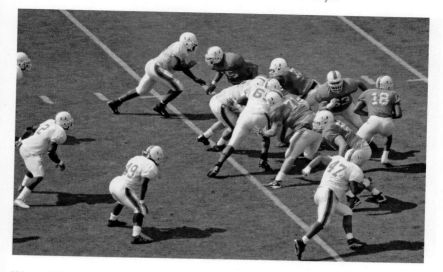

Water, Water Everywhere

Spanish explorer Ponce de León didn't find the Fountain of Youth when he swung through Florida in 1513. But if he'd lingered longer, he could have located 7,700 lakes, 1,700 rivers and creeks, and more than 700 springs. Over the centuries these have attracted American Indians, immigrants, opportunists, and countless outdoor adventurers. Boaters come for inland waterways and a 1,200-mile coast, and anglers are lured by more than 500 species of fish. (Florida claims 4,780 past and present world-record catches, so concocting elaborate "fish tales" may not be necessary.) Snorkelers and divers eager to see what lies beneath can get face time with the marine life that thrives in the world's third-largest coral reef or bone up on maritime history in underwater archaeological preserves (⊕ *www.museumsinthesea.com*). Back on dry land, all those beaches are pretty impressive, too.

Superlative Sports

South Florida is teeming with teams—and residents take the games they play very seriously. Baseball fans work themselves into a fever pitch: after all, the state has a pair of Major League franchises (the Miami Marlins christened a new stadium in 2012) and hosts another 13 in spring when the Grapefruit League goes to bat (3 alone are in the Palm Beach area). Those who prefer pigskin might cheer for the Miami Dolphins. The state is also home to top-rated college teams, like the Hurricanes. Basketball lovers feel the "Heat" in Miami, especially now that Dwyane Wade, Chris Bosh, and three-time MVP LeBron James are on the roster, and hockey fans stick around to watch the Florida Panthers. The Professional Golfers Association (PGA) is headquartered here as well, and two big annual tennis tournaments serve up fun in Miami and Delray Beach each winter.

SOUTH FLORIDA TOP ATTRACTIONS

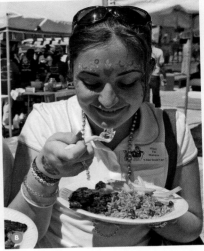

The Florida Keys

(A) Little wonder these 800-plus islands are a prime destination for divers and snorkelers: they boast the world's third-largest reef and aquarium-clear waters that are brimming with sea life. Under the turquoise-blue waters lies a colorful world populated by 60-plus species of coral and more than 500 species of fish, which means you can spot purple sea fans, blue tangs, yellowtail snappers, stoplight parrot fish, and more. Locals debate the premiere place for viewing them, but **John Pennekamp Coral Reef State Park** is high on everyone's list. Underwater excursions organized by park concessionaires let you put your best flipper forward *(Chapter 4)*.

South Beach

(B) You can't miss the distinctive forms, vibrant colors, and extravagant flourishes of SoBe's architectural gems. The world's largest concentration of art

deco edifices is right here; and the **Art Deco District,** with more than 800 buildings, has earned a spot on the National Register of Historic Places *(see "A Stroll Down Deco Lane")*. The 'hood also has enough "beautiful people" to qualify for the Register of Hippest Places. The glitterati, along with assorted vacationing hedonists, are drawn by trendy shops and a surfeit of celeb-studded clubs. Stellar eateries are the icing—make that the ganache—on South Beach's proverbial cake *(Chapter 2)*.

The Everglades

(C) No trip to southern Florida is complete without seeing the Everglades. At its heart is a river—50 miles wide but only 6 inches deep—flowing from Lake Okeechobee into Florida Bay. For an up-close look, speed demons can board an airboat that careens through the marshy waters. Purists, alternately, may placidly canoe or kayak within the boundaries of

Everglades National Park. Just remember to keep your hands in the boat. The critters that call this unique ecosystem home (alligators, Florida panthers, and cottonmouth snakes, for starters) can add real bite to your visit *(Chapter 3).*

Palm Beach

(D) If money could talk, you'd hardly be able to hear above the din in Palm Beach. The upper crust started residing there, during the winter months at least, back in the early 1900s. And today it remains a ritzy, glitzy enclave for both old money and the nouveau riche (a coterie led by "The Donald" himself). Simply put, Palm Beach is the sort of place where shopping is a full-time pursuit and people don't just wear Polo—they play it. Oooh and ahhh to your heart's content; then, for more conspicuous consumption, continue south on the aptly named Gold Coast to Boca Raton *(Chapter 6).*

Fort Lauderdale

(E) Mariners should set their compass for Fort Lauderdale (aka the Venice of America), where vessels from around the world moor along some two dozen finger isles between the beach and the mainland. Sailors can cruise Broward County's 300 miles of inland waterways by water taxi and tour boat, or bob around the Atlantic in a chartered yacht. If you're in a buying mood, come during October for the annual Fort Lauderdale International Boat Show. Billed as the world's largest, it has more than a billion dollars' worth of boats in every conceivable size, shape, and price range *(Chapter 5).*

IF YOU LIKE

Animals

The state has more than 1,200 different kinds of critters.

Alligators. "Gator spotting" in roadside waterways is itself a favorite pastime, but get a good close-up—and even hold a baby one—at **Everglades Gator Park** near Miami *(Chapter 3)*. Farther north, canoeing around the **Arthur R. Marshall Loxahatchee National Wildlife Refuge** or the **Jonathan Dickinson State Park** will almost definitely yield a sighting *(Chapter 6)*.

Birds. The state draws hundreds of species, from bald eagles and burrowing owls to bubblegum-pink flamingos, and the 2,000-mile **Great Florida Birding Trail** (⊕ *www.floridabirdingtrail.com*) with locations all over the Southeast helps you find them. For a squawkishly good time, feed parrots and budgies at **Lion Country Safari** *(Chapter 6)*.

Manatees. Florida's official marine mammals are nicknamed sea cows and resemble walruses, and you can scan canals for a telltale glassy "footprint" patch indicating one is swimming below; however, for a surefire viewing, visit the gentle giants who live at the **Miami Seaquarium** *(Chapter 2)*.

Sea Turtles. Ready for a late-night rendezvous with loggerheads that lumber ashore to lay eggs? Walks are organized throughout South Florida in June and July, but the **Treasure Coast** has a trove of spots *(Chapter 6)*. Elsewhere try the **Museum of Discovery and Science** in Fort Lauderdale *(Chapter 5)* and **Gumbo Limbo Nature Center** in Boca Raton *(Chapter 6)*.

Beaches

Each of us defines the "perfect" beach differently. But whether you want to swim, surf, lounge, or leer, Florida has one to suit your preference. Best of all, in this skinny state—bounded by the Atlantic *and* Gulf of Mexico—the coast is never more than 60 miles away.

South Beach, Miami. Over the past 20 years, no American beach has generated as much buzz as the one that hugs Ocean Drive, and it's easy to see why. Fringed with palms, backed by art deco architecture, and pulsating with urban energy, South Beach is the place to stretch out or strut *(Chapter 2)*.

Crandon Park Beach, Key Biscayne. You'll see why this beach is continually ranked among the nation's top ten. After 2 miles of lagoon-style beach, there's an amusement center and gardens to explore *(Chapter 2)*.

Delray Municipal Beach, Delray Beach. This super-popular stretch of sand dotted with trademark royal blue umbrellas intersects trendy Atlantic Avenue in the alluring Village by the Sea; delicious nosh and cute boutiques are a short stroll from the waves *(Chapter 6)*.

Matheson Hammock Park Beach, Miami. Pack a picnic and bring the family to the safe, warm waters of this palm-tree fringed beach. Loll in the balmy breezes as you take in the amazing views or hit up the nature trails, full-service marina, and restaurant built into a historic coral rock building *(Chapter 2)*.

Dry Tortugas National Park, the Florida Keys. Forget lazily reading a book on these shores. Come here if you're looking for a beach where you can dive in—literally. Set among coral reefs, this cluster of seven islands (accessible only by boat or seaplane) offers outstanding snorkeling and diving *(Chapter 4)*.

Golf

With more than 1,200 courses (and counting), Florida has more greens than any other state in the Union. Palm Beach County alone is home to more than 140 courses. The trend began in 1897, when Florida's first golf course opened in Palm Beach at The Breakers, whose guests included the Rockefellers, Vanderbilts, and Astors. In Southeast Florida there are enough golf courses to allow you to play a new course every week for two years. Even if you're new to the game, you can tee up with a PGA pro for a lesson and soak in the beauty of Florida's tropical flora from one of the country's most exquisitely designed courses. Floridians play golf 12 months out of the year, although the courses are less crowded (and cheaper) between May and October.

Boca Raton Resort & Club. This scenic course has some of the most exotic terrain, water features, and floral landscapes outside of Hawaii *(Chapter 6)*.

The Breakers, Palm Beach. The 70-par Ocean Course offers spectacular views of the Atlantic and challenging shots on 140 acres *(Chapter 6)*.

Trump National Doral Miami. Home of the "Blue Monster": Doral's famous 18th hole has been ranked the best in South Florida. The par-4 hole leaves little room for error with bunkers aplenty and a green that slopes toward water *(Chapter 2)*.

PGA National Resort & Spa. Its five championship courses were all done by master designers, plus the pro tour's Honda Classic is held here *(Chapter 6)*.

Scenic Views

Florida is more than its sunsets, from aerial panoramic views to architectural wonders to nature's many surprises. Here are some views we find delightful.

Everglades National Park, from the tower on Shark Valley loop. This 50-foot observation tower, about 35 miles from downtown Miami, yields a splendid panorama of the wide River of Grass as it sweeps southward toward the Gulf of Mexico. To get to the tower, you can hike or take the tram *(Chapter 3)*.

Ocean Drive in the Art Deco District, Miami Beach. Feast your eyes on brilliantly restored vintage art deco hotels at every turn. The palm-lined beachfront that the hotels are set along hops 24 hours a day. And when you're finished looking at the colorful hotels, you can catch the sea of colorful swimsuits parading by on nearby South Beach *(see "A Stroll Down Deco Lane" in Chapter 2)*.

The Mansions of Palm Beach, from South Ocean Boulevard. Some old, some new. Some ginormous—and the very definition of over-the-top—others a bit more subdued. But all are incredible, particularly the historic Mediterranean-inspired ones built by Addison Mizner and his Gilded Age peers *(Chapter 6)*.

Sunset scene at Mallory Square, Key West. Don't be surprised if someone claps for the sunset in Key West. It's that amazing, and those watching can't help but applaud. Along the waterfront the sunset draws street performers, vendors, and thousands of onlookers to the dock at Mallory Square. Fun attractions, like the Florida Keys Aquarium Encounters, are nearby *(Chapter 4)*.

GREAT ITINERARIES

2 to 3 Days: Gold Coast and Treasure Coast

The opulent mansions of Palm Beach's Ocean Boulevard give you a glimpse of how the richer half lives. For exclusive boutique shopping, art gallery browsing, and glittery sightseeing, sybarites should wander down "The Avenue" (that's Worth Avenue to non–Palm Beachers). The sporty set will find dozens of places to tee up (hardly surprising given that the PGA is based here), along with tennis courts, polo clubs, and even a croquet center. Those who'd like to see more of the Gold Coast can continue traveling south through Boca Raton to Fort Lauderdale (known as the "Yachting Capital of the World"). But to balance the highbrow with the low-key, turn northward for a tour of the Treasure Coast. You can also look for the sea turtles that lay their own little treasures in the sands from May through October.

2 to 3 Days: Miami Area

Greater Miami lays claim to the country's most celebrated strand—South Beach—and lingering on it tops most tourist itineraries. (The Ocean Drive section, lined with edgy clubs, boutiques, and eateries, is where the see-and-be-seen crowd gathers.) Once you've checked out the candy-colored art deco architecture, park yourself to ogle the parade of stylish people, or join them by browsing Lincoln Road Mall, and admire its latest addition, the gleaming Frank Gehry–designed New World Symphony. Later, merengue over to Calle Ocho, the epicenter of Miami's Cuban community. Elsewhere in the area, Coconut Grove, Coral Gables, and the Miami Design District (an 18-block area crammed with showrooms and galleries) also warrant a visit. Miami is a convenient base for eco-excursions, too. You can

TIPS

Now that one-way airfares are commonplace, vacationers visiting multiple destinations can fly into and out of different airports. Rent a car in between, picking it up at your point of arrival and leaving it at your point of departure. If you do these itineraries as an entire vacation, your best bet is to fly into and out of Miami and rent a car from there.

take a day trip to the Everglades or get a spectacular view of the reefs from a glass-bottom boat in Biscayne National Park.

2 to 3 Days: Florida Keys

Some dream of "sailing away to Key Largo," others of "wasting away again in Margaritaville." In any case, almost everybody equates the Florida Keys with relaxation. And they live up to their reputation, thanks to offbeat attractions and that fabled come-as-you-are, do-as-you-please vibe. Key West, alternately known as the Conch Republic, is a good place to get initiated. The Old Town has a funky, laid-back feel. So take a leisurely walk; pay your regards to "Papa" (Hemingway, that is); then rent a moped to tour the rest of the island. Clear waters and abundant marine life make underwater activities another must. After scoping out the parrot fish, you can always head back into town and join local "Parrotheads" in a Jimmy Buffett sing-along. When retracing your route to the mainland, plan a last pit stop at Bahia Honda State Park (it has ranger-led activities plus the Keys' best beach) or John Pennekamp Coral Reef State Park, which offers unparalleled snorkeling and scuba-diving opportunities.

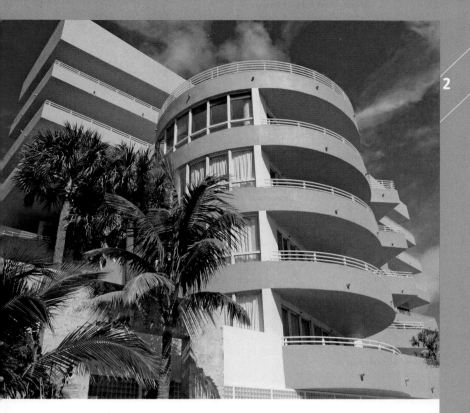

MIAMI AND
MIAMI BEACH

WELCOME TO MIAMI AND MIAMI BEACH

TOP REASONS TO GO

★ **The beach:** Miami Beach has been rated as one of the 10 best beaches in the world. White sand, warm water, and bronzed bodies everywhere provide just the right mix of relaxation and people-watching.

★ **Dining delights:** Miami's eclectic residents have transformed the city into a museum of epicurean wonders, ranging from Cuban and Argentine fare to fusion haute cuisine.

★ **Wee-hour parties:** A 24-hour liquor license means clubs stay open until 5 am, and after-parties go until noon the following day.

★ **Picture-perfect people:** Miami is a watering hole for the vain and beautiful of South America, Europe, and the Northeast. Watch them—or join them—as they strut their stuff and flaunt their tans on the white beds of renowned art deco hotels.

★ **Art Deco District:** Iconic pastels and neon lights accessorize the architecture that first put South Beach on the map in the 1930s.

1 Downtown. Weave through the glass-and-steel labyrinth of new condo construction to catch a game or a new exhibition.

2 Coconut Grove. Catch dinner and a movie, listen to live music, or cruise the bohemian shops.

3 Coral Gables. Dine and shop on family-friendly Miracle Mile, and take a driving tour of the surrounding neighborhoods.

4 Key Biscayne. Explore the pristine parks and stretches of award-winning beaches by boat, kayak, or foot.

5 Wynwood. Eat, shop, and gawk your way through this trendy, creative neighborhood north of Downtown.

6 Midtown. Experience yuppie life in this residential enclave chock-full of fabulous restaurants and lounges.

7 Design District. Browse the design showrooms and haute boutiques before dining at Miami's trendiest restaurants.

8 Little Haiti. Practice your Creole, sample Haitian food, and look for MiMo architecture around this interesting ethnic neighborhood.

9 Little Havana. Sip Cuban coffee, roll cigars,

2

N.W. 79th St.

N.W. 62nd St. · **LITTLE** 8
HAITI

N.W. 54th St.

Robert Frost Expwy. **DESIGN**
DISTRICT 7

N. 36th St. 6 **MIDTOWN**

WYNWOOD
N.W. 20th St. 5

DOWNTOWN 95

W. Flagler St.
S.W. 8th St.

LITTLE 9
HAVANA
S.W. 22nd St.

COCONUT
2 GROVE

Grove Isle
Coco Walk

Biscayne
Bay

4
KEY
BISCAYNE

JFK Causeway

↑**NORTH**
BEACH & 13
AVENTURA

MID- 11
BEACH

Julia Tuttle Causeway

Arsht
Center

Venetian Causeway 12 **SOUTH** 10
BEACH

Watson
Island

*MacArthur
Causeway* 41

Belle
Isle A1A

Art Deco
District ◆

American
Airlines
Arena 1

Port
Miami

12

Fisher
Island

Rickenbacker
Causeway

Virginia
Key

Cape Florida
Lighthouse

0 _____ 2 mi
0 _____ 2 km

GETTING
ORIENTED

Long considered the gateway
to Latin America, Miami is
as close to Cuba and the
Caribbean as you can get
within the United States. The
36-square-mile city is at the
southern tip of the Florida
peninsula, bordered on
the east by Biscayne Bay.
Over the bay lies a series of
barrier islands, the largest
being a thin 18-square-mile
strip called Miami Beach. To
the east of Miami Beach is
the Atlantic Ocean. To the
south are the Florida Keys.

and play dominoes in the
heart and soul of Cuba's
exile community.

🔟 **South Beach.** People-
watch from sidewalk cafés,
admire art deco, and party
'til dawn at the nation's
hottest clubs.

⓫ **Mid-Beach.** Experience
the booming restaurant
scene and trendy hotels just
beyond South Beach.

⓬ **Fisher and Belle Isle.**
Be near the pulse of Miami
Beach but a man-made
island away.

⓭ **North Beach.** Shop and
relax in the quieter northern
end of Miami Beach, which
also encompasses Aventura,
Bal Harbour, and Sunny Isles.

CUBAN FOOD

If the tropical vibe has you hankering for Cuban food, you've come to the right place. Miami is the top spot in the country to enjoy authentic Cuban cooking.

The flavors and preparations of Cuban cuisine are influenced by the island nation's natural bounty (yuca, sugarcane, guava), as well as its rich immigrant history, from near (Caribbean countries) and far (Spanish and African traditions). Chefs in Miami tend to stick with the classic versions of beloved dishes, though you'll find some variation from restaurant to restaurant, as recipes have often been passed down through generations of home cooks. For a true Cuban experience, try either the popular **Versailles** (⊠ *3555 S.W. 8th St.* ☎ *305/444-0240* ⊕ *www.versaillesrestaurant.com*) or classic **La Carreta** (⊠ *3632 S.W. 8th St.* ☎ *305/444-7501*) in Little Havana, appealing to families seeking a home-cooked, Cuban-style meal. For a modern interpretation of Cuban eats, head to Coral Gable's **Havana Harry's** (⊠ *4612 S. Le Jeune Rd.* ☎ *305/661-2622*). South Beach eatery **Puerto Sagua Restaurant** (⊠ *700 Collins Ave.* ☎ *305/673-1115*) is the beach's favorite Cuban hole-in-the-wall, open daily from 7 am to 2 am.

THE CUBAN SANDWICH

A great *cubano* (Cuban sandwich) requires pillowy Cuban bread layered with ham, garlic-citrus-marinated slow-roasted pork, Swiss cheese, and pickles (plus salami in Tampa, lettuce and tomatoes in Key West), with butter and/or mustard. The sandwich is grilled in a sandwich press until the cheese melts and all the elements are fused together. Try one at **Enriqueta's Sandwich Shop** (⊠ *186 N.E. 29 St.* ☎ *305/573-4681* ⊙ Weekdays 6 am–4 pm, Sat. 6 am–2 pm) in Wynwood, or **Exquisito Restaurant** (⊠ *1510 S.W. 8th St.* ☎ *305/643-0227* ⊙ Daily 7 am–11 pm) in Little Havana.

KEY CUBAN DISHES

ARROZ CON POLLO

This chicken-and-rice dish is Cuban comfort food. Found throughout Latin America, the Cuban version is typically seasoned with garlic, paprika, and onions, then colored golden or reddish with saffron or achiote (a seed paste), and enlivened with a sizable splash of beer near the end of cooking. Green peas and sliced, roasted red peppers are standard toppings.

BISTEC DE PALOMILLA

This thinly sliced sirloin steak is marinated in lime juice and garlic and fried with onions. The steak is often served with *chimichurri* sauce, an olive oil, garlic, and cilantro sauce that sometimes comes with bread (slather bread with butter and dab on the chimichurri). Also try *ropa vieja,* a slow-cooked, shredded flank steak in a garlic-tomato sauce.

DESSERTS

Treat yourself to a slice of *tres leches* cake. The "three milks" come from the sweetened condensed milk, evaporated milk, and heavy cream that are poured over the cake until it's an utterly irresistible gooey mess. Also, don't miss the *pastelitos,* Cuban fruit-filled turnovers. Traditional flavors include plain guava, guava with cream cheese, and cream cheese with coconut.

DRINKS

Sip *guarapo* (gwa-RA-poh), a fresh sugarcane juice that isn't really as sweet as you might think, or grab a straw and enjoy a frothy *batido* (bah-TEE-doe), a Cuban-style milk shake made with tropical fruits like mango, *piña* (pineapple), or *mamey* (mah-MAY, a tropical fruit with a melon-cherry taste). For a real twist, try the *batido de trigo*—a wheat shake that will remind you of sugarglazed breakfast cereal.

FRITAS

If you're in the mood for an inexpensive, casual Cuban meal, have a *frita*—a hamburger with distinctive Cuban flair. It's made with ground beef that's mixed with ground or finely chopped chorizo, spiced with pepper, paprika, and salt, topped with sautéed onions and shoestring potato fries, and then served on a bun slathered with a special tomatobased ketchup-like sauce.

LECHON ASADO

Fresh ham or an entire suckling pig marinated in *mojo criollo* (parsley, garlic, sour orange, and olive oil) is roasted until fork tender and served with white rice, black beans, and *tostones* (fried plantains) or yuca (pronounced YU-kah), a starchy tuber with a mild nut taste that's often sliced into fat sticks and deep-fried like fries.

Updated by
Paul Rubio

Three-quarters of a century after the art deco movement, Miami remains one of the world's trendiest and flashiest hot spots. Luckily for visitors, South Beach is no longer the only place to stand and pose in Miami. North of Downtown, the growing Wynwood and Design districts—along with nearby Midtown—are home to Miami's hipster and fashionista movements, and the South Beach "scene" continues to extend both north and west, with the addition of new venues north of 20th Street, south of 5th Street, and along the bay on West Avenue. The reopening of the mammoth Fontainebleau and its enclave of nightclubs and restaurants along Mid-Beach paved the way for a Mid-Beach renaissance, luring other globally renowned resorts, lounges, and restaurants into the neighborhood, such as the Soho Beach House and the Faena District Miami Beach, a multiblock project in Mid-Beach by Argentinean icon and developer Alan Faena.

Visit Miami today and it's hard to believe that 100 years ago it was a mosquito-infested swampland, with an Indian trading post on the Miami River. Then hotel builder Henry Flagler brought his railroad to the outpost known as Fort Dallas. Other visionaries—Carl Fisher, Julia Tuttle, William Brickell, and John Sewell, among others—set out to tame the unruly wilderness. Hotels were erected, bridges were built, the port was dredged, and electricity arrived. The narrow strip of mangrove coast was transformed into Miami Beach—and the tourists started to come. They haven't stopped since!

Greater Miami is many destinations in one. At its best it offers an unparalleled multicultural experience: melodic Latin and Caribbean tongues, international cuisines and cultural events, and an unmistakable joie de vivre—all against a beautiful beach backdrop. In Little Havana the air is tantalizing with the perfume of strong Cuban coffee. In Coconut Grove, Caribbean steel drums ring out during the Miami/Bahamas Goombay Festival. Anytime in colorful Miami Beach, restless crowds wait for entry to the hottest new clubs.

Many visitors don't know that Miami and Miami Beach are really separate cities. Miami, on the mainland, is South Florida's commercial hub. Miami Beach, on 17 islands in Biscayne Bay, is sometimes considered America's Riviera, luring refugees from winter with its warm sunshine; sandy beaches; graceful, shady palms; and tireless nightlife. The natives know well that there's more to Greater Miami than the bustle of South Beach and its Art Deco District. In addition to well-known places such as Ocean Drive and Lincoln Road, the less reported spots—like the burgeoning Design District in Miami, the historic buildings of Coral Gables, and the secluded beaches of Key Biscayne—are great insider destinations.

PLANNING

WHEN TO GO

Miami and Miami Beach are year-round destinations. Most people come from November through April, when the weather is close to perfect; hotels, restaurants, and attractions are busiest; and each weekend holds a festival or event. High season kicks off in December with Art Basel Miami Beach, and hotel rates don't come down until after the college kids have left after spring break in late March.

It's hot and steamy May through September, but nighttime temperatures are usually pleasant. Also, summer is a good time for the budget traveler. Many hotels lower their rates considerably, and many restaurants offer discounts—especially during Miami Spice in August and September, when a slew of top restaurants offer special tasting menus at a steep discount.

GETTING HERE AND AROUND

You'll need a car to visit many attractions and points of interest. If possible, avoid driving during the rush hours of 7–9 am and 5–7 pm—the hour just after and right before the peak times also can be slow going. During rainy weather, be especially cautious of flooding in South Beach and Key Biscayne.

AIR TRAVEL

Miami is serviced by Miami International Airport (MIA), 8 miles northwest of Downtown, and Fort Lauderdale–Hollywood International Airport (FLL), 26 miles northeast. Many discount carriers, like Spirit Airlines, Southwest Airlines, and JetBlue, fly into FLL, making it a smart bargain if you're renting a car. Otherwise, look for flights to MIA, which has undergone an extensive face-lift, improving facilities, common spaces, and the overall aesthetic of the airport.

CAR TRAVEL

Interstate 95 is the major expressway connecting South Florida with points north; State Road 836 is the major east–west expressway and connects to Florida's Turnpike, State Road 826, and Interstate 95. Seven causeways link Miami and Miami Beach, with Interstate 195 and Interstate 395 offering the most convenient routes; the Rickenbacker Causeway extends to Key Biscayne from Interstate 95 and U.S. 1. The high-speed lanes on the left-hand side of Interstate 95 require a prepaid toll pass called a Sunpass, available in most drug and grocery stores, or it can be ordered by mail before your trip. It is available with all rental cars (but you are billed for the tolls and associated fees later).

PUBLIC TRANSPORTATION

Some sights are accessible via the public transportation system, run by the **Metro-Dade Transit Agency,** which maintains 740 Metrobuses on 90 routes; the 23-mile Metrorail elevated rapid-transit system; and the Metromover, an elevated light-rail system. Those planning to use public transportation should get an EASY Card or EASY Ticket available at any Metrorail station and most supermarkets. Fares are discounted, and transfer fees are nominal. The bus stops for the **Metrobus** are marked with blue-and-green signs with a bus logo and route information. The fare is $2.25 (exact change only). Cash-paying customers must pay for another ride if transferring. Some express routes carry a surcharge of 40¢. Elevated **Metrorail** trains run from downtown Miami north to Hialeah and south along U.S. 1 to Dadeland. The system operates daily 5 am–midnight. The fare is $2.25; $0.60 transfers to Metrobus are available only for EASY Card and EASY Ticket holders. The free **Metromover** resembles an airport shuttle and runs on two loops around downtown Miami, linking major hotels, office buildings, and shopping areas. The system spans about 4½ miles, including the 1-mile Omni Loop and the 1-mile Brickell Loop. **Tri-Rail,** South Florida's commuter-train system, stops at 18 stations north of MIA along a 71-mile route. There's a Metrorail transfer station two stops north of MIA. Prices range from $2.50 to $6.90 for a one-way ticket.

Contacts Metro-Dade Transit Agency. ☎ 305/891–3131 ⊕ www.miamidade. gov/transit/. **Tri-Rail.** ☎ 800/874–7245 ⊕ www.tri-rail.com.

TAXI TRAVEL

Except in South Beach, it's difficult to hail a cab on the street; in most cases you'll need to call a cab company or have a hotel doorman hail one for you. Taxi drivers in Miami are notorious for bad customer service and not having credit card machines in their vehicles. These days, many people use Uber or Lyft to avoid this taxi drama, and for reasonable prices; however, in order to use Uber you must sign up with the company and have the Uber app installed on your smartphone. If using a regular taxi, note that fares run $2.50 for the first 1/6 of a mile and $0.40 for every additional 1/6 of a mile. Waiting time is $0.40 per minute. Flat-rate fares are also available from the airport to a variety of zones (including Miami Beach) for $35. Expect a $2 surcharge on rides leaving from Miami International Airport or the Port of Miami.

For those heading from MIA to Downtown, the 15-minute, 7-mile trip costs around $22. Some but not all cabs accept credit cards, so ask when you get in.

Taxi Companies Central Cab. *☎ 305/532–5555 ⊕ www.centralcab.com.* **Uber.** *⊕ www.uber.com.* **Yellow Cab.** *☎ 305/444–4444.*

TRAIN TRAVEL
New, privately operated high-speed Brightline service began in summer 2017, connecting downtown Miami, Fort Lauderdale, and West Palm Beach. The trip from downtown Miami to Fort Lauderdale takes about 30 minutes; it's another 30 minutes to West Palm Beach.

Amtrak provides service from 500 destinations to the Greater Miami area. The trains make several stops along the way; north–south service stops in the major Florida cities of Jacksonville, Orlando, Tampa, West Palm Beach, and Fort Lauderdale, but stations are not always conveniently located. The Auto Train (where you bring your car along) travels from Lorton, Virginia, just outside Washington, D.C., to Sanford, Florida, just outside Orlando. From there it's less than a four-hour drive to Miami. Fares vary, but expect to pay between around $275 and $350 for a basic sleeper seat and car passage each way. ■ TIP➜ **You must be traveling with an automobile to purchase a ticket on the Auto Train.**

Contacts Brightline. *⊕ gobrightline.com.*

VISITOR INFORMATION
For additional information about Miami and Miami Beach, contact the city's visitor bureaus. You can also pick up a free Miami Beach INcard at the Miami Beach Visitors Center 10–4, seven days a week, entitling you to discounts and offers at restaurants, shops, galleries, and more.

Contacts City of Coral Gables. *⊠ Coral Gables City Hall, 405 Biltmore Way, Coral Gables ☎ 305/446–6800 ⊕ www.coralgables.com.* **Coconut Grove Business Improvement District.** *⊠ 3390 Mary St., Suite 130, Coconut Grove ☎ 305/461–5506 ⊕ www.coconutgrove.com.* **Greater Miami Convention & Visitors Bureau.** *⊠ 701 Brickell Ave., Suite 2700 ☎ 305/539–3000, 800/933–8448 in U.S. ⊕ www.miamiandbeaches.com.* **Key Biscayne Chamber of Commerce and Visitors Center.** *⊠ 88 W. McIntyre St., Suite 100, Key Biscayne ☎ 305/361–5207 ⊕ www.keybiscaynechamber.org.* **Visit Miami Beach.** *⊠ Visitor Center, 1901 Convention Center Dr., Hall C, Miami Beach ☎ 786/276–2763, 305/673–7400 Miami Beach tourist hotline ⊕ www.miamibeachguest.com.*

EXPLORING

If you'd arrived here 50 years ago with a guidebook in hand, chances are you'd be thumbing through listings looking for alligator wrestlers and you-pick strawberry fields or citrus groves. Things have changed. While Disney sidetracked families in Orlando, Miami was developing a unique culture and attitude that's equal parts beach town/big business, Latino/Caribbean meets European/American—all of which fuels a great art and food scene, as well as exuberant nightlife and myriad festivals.

To find your way around Greater Miami, learn how the numbering system works (or better yet, use your phone's GPS). Miami is laid out on a grid with four quadrants—northeast, northwest, southeast, and southwest—that meet at Miami Avenue and Flagler Street. Miami Avenue separates east from west, and Flagler Street separates north from south. Avenues and courts run north–south; streets, terraces, and ways run east–west. Roads run diagonally, northwest–southeast. But other districts—Miami Beach, Coral Gables, and Hialeah—may or may not follow this system, and along the curve of Biscayne Bay the symmetrical grid shifts diagonally. If you do get lost, make sure you're in a safe neighborhood or public place when you seek guidance; cabdrivers and cops are good resources.

DOWNTOWN

Downtown Miami dazzles from a distance. America's third-largest skyline is fluid, thanks to the sheer number of sparkling glass high-rises between Biscayne Boulevard and the Miami River. Business is the key to downtown Miami's daytime bustle. However, the influx of massive, modern, and once-affordable condos has lured a young and trendy demographic to the areas in and around Downtown, giving Miami much more of a "city" feel come nightfall. In fact, Downtown has become a nighttime hot spot in recent years, inciting a cultural revolution that has fostered burgeoning areas north in Wynwood, Midtown, and the Design District, and south along Brickell Avenue. The pedestrian streets here tend to be very restaurant-centric, complemented by lounges and nightclubs.

The free, 4½-mile, elevated commuter system known as the Metromover runs inner and outer loops through Downtown and to nearby neighborhoods south and north. Many attractions are conveniently located within a few blocks of a station.

TOP ATTRACTIONS

Adrienne Arsht Center. Culture vultures and other artsy types are drawn to this stunning performing arts center, which includes the 2,400-seat Ziff Ballet Opera House, the 2,200-seat John S. and James L. Knight Concert Hall, the black-box Carnival Studio Theater, and an outdoor Plaza for the Arts. Throughout the year, you'll find top-notch performances by local and national touring groups, including Broadway hits like *Wicked* and *Jersey Boys,* intimate music concerts, and showstopping ballet. Think of it as a sliver of savoir faire to temper Miami's often-over-the-top vibe. The massive development was designed by architect César Pelli, and stands as the largest American performing arts center constructed since the 1980s. Complimentary one-hour tours of the Arsht Center, highlighting the architecture and its public art, are offered every Saturday and Monday at noon. Arrive early for your performance to dine at BRAVA By Brad Kilgore, located within the Arsht center and currently one of Miami's hottest restaurants. ⊠ *1300 Biscayne Blvd., at N.E. 13th St., Downtown* ☎ *305/949–6722 box office* ⊕ *www.arshtcenter.org.*

2

Downtown Miami

KEY

- 🅜 Metromover Station
- - - - Metromover

Freedom Tower. In the 1960s this ornate Spanish-baroque structure was the Cuban Refugee Center, processing more than 500,000 Cubans who entered the United States after fleeing Fidel Castro's regime. Built in 1925 for the *Miami Daily News,* it was inspired by the Giralda, an 800-year-old bell tower in Seville, Spain. Preservationists were pleased to see the tower's exterior restored in 1988. Today, it is owned by Miami Dade College (MDC), functioning as a cultural and educational center; it's also home to the MDC Museum of Art + Design, which showcases a broad collection of contemporary Latin art as well works in the genres of minimalism and pop art. ■TIP→ **Admission is free to both the tower and museum.** ⊠ *600 Biscayne Blvd., at N.E. 6th St., Downtown* ☎ *305/237-7700* ⊕ *www.mdcmoad.org.*

FAMILY **HistoryMiami.** Discover a treasure trove of colorful stories about the region's history at HistoryMiami, formerly known as the Historical Museum of Southern Florida. Exhibits celebrate the city's multicultural heritage, including an old Miami streetcar and unique items chronicling the migration of Cubans to Miami. Though HistoryMiami is not wildly popular with tourists, the museum's tours certainly are. You can take a wide range of walking, boat, coach, bike, gallery, and eco-history tours with varying prices, including culture walks through Little Haiti, informative and exciting Little Havana Arts and Culture Walks, and an evening of storytelling during the "Moon Over Miami" tour led by HistoryMiami historian Dr. Paul George, where you'll float through Downtown on the Miami River, learning all about Miami's early history circa the Tequesta Indians' days. ⊠ *101 W. Flagler St., between N.W. 1st and 2nd Aves., Downtown* ☎ *305/375–1492* ⊕ *www.historymiami. org* ⊑ *$10; tour costs vary.*

FAMILY
Fodor'sChoice
★ **Pérez Art Museum Miami (PAMM).** Opened in December 2013, the Pérez Art Museum Miami, known locally as PAMM, shines as the city's first true world-class museum. This über-high-design architectural masterpiece on Biscayne Bay is a sight to behold. Double-story, cylindrical hanging gardens sway from high atop the museum, anchored to stylish wood trusses that help create this gotta-see-it-to-believe-it indoor-outdoor museum. Large sculptures, Asian-inspired gardens, sexy white benches, and steel frames envelop the property. Inside, the 120,000-square-foot space houses multicultural art from the 20th and 21st centuries, some of which were previously on display at the Miami Art Museum (note: downtown's Miami Art Museum no longer exists, and the collection has now been incorporated into PAMM). Most of the interior space is devoted to temporary exhibitions, which have included the likes of *Ai Weiwei: According to What?* and *Edouard Duval-Carrié: Imagined Landscapes.* Even if you aren't a "museum type," come check out this magnum opus over lunch at Verde at PAMM, the museum's sensational waterfront restaurant and bar. ■TIP→ **Admission is free every first Thursday of the month and every second Saturday of the month.** ⊠ *1103 Biscayne Blvd., Downtown* ☎ *305/375–3000* ⊕ *www.pamm. org* ⊑ *$16* ⊗ *Closed Wed.*

WORTH NOTING

Bayfront Park. This pedestrian-friendly waterfront park sits on a 32-acre site smack in the heart of downtown Miami on Biscayne Bay, bordered by Bayside Marketplace to the north and the InterContinental Miami to the south. There's a small but lovely walking trail and two major event spaces—the Tina Hills Pavilion and Bayfront Park Amphitheater. American sculptor Isamu Noguchi helped redesign the park in the late 1980s, gracing the site with several works, including the white *Challenger* Memorial, commemorating the space shuttle that exploded in 1986. If you want to live like a local, join in the free yoga on the bay front Monday and Wednesday (6 pm) or Saturday (9 am). Seven blocks north of Bayfront Park is the 30-acre Museum Park (formerly Bicentennial Park), which houses the Patricia and Phillip Frost Museum of Science and the Pérez Art Museum Miami (PAMM), and is also managed by Bayfront Park Management Trust. ⊠ *301 N. Biscayne Blvd., Downtown* ☎ *305/358–7550* ⊕ *www.bayfrontparkmiami.com.*

FAMILY **Bayside Marketplace.** The Bayside Marketplace, a waterfront complex of entertainment, dining, and retail stores, was en vogue circa 1992 and remains popular due to its location near PortMiami. You'll find the area awash in cruise-ship passenger chaos on most days (it's definitely *not* a draw for locals), so expect plenty of souvenir shops, a Hard Rock Cafe, and stores like Wet Seal and Sunglass Hut. Many boat tours leave from the marinas lining the festival marketplace. ⊠ *401 Biscayne Blvd., Downtown* ☎ *305/577–3344* ⊕ *www.baysidemarketplace.com.*

Fredric Snitzer Gallery. The gallery of this longtime figure in the Miami arts scene highlights emerging and mid-career artists, providing them that tipping point needed for national and international exposure and recognition. The newly relocated space maintains its warehouse roots, letting the art speak for itself amid the raw walls and ample natural light. Though a commercial gallery, the selection is highly curated. Rotating monthly exhibitions are usually thematic, with works by one of its represented artists including Hernan Bas, Alice Aycock, Enrique Martinez Celaya, Rafael Domenech, and Jon Pylypchuk. For the art novice, the team, including Snitzer himself, are readily available and willing to share their knowledge. ⊠ *1540 N.E. Miami Ct., Downtown* ☎ *305/448–8976* ⊕ *www.snitzer.com.*

FAMILY **Jungle Island.** Originally located deep in south Miami and known as Parrot Jungle, South Florida's original tourist attraction opened in 1936 and moved closer to Miami Beach in 2003. Now on Watson Island, a small stretch of land between downtown Miami and South Beach, Jungle Island is far more than a place where cockatoos ride tricycles; this interactive zoological park is home to just about every unusual and endangered species you would want to see (if you are into seeing them in zoo-like settings, that is), including a rare albino alligator, a liger (lion and tiger mix), and myriad exotic birds. With an emphasis on the experiential versus mere observation, the park now offers several new attractions and activities, including private beaches, treetop zip-lining, aquatic activities, adventure trails, cultural activities, and enhanced VIP packages where you mingle with an array of furry and feathered friends. Jungle Island offers complimentary shuttle service to most downtown

Miami and South Beach hotels. ⊠ *Watson Island, 1111 Parrot Jungle Trail, off MacArthur Causeway (I–395), Downtown* ☎ *305/400–7000* ⊕ *www.jungleisland.com* ✑ *$39.95, plus $10 parking.*

FAMILY **Miami Children's Museum.** This Arquitectonica-designed museum, both imaginative and geometric in appearance, is directly across the MacArthur Causeway from Jungle Island. Twelve galleries house hundreds of interactive, bilingual exhibits. Children can scan plastic groceries in the supermarket, scramble through a giant sand castle, climb a rock wall, learn about the Everglades, and combine rhythms in the world-music studio. ⊠ *Watson Island, 980 MacArthur Causeway, off I–395, Downtown* ☎ *305/373–5437* ⊕ *www.miamichildrensmuseum.org* ✑ *$20, parking $1/hr.*

FAMILY **Patricia and Phillip Frost Museum of Science.** In spring 2017, the Patricia and Phillip Frost Museum of Science relocated to its much larger (250,000-square-foot), hypermodern, $300 million-plus new home in Downtown's Museum Park. Marvel at the wealth of hands-on sound, gravity, and electricity displays for children and adults alike alongside a tri-level aquarium and a 250-seat state-of-the-art planetarium. There are also exhibits dedicated to space travel, the Everglades, and mind-blowing laser shows daily. Price of admission includes access to the museum as well as one Frost Planetarium show. ⊠ *1101 Biscayne Blvd., Downtown* ☎ *305/434–9600* ⊕ *www.frostscience.org* ✑ *$27.*

COCONUT GROVE

A former haven for writers and artists, Coconut Grove has never quite outgrown its image as a small village. You can still feel the bohemian roots of this artsy neighborhood, but it has grown increasingly mainstream and residential over the past 20 years. Posh estates mingle with rustic cottages, modest frame homes, and stark modern dwellings, often on the same block. If you're into horticulture, you'll be impressed by the Garden of Eden–like foliage that seems to grow everywhere without care. In truth, residents are determined to keep up the Grove's village-in-a-jungle look, so they lavish attention on exotic plantings even as they battle to protect any remaining native vegetation.

The center of the Grove still attracts its fair share of locals and tourists who enjoy perusing the small boutiques, sidewalk cafés, and cute galleries that remind us of the old Grove. Activities here are family-friendly with easy access to bay-side parks, museums, and gardens.

TOP ATTRACTIONS

FAMILY
Fodor's Choice
★
Vizcaya Museum and Gardens. Of the 10,000 people living in Miami between 1912 and 1916, about 1,000 of them were gainfully employed by Chicago industrialist James Deering to build this European-inspired residence. Once comprising 180 acres, this National Historic Landmark now occupies a 30-acre tract that includes a rockland hammock (native forest) and more than 10 acres of formal gardens with fountains overlooking Biscayne Bay. The house, open to the public, contains 70 rooms, 34 of which are filled with paintings, sculpture, antique furniture, and other fine and decorative arts. The collection spans 2,000 years and represents the Renaissance, baroque, rococo, and neoclassical periods.

The 90-minute self-guided Discover Vizcaya Audio Tour is available in multiple languages for an additional $5. Moonlight tours, offered on evenings that are nearest the full moon, provide a magical look at the gardens; call for reservations. ✉ *3251 S. Miami Ave., Coconut Grove* ☎ *305/250–9133* ⊕ *www.vizcaya.org* ✉ *$18* ⊙ *Closed Tues.*

CORAL GABLES

You can easily spot Coral Gables from the window of a Miami-bound jetliner—just look for the massive orange tower of the Biltmore Hotel rising from a lush green carpet of trees concealing the city's gracious homes. The canopy is as much a part of this planned city as its distinctive architecture, all attributed to the vision of George E. Merrick more than a century ago.

The story of this city began in 1911, when Merrick inherited 1,600 acres of citrus and avocado groves from his father. Through judicious investment he nearly doubled the tract to 3,000 acres by 1921. Merrick dreamed of building an American Venice here, complete with canals and homes. Working from this vision, he began designing a city based on centuries-old prototypes from Mediterranean countries. Unfortunately for Merrick, the devastating no-name hurricane of 1926, followed by the Great Depression, prevented him from fulfilling many of his plans. He died at 54, an employee of the post office. Today Coral Gables has a population of about 50,000. In its bustling Downtown more than 150 multinational companies maintain headquarters or regional offices, and the University of Miami campus in the southern part of the Gables brings a youthful vibrancy to the area. A southern branch of the city extends down the shore of Biscayne Bay through neighborhoods threaded with canals.

TOP ATTRACTIONS

Biltmore Hotel. Bouncing back stunningly from its dark days as an army hospital, this hotel has become the jewel of Coral Gables—a dazzling architectural gem with a colorful past. First opened in 1926, it was a hot spot for the rich and glamorous of the Jazz Age until it was converted to an army–air force regional hospital in 1942. Until 1968, the Veterans Administration continued to operate the hospital after World War II. The Biltmore then lay vacant for nearly 20 years before it underwent extensive renovations and reopened as a luxury hotel in 1987. Its 16-story tower, like the Freedom Tower in downtown Miami, is a replica of Seville's Giralda Tower. The magnificent pool is reportedly the largest hotel pool in the continental United States. ■TIP→ Because it functions as a full-service hotel, your ticket in—if you aren't staying here—is to patronize one of the hotel's several restaurants or bars. Try to get a courtyard table for the Sunday Champagne brunch, a local legend. ✉ *1200 Anastasia Ave., near De Soto Blvd., Coral Gables* ☎ *855/311–6903* ⊕ *www.biltmorehotel.com.*

FAMILY **Fairchild Tropical Botanic Garden.** With 83 acres of lakes, sunken gardens, a 560-foot vine pergola, orchids, bellflowers, coral trees, bougainvillea, rare palms, and flowering trees, Fairchild is the largest tropical botanical garden in the continental United States. The tram tour highlights the best of South

Greater Miami

OCEAN

MIAMI BEACH

SOUTH BEACH

Art Deco District

Collins Ave.
Ocean Dr.

A1A

Alton Rd.

Belle Isle

Miami Children's Museum

Watson Island

MacArthur Causeway

Jungle Island

Venetian Causeway

Port Miami

Fisher Island

Virginia Key

Rickenbacker Causeway

10

Grove Isle

JFK Causeway

Julia Tuttle Causeway

195

Biscayne Blvd.

N.E. 2nd Ave.

N. Miami Ave.

1

DESIGN DISTRICT

MIDTOWN

LITTLE HAITI

441

WYNWOOD ARTS DISTRICT

2 3
1

395

95

41

S.W. 13th St.

Brickell Ave.

COCONUT GROVE

9

41

27

S.W. 3rd

S.W. 12th Ave.

N.W. 17th Ave.

N.W. 20th St.

N.W. 36th St.

Robert Frost Expwy.

MIAMI

LITTLE HAVANA

7

8

6

S.W. 8th St.

Coral Way

S.W. 22nd St.

N.W. 27th Ave.

1

9

N.W. 62nd St.

N.W. 54th St.

N.W. 79th St.

Hialeah Dr.

944

27

N.W. 39th Ave.

N.W. 72nd Ave.

Dairy Rd.

Miami River

East-West Expressway

Miami International Airport

836

959

968

N.W. 7th St.

W. Flagler St.

S.W. 8th St.

S.W. 24th St.

826

Tamiami Trail

Ponce de León Blvd.

Le Jeune Rd.

Granada Blvd.

972

953

S.W. 37th Ave. (Douglas Rd.)

Sevilla Ave.

5

4

CocoWalk

Grand Ave.

S. Dixie Hwy.

S.W. 57th Ave.

976

Bird Rd.

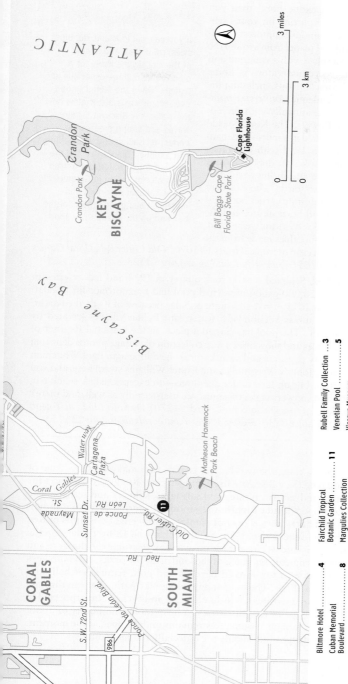

ATLANTIC

Crandon
Park

KEY
BISCAYNE

Crandon Park

Bill Baggs Cape
Florida State Park

◆ Cape Florida
  Lighthouse

Biscayne Bay

CORAL
GABLES

S.W. 72nd St.

Ponce de León Blvd.

986

Coral Gables

Maynada
St.

Sunset Dr.

León Rd.

Ponce de León Rd.

Cartagena
Plaza

Waterway

Red Rd.

Old Cutler Rd.

SOUTH
MIAMI

⑪

Matheson Hammock
Park Beach

0   3 km

0   3 miles

Florida and exotic flora; then you can set off exploring on your own. The 2-acre Simons Rainforest showcases tropical plants from around the world complete with a waterfall and stream. The conservatory is home to rare tropical plants, including the Burmese endemic *Amherstia nobilis*, flowering annually with orchid-like pink flowers. The Keys Coastal Habitat, created in a marsh and mangrove area in 1995 with assistance from the Tropical Audubon Society, provides food and shelter to resident and migratory birds. The excellent bookstore–gift shop carries books on gardening and horticulture, and the Garden Café serves sandwiches and, seasonally, smoothies made from the garden's own crop of tropical fruits. ⊠ *10901 Old Cutler Rd., Coral Gables* ☎ *305/667–1651* ⊕ *www.fairchildgarden.org* ⌨ *$25.*

FAMILY **Venetian Pool.** Sculpted from a rock quarry in 1923 and fed by artesian wells, this 820,000-gallon municipal pool had a major face-lift in 2010 and again in 2015. It remains quite popular because of its themed architecture—a fantasy version of a waterfront Italian village—created by Denman Fink. The pool has earned a place on the National Register of Historic Places and showcases a nice collection of vintage photos depicting 1920s beauty pageants and swank soirees held long ago. Paul Whiteman played here, Johnny Weissmuller and Esther Williams swam here, and you should, too (but no kids under age three—no exceptions). A snack bar, lockers, and showers make this must-see user-friendly as well, and there's free parking across De Soto Boulevard. ⊠ *2701 De Soto Blvd., at Toledo St., Coral Gables* ☎ *305/460–5306* ⊕ *www.coralgables.com* ⌨ *$13.*

KEY BISCAYNE

Once upon a time, the two barrier islands that make up the village of Key Biscayne (Key Biscayne itself and Virginia Key) were outposts for fishermen and sailors, pirates and salvagers, soldiers and settlers. The 95-foot Cape Florida Lighthouse stood tall during Seminole Indian battles and hurricanes. Coconut plantations covered two-thirds of Key Biscayne, and there were plans as far back as the 1800s to develop the picturesque island as a resort for the wealthy. Fortunately, the state and county governments set much of the land aside for parks, and both keys are now home to top-ranked beaches and golf, tennis, softball, and picnicking facilities. The long and winding bike paths that run through the islands are favorites for in-line skaters and cyclists. Incorporated in 1991, the village of Key Biscayne is a hospitable community of about 12,500, even though Virginia Key remains undeveloped at the moment. These two playground islands are especially family-friendly.

TOP ATTRACTIONS

FAMILY **Miami Seaquarium.** This classic family attraction stages shows with sea lions, dolphins, and other marine animals. The Crocodile Flats exhibit has 26 Nile crocodiles. Discovery Bay, an endangered-mangrove habitat, is home to sea turtles, alligators, herons, egrets, and ibis. You can also visit a shark pool, a tropical reef aquarium, and West Indian and Florida manatees. A popular interactive attraction is the Stingray Touch Tank, where you can touch and feed cow-nose rays and southern stingrays. Another big draw is the Dolphin Interaction program, including the quite intensive Dolphin Odyssey ($210) experience and the lighter shallow-water Dolphin Encounter ($110). Make reservations for either experience. ✉ *4400 Rickenbacker Causeway, Virginia Key* ☎ *305/361–5705* ⊕ *www.miamiseaquarium.com* 💲 *$44.99, parking $10 (cash only).*

WYNWOOD

North of Downtown, the formerly downtrodden Wynwood neighborhood has arrived, with an impressive mix of one-of-a-kind shops and art galleries, public art displays, see-and-be-seen bars, slick restaurants, and plenty of eye-popping graffiti. Wynwood's trendiness has proven infectious, also taking root in proximate neighborhoods. One thing is still missing from the emerging landscape: a decent hotel. On a positive note, it's kept the Wynwood vibe more local and less touristy. The downside: you'll need a vehicle to get here, and though in close proximity to one another, you'll also need a vehicle to get to nearby Midtown and the Design District.

Between Interstate 95 and Northeast 1st Avenue from 29th to 22nd streets lies the centerpiece of the edgy Wynwood neighborhood—the funky and edgy **Wynwood Art District** (⊕ *www.wynwoodmiami.com*), which is peppered with galleries, art studios, and private collections accessible to the public. Though the neighborhood hasn't completely shed its dodgy past, artist-painted graffiti walls and reinvented urban warehouses have transformed the area from plain old grimy to super-trendy. The Wynwood Walls on Northwest 2nd Avenue between Northeast 25th and 26th streets are a cutting-edge enclave of modern urban murals. However, these avant-garde graffiti displays by renowned artists are just the beginning; in fact, almost every street is colored with funky spray-paint art, making the neighborhood a photographer's dream. Wynwood's retail space is a hodgepodge of cheap garment stores, upscale boutiques, and contemporary galleries (some by appointment only). First-timers may want to visit during Wynwood's monthly gallery walk on the second Saturday evening of each month, when studios and galleries are all open at the same time.

TOP ATTRACTIONS

Margulies Collection at the Warehouse. Make sure a visit to Wynwood includes a stop at the Margulies Collection at the Warehouse. Martin Margulies's collection of vintage and contemporary photography, videos, and installation art in a 45,000-square-foot space makes for eye-popping viewing. Admission proceeds go to the Lotus House, a

Wynwood is famous for its walls covered by murals from famous contemporary artists, including these by Shepard Fairey.

local homeless shelter for women and children. ✉ *591 N.W. 27th St., between N.W. 5th and 6th Aves., Wynwood* ☎ *305/576–1051* ⊕ *www. margulieswarehouse.com* ✉ *$10.*

Fodor's Choice
★ **Rubell Family Collection.** Fans of edgy art will appreciate the Rubell Family Collection. Mera and Don Rubell have accumulated work by artists from the 1970s to the present, including Jeff Koons, Cindy Sherman, Damien Hirst, and Keith Haring. New exhibitions for 2017 embodied a politically charged motif, including *High Anxiety: New Acquisitions,* a vast collection of art focused on today's social and political uncertainty. Admission always includes a complimentary audio tour; however, true art lovers should opt for a complimentary guided tour of the collection, offered Wednesday through Saturday at 3 pm. The collection plans to move to a new, larger home on the outskirts of Wynwood in 2018. ✉ *95 N.W. 29th St., between N. Miami and N.W. 1st Aves., Wynwood* ☎ *305/573–6090* ⊕ *www.rfc.museum* ✉ *$10* ☉ *Closed Sept.–Nov. 2017.*

Fodor's Choice
★ **Wynwood Walls.** Between Northeast 25th and 26th streets on Northwest 2nd Avenue, the Wynwood Walls are a cutting-edge enclave of modern urban murals, reflecting diversity in graffiti and street art. More than 50 well-known and lesser-known artists have transformed 80,000 square feet of warehouse walls into an outdoor museum of sorts (bring your camera). The popularity of the walls spawned the neighboring Wynwood Doors, an industrial space rife with metal roll-down gates also used as blank canvases. The Outside the Walls project followed, which spreads the Walls love across the neighborhood, as artists are commissioned to transform Wynwood's surrounding warehouses and building spaces into singular pieces of painted art. ✉ *2520 N.W. 2nd Ave., Wynwood* ⊕ *www.thewynwoodwalls.com.*

MIDTOWN

Northeast of Wynwood, Midtown (⊕ *www.midtownmiami.com*) lies between Northeast 29th and 36th streets, from North Miami Avenue to Northeast 2nd Avenue. This subcity is anchored by a multitower residential complex with prolific retail space, often housing the latest and greatest in dining and shopping trends.

DESIGN DISTRICT

North of Midtown, from about Northeast 38th to Northeast 42nd streets and across the other side of Interstate 195, the Design District (⊕ *www.miamidesigndistrict.net*) is yet another 18 blocks of clothiers, antiques shops, design stores, and bars and eateries. The real draws here are the interior design and furniture galleries as well as über-high-end shopping that's oh-so Rodeo Drive (and rivals Bal Harbour in North Beach).

Right outside Little Haiti's boundaries, running from 50th to 77th streets along Biscayne Boulevard, is the MiMo Biscayne Boulevard Historic District, known in short as the MiMo District. This strip is noted for its Miami modernist architecture and houses a number of boutiques and design galleries. It's sometimes seen as the latest extension of the growing Design District (with much cheaper rents). Within this district and in the neighborhoods to the east—collectively known as Miami's "Upper East Side"—several new restaurants are beginning to open.

LITTLE HAITI

Once a small farming community, Little Haiti is the heart and soul of Haitian society in the United States. In fact, Miami's Little Haiti is the largest Haitian community outside of Haiti itself. While people of different ethnic backgrounds have begun to move into the neighborhood, people here are still surprised to see tourists. However, owners of shops and restaurants tend to be welcoming. Creole is commonly spoken, although some people—especially younger folks—also speak English. Its northern and southern boundaries are 85th Street and 42nd Street, respectively, with Interstate 95 to the west and Biscayne Boulevard to the east in its southern reaches, then Northeast 4th Court to the east (two blocks west of Biscayne Boulevard). The best section to visit is along North Miami Avenue from 54th to 59th streets.

LITTLE HAVANA

First settled en masse by Cubans in the early 1960s, after Cuba's Communist revolution, Little Havana is a predominantly working-class area and the core of Miami's Hispanic community. Spanish is the principal language, but don't be surprised if the cadence is less Cuban and more Salvadoran or Nicaraguan: the neighborhood is now home to people from all Latin American countries.

If you come to Little Havana expecting the Latino version of New Orleans's French Quarter, you're apt to be disappointed—it's not about the architecture here. Rather, it's a place to soak in the atmosphere.

Little Havana is more about great, inexpensive food (not just Cuban; there's Vietnamese, Mexican, and Argentinean here as well), distinctive affordable Cuban-American art, cigars, and great coffee. It's not a prefab tourist destination—this is real life in Spanish-speaking Miami. Little Havana's semiofficial boundaries are 27th Avenue to 4th Avenue on the west, Miami River to the north, and Southwest 13th Street to the south. Much of the neighborhood is residential; however, you'll quickly discover the area's flavor, both literally and figuratively, along Calle Ocho (Southwest 8th Street), between Southwest 11th and 17th avenues, which is lined with cigar factories, cafés selling guava pastries and rose-petal flan, *botanicas* brimming with candles, and Cuban clothes and crafts stores. Your "Welcome to Little Havana" photo op shines on 27th Avenue and 8th Street. Giant hand-painted roosters are found scattered throughout the entire neighborhood, an artistic nod to their real-life counterparts that roam the streets here. You'll need to drive into Little Havana, since public transportation here is limited; but once on Calle Ocho, it's best to experience the neighborhood on foot.

TOP ATTRACTIONS

Cuban Memorial Boulevard. Four blocks in the heart of Little Havana are filled with monuments to Cuba's freedom fighters. South of Calle Ocho (8th Street), Southwest 13th Avenue becomes a ceiba tree–lined parkway known as Cuban Memorial Boulevard, divided at the center by a narrow grassy mall with a walking path through the various memorials. Among them is the *Eternal Torch of the Brigade 2506*, blazing with an endless flame and commemorating those who were killed in the failed Bay of Pigs invasion of 1961. Another is a bas-relief map of Cuba depicting each of its *municipios*. There's also a bronze statue in honor of Nestory (Tony) Izquierdo, who participated in the Bay of Pigs invasion and served in Nicaragua's Somozan forces. ⊠ *S.W. 13th Ave., between S.W. 8th and S.W. 12th Sts., Little Havana.*

Domino Park. If you're not yet ready to take advantage of the relaxed restrictions on travel to Cuba, watch a slice of old Havana come to life in Miami's Little Havana. At Domino Park, officially known as Maximo Gomez Park, guayabera-clad seniors bask in the sun and play dominoes, while onlookers share neighborhood gossip and political opinions. ■TIP➔ There is a little office at the park with a window where you can get information on Little Havana; the office also stores the dominoes for the older gents who play regularly, but it's BYOD (bring your own dominoes) for everyone else. ⊠ *801 S.W. 15th Ave., Little Havana* ☎ *305/859–2717 park office.*

El Titan de Bronze. A peek at the intently focused cigar rollers through the windows doesn't prepare you for the rich, pungent scent that jolts your senses as you step inside the store. Millions of stogies are deftly hand-rolled at this family-owned cigar factory and retail store each year. Visitors are welcome to watch the rolling action (and of course buy some cigars). ⊠ *1071 S.W. 8th St., Little Havana* ☎ *305/860–1412* ⊕ *www.eltitancigars.com.*

SOUTH BEACH

Fodor's Choice
★

The hub of Miami Beach is South Beach (better known as SoBe), with its energetic Ocean Drive, Collins Avenue, and Washington Avenue. Here life unfolds 24 hours a day. Beautiful people pose in hotel lounges and sidewalk cafés, bronzed cyclists zoom past palm trees, and visitors flock to see the action. On Lincoln Road, café crowds spill onto the sidewalks, weekend markets draw all kinds of visitors and their dogs, and thanks to a few late-night lounges, the scene is just as alive at night. Farther north (in Mid-Beach and North Beach), the vibe is decidedly quieter.

TOP ATTRACTIONS

Española Way. There's a bohemian feel to this street lined with Mediterranean-revival buildings constructed in 1925. Al Capone's gambling syndicate ran its operations upstairs at what is now the Clay Hotel, a youth hostel. At a nightclub here in the 1930s, future bandleader Desi Arnaz strapped on a conga drum and started beating out a rumba rhythm. Visit this quaint avenue on a weekend afternoon, when merchants and craftspeople set up shop to sell everything from handcrafted bongo drums to fresh flowers. Between Washington and Drexel avenues the road has been narrowed to a single lane, and Miami Beach's trademark pink sidewalks have been widened to accommodate sidewalk cafés and shops selling imaginative clothing, jewelry, and art. ⊠ *Española Way, between 14th and 15th Sts. from Washington to Jefferson Aves., South Beach.*

Holocaust Memorial. A bronze sculpture depicts refugees clinging to a giant bronze arm that reaches out of the ground and 42 feet into the air. Enter the surrounding courtyard to see a memorial wall and hear the music that seems to give voice to the 6 million Jews who died at the hands of the Nazis. It's easy to understand why Kenneth Treister's dramatic memorial is in Miami Beach: the city's community of Holocaust survivors was once the second largest in the country. ⊠ *1933–1945 Meridian Ave., at Dade Blvd., South Beach* ☎ *305/538–1663* ⊕ *www.holocaustmemorialmiamibeach.org* ▭ *Free.*

FAMILY
Fodor's Choice
★

Lincoln Road Mallz. This open-air pedestrian mall flaunts some of Miami's best people-watching. The eclectic interiors of myriad fabulous restaurants, colorful boutiques, art galleries, lounges, and cafés are often upstaged by the bustling outdoor scene. It's here among the prolific alfresco dining enclaves that you can pass the hours easily beholding the beautiful people. Indeed, outdoor restaurant and café seating take center stage along this wide pedestrian road adorned with towering date palms, linear pools, and colorful broken-tile mosaics. A few of the shops on Lincoln Road are owner-operated boutiques carrying a smart variety of clothing, furnishings, jewelry, and decorative elements. But more often you'll find typical upscale chain stores—Apple Store, Nespresso, Gap, and so on. Lincoln Road is fun, lively, and friendly for people—old, young, gay, and straight—and their dogs. Lincoln Road is a great place to cool down with an icy treat while touring South Beach. If you visit on a Sunday, stop at one of the many juice vendors, who'll whip up made-to-order smoothies from mangoes, oranges, and other fresh local fruits.

Miami Beach
and South Beach

Two landmarks worth checking out at the eastern end of Lincoln Road are the massive 1940s keystone building at 420 Lincoln Road, which has a 1945 Leo Birchanky mural in the lobby, and the 1921 Mission-style Miami Beach Community Church, at Drexel Avenue. The Lincoln Theatre (541–545 Lincoln Rd.), at Pennsylvania Avenue, is a classical four-story art deco gem with friezes, which now houses H&M. At Euclid Avenue there's a monument to Morris Lapidus, the brains behind Lincoln Road Mall, who in his nineties watched the renaissance of his whimsical South Beach creation. At Lenox Avenue, a black-and-white art deco movie house with a Mediterranean barrel-tile roof is now the Colony Theater (1040 Lincoln Rd.), where live theater and experimental films are presented. ⊠ *Lincoln Rd., between Washington Ave. and Alton Rd., South Beach* ⊕ *www.lincolnroadmall.com.*

QUICK BITES

The Frieze Ice Cream Factory. A true South Beach original, this mom-and-pop ice-cream shop serves what could very well be the best ice cream in Florida (except Azucar in Little Havana). Delight in mouthwatering homemade ice cream and sorbets including Indian mango, key lime pie, cashew toffee crunch, and chocolate decadence. ⊠ *1626 Michigan Ave., just south of Lincoln Rd., South Beach* ☎ *305/538-0207.*

QUICK BITES

Gelateria 4D. Authentic Italian gelato is scooped up with plenty of authentic Miami attitude at this sleek glass-and-stainless-steel sweet spot. The gelato is delicious despite the not-so-sweet service and exorbitant price. ⊠ *670 Lincoln Rd., between Euclid and Pennsylvania Aves., South Beach* ☎ *786/276-9475* ⊕ *www.gelateria4d.com.*

WORTH NOTING

Art Deco Welcome Center and Museum. Run by the Miami Design Preservation League, the center provides information about the buildings in the district. An official art deco Museum opened within the center in October 2014, and an improved gift shop sells 1930s–50s art deco memorabilia, posters, and books on Miami's history. Several tours—covering Lincoln Road, Española Way, North Beach, and the entire Art Deco District, among others—start here. You can choose from a self-guided iPod audio tour or join one of the regular morning walking tours at 10:30 every day. On Thursday a second tour takes place at 6:30 pm. Prepurchase tickets online and arrive at the center 15 minutes beforehand; all tours leave from the gift shop. All of the options provide detailed histories of the art deco hotels as well as an introduction to the art deco, Mediterranean revival, and Miami Modern (MiMo) styles found within the Miami Beach Architectural Historic District. Don't miss the special boat tours during Art Deco Weekend, in early January. ⊠ *1001 Ocean Dr., South Beach* ☎ *305/672–2014, 305/531–3484 for tours* ⊕ *www.mdpl.org* ☞ *Tours $25.*

World Erotic Art Museum (WEAM). Late millionaire Naomi Wilzig's collection of some 4,000 erotic items is on display at this unique museum. Expect sexy art of varying quality—fertility statues from around the globe and historic Chinese *shunga* books (erotic art offered as gifts to new brides on the wedding night) share the space with some kitschy

knickknacks. If this is your thing, an original phallic prop from Stanley Kubrick's *A Clockwork Orange* and an over-the-top Kama Sutra bed is worth the price of admission. Kids 17 and under are not admitted. ✉ *1205 Washington Ave., at 12th St., South Beach* ☎ *305/532–9336* ⊕ *www.weam.com* ✉ *$15.*

MID-BEACH

Where does South Beach end and Mid-Beach begin? With the massive amount of money being spent on former 1950s pleasure palaces like the Fontainebleau and Eden Roc, it could be that Mid-Beach will soon just be considered part of South Beach. North of 23rd Street, Collins Avenue curves its way to 44th Street, where it takes a sharp left turn after running into the Soho House Miami and then the Fontainebleau resort. The area between these two points—and up until 63rd Street—is officially Mid-Beach. The area has been experiencing a renaissance since the $1 billion re-debut of the Fontainebleau resort in 2008. Investors have followed suit with major other projects to revive the Mid-Beach area. Most recently, Argentinean developer Alan Faena has embarked on the neighborhood's latest $1 billion-plus mission: to restore the historic buildings along Collins Avenue from 32nd to 36th streets, creating new hotels, condos, and cultural institutions which will collectively become the Miami Beach Faena District. And the results have been nothing short of amazing.

FISHER AND BELLE ISLANDS

A private island community near the southern tip of South Beach, Fisher Island is accessible only by the island's ferry service. The island is predominantly residential with a few hotel rooms on offer at the Resort at Fisher Island Club. Belle Island is a small island connected to both the mainland and Miami Beach by road. It is a mile north of South Beach and just west over the Venetian Causeway.

NORTH BEACH

Though often referred to collectively as "North Beach," there are several neighborhoods above Mid-Beach before reaching the Dade-Broward border. In Miami Beach proper, nearing the 63rd Street mark on Collins Avenue, Mid-Beach gives way to North Beach (until 87th Street), followed by Surfside (up until 96th Street).

BAL HARBOUR

At 96th Street, the town of Bal Harbour takes over Collins Avenue from Miami Beach. Bal Harbour is famous for its outdoor high-end shops; and if you take your shopping seriously, you may want to spend some considerable time in this area. The town runs a mere 10 blocks to the north before the bridge to another barrier island. After crossing the bridge, you'll first come to Haulover Beach Park, which is still technically in the village of Bal Harbour.

SUNNY ISLES BEACH

Beyond Haulover Beach (and on the same barrier island) is the town of Sunny Isles Beach. Once over the bridge, Collins Avenue bypasses several dozen street numbers, picking up again in the 150s; that's when you know you've arrived in the town of Sunny Isles Beach—an appealing, calm, and predominantly upscale choice for families looking for a beautiful beach, and where Russian may be heard as often as English. There's no nightlife to speak of in Sunny Isles, and yet the half dozen mega-luxurious skyscraper hotels that have sprung up here in the past decade have created a niche-resort town from the demolished ashes of much older, affordable hotels.

NORTH MIAMI

This suburban city, north of Miami proper, is comprised predominantly of older homes in its western reaches—many derelict—but also some snazzy rebuilds in the sections around Biscayne Bay and U.S.1. Several strip malls and restaurants line U.S. 1.

NORTH MIAMI BEACH

Don't let the name fool you. North Miami Beach actually isn't on the beach, but its southeastern end does abut Biscayne Bay. Beyond the popular Oleta River State Park on the bay, the city offers little in terms of touristic appeal.

AVENTURA

West of Sunny Isles Beach and on the mainland are the high-rises of Aventura. This city is the heart and soul of South Florida's Jewish community as well as Miami's growing Russian community (along with Sunny Isles Beach). It is known for its high-end shopping opportunities, from the mega Aventura Mall to smaller boutiques in eclectic strip malls.

BEACHES

CORAL GABLES

FAMILY **Matheson Hammock Park and Beach.** Kids love the gentle waves and warm (albeit often murky) waters of this beach in Coral Gables's suburbia, near Fairchild Tropical Botanic Garden. But the beach is only part of the draw—the park includes a boardwalk trail, a playground, and a golf course. Plus, the park is a prime spot for kiteboarding. The man-made lagoon, or "atoll pool," is perfect for inexperienced swimmers, and it's one of the best places in mainland Miami for a picnic. Most tourists don't make the trek here; this park caters more to locals who don't want to travel all the way to Miami Beach. The park also offers a full-service marina. ■TIP→ With an emphasis on family fun, it's not the best place for singles. **Amenities:** parking (fee); toilets. **Best for:** swimming. ⌂ *9610 Old Cutler Rd., Coral Gables* ☎ *305/665–5475* ⊕ *www.miamidade.gov/parks/matheson-hammock.asp* 🎫 *$5 per vehicle weekdays, $7 weekends.*

KEY BISCAYNE

Fodor's Choice
★
Bill Baggs Cape Florida State Park. Thanks to inviting beaches, sunsets, and a tranquil lighthouse, this park at Key Biscayne's southern tip is worth the drive. In fact, the 1-mile stretch of pure beachfront has been named several times in Dr. Beach's revered America's Top 10 Beaches list. It has 18 picnic pavilions available as daily rentals, two cafés that serve light lunches that include several Cuban specialties, and plenty of space to enjoy the umbrella and chair rentals. A stroll or ride along walking and bicycle paths provides wonderful views of Miami's dramatic skyline. From the southern end of the park you can see a handful of houses rising over the bay on wooden stilts, the remnants of Stiltsville, built in the 1940s and now protected by the Stiltsville Trust. The nonprofit group was established in 2003 to preserve the structures, because they showcase the park's rich history. Bill Baggs has bicycle rentals, a playground, fishing piers, and guided tours of the **Cape Florida Lighthouse,** South Florida's oldest structure. The lighthouse was erected in 1845 to replace an earlier one damaged in an 1836 Seminole attack, in which the keeper's helper was killed. Free tours are offered at the restored cottage and lighthouse at 10 am and 1 pm Thursday to Monday. Be there a half hour beforehand. **Amenities:** food and drink; lifeguards; parking (free); showers; toilets. **Best for:** solitude; sunset; walking. ⊠ *1200 S. Crandon Blvd., Key Biscayne* ☎ *305/361–5811* ⊕ *www.floridastateparks.org/park/Cape-Florida* ⊠ *$8 per vehicle; $2 per pedestrian.*

FAMILY
Crandon Park Beach. This relaxing oasis in northern Key Biscayne offers renowned tennis facilities, a great golf course, a family amusement center, and 2 miles of beach dotted with palm trees. The park is divided by Key Biscayne's main road, with tennis and golf on the bay side, the beaches on the ocean side. Families really enjoy the beaches here—the sand is soft, there are no riptides, there's a great view of the Atlantic, and parking is both inexpensive and plentiful. However, on weekends, be prepared for a long hike from your car to the beach. There are bathrooms, outdoor showers, plenty of picnic tables, and concession stands. The family-friendly park offers abundant options for those who find it challenging simply to sit and build sand castles. Kite-board rentals and lessons are offered from the north water-sports concessions, as are kayak rentals. Eco-tours and nature trails showcase the myriad ecosystems of Key Biscayne including mangroves, coastal hammock, and sea-grass beds. Bird-watching is great at the southern end of the park. The **Crandon's Family Amusement Center** at Crandon Park was once the site of a zoo. There are swans, waterfowl, peacocks, and dozens of huge iguanas running loose. Nearby you'll find a restored carousel (it's open weekends and major holidays), an old-fashioned outdoor roller rink, a dolphin-shape spray fountain, and a playground. **Amenities:** food and drink; lifeguards; parking (fee); showers; toilets; water sports. **Best for:** swimming; walking. ⊠ *6747 Crandon Blvd., Key Biscayne* ☎ *305/361–5421* ⊕ *www.miamidade.gov/Parks/crandon.asp* ⊠ *$5 per vehicle weekdays, $7 weekends.*

SOUTH BEACH

Fodor's Choice
★

South Beach. A 10-block stretch of white sandy beach hugging the turquoise waters along Ocean Drive—from 5th to 15th streets—is one of the most popular in America, known for drawing unabashedly model-like sunbathers and posers. With the influx of new luxe hotels and hot spots from 1st to 5th and 16th to 25th streets, the South Beach stand-and-pose scene is now bigger than ever and stretches yet another dozen-plus blocks. The beaches crowd quickly on the weekends with a blend of European tourists, young hipsters, and sun-drenched locals. Separating the sand from the traffic of Ocean Drive is palm-fringed **Lummus Park**, with its volleyball nets and chickee huts (huts made of palmetto thatch over a cypress frame) for shade. The beach at **12th Street** is popular with gays, in a section often marked with rainbow flags. Locals hang out on 3rd Street beach, in an area called **SoFi** (South of Fifth) where they watch fit Brazilians play foot volley, a variation of volleyball that uses everything but the hands. Because much of South Beach leans toward skimpy sunning—women are often in G-strings and casually topless—many families prefer the tamer sections of Mid- and North Beach (save Haulover nude beach). Metered parking spots next to the ocean are a rare find. Instead, opt for a public garage a few blocks away and enjoy the people-watching as you walk to find your perfect spot on the sand. **Amenities:** food and drink; lifeguards; parking (fee); showers; toilets. **Best for:** partiers; sunrise; swimming; walking. ⊠ *Ocean Dr., from 5th to 15th Sts., then Collins Ave. to 25th St., South Beach.*

NORTH BEACH

MIAMI BEACH

Haulover Beach Park. This popular clothing-optional beach is embraced by naturists of all ages, shapes, and sizes; there are even sections primarily frequented by families, singles, and gays. However, Haulover has more claims to fame than its casual attitude toward swimwear—it's also the best beach in the area for bodyboarding and surfing, as it gets what passes for impressive swells in these parts. Plus the sand here is fine-grain white, unusual for the Atlantic coast. Once you park in the North Lot, you'll walk through a short tunnel covered with trees and natural habitat until you emerge on the unpretentious beach, where nudity is rarely met by gawkers. There are volleyball nets, and plenty of beach chair and umbrella rentals to protect your birthday suit from too much exposure—to the sun, that is. The sections of beach requiring swimwear are popular, too, given the park's ample parking and relaxed atmosphere. Lifeguards stand watch. More active types might want to check out the kite rentals, or charter-fishing excursions. **Amenities:** food and drink; lifeguards; parking (fee); showers; toilets. **Best for:** nudists; surfing; swimming; walking. ⊠ *10800 Collins Ave., north of Bal Harbour, North Beach* ☎ *305/947–3525* ⊕ *www.miamidade.gov/parks/haulover.asp* 🅿 *Parking $5 per vehicle weekdays, $7 weekends.*

NORTH MIAMI BEACH

FAMILY **Oleta River State Park.** Tucked away in North Miami Beach, this urban park is a ready-made family getaway. Nature lovers will find it easy to embrace the 1,128 acres of subtropical beauty along Biscayne Bay. Swim in the calm bay waters and bicycle, canoe, kayak, and bask among egrets, manatees, bald eagles, and fiddler crabs. Dozens of picnic tables, along with 10 covered pavilions, dot the stunning natural habitat, which was restored with red mangroves to revitalize the ecosystem and draw endangered birds, like the roseate spoonbill. There's a playground for tots, a mangrove island accessible only by boat, 15 miles of mountain-bike trails, a half-mile exercise track, concessions, and outdoor showers. **Amenities:** food and drink; parking (fee); showers; toilets; water sports. **Best for:** solitude; sunrise; sunset; walking. ✉ *3400 N.E. 163rd St., North Miami Beach* ☎ *305/919–1844* ⊕ *www.floridastateparks.org/park/Oleta-River* 🖂 *$6 per vehicle; $2 per pedestrian.*

WHERE TO EAT

Miami's restaurant scene has exploded in the past few years, with new restaurants springing up left and right every month. The melting pot of residents and visitors has brought an array of sophisticated, tasty cuisine. Little Havana is still king for Cuban fare, and Miami Beach is swept up in a trend of fusion cuisine, which combines Asian, French, American, and Latin cooking with sumptuous—and pricey—results. Locals spend the most time in downtown Miami, Wynwood, Midtown, and the Design District, where the city's ongoing foodie and cocktail revolution is most pronounced. Since Miami dining is a part of the trendy nightlife scene, most dinners don't start until 8 or 9 pm, and may go well into the night. To avoid a long wait among the late-night partiers at hot spots, come before 7 pm or make reservations. Attire is usually casual-chic, but patrons like to dress to impress. Don't be surprised to see large tables of women in skimpy dresses—this is common in Miami. Prices tend to stay high in hot spots like Lincoln Road, but if you venture off the beaten path you can find delicious food for reasonable prices. When you get your bill, check whether a gratuity is already included; most restaurants add between 15% and 20% (ostensibly for the convenience of, and protection from, the many Latin American and European tourists who are used to this practice in their homelands), but supplement it depending on your opinion of the service.

Restaurant reviews have been shortened. For full information, visit Fodors.com. Use the coordinate (✛ C2) at the end of each review to locate a property on the Where to Eat and Stay in the Miami Area map.

WHAT IT COSTS			
$	$$	$$$	$$$$
Restaurants	under $15	$15–$20	$21–$30	over $30

Restaurant prices are the average cost of a main course at dinner or, if dinner is not served, at lunch.

DOWNTOWN

$$$$
SEAFOOD

✕ **Area 31.** High atop the 16th floor of downtown Miami's Kimpton Epic Hotel, memorable and sustainable ocean-to-table cuisine is prepared in the bustling, beautiful open kitchen. Executive chef Wolfgang Birk infuses his seafood-centric menu with innovative flavors and a hefty portion of ethos—all fruits of the sea here are certified by the Monterey Bay Aquarium's Seafood Watch. **Known for:** sustainable seafood; excellent bay-side views; artisanal cocktails. $ *Average main: $35* ✉ *Kimpton Epic Hotel, 270 Biscayne Blvd. Way, 16th fl., Downtown* ☎ *305/424–5234* ⊕ *www.area31restaurant.com* ✛ *D4.*

$$$$
ECLECTIC

✕ **Azul.** A restaurant known for producing celebrity chefs and delivering dining fantasies of Food Network proportions, Azul is a Miami foodie institution. With its Forbes five-star, award-winning team, Azul offers a haute-cuisine experience on par with a two- or three-Michelin-star restaurant. **Known for:** special-occasion dining; gastronomic excellence; sublime bay-side views. $ *Average main: $48* ✉ *Mandarin Oriental, Miami, 500 Brickell Key Dr., Downtown* ☎ *305/913–8358* ⊕ *www.mandarinoriental.com/miami* ☾ *Closed Sun. and Mon. No lunch* ✛ *D5.*

$$$
FRENCH

✕ **db Bistro Moderne Miami.** One of America's most celebrated French chefs, Daniel Boulud brings his renowned cooking to the Miami scene with a menu that pays homage to Mediterranean cuisines and the specialties of his homeland. There's a good-value prix-fixe lunch during the workweek for Miami's business crowd. **Known for:** power lunches; beautiful interiors; coq au vin. $ *Average main: $30* ✉ *JW Marriott Marquis Miami, 255 Biscayne Blvd. Way, Downtown* ☎ *305/421–8800* ⊕ *www.dbbistro.com/miami/* ✛ *D4.*

$$$
STEAKHOUSE
Fodor's Choice
★

✕ **Edge, Steak & Bar.** It's farm-to-table surf and turf at this elegantly understated restaurant in the Four Seasons Hotel Miami, where hefty portions of the finest cuts and freshest seafood headline the menu, prepared by renowned chef Aaron Brooks. The innovative tartares are a surefire way to start the night right—try the corvina with baby cucumber, green apple, and a young celery-leaf, yellow-pepper sauce, or the ahi tuna with pickled shallots, watermelon, and mint. **Known for:** crudos; Sunday brunch; outdoor terrace seating. $ *Average main: $30* ✉ *Four Seasons Miami, 1435 Brickell Ave, Downtown* ☎ *305/381–3190* ⊕ *www.edgerestaurantmiami.com* ✛ *D5.*

$$$
ECLECTIC

✕ **15th & Vine Kitchen and Bar.** The signature restaurant of the swanky W Miami wows with a trifecta of sleek decor, delicious food, and a breathtaking backdrop from the property's famed terrace and deck hovering 15 stories above Brickell Avenue and Biscayne Bay. Seasonal menus tout contemporary American cuisine under global influences, all presented tapas-style. **Known for:** coconut mojitos; ecelctic small plates; dining under the stars. $ *Average main: $27* ✉ *W Miami, 485 Brickell Ave., Downtown* ☎ *305/307–5413* ⊕ *www.wmiamihotel.com/downtown-miami-restaurants* ✛ *D4.*

$$$$
PERUVIAN
Fodor's Choice
★

✕ **La Mar by Gaston Acurio.** Don't have time to make a foodie pilgrimage to Lima, Peru? Not to worry; the next best thing beckons in downtown Miami, where Peruvian celebrity-chef Gaston Acurio dazzles with a sublime menu and an atmospheric, bay-side setting to match. **Known for:** authentic Peruvian food; alfresco dining; desserts served in dollhouses.

$ *Average main: $34* ✉ *Mandarin Oriental, Miami, 500 Brickell Key Dr., Downtown* ⊕ *www.mandarinoriental.com/miami* ✛ *D5.*

$$$$
JAPANESE

✕ **NAOE.** By virtue of its petite size (eight patrons max) and strict seating times (at 6 and 9:30 nightly), the Japanese gem will forever remain intimate and original. Chef Kevin Cory prepares a gastronomic adventure a few feet from his patrons, using only the best Japanese ingredients and showcasing family treasures, like the renowned products of his centuries-old family shoyu (soy sauce) and sake brewery. **Known for:** freshest of fresh fish; authentic Japanese taste; $240 per person price tag. $ *Average main: $240* ✉ *661 Brickell Key Dr., Downtown* ☎ *305/947–6263* ⊕ *www.naoemiami.com* ☾ *Closed Sun. No lunch* ✛ *D5.*

$$$
ITALIAN

✕ **Perricone's Marketplace and Café.** Brickell Avenue south of the Miami River is a haven for Italian restaurants, and this lunch place for local bigwigs is arguably the best and most popular. It's housed partially outdoors and partially indoors in an 1880s barn that was brought down from Vermont. **Known for:** rustic setting; tree-lined garden seating area; excellent Italian food. $ *Average main: $22* ✉ *Mary Brickell Village, 15 S.E. 10th St., Downtown* ☎ *305/374–9449* ⊕ *www.perricones.com* ✛ *D5.*

$$
ECLECTIC
Fodor'sChoice
★

✕ **Verde at PAMM.** As if the high-design Pérez Art Museum Miami (PAMM) weren't cool enough, its waterfront restaurant also makes major waves across Biscayne Bay. The slick, contemporary restaurant offers seating both indoors and out, with chic decor and accessories true to its "green" name that blend seamlessly with the living walls and hanging gardens strewn across the museum's exterior. **Known for:** fabulous bay views; light lunching; artisanal pizzas. $ *Average main: $18* ✉ *Pérez Art Museum Miami, 1103 Biscayne Blvd., Downtown* ☎ *305/375–3000* ⊕ *www.pamm.org/dining* ☾ *Closed Wed. No dinner Fri.–Tues.* ✛ *D4.*

COCONUT GROVE

$$$$
MODERN
AMERICAN
FAMILY

✕ **Glass & Vine.** With a design that fuses the indoors and outdoors, this charming restaurant by celebrity-chef Giorgio Rapicavoli (a champion on Food Network's *Chopped*) is as picturesque as it is unexpected. It happens to be smack in the middle of Coconut Grove's residential Peacock Park, fronting a playground, a baseball park, and the bay. **Known for:** local fish aguachile; locally sourced ingredients; garden atmosphere. $ *Average main: $34* ✉ *2820 McFarlane Rd., Coconut Grove* ☎ *305/200–5268* ⊕ *www.glassandvine.com* ✛ *C5.*

$$
MEDITERRANEAN

✕ **GreenStreet Cafe.** A tried-and-true locals' hangout since it was founded in the early 1990s—with regulars including athletes, politicians, entrepreneurs, artists, and other prominent area names—this cozy café serves up simple French-Mediterranean delights. Despite the restaurant's see-and-be-seen reputation, diners are encouraged to sit back and simply enjoy the experience with relaxed decor, good food, and friendly service. **Known for:** fruity cocktails; great breakfast; late-night lounging and noshing. $ *Average main: $17* ✉ *3468 Main Hwy., Coconut Grove* ☎ *305/444–0244* ⊕ *www.greenstreetcafe.net* ✛ *C5.*

$$$
SEAFOOD
FAMILY

✕ **Monty's.** Connected to Prime Marina Miami, Monty's has a Caribbean flair, thanks especially to live calypso and island music on the outdoor terrace. Though it has lost the luster it had back in the 1990s, it's still a fun, chill, kid-friendly place where Mom and Dad can kick back in the early evening and enjoy a beer and the raw bar while the kids dance to live music. **Known for:** conch fritters; tropical cocktails; waterfront dining. $ *Average main: $23* ⊠ *Prime Marina Miami, 2550 S. Bayshore Dr., at Aviation Ave., Coconut Grove* ☎ *305/856–3992* ⊕ *www.montysrawbar.com* ✛ *C5.*

$$ ✕ **Peacock Garden Café.** Reinstating the artsy and exciting vibe of Coco-
AMERICAN nut Grove circa once-upon-a-time, this lovely spot offers an indoor-
FAMILY outdoor, teatime setting for light bites. By day, it's one of Miami's most serene lunch spots as the lushly landscaped courtyard is lined with alfresco seating, drawing some of Miami's most fabulous ladies who lunch. **Known for:** old-school charm; idyllic setting for lunch; home-made soups. $ *Average main: $19* ⊠ *2889 McFarlane Rd., Coconut Grove* ☎ *305/774–3332* ⊕ *www.jaguarhg.com* ✛ *C5.*

CORAL GABLES

$$$ ✕ **eating house.** Check your calorie counter at the door when you enter the
ECLECTIC hippest eatery in Coral Gables. The ever-changing small-plates menu teems
Fodor's Choice with extreme culinary innovation and unexpected flavor combinations.
★ **Known for:** "dirt cup" dessert; innovative cuisine; foodie crowd. $ *Aver-age main: $25* ⊠ *804 Ponce de León Blvd., Coral Gables* ☎ *305/448–6524* ⊕ *www.eatinghousemiami.com* ⊗ *No lunch weekends* ✛ *B5.*

$ ✕ **El Palacio de los Jugos.** To the northwest of Coral Gables proper, this
CUBAN joint is one of the easiest and truest ways to see Miami's local Latin life in
FAMILY action. It's also one of the best fruit-shake shacks you'll ever come across (ask for a tropical juice of mamey or guanabana). **Known for:** exotic fruit shakes; no-frills feel; great market for getting produce to go. $ *Average main: $6* ⊠ *5721 W. Flagler St., Flagami, Coral Gables* ☎ *305/264–8662* ⊕ *www.elpalaciodelosjugos.com/en* ▭ *No credit cards* ✛ *B4.*

$$$ ✕ **Ortanique on the Mile.** Cascading *ortaniques,* a Jamaican hybrid orange,
CARIBBEAN are hand-painted on columns in this warm, welcoming, yellow dining room. Food is vibrant in taste and color, as delicious as it is beautiful. **Known for:** creative, tropical cocktails; colorful decor; excellent seafood. $ *Average main: $29* ⊠ *278 Miracle Mile, Coral Gables* ☎ *305/446–7710* ⊕ *www.ortaniquerestaurants.com* ⊗ *No lunch weekends* ✛ *B5.*

$$$$ ✕ **Pascal's on Ponce.** This French gem amid the Coral Gables restaurant
FRENCH district is always full, thanks to chef-proprietor Pascal Oudin's assured and consistent cuisine. Oudin forgoes the glitz and fussiness often asso-ciated with French cuisine, and instead opts for a simple, small, refined dining room that won't overwhelm patrons. **Known for:** tomato tartine; crispy duck confit; refined atmosphere. $ *Average main: $34* ⊠ *2611 Ponce de León Blvd., Coral Gables* ☎ *305/444–2024* ⊕ *www.pascalmi-ami.com* ⊗ *Closed Sun. No lunch Sat.* ✛ *B5.*

KEY BISCAYNE

$$$ ✕ **Cantina Beach.** Leave it to Ritz-Carlton to bring a small, sumptuous
MEXICAN piece of coastal Mexico to Florida's fabulous beaches. The pool- and ocean-side Cantina Beach showcases authentic and divine Mexican cui-sine, including fresh guacamole made table-side. **Known for:** top-shelf

margaritas; table-side guacamole; dining on the sand. $\boxed{\$}$ *Average main: $21* $\boxtimes$ *The Ritz-Carlton Key Biscayne, Miami, 455 Grand Bay Dr., Key Biscayne* ☎ *305/365–4500* ⊕ *www.ritzcarlton.com/keybiscayne* ✛ *D6.*

$$$
MODERN
AMERICAN
Fodor's Choice
★

✕ **Rusty Pelican.** Whether you're visiting Miami for the first or 15th time, a meal at the Rusty Pelican is a memorable experience. Vistas of the bay and Miami skyline are sensational—whether you admire them through the floor-to-ceiling windows or from the expansive outdoor seating area, lined with alluring fire pits. **Known for:** views of Miami skyline; great seafood; outdoor fire pits. $\boxed{\$}$ *Average main: $26* $\boxtimes$ *3201 Rickenbacker Causeway, Key Biscayne* ☎ *305/361–3818* ⊕ *www.therustypelican.com* ✛ *D5.*

WYNWOOD

$$$$
ECLECTIC
Fodor's Choice
★

✕ **Alter Restaurant.** Chef Bradley Kilgore has risen to local superstardom with his progressive, seasonally inspired new American hot spot. Kilgore is always changing up the menu based on ingredient availability and then taking on the awesome task of transforming food into edible art. **Known for:** tasting menus; locavore patrons; great wine pairings. $\boxed{\$}$ *Average main: $34* $\boxtimes$ *223 N.W. 23rd St., Wynwood* ☎ ⊕ *www.altermiami.com* ✛ *D4.*

$$
ITALIAN

✕ **Joey's.** This small, modern Italian café offers a full line of flatbread pizzas, including the legendary *dolce e piccante* with figs, Gorgonzola, honey, and hot pepper—it's sweet-and-spicy goodness through and through. Joey's also serves the full gamut of Italian favorites and was cited in 2016 as one of Beyoncé and Jay Z's favorite Miami haunts. Opened in 2008, it was one of the first nongallery tenants in the area and the first restaurant in the Wynwood Art District, and it remains a favorite in the neighborhood despite an onslaught of fancy newcomers. **Known for:** fig-and-Gorgonzola pizza; true local feel; affordable wine selection. $\boxed{\$}$ *Average main: $19* $\boxtimes$ *2506 N.W. 2nd Ave., Wynwood* ☎ *305/438–0488* ⊕ *www.joeyswynwood.com* ☉ *No dinner Mon.* ✛ *D4.*

$$$
ECLECTIC
Fodor's Choice
★

✕ **KYU.** Foodies and locavores love this eclectic, eco-minded restaurant in the heart of Wynwood. The small-plates menu wows with dishes from the Japanese wood-fired grill such as the epic roasted cauliflower and goat cheese, divine roasted grouper over sake-braised white beans, and simple yet delicious whole-grilled corn with miso-lime butter. **Known for:** living walls; apex of Wynwood atmosphere; flavor-rich small plates. $\boxed{\$}$ *Average main: $28* $\boxtimes$ *251 N.W. 25th St., Wynwood* ☎ *786/577–0150* ⊕ *www.kyumiami.com* ✛ *D4.*

$
CAFÉ
Fodor's Choice
★

✕ **Panther Coffee.** The eclectic coffee shop has made a triumphant return to Miami, and it goes by the name of Panther Coffee. The original location of the Miami-based specialty coffee roaster is smack in the center of the Wynwood Arts District (it has now expanded into Miami Beach and other South Florida neighborhoods), attracting a who's who of hipsters, artists, and even suburbanites to indulge in small-batch cups of joe and supermoist muffins and fresh-baked pastries. **Known for:** hipster clientele; great coffee; fabulous people-watching. $\boxed{\$}$ *Average main: $5* $\boxtimes$ *2390 N.W. 2nd Ave., Wynwood* ☎ *305/677–3952* ⊕ *www.panthercoffee.com* ✛ *D4.*

2

$$$
ECLECTIC
Fodor'sChoice
★

✕ **Wynwood Kitchen & Bar.** At the center of Miami's artsy gallery-driven neighborhood, Wynwood Kitchen & Bar offers an experience that includes both cultural and gastronomic excitement. While you enjoy Latin-inspired small plates, you can marvel at the powerful, hand-painted interior and exterior murals, which also spill out onto the captivating Wynwood Walls. **Known for:** ropa vieja empanadas; hamburguesitas; graffiti art displays. ⑤ *Average main: $22* ⊠ *2550 N.W. 2nd Ave., Wynwood* ☎ *305/722–8959* ⊕ *www.wynwoodkitchenandbar.com* ✛ *D4.*

MIDTOWN

$$$
MODERN ITALIAN

✕ **Bocce.** A splendid slice of the Italian countryside thrives in Miami's trendy Midtown area, and the impressive 3,200-square-foot enclave houses a beautifully appointed rustic Italian restaurant, Miami's first official bocce court, and a throwback-style Italian market. Mosaic-tiled floors, antique mirrors, and exposed wood beams set the scene indoors while towering cypress trees, a traditional bocce court, and alfresco seating aplenty define the front patio. **Known for:** lively bocce court; great happy hour; melanzane (eggplant) parmigiana. ⑤ *Average main: $24* ⊠ *3252 N.E. 1st Ave., No. 107, Midtown* ☎ *786/245–6211* ⊕ *www.bocceristorante.com* ✛ *D4.*

$$$$
JAPANESE
FUSION
Fodor'sChoice
★

✕ **Sugarcane Raw Bar Grill.** Midtown's most popular restaurant rages seven nights (and days) a week, and it's not hard to see why. The vibrant, supersexy, high-design restaurant perfectly captures Miami's Latin vibe while serving eclectic Latin American tapas and modern Japanese delights from three separate kitchens (*robata* grill, raw bar, and hot kitchen). **Known for:** "night crab" sushi roll; spicy local-catch crudo; high-design interiors. ⑤ *Average main: $38* ⊠ *3252 N.E. 1st Ave., Midtown* ☎ *786/369–0353* ⊕ *sugarcanerawbargrill.com* ✛ *D4.*

DESIGN DISTRICT

$$
PIZZA
FAMILY
Fodor'sChoice
★

✕ **Harry's Pizzeria.** Harry's is a neighborhood spot with some seriously good pizza, as one would expect as the second restaurant under Miami culinary darling Michael Schwartz and his team. The casual, friendly-yet-funky ambience is inviting for all diner matchups: old chums, new dates, family members young and old. **Known for:** seasonally inspired pizzas; lively atmopshere; homemade ricotta. ⑤ *Average main: $16* ⊠ *3918 N. Miami Ave., Design District* ☎ *786/275–4963* ⊕ *www.harryspizzeria.com* ✛ *D3.*

$$$
MODERN GREEK
Fodor'sChoice
★

✕ **Mandolin Aegean Bistro.** A step inside this 1940s house-turned-bistro transports you to *ya-ya* 's home along the Aegean Sea. The food is fresh and the service warm, matching its charming dining garden enlivened by an awning of trees, a rustic wooden canopy, and traditional village furnishings. **Known for:** signature Greek salad; bucolic courtyard; spectacular meze. ⑤ *Average main: $26* ⊠ *4312 N.E. 2nd Ave., Design District* ☎ *305/576–6066* ⊕ *www.mandolinmiami.com* ✛ *D3.*

$$$
AMERICAN
Fodor'sChoice
★

✕ **Michael's Genuine Food & Drink.** Michael's is often cited as Miami's top restaurant, and it's not hard to see why: this indoor-outdoor bistro in Miami's Design District is an evergreen oasis for Miami dining sophisticates. Owner and chef Michael Schwartz aims for sophisticated

American cuisine with an emphasis on local and organic ingredients, and he gets it right. **Known for:** being at the forefront of modern American cuisine; sceney alfresco dining area; innovative cocktails. ⑤ *Average main: $27* ✉ *130 N.E. 40th St., Design District* ☎ *305/573–5550* ⊕ *www.michaelsgenuine.com* ✛ *D3.*

LITTLE HAITI

$$
CARIBBEAN

✕ **Chez Le Bebe.** Chez Le Bebe offers a short menu of Haitian home cooking—it's been going strong for 30 years and has been featured on shows like the Travel Channel's *Bizarre Foods with Andrew Zimmern* and *The Layover with Anthony Bourdain.* If you want to try stewed goat, this is the place to do it! **Known for:** authentic Haitian eats; no-frills atmosphere; stewed goat. ⑤ *Average main: $15* ✉ *114 N.E. 54th St., Little Haiti* ☎ *305/751–7639* ▭ *No credit cards* ✛ *D3.*

LITTLE HAVANA

$
CAFÉ
FAMILY
Fodor's Choice
★

✕ **Azucar Ice Cream Company.** Balmy weather and sweet-tooth cravings are tempered at this ice-cream shop specializing in homemade Cuban-style scoops. More crafty than churning, flavors are inspired and derived from ingredients at nearby fruit stands, international grocery shops, and farmers' markets. **Known for:** Abuela Maria ice cream; flan ice cream; one-of-a-kind frozen indulgences. ⑤ *Average main: $6* ✉ *1503 S.W. 8th St., Little Havana* ☎ *305/381–0369* ⊕ *www.azucaricecream.com* ✛ *C5.*

$
LATIN AMERICAN

✕ **El Exquisito Restaurant.** For a true locals' spot and some substantial Cuban eats in the heart of Little Havana, pop into this local institution that's been popular since the 1970s. The unassuming Cuban café serves up delectable, authentic Cuban favorites, including a great cubano (a grilled Cuban sandwich layered with ham, garlic-and-citrus-marinated slow-roasted pork, Swiss cheese, and pickles) and succulent yuca with garlic sauce. **Known for:** chatty regulars; insanely cheap prices; Cuban sandwiches. ⑤ *Average main: $14* ✉ *1510 S.W. 8th St., Little Havana* ☎ *305/643–0227* ⊕ *www.elexquisitomiami.com* ▭ *No credit cards* ✛ *C5.*

$
CUBAN

✕ **Las Pinareños Fruteria y Floreria.** In the mood for something refreshing or a high-octane jolt? Try Las Pinareños, a *fruteria* (fruit stand) that serves *coco frio* (fresh, cold coconut juice served in a whole coconut), mango juice, and other *jugos* (juices), as well as Cuban coffees and Cuban finger foods. **Known for:** exotic juices; coco frio; friendly staff. ⑤ *Average main: $7* ✉ *1334 S.W. 8th St., Little Havana* ☎ *305/285–1135* ✛ *C5.*

$$
CUBAN
FAMILY
Fodor's Choice
★

✕ **Versailles.** To the area's Cuban population, Miami without Versailles is like rice without black beans. First-time Miami visitors looking for that "Cuban food on Calle Ocho" experience, look no further: the storied eatery, where old émigrés opine daily about all things Cuban, is a stop on every political candidate's campaign trail, and it should be a stop for you as well. **Known for:** lechon asado; Cuban coffee; take-out window. ⑤ *Average main: $15* ✉ *3555 S.W. 8th St., Little Havana* ☎ *305/444–0240* ⊕ *www.versaillesrestaurant.com* ✛ *C5.*

SOUTH BEACH

$$$
MODERN
AMERICAN
✕**Beachcraft.** Tom Colicchio made his Miami debut in late 2015 with this fabulous, farm-meets-ocean-to-table concept. A vast open kitchen anchors the restaurant, where guests can see and smell the action from their seats. **Known for:** grilled specialities; local products; intimate vibe. ⑤ *Average main: $28* ✉ *1 Hotel South Beach, 2395 Collins Ave., South Beach* ☎ *305/604–6700* ⊕ *www.beachcraftsobe.com* ✛ *E4.*

$$$$
ITALIAN
✕**Bianca at Delano South Beach.** In a hotel where style reigns supreme, this high-profile restaurant provides both glamour and solid Italian cuisine. The main attraction of dining here is to see and be seen, but you may leave talking about the shaved baby-artichoke salad and truffle tagliatelle just as much as the outfits, hairdos, and celebrity appearances. **Known for:** truffle tagliatelle; Sunday brunch; stylish crowd. ⑤ *Average main: $37* ✉ *Delano Hotel, 1685 Collins Ave., South Beach* ☎ *305/674–5752* ⊕ *www.delano-hotel.com* ✛ *H2.*

$$$
MODERN ITALIAN
Fodor's Choice
★
✕**Dolce Italian.** Best known as a top contender on the Bravo TV show *Best New Restaurant,* Dolce Italian buzzes in the center of the South Beach action, doling out an irresistible menage à trois: great food, great ambience, and an easy-on-the-eyes crowd. Italian-born chef Paolo Dorigato's menu is packed with modern incarnations of Italian classics that would make nonna proud. **Known for:** house-made mozzarella and pastas; Neopolitan-style pizzas; hot crowd. ⑤ *Average main: $29* ✉ *Gale South Beach, 1690 Collins Ave., South Beach* ☎ *786/975–2550* ⊕ *www.dolceitalianrestaurant.com* ✛ *G2.*

$$$$
MODERN
AMERICAN
✕**The Dutch Miami.** Loft meets cozy kitchen at the Miami outpost of chef Andrew Carmellini's NYC foodie hot spot in the swank W South Beach. There's a bit of everything on the "roots-inspired American menu," from local line-caught fish to homemade pastas and 28-day dry-aged steaks. **Known for:** local crowd; sweet corn mezzaluna; artisanal cocktails. ⑤ *Average main: $34* ✉ *W South Beach, 2201 Collins Ave., South Beach* ☎ *305/938–3111* ⊕ *www.thedutchmiami.com* ✛ *H1.*

$$$$
ITALIAN
✕**Gianni's at the Villa.** Set within the glitz and ostentation of Gianni Versace's former mansion, the Villa Casa Casuarina, this restaurant doles out excellent Italian eats across the mansion's most prized nooks. You can expect stellar service, bedazzling dishes, and a gold-and-diamond-encrusted atmosphere. **Known for:** haute dining; wow-factor surrounds; only-in-Miami experience. ⑤ *Average main: $48* ✉ *The Villa Casa Casuarina, 1116 Ocean Dr., South Beach* ☎ *786/485–2200* ⊕ *www.vmmiamibeach.com/restaurant* ☾ *Closed Mon.* ✛ *G3.*

$$$$
ASIAN FUSION
✕**Jaya at The Setai.** As the flagship restaurant of one of Miami's most exclusive hotels, The Setai, Jaya exceeds all expectations yet remains remarkably approachable. Chef Mathias Gervais delivers a pan-Asian extravaganza, representing the countries of Thailand, Vietnam, Singapore, Korea, India, China, and Japan, through dishes that range from tandoori sea bass to Peking duck to lobster laksa. **Known for:** beautiful interiors; tandoori sea bass; black pepper shrimp. ⑤ *Average main: $36* ✉ *The Setai, 2001 Collins Ave., South Beach* ☎ *855/923–7899* ⊕ *www.thesetaihotel.com/jaya.php* ✛ *H1.*

2

$$$$
SEAFOOD
Fodor's Choice
★

✕**Joe's Stone Crab Restaurant.** In South Beach's decidedly new-money scene, the stately Joe's Stone Crab is an old-school testament to good food and good service. Stone crabs, served with legendary mustard sauce, crispy hash brown potatoes, and creamed spinach, remain the staple. **Known for:** the best of the best stone crab claws; long waits (up to three hours on weekends); decadent side dishes. ⑤ *Average main: $49* ✉ *11 Washington Ave., South Beach* ☎ *305/673–0365, 305/673–4611 for takeout* ⊕ *www.joesstonecrab.com* ⊗ *No lunch Sun. and Mon. and mid-May–mid-Oct.* ✛ *G5.*

$$$$
JAPANESE
FUSION
Fodor's Choice
★

✕**Juvia.** High atop South Beach's design-driven 1111 Lincoln Road parking garage, Juvia commingles urban sophistication with South Beach seduction. Three renowned chefs unite to deliver an amazing eating experience that screams Japanese, Peruvian, and French all in the same breath, focusing largely on raw fish and seafood dishes. **Known for:** city and beach views; sunset cocktails on the terrace; tuna poke. ⑤ *Average main: $35* ✉ *1111 Lincoln Rd., South Beach* ☎ *305/763– 8272* ⊕ *www.juviamiami.com* ✛ *F2.*

$$$
JAPANESE
FUSION

✕**Katsuya South Beach.** Design impresario Philippe Starck opted to fill the smoking-hot SLS Hotel South Beach with a number of see-and-be-seen eateries, including Katsuya South Beach. At this popular Japanese restaurant, executive chef Jose Icardi (under the tutelage of master sushi chef Katsuya Uechi) employs four separate kitchens to serve up awesome eats like his legendary miso-marinated black cod, succulent lobster dynamite (in a creamy mushroom sauce), baked crab hand rolls, and amazing sushi rolls. **Known for:** sceney dining; baked crab hand rolls; high-design interiors. ⑤ *Average main: $28* ✉ *SLS Hotel South Beach, 1701 Collins Ave., South Beach* ⊕ *www.katsuyarestaurant.com/ southbeach* ✛ *H1.*

$$$
ITALIAN

✕**Macchialina.** Framed by exposed brick walls, decorated with daily specials chalkboards, and packed with gregarious patrons, this local foodie hangout feels like a cozy, neighborhoody, New England tavern. And with a gorgeous menu showcasing the prowess of chef Michael Pirolo, Macchialina Taverna Rustica nails the concept of modern Italian cuisine. **Known for:** Italian-imported salumi; house panna cotta; devoted local following. ⑤ *Average main: $26* ✉ *820 Alton Rd., South Beach* ☎ *305/534–2124* ⊕ *www.macchialina.com* ✛ *F3.*

$$$
THAI

✕**NaiYaRa.** Combine the pulse of Bangkok with the glitz of South Beach and undertones of Tokyo, and you get this hypercool, Thai-meets-Japanese restaurant with a sleek, retro-contemporary design in the heart of Miami's burgeoning Sunset Harbour area. The lovable and highly talented owner, Piyarat Potha Arreeratn (aka Chef Bee), guarantees a memorable night of fun, fruity and wild cocktails, and a diverse menu that spans classic Thai dishes perfected (pad thai and papaya salad) to more daring taste creations like the Naiyara roll (a sushi roll filled with salmon belly, cucumber, avocado, scallion, truffle oil, and topped with salmon belly "crème brûlée"). **Known for:** fried chicken dumplings; dynamic atmosphere; Bangkok-imbued environs. ⑤ *Average main: $28* ✉ *1854 Bay Rd., South Beach* ☎ *786/275–6005* ⊕ *www.naiyara.com* ✛ *E4.*

Where to Eat and Stay in the Miami Area

A **B** **C** **D**

1

I-95

Palmetto Expwy. 826
817

N. Miami Beach Blvd.

NORTH
MIAMI
BEACH

909

N.E. 6th Ave.

2 mi

2 km

75

Okeechobee Rd.

Palmetto Expwy.

Red Rd.

N.W. 135th St.

E. 8th Ave.

N.W. 27th Ave.

7th Ave.

N.E. 135th St.
915

2

HIALEAH

W. 49th St. E. 49th St. 932

N.W. 103rd St.

N.W. 95th St. N.E. 95th St.

Gratigny Rd.

N.W.

N.W. 2nd Ave.

NORTH
MIAMI

Biscayne Blvd.

JFK Causeway

W. 4th Ave.

N.W. 72nd Ave.

27

3

N.W. 58th St.

N.W. 87th Ave.

N.W. 39th St.

Dairy Rd.

N.W. 79th St.
9

N.W. 62nd St. 441 I-95 N. Miami Ave.

N.W. 54th St. 944

Hialeah Dr.

N.W. 40th St.
Airport Expwy.

N.W. 36th St.

Miami River

DESIGN
DISTRICT 1

Chez Le Bebe   **Mandolin
Aegean Bistro**

Harry's Pizzeria **Michael's Genuine
Food & Drink**

Bocce

Sugarcane Raw Bar Grill
Wynwood Kitchen & Bar WYNWOOD
DOWNTOWN MIAMI

Julia Tuttle
Causeway

MIDTOWN **Doubletree
by Hilton
Grand Hotel
Biscayne Bay**

KYU **Joey's**

N.W. 20th St. 27 **Alter** **Panther
Coffee**

Venetian Causeway

Miami
International
Airport

4

Dolphin Expwy. 836

I-395

MacArthur Causeway

N.W. 7th St. **db Bistro Moderne Miami**
JW Marriott Marquis Miami **Verde at
PAMM**

**El Palacio de
los Jugos**

W. Flagler St. 968

S.W. 8th St. 41

Tamiami Trail

**Azucar
Ice Cream
Company**

15th & Vine
W Miami

**Perricone's
Marketplace
and Café**

Area 31
Kimpton
EPIC Hotel

Azul
NAOE
**La Mar by
Gaston Acurio**

Versailles

W. Flagler St. 41 **El Exquisito**
eating house LITTLE HAVANA

Conrad
Miami

Mandarin
Oriental, Miami

Biltmore
Hotel

24th St. 972

**Ortanique
on the Mile**

Coral Way 959

S.W. 22nd St.

**Rusty
Pelican**

Las Pinareños
Coral Gables

COCONUT
GROVE

**Edge, Steak
and Bar**
Four Seasons
Hotel Miami

5

Bird Rd.

826

Biltmore Hotel 953

CORAL
GABLES

**Pascal's
on Ponce**

Glass & Vine
GreenStreet Café

Monty's

Rickenbacker Causeway

40th St. 976

S.W. 87th Ave.

874

S.W. 57th Ave.

S. Dixie Hwy.

Mayfair
Hotel & Spa

**Peacock
Garden Café**

The Ritz-Carlton,
Coconut Grove, Miami

Biscayne
Bay

Crandon
Park

KEY
BISCAYNE

6

973 986

N. Kendall Dr.

S.W. 72nd St.

Red Rd.

Old Cutler Rd.

S. Dixie Hwy.

1

Matheson
Hammock
Park

Cantina Beach
The Ritz-Carlton Key Biscayne, Miami

A **B** **C** **D**

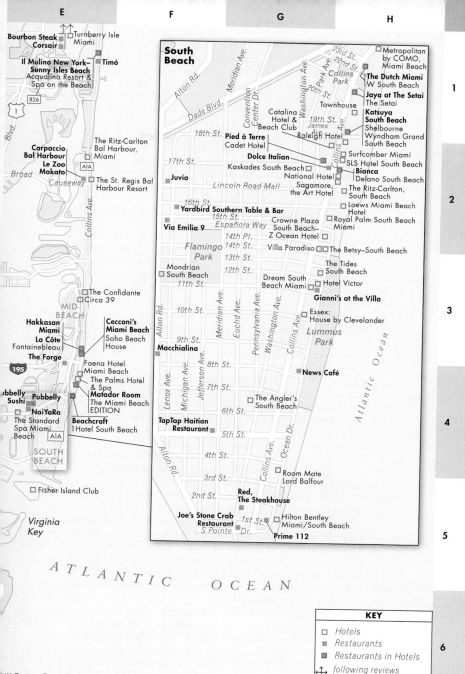

E   **F**   **G**   **H**

Bourbon Steak
Corsair   Turnberry Isle
Miami
Il Mulino New York–
Sunny Isles Beach   **Timó**
Acqualina Resort &
Spa on the Beach

826
1
Blvd.

South Beach

Collins
Park

Metropolitan
by COMO,
Miami Beach

The Dutch Miami
W South Beach

23rd St.
22nd St.
Park Ave.

Alton Rd.

Meridian Ave.

Convention
Center Dr.

Dade Blvd.

Washington Ave.

20th St.

Jaya at The Setai
The Setai

Townhouse

Catalina
Hotel &
Beach Club

19th St.

James Ave.

Katsuya
South Beach
Shelbourne
Wyndham Grand
South Beach

18th St.   **Pied à Terre**
Cadet Hotel
Raleigh Hotel

Carpaccio
Bal Harbour
Le Zoo
Makato

The Ritz-Carlton
Bal Harbour,
Miami

A1A

17th St.

Dolce Italian

Surfcomber Miami
SLS Hotel South Beach

Kaskades South Beach

Broad

Causeway

The St. Regis Bal
Harbour Resort

Juvia

Collins

Bianca
Delano South Beach

National Hotel
Sagamore,
the Art Hotel

16th St.

Yardbird Southern Table & Bar

The Ritz-Carlton,
South Beach

Loews Miami Beach
Hotel

Lincoln Road Mall

Collins Ave.

15th St.

Via Emilia 9

Española Way

Royal Palm South Beach
Miami

14th Pl.

14th St.

Flamingo
Park

Villa Paradiso

The Betsy–South Beach

13th St.

Mondrian
South Beach

12th St.

The Tides
South Beach

Dream South
Beach Miami

Hotel Victor

MID-
BEACH

The Confidante
Circa 39

11th St.

Gianni's at the Villa

Alton Rd.

Meridian Ave.

Euclid Ave.

Pennsylvania Ave.

Washington Ave.

Collins Ave.

Essex:
House by Clevelander

10th St.

Hakkasan
Miami
La Côte
Fontainebleau

Cecconi's
Miami Beach
Soho Beach
House

9th St.

Lummus
Park

The Forge

195

Macchialina

Michigan Ave.

Jefferson Ave.

Lenox Ave.

8th St.

Faena Hotel
Miami Beach
The Palms Hotel
& Spa
Matador Room
The Miami Beach
EDITION

7th St.

News Café

Pubbelly
Sushi   **Pubbelly**

The Angler's
South Beach

6th St.

NaiYaRa

The Standard
Spa Miami
Beach

5th St.

Beachcraft
1Hotel South Beach

TapTap Haitian
Restaurant

A1A

SOUTH
BEACH

4th St.

Alton Rd.

Collins Ave.

3rd St.

Fisher Island Club

2nd St.

Room Mate
Lord Balfour

Ocean Dr.

Red,
The Steakhouse

Virginia
Key

Joe's Stone Crab
Restaurant
S Pointe Dr.

1st St.

Hilton Bentley
Miami/South Beach

Prime 112

A T L A N T I C   **O C E A N**

Atlantic Ocean

ill Baggs Cape Florida
tate Recreation Area

1

2

3

4

5

6

KEY	
□	*Hotels*
■	*Restaurants*
■	*Restaurants in Hotels*
↔	*following reviews* *indicates a map-grid* *coordinate*

E   **F**   **G**   **H**

$$
AMERICAN

✕ **News Café.** No first-time trip to Miami is complete without a stop at this Ocean Drive landmark, though the food is nothing special. The 24-hour café attracts a crowd with snacks, light meals, drinks, periodicals, and the people parade on the sidewalk out front. **Known for:** late-night and early-morning dining; people-watching; newspaper selection. Ⓢ *Average main: $18* ✉ *800 Ocean Dr., South Beach* ☎ *305/538–6397* ⊕ *www.newscafe.com* ✛ *G4.*

$$$$
MODERN FRENCH

✕ **Pied à Terre.** This cozy, 36-seat, French contemporary restaurant with Mediterranean influences resides in the heart of South Beach, but it's everything the beach is not. Quiet, classic, and elegant, this hidden gastro-sanctuary within the historic Cadet Hotel forgoes glitz and gimmicks for taste and sophistication. **Known for:** romantic dining; use of seasonal ingredients; visiting French chefs from top restaurants in France. Ⓢ *Average main: $42* ✉ *Cadet Hotel, 1701 James Ave., South Beach* ☎ *305/531–4533* ⊕ *www.cadethotel.com* ☾ *Closed Mon. No lunch* ✛ *G2.*

$$$$
STEAKHOUSE
Fodor's Choice
★

✕ **Prime 112.** This wildly busy steak house is particularly prized for its highly marbleized prime beef, creamed corn, truffle macaroni and cheese, and buzzing scene. While you stand at the bar awaiting your table—everyone has to wait, at least a little bit—you'll clamor for a drink with all facets of Miami's high society, from the city's top real estate developers and philanthropists to striking models and celebrities. **Known for:** finest cuts of beef; decadent side dishes; stellar service. Ⓢ *Average main: $45* ✉ *112 Ocean Dr., South Beach* ☎ *305/532–8112* ⊕ *www.mylesrestaurantgroup.com* ☾ *No lunch weekends* ✛ *G5.*

$$$
ECLECTIC
Fodor's Choice
★

✕ **Pubbelly.** This petite eatery, on a residential street in SoBe's western reaches, still attracts the who's who of beach socialites, hipsters, and the occasional tourist coming to chow down on inventive Asian-Latin small plates, dumplings, charcuterie, and seasonal large plates by executive chef–owner Jose Mendin. From bay scallops "à la escargot" to short-rib tartare, Pubbelly constantly pushes the envelope on inventive cuisine, and locals simply can't get enough. **Known for:** chef's tasting menu; hypercreative "pb culture" small plates; modern dim sum. Ⓢ *Average main: $28* ✉ *1418 20th St., South Beach* ☎ *305/532–7555* ⊕ *www. pubbellyboys.com/miami/pubbelly* ✛ *E4.*

$$$$
JAPANESE

✕ **Pubbelly Sushi.** The team behind South Beach's wildly popular Pubbelly gastropub teamed up with sushi chef Yuki Leto to create the original Pubbelly Sushi, a 40-seat canteen doling out contemporary, Japanese-inspired sharing plates. Now there are four spread between Miami and the Dominican Republic. **Known for:** happy hour; sake cocktails; flavorful sushi rolls. Ⓢ *Average main: $35* ✉ *1424 20th St., South Beach* ☎ *305/531–9282* ⊕ *www.pubbellysushi.us* ✛ *E4.*

$$$$
STEAKHOUSE

✕ **Red, the Steakhouse.** The carnivore glamour den seduces with its red-and-black dominatrix color scheme and overloads the senses with the divine smells and tastes of the extensive menu. Red boasts an equal number of seafood and more traditional meat offerings, each delicately prepared, meticulously presented, and gleefully consumed. **Known for:** sexy interiors; decadent, caloric side dishes; sublime steaks. Ⓢ *Average main: $55* ✉ *119 Washington Ave., South Beach* ☎ *305/534–3688* ⊕ *www.redthesteakhouse.com* ✛ *G5.*

$$ ✕**Tap Tap Haitian Restaurant.** Tap
CARIBBEAN Tap is anything but SoBe glitz and
glam, but this Haitian restaurant
will instantly immerse you in Hai-
ti's cuisine and culture. An exten-
sive collection of Haitian folk art
is displayed throughout this house-
turned-restaurant—so much so that
every wall, table, and chair doubles
as a piece of colorful art. **Known for:**
unique dining experience; affordable
pricing; vegetarian menu. [$] *Aver-
age main: $15 ⊠ 819 5th St., South
Beach* ☎ *305/672–2898* ⊕ *www.
taptapmiamibeach.com* ✣ *F4.*

$$ ✕**Via Emilia 9.** If you're longing for
ITALIAN a *true* taste of Italy and a respite
Fodor's Choice from the overpriced SoBe dining
★ scene, head to this adorable hole-in-
the-wall restaurant off Alton Road.
It is owned and operated by Italian chef Wendy Cacciatori and his
lovely wife. **Known for:** authentic
Italian fare; homemade flatbreads; variety of stuffed pastas. [$] *Average
main: $17 ⊠ 1120 15th St., South Beach* ☎ *786/216–7150* ⊕ *www.
viaemilia9.com* ✣ *F2.*

$$$ ✕**Yardbird Southern Table & Bar.** There's a helluva lot of Southern lovin'
SOUTHERN from the Lowcountry at this lively and funky South Beach spot. Miami's
A-list puts calorie-counting aside for decadent nights filled with com-
fort foods and innovative drinks. **Known for:** high-calorie delights;
Mama's chicken biscuits; 27-hour marinated fried chicken. [$] *Average
main: $30 ⊠ 1600 Lenox Ave., South Beach* ☎ *305/538–5220* ⊕ *www.
runchickenrun.com* ✣ *F2.*

> CHEAP EATS ON
> SOUTH BEACH
>
> Miami Beach is notoriously
> overpriced, but locals know that
> you don't always have to spend
> $30 for lunch or $45 for a dinner
> entrée here to have a good meal.
> **Pizza Rustica** (⊠ *8th St. and
> Washington Ave. and 667 Lincoln
> Rd.*) serves up humongous slices
> overflowing with mozzarella, steak,
> olives, and barbecue chicken until
> 4 am. **La Sandwicherie** (⊠ *14th
> St. between Collins and Washing-
> ton Aves.*) is a South Beach
> classic that's been here since
> 1988, serving gourmet French
> sandwiches, a delicious prosciutto
> salad, and healthful smoothies
> from a walk-up bar.

MID-BEACH

$$$ ✕**Cecconi's Miami Beach.** The wait for a table at this outpost of the iconic
ITALIAN Italian restaurant is just as long as for its counterparts in West Hol-
lywood and London, and the dining experience just as fabulous. The
food is great, but atmosphere here is everything. **Known for:** light and
succulent fish carpaccios; hearty pastas; sceney courtyard. [$] *Average
main: $27 ⊠ Soho Beach House Miami, 4385 Collins Ave., Mid-Beach*
☎ *786/507–7902* ⊕ *www.cecconismiamibeach.com* ✣ *E3.*

$$$$ ✕**The Forge.** Legendary for its opulence, this restaurant has been wow-
STEAKHOUSE ing patrons since 1968. After a face-lift in 2010, antiques, gilt-framed
paintings, a chandelier from the Paris Opera House, and Tiffany
stained-glass windows from New York's Trinity Church are the fitting background for some of Miami's best cuts. **Known for:** expansive
enomatic wine system; dramatic interiors; prime cuts of beef. [$] *Average
main: $44 ⊠ 432 Arthur Godfrey Rd., Mid-Beach* ☎ *305/538–8533*
⊕ *www.theforge.com* ☾ *No lunch* ✣ *E4.*

$$$$
CANTONESE

✕ **Hakkasan Miami.** This stateside sibling of the Michelin-star London restaurant brings the haute-Chinese-food movement to South Florida, adding pan-Asian flair to even quite simple and authentic Cantonese recipes, and producing an entire menu that can be classified as blow-your-mind delicious. Seafood and vegetarian dishes outnumber meat options. **Known for:** well-dressed patrons; superb Cantonese cuisine; dim sum perfected. $ *Average main: $52* ✉ *Fontainebleau Miami Beach, 4441 Collins Ave., 4th fl., Mid-Beach* ☎ *786/276–1388 after 4 pm, 877/326–7412 before 4 pm* ⊕ *www.hakkasan.com/locations/ hakkasan-miami/* ☺ *No lunch weekdays* ✛ *E3.*

$$$$
FRENCH

✕ **La Côte.** With clean white lines, colorful bursts of aqua-blue cushions, and elegant umbrellas, La Côte at the Fontainebleau whisks you away to the coast of southern France. The two-level, predominantly alfresco restaurant snuggled between the beach and the Fontainebleau's pools opens its arms in a generous embrace while flirting with your taste buds, and maybe your man: the female waitstaff wear bikinis and flip-flops. **Known for:** beach cuisine; stylish, alfresco surrounds; French Riviera ambience. $ *Average main: $31* ✉ *Fontainebleau Hotel, 4441 Collins Ave., Mid-Beach* ☎ *305/674–4710* ☺ *No dinner Sun.–Wed.* ✛ *E3.*

$$$
SPANISH
Fodor'sChoice
★

✕ **Matador Room.** In one of Miami's most captivating and seductive settings, the latest headline restaurant by celebrity-chef Jean-Georges Vongerichten fuses Spanish, Caribbean, and Latin American gastronomy, presenting the result in a diverse collection of small and large plates. Though the venue plays into a sexy matador theme, the name stems from the space's former incarnation—the eponymous, superglam supper club of yesteryear. **Known for:** tropically inspired bites; the epic pineapple elixir cocktail served in a massive copper pineapple; nice terrace for outdoor dining. $ *Average main: $25* ✉ *The Miami Beach EDITION, 2901 Collins Ave., Mid-Beach* ☎ *786/257–4600* ⊕ *www. matadorroom.com* ✛ *E4.*

NORTH BEACH

BAL HARBOUR

$$$$
MODERN ITALIAN

✕ **Carpaccio Bal Harbour.** As expected for its ritzy location, this upscale restaurant matches its high-fashion neighbors, albeit in a refreshing manner. There's no funky furniture nor slick decor, just simple white-clothed tables and charming Italian touches. **Known for:** myriad carpaccios; ladies who lunch; well-heeled crowd. $ *Average main: $32* ✉ *Bal Harbour Shops, 9700 Collins Ave., Bal Harbour* ☎ *305/867–7777* ⊕ *www.carpaccioatbalharbour.com* ✛ *E2.*

$$$$
FRENCH

✕ **Le Zoo.** Following success with Makoto in the swanky Bal Harbour shops, restaurateur Stephen Starr has shifted gears from Japan to France, bringing a bona fide Parisian brasserie—inclusive of vintage decorations, furnishings, and an entire bar, all of which were imported from France—to Miami's poshest region. Expect classics perfected such as onion soup gratiné, steak frites, and seafood plateaux (towers); a few delicious deviations like the escargots in hazelnut butter (rather than garlic butter); and plenty of excellent people-watching. **Known**

for: Parisian flair; seafood towers; outdoor seating. $ *Average main: $42* ✉ *Bal Harbour Shops, 9700 Collins Ave. No. 135, North Beach* ☎ *305/602–9663* ⊕ *www.lezoo.com* ✥ *E2.*

$$$$

JAPANESE

Fodor'sChoice

★

✕**Makoto.** Stephen Starr's Japanese headliner, executed by celebrity-chef Makoto Okuwa, is one of the most popular restaurants in all of South Florida (and in this swanky shopping center, too). There are two menus: one is devoted solely to sushi, sashimi, and maki, the other to Japanese cold and hot dishes. **Known for:** superfresh sushi; artistic presentation; well-dressed crowd. $ *Average main: $31* ✉ *Bal Harbour Shops, 9700 Collins Ave., Bal Harbour* ☎ *305/864–8600* ⊕ *www. makoto-restaurant.com* ✥ *E2.*

SUNNY ISLES BEACH

$$$$

ITALIAN

✕**Il Mulino New York – Sunny Isles Beach.** For more than two decades, Il Mulino New York has ranked among the top Italian restaurants in Gotham, so it's no surprise that the Miami outposts (one in Sunny Isles, one in South Beach) are similarly good. Everything that touches your palate will be perfectly executed, from simply prepared fried calamari and gnocchi pomodoro to the more complex scampi oreganata and ever-changing risottos. **Known for:** seasonal primavera risotto; fried zucchini and bruschetta; consistency. $ *Average main: $45* ✉ *Acqualina Resort, 17875 Collins Ave., Sunny Isles Beach* ☎ *305/466–9191* ⊕ *www.ilmulino.com/miami* ✥ *E1.*

$$$

ITALIAN

✕**Timó.** In a glorified strip mall, Timó (Italian for "thyme") is worth the trip from anywhere in South Florida. It's a kind of locals' secret. **Known for:** brick-oven pizza; seafood antipasto; vegetarian tasting menu. $ *Average main: $28* ✉ *17624 Collins Ave., Sunny Isles Beach* ☎ *305/936–1008* ⊕ *www.timorestaurant.com* ☾ *No lunch weekends* ✥ *E1.*

AVENTURA

$$$$

STEAKHOUSE

✕**Bourbon Steak.** Michael Mina's long-standing South Florida steak house has never gone out of style. The restaurant design is seductive, the clientele sophisticated, the wine list outstanding, the service phenomenal, and the food exceptional. **Known for:** duck-fat fries; Maine lobster potpie; apex of Aventura "scene". $ *Average main: $60* ✉ *Turnberry Isle Miami, 19999 W. Country Club Dr., Aventura* ☎ *786/279–6600* ⊕ *www.michaelmina.net* ✥ *E1.*

$$$

MEDITERRANEAN

FAMILY

✕**Corsair.** At Corsair, *Chopped* judge Scott Conant doles out experiential, seasonally inspired farm-to-table fare prepared in Mediterranean style. From start to finish, each course serves as testimony to his well-deserved win on *Chopped All-Stars*, where he competed against other celebrity chefs to prove himself best of the best. **Known for:** complex flavors; fresh ingredients; skillful preparation of dishes. $ *Average main: $28* ✉ *Turnberry Isle Miami, 19999 W. Country Club Dr., Aventura* ☎ *786/279–6800* ⊕ *www.turnberryislemiami.com* ✥ *E1.*

WHERE TO STAY

Room rates in Miami tend to swing wildly. In high season, which is January through May, expect to pay at least $250 per night, even at value-oriented hotels. In fact, it's common nowadays for rates to begin around $500 at Miami's top hotels. In summer, however, prices can be as much as 50% lower than the dizzying winter rates. You can also find great deals between Easter and Memorial Day, which is actually a delightful time in Miami. Business travelers tend to stay in downtown Miami, and most vacationers stay on Miami Beach, as close as possible to the water. South Beach is no longer the only "in" place to stay. Mid-Beach and Downtown have taken the hotel scene by storm in the past few years and become home to some of the region's most avant-garde and luxurious properties to date. If money is no object, stay in one of the glamorous hotels lining Collins Avenue between 15th and 23rd streets or between 29th and 44th streets. Otherwise, stay on the quiet beaches farther north, or in one of the small boutique hotels on Ocean Drive, Collins, or Washington avenues between 10th and 15th streets. Two important considerations that affect price are balcony and view. If you're willing to have a room without an ocean view, you can sometimes get a much lower price than the standard rate, even at an oceanfront hotel.

Hotel reviews have been shortened. For full information, visit Fodors. com. Use the coordinate (⊕ C2) at the end of each review to locate a property on the Where to Eat and Stay in the Miami Area map.

WHAT IT COSTS			
$	**$$**	**$$$**	**$$$$**
Hotels under $200	$200–$300	$301–$400	over $400

Hotel prices are the lowest cost of a standard double room in high season.

DOWNTOWN

Miami's skyline continues to grow by leaps and bounds. With Downtown experiencing a renaissance of sorts, the hotel scene here isn't just for business anymore. In fact, hotels that once relied solely on their Monday–Thursday traffic are now bustling on weekends, with a larger focus on cocktails around the rooftop pool and less on the business center. These hotels offer proximate access to Downtown's burgeoning food and cocktail scene, and historic sights, and are a short Uber ride away from Miami's beaches.

$$$
HOTEL   ☗ **Conrad Miami.** Occupying floors 16 to 26 of a 36-story skyscraper in Miami's burgeoning city center, this hotel mixes business with pleasure, offering easy access to the best of Downtown. **Pros:** central Downtown location; excellent service; good spa. **Cons:** poor views from some rooms; expensive parking. $ *Rooms from: $319* ⊠ *Espirito Santo Plaza, 1395 Brickell Ave., Downtown* ☎ *305/503–6500* ⊕ *www.conradmiami.com* ⊅ *201 rooms* ¶◎¶ *No meals* ⊕ *D5.*

2

$$
HOTEL

🏨 **DoubleTree by Hilton Grand Hotel Biscayne Bay.** Just 1 mile from Port-Miami at the north end of Downtown, this waterfront hotel offers relatively basic, spacious rooms and convenient access to and from the cruise ships, making it a good crash pad for budget-conscious cruise passengers. **Pros:** marina; proximity to cruise port; spacious rooms. **Cons:** still need a cab to get around; dark lobby and neighboring arcade of shops; worn rooms. 💲 *Rooms from: $279* ✉ *1717 N. Bayshore Dr., Downtown* ☎ *305/372–0313* ⊕ *www.doubletree.com* ⌿ *202 rooms* ⏅ *No meals* ✛ *D4.*

$$$$
HOTEL
Fodor's Choice
★

🏨 **Four Seasons Hotel Miami.** A favorite of business travelers visiting Downtown's busy, business-centric Brickell Avenue, this plush sanctuary offers a respite from the nine-to-five mayhem—a soothing water wall greets you, the understated rooms impress you, and the seventh-floor, 2-acre-pool terrace relaxes you. **Pros:** sensational service; window-side daybeds; amazing gym and pool deck. **Cons:** no balconies; not near the beach. 💲 *Rooms from: $519* ✉ *1435 Brickell Ave., Downtown* ☎ *305/358–3535* ⊕ *www.fourseasons.com/miami* ⌿ *221 rooms* ⏅ *No meals* ✛ *D5.*

$$$$
HOTEL

🏨 **JW Marriott Marquis Miami.** The marriage of Marriott's JW and Marquis brands created a truly high-tech, contemporary, and stylish business-minded hotel—you may never have seen another Marriott quite like this one. **Pros:** entertainment center; amazing technology; pristine rooms. **Cons:** swimming pool receives limited sunshine; lots of conventioneers on weekdays; congestion at street entrance. 💲 *Rooms from: $499* ✉ *255 Biscayne Blvd. Way, Downtown* ☎ *305/421–8600* ⊕ *www.jwmarriottmarquismiami.com* ⌿ *313 rooms* ⏅ *No meals* ✛ *D4.*

$$$
HOTEL

🏨 **Kimpton EPIC Hotel.** In the heart of Downtown, Kimpton's pet-friendly, artful EPIC Hotel offers rooms with spacious balconies (many of them overlook Biscayne Bay) and fabulous modern amenities—Frette linens, iPod docks, spa-inspired luxury bath products—that match the modern grandeur of the trendy common areas, which include a supersexy rooftop pool. **Pros:** sprawling rooftop pool deck; balcony in every room; complimentary wine hour, coffee, and Wi-Fi. **Cons:** some rooms have inferior views; congested valet area. 💲 *Rooms from: $319* ✉ *270 Biscayne Blvd. Way, Downtown* ☎ *305/424–5226* ⊕ *www.epichotel.com* ⌿ *411 rooms* ⏅ *No meals* ✛ *D4.*

$$$$
HOTEL
Fodor's Choice
★

🏨 **Mandarin Oriental, Miami.** At the tip of prestigious Brickell Key in Biscayne Bay, the Mandarin Oriental feels as exclusive as it does glamorous, with luxurious rooms, exalted restaurants, and the city's top spa, all of which marry the brand's signature Asian style with Miami's bold tropical elegance. **Pros:** impressive lobby; intimate vibe; ultraluxurious. **Cons:** man-made beach; small infinity pool; few beach cabanas. 💲 *Rooms from: $599* ✉ *500 Brickell Key Dr., Downtown* ☎ *305/913–8288, 866/888–6780* ⊕ *www.mandarinoriental.com/miami* ⌿ *357 rooms* ⏅ *No meals* ✛ *D5.*

$$$$
HOTEL

🏨 **W Miami.** Formerly the Viceroy, Miami's second W hotel cultivates a brash, supersophisticated Miami attitude, likely stemming from its guest rooms decked out with dramatic Kelly Wearstler, Asian-inspired interiors and larger-than-life common areas designed by Philippe Starck. **Pros:** amazing design elements; exceptional pool deck and spa; sleek rooms. **Cons:** serious traffic getting in and out of hotel entrance; tiny lobby; some amenities shared with ICON Miami residents. Ⓢ *Rooms from: $528* ☒ *485 Brickell Ave., Downtown* ☎ *305/503–4400* ⊕ *www.wmiamihotel.com* ⟿ *168 rooms* ⧖ *No meals* ✛ *D4.*

COCONUT GROVE

Although this area certainly can't replace the draw of Miami Beach or the business convenience of Downtown, about 20 minutes away, it's an exciting bohemian-chic neighborhood with a gorgeous waterfront.

$$　**Mayfair Hotel & Spa.** Some 30 years strong, the five-story Mayfair
HOTEL　Hotel & Spa still reflects Coconut Grove's bohemian roots, best exemplified by its eclectic exteriors: handcrafted wooden doors, one-of-a-kind decorative moldings, mosaic tiles inspired by Spain's Alhambra, and Gaudi-like ornaments adorning the rooftop pool deck. **Pros:** in the heart of walkable Coconut Grove; details in exterior design; in-house spa. **Cons:** limited lighting within rooms; interiors not as exciting as exteriors; car needed to get to the beach. Ⓢ *Rooms from: $258* ☒ *3000 Florida Ave., Coconut Grove* ☎ *800/433–4555 reservations, 305/441–0000* ⊕ *www.mayfairhotelandspa.com* ⟿ *179 rooms* ⧖ *No meals* ✛ *C5.*

$$$$　**The Ritz-Carlton Coconut Grove, Miami.** This business-centric Ritz-Carl-
HOTEL　ton hotel in the heart of Coconut Grove has a lively lobby and lounge that complements its sophisticated guest rooms—all with marble baths and private balconies. **Pros:** elevated pool deck; near Coconut Grove and Coral Gables shopping; excellent service. **Cons:** near residential area; more business than leisure oriented. Ⓢ *Rooms from: $499* ☒ *3300 S.W. 27th Ave., Coconut Grove* ☎ *305/644–4680, 800/241–3333* ⊕ *www.ritzcarlton.com/coconutgrove* ⟿ *115 rooms* ⧖ *No meals* ✛ *C5.*

CORAL GABLES

Beautiful Coral Gables is set around its beacon, the national landmark Biltmore Hotel. It also has a couple of big business hotels and one smaller boutique property. The University of Miami is nearby.

$$$$　**Biltmore Hotel.** Built in 1926, this landmark hotel has had several
HOTEL　incarnations over the years—including a stint as a hospital during World War II—but through it all, this grande dame has remained an opulent reminder of yesteryear, with its palatial lobby and grounds, enormous pool (largest in the Lower 48), and distinctive 315-foot tower, which rises above the canopy of trees shading Coral Gables. **Pros:** historic property; gorgeous pool; great tennis and golf. **Cons:** in the suburbs; a car is necessary to get around. Ⓢ *Rooms from: $469* ☒ *1200 Anastasia Ave., Coral Gables* ☎ *855/311–6903* ⊕ *www.biltmorehotel.com* ⟿ *312 rooms* ⧖ *No meals* ✛ *B5.*

$$$　**Hyatt Regency Coral Gables.** Within walking distance to the shops and
HOTEL　businesses of Miami's most prestigious suburb and just 4 miles from Miami International Airport, the 250-room, Moorish-inspired Hyatt Regency Coral Gables mingles European charm with functionality. **Pros:** easy access to MIA; meets rigorous "green" standards; walking

distance to several local restaurants. **Cons:** small bathrooms; in suburbs; no spa. $ *Rooms from: $310* ⊠ *50 Alhambra Plaza, Coral Gables* ☎ *305/441–1234* ⊕ *www.coralgables.regency.hyatt.com* ⤳ *253 rooms* ❍❉ *No meals* ✛ *B5.*

KEY BISCAYNE

There's probably no other place in Miami where slowness is lifted to a fine art. On Key Biscayne there are no pressures, there's no nightlife outside of the Ritz-Carlton's great live Latin music weekends, and the dining choices are essentially limited to the hotel (which has four dining options, including the languorous, Havana-style RUMBAR).

$$$$
RESORT
FAMILY
Fodor's Choice
★

The Ritz-Carlton Key Biscayne, Miami. In this ultra-laid-back setting, it's natural to appreciate the Ritz brand of pampering with luxurious rooms, attentive service, five on-property dining options, and ample recreational activities for the whole family. **Pros:** on the beach; quiet; luxurious family retreat. **Cons:** far from South Beach; beach sometimes seaweed strewn; rental car almost a necessity. $ *Rooms from: $499* ⊠ *455 Grand Bay Dr., Key Biscayne* ☎ *305/365–4500, 800/241–3333* ⊕ *www.ritzcarlton.com/keybiscayne* ⤳ *402 rooms* ❍❉ *No meals* ✛ *D6.*

SOUTH BEACH

If you are looking to experience the postcard image of Miami, look no further than South Beach. Most of the hotels along Ocean Drive, Collins Avenue, and Washington Avenue are housed in history-steeped art deco buildings, each one cooler than the next. From boutique hotels to high-rise structures, all South Beach hotels are in close proximity to the beach and never far from the action. Most hotels here cost a pretty penny, and for good reason. They are more of an experience than a place to crash (think designer lobbies, some of the world's best pool scenes, and unparalleled people-watching).

$$$
HOTEL

The Angler's South Beach. This boutique hotel, one of several in Miami under the Kimpton brand, has an air of serenity and privacy that pervades this discreet little oasis of personality-driven villas (built in 1930 by architect Henry Maloney) and modern tower units, together capturing the feel of a sophisticated private Mediterranean villa community. **Pros:** gardened private retreat; excellent service; daily complimentary wine hour. **Cons:** on busy Washington Avenue; not directly on beach. $ *Rooms from: $379* ⊠ *660 Washington Ave., South Beach* ☎ *305/534–9600* ⊕ *www.anglershotelmiami.com* ⤳ *44 rooms* ❍❉ *No meals* ✛ *G4.*

$$$
HOTEL
Fodor's Choice
★

The Betsy—South Beach. After a two-year expansion, the original Betsy Ross Hotel (now christened the "Colonial" wing) has been joined with what was the neighboring, historic Carlton Hotel to create a retro-chic, art deco treasure that delivers the full-throttle South Beach experience with style, pizzazz, and cultural twist. **Pros:** unbeatable location; superfashionable; great beach club. **Cons:** some small rooms; service can be hit or miss. $ *Rooms from: $315* ⊠ *1440 Ocean Dr., South Beach* ☎ *305/531–6100* ⊕ *www.thebetsyhotel.com* ⤳ *130 rooms* ❍❉ *No meals* ✛ *G2.*

$
HOTEL
Fodor's Choice
★

Cadet Hotel. A former home to World War II air force cadets, this gem has been reimagined as an oasis in South Beach, offering the antithesis of the sometimes maddening jet-set scene, with 34 distinctive rooms exuding understated luxury. **Pros:** excellent service; lovely garden and spa pool; originality. **Cons:** tiny swimming pool; limited appeal for the party crowd. ⑤ *Rooms from: $189* ✉ *1701 James Ave., South Beach* ☎ *305/672–6688* ⊕ *www.cadethotel.com* ⤴ *34 rooms* ⍾❶ *No meals* ✛ *G2.*

$
HOTEL

Catalina Hotel & Beach Club. The Catalina is the budget party spot in the heart of South Beach's hottest block and attracts plenty of twentysomethings with its free nightly drink hour, airport shuttles, fitness classes, two fun pools, and beach chairs. **Pros:** free drinks; free airport shuttle; good people-watching. **Cons:** service not a high priority; loud; not all rooms well maintained. ⑤ *Rooms from: $183* ✉ *1720–1756 Collins Ave., South Beach* ☎ *305/674–1160* ⊕ *www.catalinahotel.com* ⤴ *190 rooms* ⍾❶ *No meals* ✛ *G2.*

$$
HOTEL

Crowne Plaza South Beach – Z Ocean Hotel. This is definitely not your grandmother's Crowne Plaza: the lauded firm of Arquitectonica designed this glossy and bold all-suites hideaway, including 27 rooftop suites endowed with terraces, each complete with Jacuzzi, plush chaise lounges, and a view of the South Beach skyline. **Pros:** incredible balconies; huge rooms; space-maximizing closets. **Cons:** gym is tiny and basic; not much privacy on rooftop suite decks. ⑤ *Rooms from: $263* ✉ *1437 Collins Ave., South Beach* ☎ *305/672–4554* ⊕ *www.ihg.com* ⤴ *79 suites* ⍾❶ *No meals* ✛ *G2.*

$$$$
HOTEL

Delano South Beach. The hotel that single-handedly made South Beach cool again in the 1990s is still making major waves across the beach as this Philippe Starck powerhouse continues to define the paradigm of South Beach decor and glamour. **Pros:** electrifying design; lounging among the beautiful and famous. **Cons:** crowded; scene-y; entry-level rooms are on small side. ⑤ *Rooms from: $409* ✉ *1685 Collins Ave., South Beach* ☎ *305/672–2000, 800/555–5001* ⊕ *www.morganshotel-group.com/delano/delano-south-beach* ⤴ *208 rooms* ⍾❶ *No meals* ✛ *H2.*

$$$
HOTEL

Dream South Beach Miami. This trendy boutique hotel, which is right in the center of the South Beach action, merges two refurbished, archetypal, 1939 art deco buildings into a single project of eclectic modernism, with whimsically decorated interiors—and the result is at once trippy and cool. **Pros:** awesome interior design; easy-on-the-eyes crowd; amazing location. **Cons:** limited natural light in some rooms; lack of bathroom privacy; small pool. ⑤ *Rooms from: $309* ✉ *1111 Collins Ave., South Beach* ☎ *305/673–4747* ⊕ *www.dreamhotels.com/south-beach* ⤴ *108 rooms* ⍾❶ *No meals* ✛ *G3.*

$$
HOTEL

Essex: House by Clevelander. This restored art deco gem is a favorite with Europeans desiring good location and a relatively no-frills, practical base—expect average-size rooms with mid-century-style red furniture and marble tubs. **Pros:** a social, heated pool; access to amenities at neighboring Clevelander hotel; in-house sushi restaurant Zen Sai. **Cons:** small pool; not on the beach. ⑤ *Rooms from: $254* ✉ *1001 Collins Ave., South Beach* ☎ *877/532–4006* ⊕ *www.clevelander.com/essex-house.htm* ⤴ *70 rooms* ⍾❶ *No meals* ✛ *G3.*

Continued on page 75

A STROLL DOWN

DECO LANE

by Susan MacCallum Whitcomb

"It was an age of miracles, it was an age of art,

it was an age of excess, and it was an age of satire."

—F. Scott Fitzgerald, *Echoes of the Jazz Age*

The 1920s and '30s brought us flappers and gangsters, plunging stock prices and soaring skyscrapers, and plenty of headline-worthy news from the arts scene, from talking pictures and the jazz craze to fashions where pearls piled on and sequins dazzled. These decades between the two world wars also gave us an art style reflective of the changing times: art deco.

Distinguished by geometrical shapes and the use of industrial motifs that fused the decorative arts with modern technology, art deco became the architectural style of choice for train stations and big buildings across the country (think New york's Radio City Music Hall and Empire State Building).

Using a steel-and-concrete box as the foundation, architects dipped into art deco's grab bag of accessories, initially decorating facades with spheres, cylinders, and cubes. They later borrowed increasingly from industrial design, stripping elements used in ocean liners and automobiles to their streamlined essentials.

The style was also used in jewelry, furniture, textiles, and advertising. The fact that it employed inexpensive materials, such as stucco or terrazzo, helped art deco thrive during the Great Depression.

MIAMI BEACH'S ART DECO DISTRICT

With its warm beaches and tropical surroundings, Miami Beach in the early 20th century was establishing itself as America's winter playground. During the roaring '20s luxurious hostelries resembling Venetian palaces, Spanish villages, and French châteaux sprouted up. In the 1930s, middle-class tourists started coming, and more hotels had to be built. Designers like Henry Hohauser chose art deco for its affordable yet distinctive design.

An antidote to the gloom of the Great Depression, the look was cheerful and tidy. And with the whimsical additions of portholes, colorful racing bands, and images of rolling ocean waves painted or etched on the walls, these South Beach properties created an oceanfront fantasy world for travelers.

Many of the candy-colored hotels have survived and been meticulously restored. They are among the more than 800 buildings of historical significance in South Beach's art deco district. Composing much of South Beach, the 1-square-mile district is bounded by Dade Boulevard on the north, the Atlantic Ocean on the east, 6th Street on the south, and Alton Road on the west.

Because the district as a whole was developed so rapidly and designed by like-minded architects—**Henry Hohauser, L. Murray Dixon, Albert Anis,** and their colleagues—it has amazing stylistic unity. Nevertheless, on this single street you can trace the evolution of period form from angular, vertically emphatic early deco to aerodynamically rounded Streamline Moderne. The relatively severe Cavalier and more curvaceous Cardozo are fine examples of the former and latter, respectively.

To explore the district, begin by loading up on literature in the **Art Deco Welcome Center** (⊠ *1001 Ocean Dr.* ☎ *305/763–8026* ⊕ *www.mdpl.org*). If you want to view these historic properties on your own, just start walking. A four-block stroll north on Ocean Drive gets you up close to camera-ready classics: the **Clevelander** (1020), the **Tides** (1220), the **Leslie** (1244), the **Carlyle** (1250), the **Cardozo** (1300), the **Cavalier** (1320), and the **Winter Haven** (1400).

ARCHITECTURAL HIGHLIGHTS

FRIEZE DETAIL, CAVALIER HOTEL

The decorative stucco friezes outside the Cavalier Hotel at 1320 Ocean Drive are significant for more than aesthetic reasons. Roy France used them to add symmetry (adhering to the "Rule of Three") and accentuate the hotel's verticality by drawing the eye upward. The pattern he chose also reflected a fascination with ancient civilizations engendered by the recent rediscovery of King Tut's tomb and the Chichén Itzá temples.

Cavalier Hotel

LOBBY FLOOR, THE RALEIGH HOTEL

Terrazzo—a compound of cement and stone chips that could be poured, then polished—is a hallmark of deco design. Terrazzo floors typically had a geometric pattern, like this one in The Raleigh Hotel, a 1940 building by L. Murray Dixon at 1775 Collins Avenue.

The Raleigh Hotel

CORNER FACADE, ESSEX HOUSE HOTEL

Essex House Hotel, a 1938 gem that appears permanently anchored at 1001 Collins Avenue, is a stunning example of Maritime deco (also known as Nautical Moderne). Designed by Henry Hohauser to evoke an ocean liner, the hotel is rife with marine elements, from the rows of porthole-style windows and natty racing stripes to the towering smokestack-like sign. With a prow angled proudly into the street corner, it seems ready to steam out to sea.

Essex House Hotel

NEON SPIRE, THE HOTEL

The name spelled vertically in eye-popping neon on the venue's iconic aluminum spire—Tiffany—bears evidence of the hotel's earlier incarnation. When the L. Murray Dixon–designed Tiffany Hotel was erected at 801 Collins Avenue in 1939, neon was still a novelty. Its use, coupled with the spire's rocket-like shape, combined to create a futuristic look influenced by the sci-fi themes then pervasive in popular culture.

The Hotel

ENTRANCE, SEÑOR FROG'S

Inspired by everything from car fenders to airplane noses, proponents of art deco's Streamline Moderne look began to soften buildings' hitherto boxy edges. But when Henry Hohauser designed Hoffman's Cafeteria in 1940 he took moderne to the max. The landmark at 1450 Collins Avenue (now Señor Frog's) has a sleek, splendidly curved facade. The restored interior echoes it through semicircular booths and rounded chair backs.

Señor Frog's

ARCHITECTURAL TERMS

The Rule of Three: Early deco designers often used architectural elements in multiples of three, creating tripartite facades with triple sets of windows, eyebrows, or banding.

Eyebrows: Small shelf-like ledges that protruded over exterior windows were used to simultaneously provide much-needed shade and serve as a counterpoint to a building's strong vertical lines.

Tropical Motifs: In keeping with the setting, premises were plastered, painted, or etched with seaside images. Palm trees, sunbursts, waves, flamingoes, and the like were particularly common.

Banding: Enhancing the illusion that these immobile structures were rapidly speeding objects, colorful horizontal bands (also called "racing stripes") were painted on exteriors or applied with tile.

Stripped Classic: The most austere version of art deco (sometimes dubbed Depression Moderne) was used for buildings commissioned by the Public Works Administration.

(top) Hotel Marlin; (left) Sherbrooke Hotel; (right) U.S. Post Office in Miami Beach.

2

$$$$
HOTEL
FAMILY

🏨 **Hilton Bentley Miami/South Beach.** Not to be confused with the budget-oriented Bentley Hotel down the street, the Hilton Bentley Miami is a contemporary, design-driven, and artsy boutique hotel in the emerging and trendy SoFi (South of Fifth) district, offering families just the right mix of South Beach flavor and wholesome fun while still providing couples a romantic base without any party madness. **Pros:** quiet location; style and grace; family-friendly. **Cons:** small pool; small lobby; daily resort charge. $ *Rooms from: $429* ✉ *101 Ocean Dr., South Beach* ☎ *305/938–4600* ⊕ *www.hilton.com* 🛏 *109 rooms* ⦿ *No meals* ✛ *G5.*

$$
HOTEL

🏨 **Hotel Victor.** After a Yabu Pushelberg face-lift in late 2013, the sleek Hotel Victor, originally influenced by Parisian designer Jacques Garcia, has replaced the dated jellyfish motif with a newer incarnation of bold modernism. **Pros:** views from pool deck; high hip factor; good service. **Cons:** small rooms; street noise from some rooms. $ *Rooms from: $269* ✉ *1144 Ocean Dr., South Beach* ☎ *305/908–1462, 844/319–3854* ⊕ *www.hotelvictorsouthbeach.com* 🛏 *91 rooms* ⦿ *No meals* ✛ *G3.*

$$
HOTEL

🏨 **Kaskades South Beach.** Though it's not directly on the beach—it's across the street—this boutique hotel offers fabulous, style- and value-conscious accommodations in the heart of South Beach. **Pros:** awesome bathrooms; central location; complimentary wine hour. **Cons:** rooftop deck often quiet; most amenities in sister hotel. $ *Rooms from: $240* ✉ *300 17th St., South Beach* ☎ *305/673–0199* ⊕ *www.kaskadeshotel. com* 🛏 *24 rooms* ⦿ *Breakfast* ✛ *G2.*

$$$$
HOTEL
FAMILY

🏨 **Loews Miami Beach Hotel.** Loews Miami Beach, a two-tower mega-hotel with top-tier amenities, a massive spa, a great pool, and direct beachfront access, is a good choice for families, businesspeople, groups, and pet lovers. **Pros:** excellent on-site seafood restaurant; immense spa; pets welcome. **Cons:** insanely large size; constantly crowded; pets desperate to go will need to wait several minutes to make it to the grass. $ *Rooms from: $449* ✉ *1601 Collins Ave., South Beach* ☎ *305/604–1601, 800/235–6397* ⊕ *www.loewshotels.com/miami-beach* 🛏 *790 rooms* ⦿ *No meals* ✛ *H2.*

$$$
RESORT

🏨 **Metropolitan by COMO, Miami Beach.** The luxury COMO brand brings its Zen-glam swagger to South Beach, reinventing the art deco Traymore hotel into a 74-room, Paola Navone–designed boutique hotel that commingles brand signatures (excellent, health-driven cuisine, and myriad spa elements) with Miami panache. **Pros:** easy access to both South Beach and Mid-Beach; Como Shambhala toiletries; stylish "P" and "C" door magnets signal "Clean" or "Privacy". **Cons:** two people per room max; limited number of rooms with good views; small bathrooms. $ *Rooms from: $383* ✉ *2445 Collins Ave., South Beach* ☎ *305/695–3600* ⊕ *www.comohotels.com/metropolitanmiamibeach* 🛏 *74 rooms* ⦿ *No meals* ✛ *H1.*

$$
HOTEL

🏨 **Mondrian South Beach.** The Mondrian South Beach infuses life into the beach's lesser-known western perimeter and rises as a poster child of SoBe design glam—head to toe, the hotel is a living and functioning work of art, an ingenious vision of provocateur Marcel Wanders. **Pros:** great pool scene; perfect sunsets; party vibe. **Cons:** could still use a bit more refreshing; a short walk from most of the action; no direct beach access.

$ *Rooms from: $229* ✉ *1100 West Ave., South Beach* ☎ *305/514–1500* ⊕ *www.meninhospitality.com* ⮑ *335 rooms* ⦿ *No meals* ✛ *F3.*

$$ **National Hotel.** Fully renovated in 2014, the National Hotel maintains
HOTEL   its distinct art deco heritage (the chocolate- and ebony-hued pieces in
the lobby date back to the 1930s, and the baby grand piano headlines
the throwback Blues Bar) while trying to keep up with SoBe's glossy
newcomers. **Pros:** stunning pool; perfect location; Blues Bar. **Cons:**
street noise on the weekends; smaller rooms in art deco tower; $19/
day resort fee. $ *Rooms from: $295* ✉ *1677 Collins Ave., South Beach*
☎ *305/532–2311, 800/327–8370 reservations* ⊕ *www.nationalhotel.*
com ⮑ *152 rooms* ⦿ *No meals* ✛ *H2.*

$$$$ **1 Hotel South Beach.** This snazzy eco-minded hotel is one of Miami's
RESORT   all-around best. **Pros:** even basic level rooms are great; vibrant crowd;
Fodor's Choice   sustainability mantra. **Cons:** many rooms face street; constantly busy.
★ $ *Rooms from: $416* ✉ *2341 Collins Ave., South Beach* ☎ *305/604–*
1000 ⊕ *www.1hotels.com/south-beach* ⮑ *426 rooms* ⦿ *No meals* ✛ *E4.*

$$$ **Raleigh Hotel.** This classy art deco gem, part of the sbe hotel group,
HOTEL   balances the perfect amount of style, comfort, and South Beach sultri-
ness, highlighted by the beach's sexiest pool, which was created for
champion swimmer Esther Williams. **Pros:** amazing historic swimming
pool; art deco design; beautiful courtyard. **Cons:** lobby is a bit dark;
not as social as other South Beach hotels; in need of soft renovation.
$ *Rooms from: $385* ✉ *1775 Collins Ave., South Beach* ☎ *305/534–*
6300, 800/848–1775 reservations ⊕ *www.raleighhotel.com* ⮑ *105*
rooms ⦿ *No meals* ✛ *H2.*

$$$ **The Ritz-Carlton, South Beach.** The Ritz-Carlton is a surprisingly trendy
HOTEL   beachfront bombshell, with a dynamite staff, a snazzy Club Lounge,
FAMILY   and a long pool deck that leads right out to the beach. **Pros:** great
service; pool with VIP cabanas; great location. **Cons:** larger property;
in-house restaurant Bistro ONE LR often quiet; $28/night resort fee.
$ *Rooms from: $391* ✉ *1 Lincoln Rd., South Beach* ☎ *786/276–4000,*
800/542–8680 reservations ⊕ *www.ritzcarlton.com/southbeach* ⮑ *375*
rooms ⦿ *No meals* ✛ *H2.*

$$ **Room Mate Lord Balfour.** Quickly making a name for itself in South
HOTEL   Beach's emerging SoFi (South of Fifth) neighborhood, the luxurious, bou-
tique, and retro-chic Lord Balfour hotel—part of the Spain's RoomMate
brand—exudes style, sophistication, and the full-throttle, present-day
Miami Beach experience. **Pros:** great European crowd; whimsical interior
design; excellent service. **Cons:** rooms on smaller side; occasional street
noise from some rooms; small resort fee. $ *Rooms from: $219* ✉ *350*
Ocean Dr., South Beach ☎ *855/471–2739, 305/673–0401* ⊕ *www.lord-*
balfour.room-matehotels.com ⮑ *64 rooms* ⦿ *No meals* ✛ *G4.*

$$$ **Royal Palm South Beach Miami.** The Royal Palm South Beach Miami,
RESORT   now part of Starwood's Tribute Portfolio, is a daily celebration of art
Fodor's Choice   deco, Art Basel, modernity, and design detail. **Pros:** design blending
★   contemporary style with South Beach identity; impressive spa; multiple
pools; unbeatable location. **Cons:** small driveway for entering; older
elevators. $ *Rooms from: $338* ✉ *1545 Collins Ave., South Beach*
☎ *305/604–5700, 866/716–8147 reservations* ⊕ *www.royalpalmsouth-*
beach.com ⮑ *393 rooms* ⦿ *No meals* ✛ *G2.*

$$$$
HOTEL

Sagamore, the Art Hotel. This supersleek, all-white, all-suites hotel in the middle of the action looks and feels like an edgy art gallery, filled with brilliant contemporary works, the perfect complement to the posh, gargantuan, 500-square-foot crash pads. **Pros:** sensational pool; great location; good rate specials. **Cons:** can be quiet on weekdays; rooms could use some refreshing. $ *Rooms from: $429* ✉ *1671 Collins Ave., South Beach* ☎ *305/535–8088* ⊕ *www.sagamorehotel.com* ⌑ *93 suites* ⏐⊙⏐*No meals* ✛ *H2.*

$$$$
RESORT
Fodor'sChoice
★

The Setai Miami Beach. This opulent, all-suites hotel feels like an Asian museum: serene and beautiful, with heavy granite furniture lifted by orange accents, warm candlelight, and the soft bubble of seemingly endless ponds complemented by three oceanfront infinity pools (heated to different temperatures) that further spill onto the beach's velvety sands. **Pros:** quiet and classy; beautiful grounds; great celeb spotting. **Cons:** TVs are far from the beds; extremely high price point; many rooms lack ocean views. $ *Rooms from: $875* ✉ *2001 Collins Ave., South Beach* ☎ *305/520–6111, 888/625–7500 reservations* ⊕ *www.thesetaihotel. com* ⌑ *130 suites* ⏐⊙⏐*No meals* ✛ *H1.*

$$$
RESORT

Shelborne Wyndham Grand South Beach. After a major cash infusion from Wyndham hotels, the iconic Morris Lapidus–designed Shelborne hotel has reemerged as the retro-chic 200-room Shelborne Wyndham Grand South Beach, ushering in a new era of glory for both the brand and the hotel. **Pros:** location; prolific common spaces; Frette linens. **Cons:** entry-level rooms small; lack of balconies. $ *Rooms from: $389* ✉ *1801 Collins Ave., South Beach* ☎ *305/531–1271* ⊕ *www. shelbornewyndhamgrand.com* ⌑ *200 rooms* ⏐⊙⏐*No meals* ✛ *H1.*

$$$
RESORT
Fodor'sChoice
★

SLS Hotel South Beach. Smack in the center of South Beach, the SLS Hotel marks designer Philippe Starck's triumphant, large-scale return to South Beach; but this time he's teamed up with Sam Nazarian and chefs José Andrés and Katsuya Uech for the whimsical trip down the rabbit hole, creating the latest and greatest in the evolution of Miami's happening hotel-food-pool-beach scene. **Pros:** great in-house restaurants; masterful design; fun pool scene. **Cons:** some small rooms; no lobby per se; $30 per night resort fee. $ *Rooms from: $395* ✉ *1701 Collins Ave., South Beach* ☎ *305/674–1701* ⊕ *www.slshotels.com/southbeach* ⌑ *140 rooms* ⏐⊙⏐*No meals* ✛ *H2.*

$$
HOTEL

Surfcomber Miami, South Beach. As part of the hip Kimpton Hotel group, South Beach's legendary Surfcomber hotel reflects a vintage luxe aesthetic and an ocean-side freshness as well as a reasonable price point that packs the place with a young, sophisticated, yet unpretentious crowd. **Pros:** stylish but not pretentious; pet-friendly; on the beach. **Cons:** small bathrooms; front desk often busy. $ *Rooms from: $279* ✉ *1717 Collins Ave., South Beach* ☎ *305/532–7715* ⊕ *www.surf-comber.com* ⌑ *186 rooms* ⏐⊙⏐*No meals* ✛ *H2.*

$$$$
HOTEL

The Tides South Beach. The Tides South Beach, which celebrated its 80th anniversary in 2016, is an exclusive Ocean Drive art deco hotel of all ocean-facing suites adorned with soft pinks and corals, gilded accents, and marine-inspired decor. **Pros:** superior service; great beach location; ocean views from all suites plus the terrace restaurant (where we recommend cocktails only). **Cons:** tiny elevators; on touristy Ocean

Drive; taxidermy in rooms and common areas. $ *Rooms from: $445* ⊠ *1220 Ocean Dr., South Beach* ☎ *305/604–5070* ⊕ *www.tidessouthbeach.com* ⇒ *45 suites* ✱❍✱ *No meals* ✤ *G3.*

$ ☐ **Townhouse.** Though sandwiched between the glitzy high-rises of Col-
HOTEL   lins Avenue, Townhouse doesn't try to act all dolled up: it's comfortable being the shabby-chic, lighthearted, relaxed, fun hotel on South
Beach. **Pros:** a great budget buy for the style hungry; easy beach access;
hot rooftop lounge. **Cons:** no pool; small rooms not designed for long
stays; resort fee. $ *Rooms from: $195* ⊠ *150 20th St., east of Collins
Ave., South Beach* ☎ *305/534–3800* ⊕ *www.townhousehotel.com* ⇒ *70
rooms* ✱❍✱ *No meals* ✤ *H1.*

$ ☐ **Villa Paradiso.** This hotel is one of South Beach's best deals for budget
B&B/INN   travelers (and for those who don't plan on lingering in their rooms all
day), with huge (but basic) rooms with kitchens and a charming tropical courtyard with benches for hanging out at all hours. **Pros:** great
hangout spot in courtyard; good value; great location. **Cons:** no pool;
no restaurant; not trendy. $ *Rooms from: $139* ⊠ *1415 Collins Ave.,
South Beach* ☎ *305/532–0616* ⊕ *www.villaparadisohotel.com* ⇒ *17
rooms* ✱❍✱ *No meals* ✤ *G2.*

$$$$ ☐ **W South Beach.** Fun, fresh, and funky, the W South Beach represents
HOTEL   the brand's evolution towards young sophistication, which means less
Fodor's Choice   club music in the lobby, more lighting, and more attention to the mul-
★   timillion-dollar art collection lining the lobby's expansive walls. **Pros:**
pool scene; masterful design; ocean-view balconies in each room. **Cons:**
not a classic art deco building; hit-or-miss service; room rates for top-
level suites can be $1,000 per night in high season. $ *Rooms from: $429*
⊠ *2201 Collins Ave., South Beach* ☎ *305/938–3000* ⊕ *www.wsouth-
beach.com* ⇒ *248 rooms* ✱❍✱ *No meals* ✤ *H1.*

MID-BEACH

The stretch of Miami Beach called Mid-Beach is undergoing a renaissance, as formerly run-down hotels are renovated and new hotels and
condos are built.

$ ☐ **Circa 39 Hotel.** Located in the heart of Mid-Beach, this stylish yet
HOTEL   affordable boutique hotel pays attention to every detail and gets them
all right, with amenities that include a swimming pool and sundeck
complete with cabanas and umbrella-shaded chaises that invite all-day
lounging. **Pros:** affordable; beach chairs provided; art deco fireplace.
Cons: not on the beach side of Collins Avenue. $ *Rooms from: $170*
⊠ *3900 Collins Ave., Mid-Beach* ☎ *305/538–4900* ⊕ *www.circa39.com*
⇒ *96 rooms* ✱❍✱ *No meals* ✤ *E4.*

$$$ ☐ **The Confidante.** Formerly the Thompson, this hotel in Miami's bur-
RESORT   geoning Mid-Beach district is a beachfront classic art deco building
reinvented by Martin Brudnizki to channel a colorful, modern incar-
nation of 1950s Florida glamour. **Pros:** valet only $15 for visitors din-
ing on-property; rooftop spa; USB ports built into wall. **Cons:** small
driveway; entry-level rooms are on the small side. $ *Rooms from: $379*
⊠ *4041 Collins Ave., Mid-Beach* ☎ *786/605–4041* ⊕ *www.theconfi-
dante.unbound.hyatt.com* ⇒ *363 rooms* ✱❍✱ *No meals* ✤ *E3.*

2

$$$$
RESORT
Fodor'sChoice
★
Faena Hotel Miami Beach. Hotelier Alan Faena delivers on the high expectations of his Miami debut with the jaw-dropping, larger-than-life principal hotel within his in-progress, billion-dollar Faena Arts District in Miami Beach. **Pros:** incredible design; excellent service; spectacular beach club. **Cons:** pricey; construction in neighborhood. $ *Rooms from: $609* ✉ *3201 Collins Ave., Mid-Beach* ☎ *305/535–4697* ⊕ *www. faena.com/miami-beach* ➭ *169 rooms* ⦿ *No meals* ✛ *E4.*

$$$$
RESORT
FAMILY
Fodor'sChoice
★
Fontainebleau Miami Beach. Vegas meets art deco at this colossal classic hotel, Miami's largest, which has undergone a $1 billion reinvention. **Pros:** excellent restaurants; historic design mixed with all-new facilities; fabulous pools. **Cons:** away from the South Beach pedestrian scene; massive size; wide mix of guests. $ *Rooms from: $449* ✉ *4441 Collins Ave., Mid-Beach* ☎ *305/535–3283, 800/548–8886* ⊕ *www.fontainebleau.com* ➭ *1504 rooms* ⦿ *No meals* ✛ *E3.*

$$$$
RESORT
Fodor'sChoice
★
The Miami Beach EDITION. At this reinvention of the 1955 landmark Seville Hotel by unlikely hospitality duo Ian Schrager and Marriott, historic glamour parallels modern relaxation from the palm-fringed marble lobby to the beachy guest rooms. **Pros:** hotel's got incredible swagger; hanging gardens in the alfresco area; great beachfront service. **Cons:** a bit pretentious; open bathroom setup in select rooms offers little privacy; near a particularly rocky part of Miami Beach. $ *Rooms from: $459* ✉ *2901 Collins Ave., Mid-Beach* ☎ *786/257–4500* ⊕ *www. editionhotels.com/miami-beach* ➭ *294 rooms* ⦿ *No meals* ✛ *E4.*

$$
HOTEL
The Palms Hotel & Spa. If you're seeking an elegant, relaxed property away from the noise but close to both Mid-Beach and South Beach nightlife, you'll find an exceptional beach, an easy pace, and beautiful gardens with soaring palm trees and inviting hammocks here, with rooms as fabulous as the grounds. **Pros:** tropical garden; relaxed and quiet. **Cons:** standard rooms do not have balconies (but suites do); need a taxi or Uber to get most places. $ *Rooms from: $238* ✉ *3025 Collins Ave., Mid-Beach* ☎ *305/534–0505, 800/550–0505* ⊕ *www.thepalmshotel.com* ➭ *242 rooms* ⦿ *No meals* ✛ *E4.*

$$$$
HOTEL
Soho Beach House. The Soho Beach House is a throwback to swanky vibes of bygone decades, bedazzled in faded color palates, maritime ambience, and circa-1930s avant-garde furnishings, luring both somebodies and wannabes to indulge in the amenity-rich, retro-chic rooms as long as they follow stringent "house rules" (no photos, no mobile phones, no suits, and one guest only). **Pros:** two pools; fabulous restaurant; full spa. **Cons:** members have priority for rooms; lots of pretentious patrons; house rules are a bit much. $ *Rooms from: $545* ✉ *4385 Collins Ave., Mid-Beach* ☎ *786/507–7900* ⊕ *www.sohobeachhouse. com* ➭ *55 rooms* ⦿ *No meals* ✛ *E3.*

FISHER AND BELLE ISLANDS

$$$$
RESORT
Fisher Island Club. An exclusive private island, just south of Miami Beach but accessible only by ferry, Fisher Island houses an upscale residential community that includes a small inventory of overnight accommodations, including opulent cottages, villas, and junior suites, which surround the island's original 1920s-era Vanderbilt mansion. **Pros:** great private beaches; never crowded; varied on-island dining choices. **Cons:**

not the warmest fellow guests; ferry ride to get on and off island; limited cell service. ⓢ *Rooms from: $1375* ⊠ *1 Fisher Island Dr., Fisher Island* ☎ *305/535–6000, 800/537–3708* ⊕ *www.fisherislandclub.com* ☞ *60 rooms* �'◎' *No meals* ✛ *E5.*

$$
RESORT

⊡ **The Standard Spa Miami Beach.** An extension of André Balazs's trendy and hip—yet budget-conscious—brand, this shabby-chic boutique spa hotel is a mile from South Beach on an island just over the Venetian Causeway and boasts one of South Florida's most renowned spas, trendiest bars, and hottest pool scenes. **Pros:** free bike and kayak rentals; swank pool scene; great spa. **Cons:** slight trek to South Beach; small rooms with no views. ⓢ *Rooms from: $263* ⊠ *40 Island Ave., Belle Isle* ☎ *305/673–1717* ⊕ *www.standardhotels.com* ☞ *105 rooms* �'◎' *No meals* ✛ *E4.*

NORTH BEACH

BAL HARBOUR

$$$$
RESORT
FAMILY

⊡ **The Ritz-Carlton Bal Harbour, Miami.** In one of South Florida's poshest neighborhoods, the former ONE Bal Harbour exudes contemporary beachfront luxury design with decadent mahogany-floor guest rooms featuring large terraces with panoramic views of the water and city, over-the-top bathrooms with 10-foot floor-to-ceiling windows, and LCD TVs built into the bathroom mirrors. **Pros:** proximity to Bal Harbour Shops; beachfront; great contemporary-art collection. **Cons:** narrow beach is a bit disappointing; far from nightlife; $25 daily resort fee. ⓢ *Rooms from: $518* ⊠ *10295 Collins Ave., Bal Harbour* ☎ *305/455–5400* ⊕ *www.ritzcarlton.com/en/hotels/miami/bal-harbour* ☞ *187 rooms* �'◎' *No meals* ✛ *E2.*

$$$$
RESORT
Fodor's Choice
★

⊡ **The St. Regis Bal Harbour Resort.** When this $1 billion–plus resort opened in 2012, Miami's North Beach entered a new era of glamour and haute living, with A-list big spenders rushing to stay in this 27-story, triple-glass-tower masterpiece. **Pros:** beachfront setting; beyond glamorous; large rooms. **Cons:** limited lounge space around main pool; limited privacy on balconies. ⓢ *Rooms from: $929* ⊠ *9703 Collins Ave., Bal Harbour* ☎ *305/993–3300, 866/716–8116* ⊕ *www.stregisbalharbour. com* ☞ *280 rooms* ⑥ *No meals* ✛ *E2.*

SUNNY ISLES BEACH

$$$$
RESORT
FAMILY
Fodor's Choice
★

⊡ **Acqualina Resort & Spa on the Beach.** Following a complete room redesign in late 2014, Acqualina continues to raise the bar for Miami beachfront luxury, delivering a fantasy of modern Mediterranean opulence, with sumptuously appointed, striking gray- and silver-accented interiors, and expansive facilities. **Pros:** excellent beach; in-room check-in; huge spa. **Cons:** no nightlife near hotel; hotel's towering height shades the beach by early afternoon. ⓢ *Rooms from: $846* ⊠ *17875 Collins Ave., Sunny Isles Beach* ☎ *305/918–8000* ⊕ *www.acqualinaresort.com* ☞ *97 rooms* ⑥ *No meals* ✛ *E1.*

AVENTURA

$$$$
RESORT
FAMILY

⊡ **Turnberry Isle Miami.** Golfers and families favor this 300-acre tropical resort with jumbo-size rooms and world-class amenities, including a majestic lagoon pool (winding waterslide and lazy river included), an

Cars whiz by the Avalon hotel and other art deco architecture on Ocean Drive, Miami South Beach.

acclaimed three-story spa and fitness center, and two celeb-chef restaurants—Michael Mina's Bourbon Steak and Scott Conant's Corsair restaurant. **Pros:** great golf, pools, and restaurants; free shuttle to Aventura Mall; situated between Miami and Fort Lauderdale. **Cons:** not on the beach; no nightlife. $ *Rooms from: $548* ⊠ *19999 W. Country Club Dr., Aventura* ☎ *305/932–6200, 866/612–7739* ⊕ *www.turnberryislemiami.com* ⇰ *437 rooms* ⦶ *No meals* ✢ *E1.*

NIGHTLIFE

One of Greater Miami's most popular pursuits is barhopping. Bars range from intimate enclaves to showy see-and-be-seen lounges to loud, raucous frat parties. There's a New York–style flair to some of the newer lounges, which are increasingly catering to the Manhattan party crowd who escape to Miami and Miami Beach for long weekends. No doubt, Miami's pulse pounds with nonstop nightlife that reflects the area's potent cultural mix. On sultry, humid nights with the huge full moon rising out of the ocean and fragrant nightblooming jasmine intoxicating the senses, who can resist Cuban salsa with some disco and hip-hop thrown in for good measure? When this place throws a party, hips shake, fingers snap, bodies touch. It's no wonder many clubs are still rocking at 5 am. If you're looking for a relatively nonfrenetic evening, your best bet is one of the chic hotel bars on Collins Avenue, or a lounge away from Miami Beach in Wynwood, the Design District, or Downtown.

THE VELVET ROPES

How to get past the velvet ropes at the hottest South Beach night spots? First, if you're staying at a hotel, use the concierge. Decide which clubs you want to check out (consult *Ocean Drive* magazine celebrity pages if you want to be among the glitterati), and the concierge will email, fax, or call in your names to the clubs so you'll be on the guest list when you arrive. This means much easier access and usually no cover charge (which can be upward of $20) if you arrive before midnight. Guest list or no guest list, follow these pointers: Make sure there are more women than men in your group. Dress up: casual chic is the dress code. For men this means no sneakers, no shorts, no sleeveless vests, and no shirts unbuttoned past the top button. For women, provocative and seductive is fine; overly revealing is not. Black is always right. At the door: don't name-drop—no one takes it seriously. Don't be pushy while trying to get the doorman's attention. Wait until you make eye contact, then be cool and easygoing. If you decide to tip him (which most bouncers don't expect), be discreet and pleasant, not big-bucks obnoxious—a $10 or $20 bill quietly passed will be appreciated, however. With the right dress and the right attitude, you'll be on the dance floor rubbing shoulders with South Beach's finest clubbers in no time.

The *Miami Herald* (⊕ *www.miamiherald.com*) is a good source for information on what to do in town. The Weekend section of the newspaper, included in the Friday edition, has an annotated guide to everything from plays and galleries to concerts and nightclubs. The "Ticket" column details the week's entertainment highlights. Or you can pick up the *Miami New Times* (⊕ *www.miaminewtimes.com*), the city's largest free alternative newspaper, published each Thursday. It lists nightclubs, concerts, and special events; reviews plays and movies; and provides in-depth coverage of the local music scene. *MIAMI* (⊕ *www.modernluxury.com/miami*) and *Ocean Drive* (⊕ *www.oceandrive.com*), Miami's model-strewn, upscale fashion and lifestyle magazines, squeeze club, bar, restaurant, and events listings in with fashion spreads, reviews, and personality profiles. Paparazzi photos of local party people and celebrities give you a taste of Greater Miami nightlife before you even dress up to paint the town.

The Spanish-language *El Nuevo Herald* (⊕ *www.elnuevoherald.com*), published by the *Miami Herald*, has extensive information on Spanish-language arts and entertainment, including dining reviews, concert previews, and nightclub highlights.

DOWNTOWN

BARS AND LOUNGES

Bin No.18. Pop into this bistro and wine bar before or after a show at the nearby Adrienne Arsht Center, or simply while the evening away here. The setting masterfully fuses style with charm: wine barrels double as table bases, intimate and communal seating blend, a bar reveals an

2

open kitchen, and chandeliers add a hint of luxe. The menu provides a good mix of seafood and meat, to share or not, but the real highlight is the wine list. Owner-chef Alfredo Patino handpicks from boutique wineries, finding gems from the most famed regions to remote locations around the globe. ■TIP➔ **The best time to explore new varietals is Tuesday, when all bottles under $50 are half price.** ✉ *1800 Biscayne Blvd., Downtown* ☎ *786/235–7575* ⊕ *www.bin18miami.com.*

Fodor'sChoice
★
Blackbird Ordinary. This local watering hole has been around since 2011, but it became supertrendy in 2015 and hasn't looked back since. With a vibe that's a bit speakeasy, a bit dive bar, a bit hipster hangout, and a bit Miami sophisticate, it's hands down one of the coolest places in the city and clearly appeals to a wide range of demographics. Mixology is a huge part of the Blackbird experience—be prepared for some awesome artisanal cocktails. There's something going on every night of the week, and the stylish outdoor space is great for cocktails under the stars, movie screenings, and live music. ✉ *729 S.W. 1st Ave., Downtown* ☎ *305/671–3307* ⊕ *www.blackbirdordinary.com.*

Fodor'sChoice
★
Sugar. This skyscraping rooftop bar is the essence of the new downtown Miami: futuristic, worldly, and beyond sleek. It crowns the 40th floor of East, Miami, the luxury hotel tucked inside one of Miami's most ambitious multiuse endeavors: the billion-dollar-plus Brickell City Centre complex. The sunsets here are spectacular, as are the Southeast Asian bites and the exotic cocktails. ✉ *East, Miami, 788 Brickell Plaza, Downtown* ☎ *305/712–7000* ⊕ *www.east-miami.com.*

DANCE CLUBS

Club Space. Want 24-hour partying? Here's the place, which revolutionized the Miami party scene back in 2000 and still gets accolades as one of the country's best dance clubs. But depending on the month, Space wavers between trendy and empty, depending on the DJ or the special event, so make sure you get the up-to-date scoop from your hotel concierge. Created from four Downtown warehouses, it has two levels, an outdoor patio, a New York–style industrial look, and a 24-hour liquor license. It's open on weekends only, and you'll need to look good to be allowed past the velvet ropes. Note that the crowd can sometimes be sketchy, and take caution walking around the surrounding neighborhood. ✉ *34 N.E. 11th St., Downtown* ☎ *305/375–0001* ⊕ *www.clubspace.com.*

Fodor'sChoice
★
E11EVEN Miami. The former Gold Rush building has been transformed into an ultraclub with LED video walls, intelligent lighting, and a powerful sound system that pulses sports by day and beats by night, providing partygoers the 24/7 action they crave. Hospitality and VIP experiences are ample throughout the private lounges and second-level Champagne room; however, the real action is in "The Pit," featuring burlesque performances and intermittent Cirque du Soleil–style shows from a hydraulic-elevating stage. The fusion of theatrics and technology attracts an A-list clientele, and it's not unusual to catch a celebrity or two sporadically jumping on the decks. On the roof, the intimate 50-seat Touché restaurant serves a tapas menu. Live music on the adjacent rooftop lounge warms you up for the long evening—or morning—ahead. ✉ *29 N.E. 11th St., Downtown* ☎ *305/829–2911* ⊕ *www.11miami.com.*

COCONUT GROVE

BARS AND LOUNGES

Vinos in the Grove. There's no swirling, sniffing, or pondering (unless you want to, of course); most are here to simply lean back and recoup from the day. Indeed this is a place to enjoy good wine without any airs. Socialization is easy via the staff, who are genuinely conversational with their wine knowledge; you can meet the locals in the casual outdoor seating area, which is front and center for the Grove activity. Inside, punched-out brick walls, chandeliers fastened from wineglasses, and chalkboard menus highlighting cheese plates add a quirky charm. ✉ *3409 Main Hwy., Coconut Grove* ☎ *305/442–8840* ⊕ *www.vinosinthegrove.com.*

CORAL GABLES

BARS AND LOUNGES

The Bar. One of the oldest bars in South Florida (est. 1946), the old Hofbrau has been reincarnated a few times and now goes by the name "The Bar." The no-frills joint has become an institution in the South Florida bar scene, though it remains totally nontouristy. A massive American flag hangs on the wall of this locals' hangout, arguably the only "cool" nightlife in suburban Coral Gables. Owned by the same folks as Blackbird Ordinary in Downtown, The Bar delivers DJ-led tunes Wednesday through Saturday night and karaoke on Tuesday night. Oh, and they have pretty awesome, farm-fresh bar food, too, for both lunch and dinner. ✉ *172 Giralda Ave., at Ponce de León Blvd., Coral Gables* ☎ *305/442–2730* ⊕ *www.thebargables.com.*

Fodor's Choice
★
El Carajo. The back of a Mobil gas station is perhaps the most unexpected location for a wine bar, yet for nearly 25 years a passion for good food and drink has kept this family-run business among Miami's best-kept secrets. Tables are in the Old World–style wine cellar, stocked with bottles representing all parts of the globe (and at excellent prices). A waiter takes your order from the menu of exquisite cheeses and charcuterie, hot and cold tapas, paellas, and, of course, wine. Note that though this is an elusive spot, oenophiles are hardly deterred. Reservations are a must, as the place fills up quickly, especially since it closes by 10 pm weekdays, 11 pm weekends. ✉ *2465 S.W. 17th Ave, Coral Gables* ☎ *305/856–2424* ⊕ *www.el-carajo.com.*

WYNWOOD

BARS AND LOUNGES

Cafeina Wynwood Lounge. This awesome Wynwood watering hole takes center stage during the highly social Gallery Night and Artwalk through the Wynwood Art District (⊕ *www.wynwoodartwalk.com*), the second Saturday of every month, which showcases the cool and hip art galleries between Northwest 20th and Northwest 36 streets west of North Miami Avenue. For those in the know, on any given Miami weekend, the evening either begins or ends this seductive, design-driven lounge with a gorgeous patio and plenty of art on display. It's simply a great place to hang out and get a true feel for Miami's cultural revolution. It's open only Thursday–Saturday (5 pm to midnight Thursday, 5 pm to 3 am Friday, 9 pm to 3 am Saturday). ✉ *297 N.W. 23rd St., Wynwood* ☎ *305/438–0792* ⊕ *www.cafeinamiami.com.*

Wood Tavern. This is a neighborhood hangout where anything—and anyone—goes: suits mix with hoodies, fashionistas mingle with hipsters, but everyone in the crowd gives off a warm, welcoming vibe. The outdoor terrace is a block party scene with Latin bites served from graffiti-covered car countertops and bleacher-style stairs from which to people-watch or bob to the beats as the DJ jumps from Cypress Hill to Led Zepplin. The scene is a bit of a departure from the sultry nightlife typically associated with the Magic City (wine and cocktails are served in red plastic cups), but all in all it's an experience definitely worth checking out. ✉ *2531 N.W. 2nd Ave., Wynwood* ☎ *305/748–2828* ⊕ *www.woodtavern.com.*

Wynwood Brewing Company. This family-owned craft brewery is hidden among the towering graffiti arts walls of Wynwood. Communal tables and ever-changing pop-up galleries by neighborhood artists make the taproom cozy; however, a peek through the window behind the bar reveals there is much more to the establishment: 15 pristine silver vats are constantly brewing variations of blond ale, IPA, barrel-aged strong ales, seasonal offerings, and national Gold Medalist the Robust Porter. All staff members are designated "Beer Servers" under the Cicerone Certification Program, ensuring knowledgeable descriptions and recommendations to your liking. ✉ *565 N.W. 24 St., Wynwood* ☎ *305/982–8732* ⊕ *www.wynwoodbrewing.com.*

MIDTOWN

BARS AND LOUNGES

Fodor's Choice ★ **Lagniappe.** You may stumble upon this unassuming yet intriguing den across from the Midtown railroad tracks. Shelves house a selection of boutique-label wines with no corkage fee. Artisanal cheeses and meats are also available for the plucking and can be arranged into tapas-board displays. Once your selection is complete, take it back into the "living room" of worn sofas, antique lamps, and old-fashioned wall photos. Live musicians croon from the corner, with different bands each evening. Additional socializing can be found out in the "backyard" of mismatched seating and strung lighting, where as the evening wears on, you're apt to mingle and table-hop among the international crowd. ✉ *3425 N.E. 2nd Ave., Midtown* ☎ *305/576–0108* ⊕ *www.lagniappehouse.com.*

LITTLE HAVANA

LIVE MUSIC

Fodor's Choice ★ **Ball & Chain.** Established in 1935 and steeped in legends of gambling, Prohibition protests, the rise of budding entertainers Billie Holiday, Count Basie, and Chet Baker, and the development of Cuban-centric Calle Ocho, this storied nightlife spot has now been renovated and reestablished under its original name. The high-vaulted ceilings, floral wallpaper, black-and-white photos, and palm-fringed outdoor lounge nod to its torrid history and the glamour of Old Havana. Live music flows freely, as do the Latin-inspired libations and tapas of traditional Cuban favorites for an experience equally cultural as it is enjoyable. Reserved seating is available for a reasonable minimum. ✉ *1513 S.W. 8th St., Little Havana* ☎ *305/643–7820* ⊕ *www.ballandchainmiami.com.*

SOUTH BEACH

BARS AND LOUNGES

Fodor's Choice ★ **Blues Bar.** Dedicate at least one night of your Miami vacation to an art deco pub crawl, patronizing the hotel bars and lounges of South Beach's most iconic buildings, including the National Hotel. Though it's a low-key affair, the nifty wooden Blues Bar here is well worth a stop. The bar is one of many elements original to the 1939 building that give it such a sense of its era that you'd expect to see Ginger Rogers and Fred Astaire hoofing it along the polished terrazzo floor. Live music begins nightly at 8 pm. The adjoining Martini Room has a great collection of cigars, old airline stickers, and vintage Bacardi ads on the walls, but it's only available for private events (but if you ask for a peek, your request might be granted). ✉ *National Hotel, 1677 Collins Ave., South Beach* ☎ *305/532–2311* ⊕ *www.nationalhotel.com/food/blues.*

FDR at Delano. Top DJs are on tap at this überexclusive subterranean lounge that caters to a stylish see-and-be-seen crowd. Seductive lighting illuminates the two-room, 200-person watering hole, decked out in dark and sexy decor. Bottle service is available for those with deep pockets. ✉ *1685 Collins Ave., South Beach* ☎ *305/924–4071* ⊕ *www.morganshotelgroup.com/delano/delano-south-beach.*

Haven. This hipster-frequented gastrolounge may be cozy by South Beach standards, but it's just as flashy under the glow of backlit architecture, main bar, and lounge tables in ever-changing hues. Wall-to-wall TVs that double as light installations provide additional hypnotic entertainment. Clever mixology matches the innovative ambience with smoky craft cocktails fusing fresh-fruit flavors with herbs. Hungry? Your palate will be further appeased with the all-night menu of sushi and Asian-inspired bites, interspersed with fresh interpretations of American classics (including duck burgers and Maytag blue tater tots). ✉ *1237 Lincoln Rd., South Beach* ☎ *305/987–8885.*

Lost Weekend. Slumming celebs and locals often patronize this pool hall–resto–dive bar on quaint Española Way. The hard-core locals are serious about their pastime, so it can be challenging to get a table on weekends. However, everyone can enjoy the pinball machines, the air hockey table, the bar grub, and the full bar, which has 150 kinds of beer (a dozen of which are on tap). Each night, Lost Weekend draws an eclectic crowd, from yuppies to drag queens to celebs on the down-low (and everyone gets equally bad service). So South Beach! ✉ *218 Española Way, South Beach* ☎ *305/672–1707.*

Mac's Club Deuce Bar. Smoky, dark, and delightfully unpolished, this complete dive bar is anything but what you'd expect from glitzy South

Beach. The circa-1964 pool hall attracts a colorful crowd of clubbers, locals, celebs, and just about anyone else. Locals consider it a top spot for an inexpensive drink and cheap thrills. Visitors love it as a true locals' hangout. ✉ *222 14th St., at Collins Ave., South Beach* ☎ *305/531–6200* ⊕ *www.macsclubdeuce.com.*

Onyx Bar. Fanny-packed tourists are sure to stop and pose outside the Villa Casa Casuarina, the 1930s-era oceanfront mansion that once belong to late fashion designer Gianni Versace. But travelers know the true way to explore Versace's eccentric and bold Mediterranean mansion: by grabbing a drink at this six-seat bar, a conversion of Versace's former kitchen. The drinks are as opulent as you'd expect from the locale, with gold-leafed accessories and over-the-top taste sensations (think: Berissace Collins—a vodka-and-blackberry-based libation, topped with gold flakes). ✉ *1116 Ocean Dr., South Beach* ☎ *786/485–2200* ⊕ *www.vmmiamibeach.com.*

Palace Bar. South Beach's gay heyday continues at this fierce oceanfront bar where folks both gay and straight come to revel in good times, cheap cocktails, and great drag performances. Everyone's welcome, and there's no formal dress code. So for many, Speedos, tank tops, and two-pieces will do. The bar gets busiest in the afternoon and early evening; it's not really a late-night place. For out-of-towners, the Sunday Funday drag brunch is a must. It's a true showstopper—or car-stopper, shall we say: using Ocean Drive as a stage, drag queens direct oncoming traffic with street-side splits and acrobatic tricks in heels. ✉ *1200 Ocean Dr., South Beach* ☎ *305/531–7234* ⊕ *www.palacesouthbeach.com.*

Fodor's Choice ★ **Radio Bar.** What began as a pop-up bar in South Beach's emerging SoFi district in 2013 has evolved into a permanent local favorite, offering a basement-style party where the cool kids love to party, drink, and play. Radio Bar draws a diverse crowd of dressed-down locals, stylish yuppies, and consignment-shop junkies. You'll quickly recognize the bar by the 600-foot radio tower that marks the back-door entrance. Inside, the bar serves awesome craft cocktails, local brews, and small bites. ✉ *814 1st St., South Beach* ☎ *305/397–8382* ⊕ *www.radiosouthbeach.com.*

Fodor's Choice ★ **The Regent Cocktail Club.** This classic cocktail bar recalls an intimate gentleman's club (and not the stripper kind) with strong masculine cocktails, dark furnishings, bartenders dressed to the nines, and the sounds of jazz legends in the background. The intimate space exudes elegance and timelessness. It's a welcome respite from South Beach's predictable nightlife scene. Cocktails—each with bespoke ice cubes—change daily and are posted on the house blackboard. ✉ *Gale South Beach, 1690 Collins Ave., South Beach* ☎ *786/975–2555* ⊕ *www.galehotel.com/nightlife.*

Rose Bar. Tucked away inside the chic Delano South Beach, Rose Bar is a Miami mainstay and an essential stop on any South Beach crawl, mixing classic art deco architecture with the best in mixology (and a bit of Vegas bling). Embodying Philippe Starck's original, iconic vision and design for the Delano South Beach, the bar features a rose quartz bar top, velvet wall curtains, and striking chandeliers. ✉ *Delano Hotel, 1685 Collins Ave., South Beach* ☎ *305/674–5752* ⊕ *www.morganshotelgroup.com/delano/delano-south-beach.*

Sweet Liberty. Miami's bartender of-the-moment, John Lermayer, proves that he's in it for the long haul at this neighborhood hot spot, which took home the prize for Best New American Cocktail Bar 2016 in the Spirited Awards (the ultimate accolade in American bar scene). The bar is a tropical-chic, come-as-you-are joint with incredible spirit-forward cocktails. For something extra special, reserve the "Bartender's Table," which operates like a chef's table, but here you're in the thick of the bar action, tasting libations. ⊠ *237-B 20th St., South Beach* ☎ *305/763–8217* ⊕ *www.mysweetliberty.com.*

Tom on Collins. This lobby bar at the supersexy 1 Hotel South Beach is the brainchild of celebrity-chef Tom Colicchio. Don't expect a wild scene here. It has more of a sultry, laid-back vibe, a young-professional crowd, and plenty of conversation-worthy libations with cute names to match (like "Shiso-Pretty"). ⊠ *1 Hotel South Beach, 2341 Collins Ave., South Beach* ☎ *305/604–1000* ⊕ *www.beachcraftsobe.com/spaces/tom-on-collins/.*

DANCE CLUBS

Nikki Beach Miami Beach. Smack-dab on the beach, the full-service Nikki Beach Club was once upon a time a favorite of SoBe's pretty people and celebrities. Nowadays, it's filled with more suburbanites than the "in" crowd. Nikki's late-night parties are reserved for Sunday only. On Friday and Saturday, the Beach Club is open from noon to 11 pm, and closes at 6 pm on weekdays. Visitors can eat at the Nikki Beach Restaurant and get their food and drink on in the tepees, hammocks, and beach beds (expect rental fees). Sunday brunch at the club's restaurant is pretty spectacular. ⊠ *1 Ocean Dr., South Beach* ☎ *305/538–1111* ⊕ *www.nikkibeach.com.*

Fodor'sChoice ★ **Rec Room.** Entering Rec Room is like stumbling upon an awesome basement party that just happens to be packed with the hottest people ever. Amy Sacco's subterranean space at the Gale pays homage to everything 1977 (memorabilia included) and features a collection of more than 3,000 vinyl records at the disposal of resident DJs. The vibe is totally speakeasy meets modern day—the easy-on-the-eyes crowd lets loose, free of inhibitions, jamming out to old-school hip-hop and '80s and '90s throwbacks. ⊠ *Gale South Beach, 1690 Collins Ave., South Beach* ☎ *786/975–2555* ⊕ *www.recroomies.com.*

Score. Since the 1990s, Score has been the see-and-be-seen HQ of Miami's gay community, with plenty of global hotties coming from near and far to show off their designer threads and six-pack abs. After moving in 2013 to Washington Avenue from its longtime Lincoln Road location, this South Beach powerhouse shows no signs of slowing down. DJs spin five nights a week, but Planeta Macho Latin Tuesday is exceptionally popular, as are the weekend dance-offs, especially circuit-party-style "Bigger Saturdays." Dress to impress (and then be ready to go shirtless and show off your abs). ⊠ *1437 Washington Ave., South Beach* ☎ *305/535–1111* ⊕ *www.scorebar.net* ☾ *Closed Mon. and Wed.*

Twist. Twist is a gay institution in South Beach, having been the late-night go-to place for decades, filling to capacity around 2 am after the beach's fly-by-night bars and more established lounges begin to die down (though it's in fact open daily from 1 pm to 5 am). There's never a cover here—not even on holidays or during gay-pride events. The dark club has several rooms spread over two levels and patios, pumping out different tunes and attracting completely disparate groups. It's not uncommon to have college boys partying to Top 40 in one room and strippers showing off their stuff to the straight girls in another area, while an electronic dance throwdown is taking place upstairs. ⊠ *1057 Washington Ave., South Beach* ☎ *305/538–9478* ⊕ *www.twistsobe.com.*

MID-BEACH

BARS AND LOUNGES

Fodor'sChoice
★
The Broken Shakerbooks. Popular with Miami's cool crowd, this indoor-outdoor craft cocktail joint lures in droves to the adult-chic Freehand hostel to revel in the art of mixology and people-watching. The vibe is Brooklyn meets Miami: everyone's Instagraming everything in faded filters, and there's lots of man buns, facial hair, and girls that look like Lana del Rey (though they may claim they don't like her music). The drinks are pretty daring and definitely awesome with ingredients like green bean juice and kale juice complementing the top-shelf liquors. It's no wonder the venue has been awarded national titles such as America's Best Bar. ⊠ *Freehand Miami, 2727 Indian Creek Dr., Mid-Beach* ☎ *786/476–7011* ⊕ *www.thefreehand.com.*

DANCE CLUBS

Fodor'sChoice
★
LIV. Since its 2009 opening, this snazzy nightclub located at the Fontainebleau Miami Beach has garnered tons of global attention, and it shows no signs of stopping. It's not hard to see why LIV often makes lists of the world's best clubs—if you can get in, that is (LIV is notorious for lengthy lines, so don't arrive fashionably late). Past the velvet ropes, the dance palladium impresses with its lavish decor, well-dressed international crowd, sensational light-and-sound system, and seductive bi-level club experience. Sometimes the lobby bar, filled with LIV's overflow (and rejects), is just as fun as the club itself. ■TIP→ **Men beware: groups of guys entering LIV are often coerced into insanely priced bottle service.** ⊠ *Fontainebleau Miami Beach, 4441 Collins Ave., Mid-Beach* ☎ *305/674–4680 for table reservations* ⊕ *www.livnightclub.com.*

FISHER AND BELLE ISLANDS

BARS AND LOUNGES

Fodor'sChoice
★
The Lido Bayside Grill. With all due respect to wonderful food by executive-chef Mark Zeitouni, many locals come to this eatery with drinking as their top priority. By day, the colorful and chic waterfront alfresco restaurant is idyllic for watching the bay-side boats and poolside hotties go by. In the evening, lights braided into the surrounding trees illuminate the terrace, sparking a seductive ambience. On weekdays from 4 to 7, the bar offers a SunDown'er Happy Hour menu. ■TIP→ **The indoor, lobby-side Lido Bar and Lounge is great for a craft cocktail and a round of Ping-Pong, but the real scene is outdoors, on the opposite side of the hotel, at The Lido Bayside Grill.** ⊠ *The Standard Spa, Miami Beach, 40 Island Ave., Belle Isle* ☎ *786/245–0880* ⊕ *www.standardhotels.com.*

SHOPPING

Beyond its fun-in-the-sun offerings, Miami has evolved into a world-class shopping destination. People fly to Miami from all over the world just to shop. The city teems with sophisticated malls—from multistory, indoor climate-controlled temples of consumerism to sun-kissed, open-air retail enclaves—and bustling avenues and streets, lined at once with affordable chain stores, haute couture boutiques, and one-off, "only in Miami"–type shops.

Following the incredible success of the Bal Harbour Shops in the highest of the high-end market (Chanel, Alexander McQueen, ETRO), the Design District has followed suit. Beyond fabulous designer furniture showrooms, the district's tenants now include Hermès, Dior Homme, Rolex, and Prada.

If you're from a region ripe with the climate-controlled slickness of shopping malls and food-court "meals," you'll love the choices in Miami. Head out into the sunshine and shop the city streets, where you'll find big-name retailers and local boutiques alike. Take a break at a sidewalk café to power up on some Cuban coffee or fresh-squeezed OJ and enjoy the tropical breezes.

Beyond clothiers and big-name retailers, Greater Miami has all manner of merchandise to tempt even the casual browser. For consumers on a mission to find certain items—art deco antiques or cigars, for instance—the city streets burst with a rewarding collection of specialty shops.

Stroll through Spanish-speaking neighborhoods where shops sell clothing, cigars, and other goods from all over Latin America or even head to Little Haiti for rare vinyl records.

COCONUT GROVE

CLOTHING

The Griffin. This small boutique packs a big punch with the most coveted shoe styles, from Aquazarra to Chloe to Valentino and Loeffler Randall. Walk around once, then do it again, and you're sure to find another style urging you to try it on. Need help pulling the trigger? The boutique's stocked bar eases the pain of pricey purchases. ⊠ *3112 Commodore Plaza, Coconut Grove* ☎ *786/631–3522.*

Maui Nix. Anchoring the corner of CocoWalk plaza, this Florida-based store sells anything and everything you might need for a trip to the beach. More beach storehouse than shack, the bleached blond-wood walls and racks display 100 surf and skate brands of apparel, shoes, accessories, and gear. Pair a Billabong sundress with a pooka bead necklace, Hurley hoodie with skateboard, Vans slip-ons with Oakely sunglasses or Beats headphones—the possibilities are endless for looking like a true "Grovite." ⊠ *CocoWalk, 3015 Grand Ave., No. 145, Coconut Grove* ☎ *305/444–6919* ⊕ *www.mauinix.com.*

Unika. A longtime fashion resident of Coconut Grove (circa 1989), Unika takes shoppers from day to night, and all affairs in between, with a wide range of inventory for men and women. The contemporary boutique has an it-girl vibe, but the cool, relaxed one you'd actually want to be friends with. High–low pricing appeases all budgets; expect to uncover up-and-coming designer gems tucked within the racks of well-known brands. Bonus: the staff is great with styling for a head-to-toe look. ⊠ *3444 Main Hwy., Suite 2, Coconut Grove* ☎ *305/445–4752.*

MALLS

CocoWalk. Though this three-story, indoor-outdoor mall anchors the Grove's shopping scene, but it's long passed its 1990s heydey. Some chain stores like Victoria's Secret and Gap remain alongside a few specialty shops like Maui Nix. Touristy kiosks with cigars, beads, incense, herbs, and other small items are scattered around the ground level, and commercial restaurants and nightlife (Cheesecake Factory, Fat Tuesday, and Cinépolis Coconut Grove—a multiscreen, state-of-the-art movie theater with a wine bar and lounge and in-seat food service) line the upstairs perimeter. Overall, the space mixes the bustle of a mall with the breathability of an open-air market. Note that hanging out and people-watching is something of a pastime here for Miami suburbanites. ⊠ *3015 Grand Ave., Coconut Grove* ☎ *305/444–0777* ⊕ *www. cocowalk.net.*

CORAL GABLES

BOOKS

FAMILY

Fodor's Choice

★

Books & Books, Inc. Long live the classic bookstore! Greater Miami's only independent English-language bookshop, Books & Books, specializes in contemporary and classical literature as well as in books on the arts, architecture, Florida, and Cuba. The Coral Gables store is the largest of its four South Florida locations. Here, you can sip 'n' read in the courtyard lounge or dine at the old-fashioned in-store café while browsing the photography gallery. Multiple rooms are filled with myriad genres, making for a fabulous afternoon of book shopping; plus there's an entire area dedicated to kids. There are book signings, literary events, poetry, and other readings, too. Two smaller locations on Lincoln Road in South Beach and at the Bal Harbour Shops also carry great reads as does a petite outpost at the Miami International Airport. ⊠ *265 Aragon Ave., Coral Gables* ☎ *305/442–4408* ⊕ *www. booksandbooks.com.*

CLOTHING

Koko & Palenki. Shoe shopaholics come here for the well-edited selection of trendy footwear by Giuseppe Zanotti, Lola Cruz, Rachel Zoe, Rebecca Minkoff, and others. Handbags and belts add to the selection. Clothing hails from designers like Diane von Furstenberg, Misa, and J Brand. Koko & Palenki also has a store in Aventura Mall and a great online selection (they ship anywhere in the world). ⊠ *Village of Merrick Park, 342 San Lorenzo Ave., Suite 1090, Coral Gables* ☎ *305/444–0626* ⊕ *www.kokopalenki.com.*

FAMILY

Fodor's Choice

★

Nic Del Mar. Attending one of Miami's famed pool parties practically requires a trip to this upscale swimwear boutique. From the teeny weeny to innovative one-pieces to sporty cuts, the varied suit selection includes Mara Hoffman, Tori Praver, Acacia, and Zimmerman, many of which include matching children's styles for mini beach babes. Flowy cover-ups by the same labels and more can easily double as dinner dresses, while hats, totes, lotions, and even metallic temporary tattoos add a sun-kissed touch. Men's styles are also available. ⊠ *475 Biltmore Way, Suite 105, Coral Gables* ☎ *305/442–8080* ⊕ *www.nicdelmar.com.*

Silvia Tcherassi. The famed, Miami-based Colombian designer's signature boutique in the Village of Merrick Park features ready-to-wear, feminine, and frilly dresses and separates accented with chiffon, toile, and sequins. You'll see plenty of Tcherassi's designs on Miami's Latin power players at events and A-list parties. A neighboring atelier at 270 San Lorenzo Avenue showcases the designer's bridal collection. ⊠ *Village of Merrick Park, 350 San Lorenzo Ave., No. 2140, Coral Gables* ☎ *305/461–0009* ⊕ *www.silviatcherassi.com.*

MALLS

Village of Merrick Park. At this open-air Mediterranean-style, tri-level, shopping-and-dining venue, Neiman Marcus and Nordstrom anchor 115 specialty shops. Outposts by Michael Kors, Jimmy Choo, Tiffany &Co., Burberry, CH Carolina Herrera, and Gucci fulfill most high-fashion needs, and haute-decor shopping options include Brazilian contemporary-furniture designer Artefacto. International food favorite C'est Bon offers further indulgences. ⊠ *358 San Lorenzo Ave., Coral Gables* ☎ *305/529–1215* ⊕ *www.villageofmerrickpark.com.*

ONLY IN MIAMI

Ramon Puig Guayaberas. This clothing shop sells custom-made Ramon Puig guayaberas, the natty four-pocket dress shirts favored by older Cuban men and hipsters alike. Ramon Puig is known as "the King of Guayaberas," and his shirts are top of the line as far as guayaberas go. Hundreds are available off the rack. There are styles for women, too. ⊠ *5840 S.W. 8th St., Coral Gables* ☎ *305/ 266–9680* ⊕ *www.ramonpuig.com.*

SHOPPING DISTRICTS

Miracle Mile. The centerpiece of the downtown Coral Gables shopping district, lined with trees and busy with strolling shoppers, is home to a host of exclusive couturiers and bridal shops as well as some men's and women's boutiques, jewelry, and home-furnishings stores. The half-mile "mile" runs from Douglas Road to LeJeune Road and Aragon Avenue to Andalusia Avenue, but many of the Gables' best non-bridal shops are found on side streets, off the actual mile. In addition, the street itself teems with first-rate restaurants—more than two dozen—facilitating a fabulous afternoon of shopping and eating. ■ TIP→ If debating Miracle Mile versus Bal Harbour or the Design District, check out the others first. ⊠ *Miracle Mile (Coral Way), Douglas Rd. to LeJeune Rd., and Aragon Ave. to Andalusia Ave., Coral Gables* ⊕ *www.shopcoralgables.com.*

WYNWOOD

ONLY IN MIAMI

FAMILY **Genius Jones.** This is a modern design store for kids and parents. It's the best—and one of the few—places to buy unique children's gifts in Miami. Pick up furniture, strollers, clothing, home accessories, and playthings, including classic wooden toys, vintage-rock T-shirts by Claude and Trunk, and toys designed by Takashi Murakami and Keith Haring. ⊠ *2800 N.E. 2nd Ave., Wynwood* ☎ *305/571–2000* ⊕ *www. geniusjones.com.*

DESIGN DISTRICT

Fodor'sChoice ★ Miami is synonymous with good design, and this ever-expanding visitor-friendly shopping district—officially from Northeast 38th to Northeast 42nd streets, between North Miami Avenue and Northeast 2nd Avenue (though unofficially beyond)—is an unprecedented melding of public space and the exclusive world of design. High-design buildings don the creativity of architects like Aranda & Lasch, Sou Fujimoto, and the Leong Leong firm. Throughout the district, there are more than 100 showrooms and galleries, including Baltus, Animadomus, Kartell, Ann Sacks, Poliform USA, and Luminaire Lab. Upscale retail outlets also grace the district. Cartier, Dolce & Gabbana, Fendi, Marc Jacobs, Valentino, Giorgio Armani, Louis Vuitton, Prada, Rolex, and Scotch & Soda sit next to design showrooms. Meanwhile, restaurants like Michael's Genuine Food & Drink and Mandolin Aegean Bistro also make this trendy neighborhood a hip place to dine. Unlike most showrooms, which are typically the beat of decorators alone, the Miami Design District's showrooms are open to the public and occupy windowed, street-level spaces. The area also has its own website: ⊕ *www. miamidesigndistrict.net.*

CLOTHING

En Avance. This boutique offers a feminine compilation of on-the-cusp designers like Alexis, MSGM, Protagonist, Anjuna, and other young brands. Style and beauty enthusiasts will also enjoy the roving table displays of bespoke baubles, handbags, Assouline lifestyle books, and delicate lotions and potions. The owner's close connection with decorative artist Fornasetti brings to the store an extensive and exclusive selection of fashion-inspired furniture and accessories for the home. ⊠ *53 N.E. 40th St., Design District* ☎ *305/576–0056* ⊕ *www.enavance.com.*

ONLY IN MIAMI

The Bazaar Project. Those looking for the rare and special need look no further than this boutique, curated by owner and Turkey-native Yeliz Titiz via her travels around the globe. Fashions, beauty, decor, and the wonderfully unusual exude the culture and craft akin to their respective regions. Highlights include whimsical housewares and candles by Seletti, linens and Turkish rugs by Haremlique, French wallpapers by Koziel, and intriguing jewelry by Titiz's own line, Sura. ⊠ *4308 N.E. 2nd Ave., Design District* ☎ *786/703–6153* ⊕ *www.thebazaarproject-shop.com.*

V°73. Though high rents in Miami's Design District have translated to more big-name tenants like Fendi and Giorgio Armani, a number of more singular offerings still thrive. One case in point is the exquisite boutique by Italian handbag designer Elisabetta Armellin. It's the artist's only U.S. store and offers a wealth of colorful and understated leather totes and accessories at a number of different price points, catering to a broader demographic than the Design District's typical black-card holders. ⊠ *4218 N.E. 2nd Ave., Design District* ☎ *786/536–4140* ⊕ *www.v73.it/en.*

LITTLE HAITI

VINTAGE CLOTHING

Fly Boutique. After 13 years on South Beach, Fly Boutique found its new home in Miami's up-and-coming MIMO district, north of the Design District and bordering Little Haiti. This resale boutique is where Miami hipsters flock for the latest arrival of used clothing. 1980s glam designer pieces fly out at a premium price, but vintage camisoles and Levi's corduroys are still a resale deal. You'll find supercool art, furniture, luggage, and collectibles throughout the boutique. And be sure to look up—the eclectic lanterns are also for sale. ⊠ *7235 Biscayne Blvd., Little Haiti* ☎ *305/604–8508* ⊕ *www.flyboutiquevintage.com.*

Rebel. Rebel might be a little off the beaten path, though the trip here is well worth it. Half new, half vintage consignment, the goods offered here make you feel as if you are raiding your stylish friend's closet. Racks are packed with all different types of styles and designers—Flying Monkey, Ark & Co., Indah, Karina Grimaldi—requiring a little patience when sifting though. The store has a particularly strong collection of jeans, funky tees, and maxi dresses. ∎**TIP→ Be thorough, as cute finds are within every nook and corner.** ⊠ *6621 Biscayne Blvd., Upper East Side, Little Haiti* ☎ *305/793–4104.*

LITTLE HAVANA

ONLY IN MIAMI

FAMILY **La Casa de los Trucos.** This popular costume store first opened in Cuba in the 1920s; the exiled owners reopened it here in the 1970s. You'll find cartoon costumes, rock star costumes, pet costumes, couples costumes, you name it. If you come any time near Halloween, expect to stand in line just to enter the tiny store. Wooden, life-sized costume cut-outs in the parking lot make for great photo ops. ⊠ *1343 S.W. 8th St., Little Havana* ☎ *305/858–5029* ⊕ *www.crazyforcostumes.com.*

SOUTH BEACH

ART GALLERIES

Fodor's Choice
★
Romero Britto Gallery. Though exhibited throughout galleries and museums in more than 100 countries, the vibrant, pop art creations by Brazilian artist Romero Britto have become most synonymous with Miami's playful spirit. His flagship gallery and store are now split between two locations on Lincoln Road. Together they carry the full range of his portfolio, but you'll find original paintings and limited-edition

sculptures at the gallery location at 1102 Lincoln Road. Collectibles, fine art prints, and his signature interpretations in collaboration with some of America's most iconic characters and brands, including Disney and Coco-Cola, can be found at the Britto store at 532 Lincoln Road. Home-decor accessories and tech gadgets with Britto's artistic touch are also available. ⊠ *1102 Lincoln Rd., South Beach* ☎ *305/531–8821,* ⊕ *www.britto.com.*

CLOTHING

Fodor'sChoice **Alchemist.** Synonymous with the pinnacle of design and fashion in the
★ Magic City, this boutique has so much personality that it requires not one but two cutting-edge spaces in the retail section of Lincoln Road's trendy Herzog and de Meuron–designed parking garage. There's an anchor store on street level as well as a glass-encased studio for men's clothing and jewelry on the fifth floor. The price tags skew high, yet represent brands known for innovation and edge. Selections span statement pieces and accessories by Alaia, Givenchy, Moschino; jewelry on an artistry level including Cristina Ortiz, Lydia Courteille, and Stephen Webster; and fashions for the home by Tom Dixon. In 2015, Alchemist opened a fine jewelry-focused outpost in the Design District at 140 Northeast 39th Street. ⊠ *1111 Lincoln Rd., Carpark Level 5, South Beach* ☎ *305/531–4643* ⊕ *www.alchemist.miami.*

Base Superstore. This is the quintessential South Beach fun-and-funky boutique experience. Stop here for men's eclectic clothing, shoes, jewelry, and accessories that mix Japanese design with Caribbean-inspired materials. Constantly evolving, this shop features an intriguing magazine section, a record section, groovy home accessories, and the latest in men's swimwear and sunglasses. The often-present house-label designer may help select your wardrobe's newest addition. ⊠ *927 Lincoln Rd., South Beach* ☎ *305/531–4982* ⊕ *www.baseworld.com.*

frankie. miami. Expect high style at moderate prices at this boutique. The studio-like ambience matches the highly edited collection of fashionista favorites Beck & Bridge, Sam & Lavi, Iro, For Love & Lemons, and Loeffers. Co-owner Cheryl Herger also designs her own private-label line especially for frankie. miami. Skirts and dresses with interesting silhouettes, uniquely cut tops, and swimwear almost too good for just the pool are interspersed with easy-chic basics and the boutique's renowned selection of denim shorts (it is a Miami Beach fashion staple, after all). Delicate jewelry and statement clutches provide that polished edge to your final look. ⊠ *1891 Purdy Ave., South Beach* ☎ *786/479–4898* ⊕ *www.frankiemiami.com.*

Intermix. This modern New York–based boutique has the variety of a department store. You'll find fancy dresses, stylish shoes, slinky accessories, and trendy looks by sassy and somewhat pricey designers like Chloé, Stella McCartney, Marc Jacobs, Moschino, and Diane von Furstenberg. Its popularity on Collins Avenue has translated into a second outpost down the beach at Lincoln Road Mall, which opened in late 2014. There is yet another branch at the Bal Harbour Shops at 9700 Collins Avenue. ⊠ *634 Collins Ave., South Beach* ☎ *305/531–5950* ⊕ *www.intermixonline.com.*

ONLY IN MIAMI

Dog Bar. Just north of Lincoln Road's main drag, this over-the-top pet boutique caters to enthusiastic animal owners with a variety of unique items for the superpampered pet. From luxurious, vegan "leather" designer dog purse/carriers to bling-bling-studded collars to chic poopy bag holders, Miami's "original pet boutique" carries pretty much every pet accessory imaginable. You'll also find plenty of gourmet food and treats as well as a wide variety of fancy toys for dogs, large and small. ⊠ *1684 Jefferson Ave., South Beach* ☎ *305/532–5654* ⊕ *www.dogbar.com.*

Fodor's Choice   **The Webster Miami.** Occupying an entire circa-1939 art deco build-
★   ing, The Webster is a tri-level, 20,000-square-foot, one-stop shop for fashionistas. This retail sanctuary carries ready-to-wear fashions by more than 100 top designers, plus in-store exclusive shirts, candles, books, and random trendy items you might need for your South Beach experience—a kind of haute Urban Outfitters for grown-ups. Too many choices? Sit down for a café au lait and pastry inside the store to mull over your future purchases. ⊠ *1220 Collins Ave., South Beach* ☎ *305/674–7899* ⊕ *www.thewebstermiami.com.*

SHOPPING DISTRICTS

Collins Avenue. Give your plastic a workout in South Beach shopping at the many high-profile tenants on this densely packed stretch of Collins between 5th and 10th streets, with stores like Steve Madden, Club Monaco, The Webster, MAC Cosmetics, Ralph Lauren, and Intermix. Sprinkled among the upscale vendors are hair salons, spas, cafés, and such familiar stores as the Gap and Sephora. Be sure to head over one street east to Ocean Drive or west to Washington Avenue for a drink or a light bite, or go for more retail therapy on Lincoln Road. ⊠ *Collins Ave. between 5th and 10th Sts., South Beach* ⊕ *www.lincolnroadmall. com/shopping/collins-avenue.*

Fodor's Choice   **Lincoln Road Mall.** The eight-block-long pedestrian mall between Alton
★   Road and Washington Avenue is the trendiest place on Miami Beach. Home to more than 200 shops, art galleries, restaurants and cafés, and the renovated Colony Theatre, Lincoln Road is like the larger, more sophisticated cousin of Ocean Drive. The see-and-be-seen theme is furthered by outdoor seating at every restaurant, where tourists and locals lounge and discuss the people (and pet) parade passing by. An 18-screen movie theater anchors the west end of the street, which is where most of the worthwhile shops are; the far east end is mostly discount and electronics shops. Due to higher rents, you are more likely to see big corporate stores like Armani, H&M, and Victoria's Secret than original boutiques. However, a few emporiums and stores with unique personalities, like Alchemist, Base, and Books & Books, remain. ⊠ *Lincoln Rd. between Alton Rd. and Washington Ave., South Beach* ⊕ *www.lincolnroadmall.com.*

NORTH BEACH

BAL HARBOUR
CLOTHING

Le Beau Maroc. Shoppers can snag a piece of Moroccan exoticism and regality via pieces introduced to the United States for the very first time and available only within the boutique. Lavishly embellished couture kaftans by Souad Chraïbi and Siham Tazi, two of Morocco's most famed designers commissioned by a royal and celebrity clientele, can work for beach, day, and evening wear. Special orders created from the finest fabrics sourced from fashion houses Dior, Valentino, Hermès, Pucci, La Croix, Yves St. Laurent, Jakob Schlaepfer, and Ungaro are also available. Additional exclusive treasures are found at the "beauty bar," where you can adorn yourself with 18-carat-gold Moroccan jewelry and the "liquid gold" of Marokissime, an elixir of 100% pure Moroccan argan and prickly-pear oils coveted by Moroccan women for centuries for their beauty regimens. ✉ *9507 Harding Ave., Bal Harbour* ☎ *305/763–8847* ⊕ *www.lebeaumaroc.com.*

100% Capri. This shop is one of only two stores by this Italian brand in the United States (the other is in Los Angeles). The collection is all pure linen (including the shopping bags). Designer Antonio Aiello sources and produces all pieces in Capri for an exciting interpretation that takes its wearers to exotic beach locales style-wise—and quite literally, given its clientele. You'll find clothing for women, men, and children, and even home goods with curated glass accessories brought over from Italy. Displays of gray, wood-slatted wall panels and pools of water build up the ambience, prompting you to linger longer. Now if only there was rosé. ✉ *Bal Harbour Shops, 9700 Collins Ave., No. 236, Bal Harbour* ☎ *305/866–4117* ⊕ *www.100capri.com/en.*

Fodor's Choice
★ **The Webster Bal Harbour.** Though smaller than its sister store in South Beach, The Webster Bal Harbour is still sizable with 2,600 square feet to house high-level fashions for both men and women. Nearly every great contemporary luxury designer is represented (Chanel, Céline, Alaia, Valentino, Givenchy, Proenza Schouler, Stella McCartney, etc.), as well as emerging runway darlings. Fashionably impatient? The store can snag ready-to-wear pieces from the latest shows. It also carries exclusive pieces, a real feat considering its influential mall neighbors, including a continuous flow of capsule collections in collaboration with the likes of Calvin Klein, Marc Jacobs, and Anthony Vaccarello, to name a few. ✉ *Bal Habour Shops, 9700 Collins Ave., No. 204, Bal Harbour* ☎ *305/868–6544* ⊕ *www.thewebstermiami.com.*

SHOPPING CENTERS AND MALLS

Fodor's Choice
★ **Bal Harbour Shops.** Beverly Hills meets the South Florida sun at this swank collection of 100 high-end shops, boutiques, and department stores, which currently holds the title as the country's greatest revenue-earner per square foot. Many European designers open their first North American signature store at this outdoor, pedestrian-friendly mall, and many American designers open their first boutique outside of New York here. The open-air enclave includes Florida's largest Saks Fifth Avenue; an 8,100-square-foot, two-story flagship Salvatore Ferragamo

store; and stores by Alexander McQueen, Gucci, Valentino, and local juggernaut The Webster. Restaurants and cafés, in tropical garden settings, overflow with style-conscious diners; in fact, people-watching on the terrace of the Japanese restaurant Makoto and Italian restaurant Carpaccio might be the best in Miami (even trumping South Beach). ✉ *9700 Collins Ave., Bal Harbour* ☎ *305/866–0311* ⊕ *www.balharbourshops.com.*

AVENTURA

JEWELRY

MIA Jewels. This jewelry and accessories boutique is known for its colorful gem- and bead-laden, gold and silver earrings, necklaces, bracelets, and brooches by lines such as Cousin Claudine, Amrita, and Alexis Bittar. This is a shoo-in store for everyone: you'll find things for trend lovers (gold-studded chunky Lucite bangles), classicists (long, colorful, wraparound beaded necklaces), and ice lovers (long Swarovski crystal cabin necklaces) alike. ✉ *Aventura Mall, 19575 Biscayne Blvd., No. 1061, Aventura* ☎ *305/931–2000.*

SHOPPING CENTERS AND MALLS

Fodor'sChoice ★ **Aventura Mall.** This three-story megamall offers the ultimate in South Florida retail therapy and welcomes more than 29 million visitors annually. Aventura houses many global top performers including the most lucrative outposts of several U.S. chain stores, a supersize Nordstrom and Bloomingdale's, and 300 other shops like a two-story flagship Louis Vuitton, Façonnable, Fendi, and MIA Jewels, which together create the third-largest mall in the United States. This is the one-stop, shop-'til-you-drop retail mecca for locals, out-of-towners, and—frequently—celebrities. ✉ *19501 Biscayne Blvd., Aventura* ☎ *305/935–1110* ⊕ *www.aventuramall.com.*

SPORTS AND THE OUTDOORS

Sun, sand, and crystal-clear water mixed with an almost nonexistent winter and a cosmopolitan clientele make Miami and Miami Beach ideal for year-round sunbathing and outdoor activities. Whether the priority is showing off a toned body, jumping on a Jet Ski, or relaxing in a tranquil natural environment, there's a beach tailor-made to please. But tanning and water sports are only part of this sun-drenched picture. Greater Miami has championship golf courses and tennis courts, miles of bike trails along placid canals and through subtropical forests, and skater-friendly concrete paths amidst the urban jungle. For those who like their sports of the spectator variety, the city offers up a bonanza of pro teams for every season. There's even a crazy ball-flinging game called jai alai that's billed as the fastest sport on Earth.

BASEBALL

FAMILY **Marlins.** Miami's baseball team, formerly known as the Florida Marlins, then the Miami Marlins, and now simply the Marlins, plays at the state-of-the-art Marlins Park—a 37,442-seat retractable-roof, air-conditioned baseball stadium on the grounds of Miami's famous

Orange Bowl. Go see the team that came out of nowhere to beat the New York Yankees and win the 2003 World Series. Home games are April through early October. ⊠ *Marlins Park, 501 Marlins Way, Little Havana* ☎ *305/480–1300, 877/627–5467 for tickets* ⊕ *miami. marlins.mlb.com* ☒ *$10–$395; parking from $20 and should be pre-purchased online.*

BIKING

Perfect weather and flat terrain make Miami–Dade County a popular place for cyclists; however, biking here can also be quite dangerous. Be very vigilant when biking on Miami Beach, or better yet, steer clear and bike the beautiful paths of Key Biscayne instead.

Key Cycling. On an island where biking is a way of life, this Key Biscayne bike shop carries a wide range of amazing bikes in its showroom, as well as any kind of bike accessory imaginable. Out-of-towners can rent mountain or hybrid bikes for $20 for two hours, $25 for the day, and $100 for the week. ⊠ *Galleria Shopping Center, 328 Crandon Blvd., Suite 121, Key Biscayne* ☎ *305/361–0061* ⊕ *www.keycycling.com.*

Miami Beach Bicycle Center. If you don't want to opt for the hassle of CitiBike or if you want wheels with some style, the easiest and most economical place for a bike rental on South Beach is this shop near Ocean Drive. Rent a bike starting at $5 per hour, $18 per day, or $80 for the week. All bike rentals include locks, helmets, and baskets. ⊠ *601 5th St., South Beach* ☎ *305/674–0150* ⊕ *www.bikemiamibeach.com.*

BOATING AND SAILING

Boating, whether on sailboats, powerboats, luxury yachts, WaveRunners, or windsurfers, is a passion in Greater Miami. The Intracoastal Waterway, wide and sheltered Biscayne Bay, and the Atlantic Ocean provide ample opportunities for fun aboard all types of watercraft.

The best windsurfing spots are on the north side of the Rickenbacker Causeway at Virginia Key Beach or to the south at, go figure, Windsurfer Beach.

GOLF

Greater Miami has more than 30 private and public courses. Costs at most courses are higher on weekends and in season, but you can save by playing on weekdays and after 1 or 3 pm, depending on the course. Call ahead to find out when afternoon-twilight rates go into effect. For information on most courses in Miami and throughout Florida, you can visit ⊕ *www.floridagolferguide.com.*

Biltmore Golf Course. On the grounds of the historic circa 1926 Biltmore hotel, the Biltmore Golf Course provides a golf experience primarily for in-house guests, local residents, and those visiting the Coral Gables area. The 6,800-yard, 18-hole, par-71, championship golf course was designed in 1925 by Scotsman Donald Ross, the "it" golf designer of the Roaring '20s. Today, the lush, well-maintained course is easily accessible thanks to its advanced online booking system, where you can easily reserve your tee time and decide between pricing, depending on the time of day and year (weekdays are cheaper; and the later, the cheaper it gets). There's a pro shop on-site, and golf instruction is available through the Biltmore Golf Academy or the more extensive on-site Golf Channel Academy. ⊠ *The Biltmore Hotel, 1210 Anastasia Ave., Coral Gables* ☎ *305/460–5364* ⊕ *www. biltmorehotel.com/golf* ✉ *$122 for 9 holes, $200 for 18 holes* ⅃ *18 holes, 6800 yards, par 71.*

Fodor'sChoice ★ **Crandon Golf at Key Biscayne.** On the serene island of Key Biscayne, overlooking Biscayne Bay, this top-rated, championship municipal golf course is considered one of the state's most challenging par-72 courses. Enveloped by tropical foliage, mangroves, saltwater lakes, and bay-side waters, the course also happens to be the only one in North America with a subtropical lagoon. The Devlin/Von Hagge–designed course has a USGA rating of 75.4 and a slope rating of 129 and has received national awards from both *Golfweek* and *Golf Digest*. The course is located on the south side of Crandon Park. Nonresidents should expect to pay $200 for a round during peak hours in peak season (mid-December–mid-April) and roughly half that off-season. Deeply discounted twilight rates of $65 apply after 2 pm. Tee times can be booked online. ⊠ *Crandon Park, 6700 Crandon Blvd., Key Biscayne* ☎ *305/361–9129, 855/465–3305 for tee times* ⊕ *www.golfcrandon. com* ✉ *$200* ⅃ *18 holes, 7400 yards, par 72.*

The Senator Course at Shula's Golf Club. Deep in the suburbs of west Miami, the Senator Course at Shula's Golf Club boasts the longest championship course in the area (7,055 yards, par 72), a lighted par-3 course, and a golf school. The championship, classic-style Senator Course was originally designed in 1962 by Bill Watts, updated by Kipp Schulties in 1998, and completely refreshed in late 2013, with improvements that included sparkling new Champion Bermuda greens and new Celebration Bermuda tees. The club hosts dozens of tournaments yearly. Because of its remote location, greens fees tend to be on the lower side, varying by season and time. You'll pay in the lower range on weekdays, more on weekends, and a third of prime-time rates after 2 pm. Golf carts are included. For true golf enthusiasts, there's the on-site Don Shula hotel—a comfortable base to eat, live, and breathe golf. ⊠ *7601 Miami Lakes Dr., 154th St. exit off Rte. 826, Miami Lakes* ☎ *305/820–8088* ⊕ *www.shulasgolfclub.com* ✉ *$130* ⅃ *18 holes, 7055 yards, par 70.*

GUIDED TOURS

BOAT TOURS

FAMILY **Island Queen Cruises.** Working with nine boats, experiences on the very touristy Island Queen Cruises run the gamut—sunset cruises, dance cruises, fishing cruises, speedboat rides, and their signature, tours of Millionaire's Row, Miami's waterfront homes of the rich and famous. The *Island Queen, Island Lady,* and *Miami Lady* are three double-decker, 140-passenger tour boats docked at Bayside Marketplace that set sail daily for 90-minute narrated tours of the Port of Miami and Millionaires' Row. ⊠ *401 Biscayne Blvd., Downtown* ☏ *800/910–5119* ⊕ *www.islandqueencruises.com* ✉ *From $19.*

WALKING TOURS

FAMILY **Art Deco District Walking Tour.** Operated by the Miami Design Preservation League, this is a 90-minute guided walking tour that departs from the league's welcome center at Ocean Drive and 10th Street. It starts at 10:30 am daily, with an extra tour at 6:30 pm Thursday. Alternatively, you can go at your own pace with the league's self-guided iPod audio tour, which also takes roughly an hour and a half. ⊠ *1001 Ocean Dr., South Beach* ☏ *305/763–8026* ⊕ *www.mdpl.org* ✉ *$25 guided tour, $20 self-guided audio tour.*

Little Havana Arts & Culture Walk. Cultural institution HistoryMiami (formerly the Historical Museum of Southern Florida) runs some fabulous art and cultural tours of Little Havana (spiked with plenty of Cuban coffees and cigars, of course). Enjoy the unique architecture of this ethnic enclave and community history by visiting art galleries, botanicas, cigar factories, and the Cuba Ocho Art and Research Center, featuring rare Cuban art from early 19th and 20th century. The two-hour tour is offered monthly and leaves from the juice stand and market Los Pinareños Fruteria at 6 pm. Tours aren't available every month, so check the HistoryMiami calendar on the website ahead of time to book. ⊠ *1334 S.W. 8 St., Little Havana* ☏ *305/375–1492* ⊕ *www.historymiami.org* ✉ *$30.*

SCUBA DIVING AND SNORKELING

Diving and snorkeling on the offshore coral wrecks and reefs on a calm day can be very rewarding. Chances are excellent that you'll come face-to-face with a flood of tropical fish. One option is to find Fowey, Triumph, Long, and Emerald reefs in 10- to 15-foot dives that are perfect for snorkelers and beginning divers. On the edge of the continental shelf a little more than 3 miles out, these reefs are just a quarter-mile away from depths greater than 100 feet. Another option is to paddle around the tangled prop roots of the mangrove trees that line the coast, peering at the fish, crabs, and other creatures hiding there.

Perhaps the area's most unusual diving options are its artificial reefs. Since 1981, Miami-Dade County's Department of Environmental Resources Management has sunk tons of limestone boulders and a water tower, army tanks, and almost 200 boats of all descriptions to create a "wreckreational" habitat where divers can swim with yellow tang, barracudas, nurse sharks, snapper, eels, and grouper. The website offers an interactive map of wreck locations. ⇨ *For the best snorkeling in Miami–Dade, head to Biscayne National Park. See the Everglades, Chapter 3, for more information.*

Divers Paradise of Key Biscayne. This complete dive shop and diving-charter service, next to the Crandon Park Marina, includes equipment rental and scuba instruction with PADI and NAUI affiliation. Four-hour dive trips are offered on weekends at 8:30 and 1:30. Night dives are offered Thursday at 5:30; the company is generally closed on Mondays. ⊠ *Crandon Park Marina, 4000 Crandon Blvd., Key Biscayne* ☎ *305/361–3483* ⊕ *www.keydivers.com* ✉ *$60.*

Fodor'sChoice   **South Beach Dive and Surf.** Dedicated to all things ocean, this PADI five-
★   star dive shop offers multiple diving and snorkeling trips weekly as well
as surfboard, paddleboard, and skateboard sales, rentals, and lessons.
The Discover Scuba course (for noncertified divers) trains newcomers every Monday, Tuesday, Thursday, and Saturday at 10 am, which
includes two dives in Key Largo's John Pennekamp Marine Sanctuary
that same day. In some months of the year, night dives take place on
Wednesday at 5. Wreck and reef dives take place on weekend mornings.
The center also runs dives in Key Largo's Spiegel Grove, the second-
largest wreck ever to be sunk for the intention of recreational diving,
and in the Neptune Memorial Reef, inspired by the city of Atlantis and
created in part using the ashes of cremated bodies. The dive shop itself
is located in the heart of South Beach, but boats depart from marinas
in Miami Beach and Key Largo, in the Florida Keys. ⊠ *850 Washington Ave., South Beach* ☎ *305/531–6110* ⊕ *www.southbeachdivers.com.*

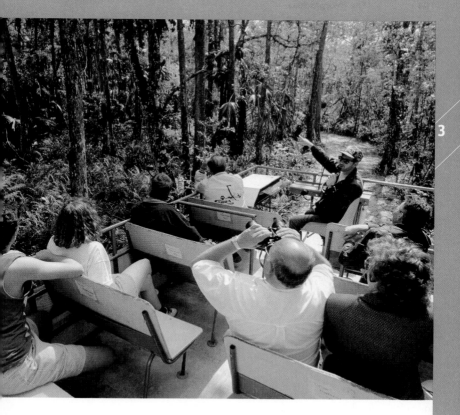

THE EVERGLADES

WELCOME TO THE EVERGLADES

TOP REASONS TO GO

★ **Fun fishing:** Cast for some of the world's fightingest game fish—600 species in all—in the Everglades' backwaters.

★ **Abundant birdlife:** Check hundreds of birds off your life list, including—if you're lucky—the rare Everglades snail kite.

★ **Cool kayaking:** Do a half-day trip in Big Cypress National Preserve or grab a paddle for the ultimate—the 99-mile Wilderness Trail.

★ **Swamp cuisine:** Want to chow down on alligator tail or frogs' legs? Or how about swamp cabbage, made from hearts of palm? Better yet, try stone-crab claws fresh from the traps.

★ **Gator-spotting:** This is ground zero for alligator viewing in the United States, and odds are you'll leave having spotted your quota.

1 Everglades National Park. Alligators, Florida panthers, black bears, manatees, dolphins, bald eagles, and roseate spoonbills call this vast habitat home.

2 Biscayne National Park. Mostly under water, here's where the string of coral reefs and islands that form the Florida Keys begins.

3 Big Cypress National Preserve. Neighbor to Everglades National Park, it's an outdoor-lover's paradise.

GETTING ORIENTED

3

The southern third of the Florida peninsula is largely taken up by protected government land that includes Everglades National Park, Big Cypress National Preserve, and Biscayne National Park. Miami lies to the northeast, with Naples and Marco Island to the northwest. Land access to Everglades National Park is primarily by two roads. The park's main road traverses the southern Everglades from the gateway towns of Homestead and Florida City to the outpost of Flamingo, on Florida Bay. To the north, Tamiami Trail (U.S. 41) cuts through the Everglades from Greater Miami on the east coast or from Naples on the west coast to the western park entrance near Everglades City at Route 29.

THE FLORIDA
EVERGLADES

by Lynne Helm

Alternately described as elixir of life or swampland muck, the Florida Everglades is one of a kind—a 50-mi-wide "river of grass" that spreads across hundreds of thousands of acres. It moves at varying speeds depending on rainfall and other variables, sloping south from the Kissimmee River and Lake Okeechobee to estuaries of Biscayne Bay, Florida Bay, and the Ten Thousand Islands.

Today, apart from sheltering some 70 species on America's endangered list, the Everglades also embraces more than 7 million residents, 50 million annual tourists, 400,000 acres of sugarcane, and the world's largest concentration of golf courses.

Demands on the land threaten the Everglades' finely balanced ecosystem. Irrigation canals for agriculture and roadways disrupt natural water flow. Drainage for development leaves wildlife scurrying for new territory. Water runoff, laced with fertilizers, promotes unnatural growth of swamp vegetation. What remains is a miracle of sorts, given decades of these destructive forces.

Creation of the Everglades required unique conditions. South Florida's geology, linked with its warm, wet subtropical climate, is the perfect mix for a marshland ecosystem. Layers of porous, permeable limestone create water-bearing rock, soil, and aquifers, which in turn affects climate, weather, and hydrology.

This rock beneath the Everglades reflects Florida's geologic history—its crust was once part of the African region. Some scientists theorize that continental shifting merged North America with Africa, and then continental rifting later pulled North America away from the African continent but took part of northwest Africa with it—the part that is today's Florida. The Earth's tectonic plates continued to migrate, eventually placing Florida at its current location as a land mass jutting out into the ocean, with the Everglades at its tip.

EXPERIENCING THE ECOSYSTEMS

Eight distinct habitats exist within Everglades National Park, Big Cypress National Preserve, and Biscayne National Park.

Carnestown ○ Ochopee ○ 41
29
Gulf Coast ○ Everglades City
Visitor Center
○ Chokoloskee
TEN THOUSAND ISLANDS

ECOSYSTEMS	EASY WAY	MORE ACTIVE WAY
COASTAL PRAIRIE: An arid region of salt-tolerant vegetation lies between the tidal mud flats of Florida Bay and dry land. **Best place to see it: The Coastal Prairie Trail**	Take a guided boat tour of Florida Bay, leaving from Flamingo Marina.	Hike the Coastal Prairie Trail from Eco Pond to Clubhouse Beach.
CYPRESS: Capable of surviving in standing water, cypress trees often form dense clusters called "cypress domes" in natural water-filled depressions. **Best place to see it: Big Cypress National Preserve**	Drive U.S. 41 (also known as Tamiami Trail—pronounced Tammy-Amee), which cuts across Southern Florida, from Naples to Miami.	Hike (or drive) the scenic Loop Road, which begins off Tamiami Trail, running from the Loop Road Education Center to Monroe Station.
FRESH WATER MARL PRAIRIE: Bordering deeper sloughs are large prairies with marl (clay and calcium carbonate) sediments on limestone. Gators like to use their toothy snouts to dig holes in prairie mud. **Best place to see it: Pahayokee Overlook**	Drive there from the Ernest F. Coe Visitor Center.	Take a guided tour, either through the park service or from permitted, licensed guides. You also can set up camp at Long Pine Key.
FRESH WATER SLOUGH AND HARDWOOD HAMMOCK: Shark River Slough and Taylor Slough are the Everglades' two sloughs, or marshy rivers. Due to slight elevation amid sloughs, dense stands of hardwood trees appear as teardrop-shaped islands. **Best place to see it: The Observation Tower**	Take a two-hour guided tram tour from the Shark Valley Visitor Center to the tower and back.	Walk or bike (rentals available) the route to the tower via the tram road and (walkers only) Bobcat Boardwalk trail and Otter Cave Hammock Trail.
MANGROVE: Spread over South Florida's coastal channels and waterways, mangrove thrives where Everglades fresh water mixes with salt water. **Best place to see it: The Wilderness Waterway**	Picnic at the area near Long Pine Key, which is surrounded by mangrove, or take a water tour at Biscayne National Park.	Boat your way along the 99-mi Wilderness Waterway. It's six hours by motorized boat, seven days by canoe.
MARINE AND ESTUARINE: Corals, sponges, mollusks, seagrass, and algae thrive in the Florida Bay, where the fresh waters of the Everglades meet the salty seas. **Best place to see it: Florida Bay**	Take a boat tour from the Flamingo Visitor Center marina.	Canoe or kayak on White Water Bay along the Wilderness Waterway Canoe Trail.
PINELAND: A dominant plant in dry, rugged terrain, the Everglades' diverse pinelands consist of slash pine forest, saw palmettos, and more than 200 tropical plant varieties. **Best place to see it: Long Pine Key trails**	Drive to Long Pine Key, about 6 mi off the main road from Ernest F. Coe Visitor Center.	Hike or bike the 28 mi of Long Pine Key trails.

Big Cypress
National Preserve

EVERGLADES
NATIONAL PARK

0   8 mi
0   8 km

Third Bay
Big Lostmans Bay

Key Loughlin

Wilderness Waterway
and Canoe Trail

Shark River Slough

**EVERGLADES
NATIONAL PARK**

Ponce De Leon
Bay

**Shark Valley
Visitor Center**

Tram tour

Overlook

Chekika

**Pa-hay-okee
Overlook**

**Long Pine
Key**

Royal Palm

Homestead
Florida City
**Ernest F Coe
Visitor Center**

9336

Biscayne
National
Park

821

997

Whitewater
Bay

**Mahogany
Hammock**

*Nine Mile Pond
Canoe Trail*

Taylor Slough

CAPE SABLE

Nine Mile Pond

West Lake

Bear Lake
Canoe Trail

Snake Bight Trail

Christian Point Trail

Flamingo   **Flamingo
Visitor Center**

Coastal Prairie
Trail

Deer Key

Eagle Key

Nest
Keys

Black Betsy
Keys

Park Key

Shell Key

Key Largo

Russell Key

Corinne Key

Florida Bay

Rabbit Keys

Panhandle
Key

Barnes Key

Islamorada

Tavernier
Plantation

1

1
TO
← KEY WEST

**Marine and Estuarine
Water Depths**
▢ 0-3 Feet
▢ 3-6 Feet
▢ over 6 Feet

Land Cover
▢ Coastal Prairie
▢ Cypress
▢ Fresh Water Marl Prairie
▢ Fresh Water Slough
▢ Hardwood Hammock
▢ Mangrove
▢ Pinelands
▢ Urban

🏠 *Ranger Station*
🛖 *Campground*
🌲 *Picnic Area*
🍴 *Restaurant*
······· *Walking/Hiking Trails*
- - - *Water/Canoe Trails*

Lake
Okeechobee

Big Cypress
National
Preserve

EVERGLADES
NATIONAL
PARK

Biscayne
National
Park

Habitats within Florida's Everglades
ecosystem support a diverse collection
of plant and animal species encountered
nowhere else. The landscape is dynamic,
and the ecosystems are in constant flux,
subject to changing elements.

FLORA

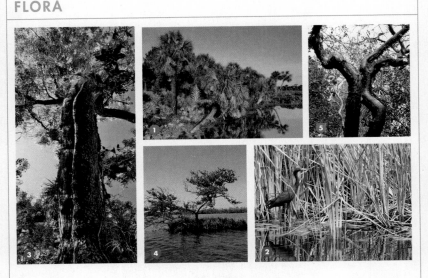

❶ Cabbage Palm

It's virtually impossible to visit the Everglades and not see a cabbage palm, Florida's official state tree. The cabbage palm (or sabal palm), graces assorted ecosystems and grows well in swamps. **Best place to see them:** At Loxahatchee National Wildlife Refuge (embracing the northern part of the Everglades, along Alligator Alley), throughout Everglades National Park, and at Big Cypress National Preserve.

❷ Sawgrass

With spiny, serrated leaf blades resembling saws, sawgrass inspired the term "river of grass" for the Everglades. **Best place to see them:** Both Shark Valley and Pahayokee Overlook provide terrific vantage points for gazing over sawgrass prairie; you also can get an eyeful of sawgrass when crossing Alligator Alley, even when doing so at top speeds.

❸ Mahogany

Hardwood hammocks of the Everglades live in areas that rarely flood because of the slight elevation of the sloughs, where they're typically found. **Best place to see them:** Everglades National Park's Mahogany Hammock Trail (which has a boardwalk leading to the nation's largest living mahogany tree).

❹ Mangrove

Mangrove forest ecosystems provide both food and protected nursery areas for fish, shellfish, and crustaceans. **Best place to see them:** Along Biscayne National Park shoreline, at Big Cypress National Preserve, and within Everglades National Park, especially around the Caple Sable area.

❺ Gumbo Limbo

Sometimes called "tourist trees" because of peeling reddish bark (not unlike sunburns). **Best place to see them:** Everglades National Park's Gumbo Limbo Trail and assorted spots throughout the expansive Everglades.

FAUNA

❶ American Alligator

In all likelihood, on your visit to the Everglades you'll see at least a gator or two. These carnivorous creatures can be found throughout the Everglades swampy wetlands.

Best place to see them: Loxahatchee National Wildlife Refuge (also sheltering the endangered Everglades snail kite) and within Everglades National Park at Shark Valley or Anhinga Trail. Sometimes (logically enough) gators hang out along Alligator Alley, basking in early morning or late-afternoon sun along four-lane I–75.

❷ American Crocodile

Crocs gravitate to fresh or brackish water, subsisting on birds, fish, snails, frogs, and small mammals.

Best place to see them: Within Everglades National Park, Big Cypress National Preserve, and protected grounds in or around Billie Swamp Safari.

❸ Eastern Coral Snake

This venomous snake burrows in underbrush, preying on lizards, frogs, and smaller snakes.

Best place to see them: Snakes typically shy away from people, but try Snake Bight or Eco Pond near Flamingo, where birds are also prevalent.

❹ Florida Panther

Struggling for survival amid loss of habitat, these shy, tan-colored cats now number around 100, up from lows of near 30.

Best place to see them: Protected grounds of Billie Swamp Safari sometimes provide sightings during tours. Signage on roadway linking Tamiami Trail and Alligator Alley warns of panther crossings, but sightings are rare.

❺ Green Tree Frog

Typically bright green with white or yellow stripes, these nocturnal creatures thrive in swamps and brackish water.

Best place to see them: Within Everglades National Park, especially in or near water.

● =Extremely Common ● =Very Common ● =Somewhat Common ● =Rare

BIRDS

❶ Anhinga

The lack of oil glands for waterproofing feathers helps this bird to dive as well as chase and spear fish with its pointed beak. The Anhinga is also often called a "water turkey" because of its long tail, or a "snake bird" because of its long neck.

Best place to see them: The Anhinga Trail, which also is known for attracting other wildlife to drink during especially dry winters.

❷ Blue-Winged Teal

Although it's predominantly brown and gray, this bird's powder-blue wing patch becomes visible in flight. Next to the mallard, the blue-winged teal is North America's second most abundant duck, and thrives particularly well in the Everglades.

Best place to see them: Near ponds and marshy areas of Everglades National Park or Big Cypress National Preserve.

❸ Great Blue Heron

This bird has a varied palate and enjoys feasting on everything from frogs, snakes, and mice to shrimp, aquatic insects, and sometimes even other birds! The all-white version, which at one time was considered a separate species, is quite common to the Everglades.

Best place to see them: Loxahatchee National Wildlife Refuge or Shark Valley in Everglades National Park.

❹ Great Egret

Once decimated by plume hunters, these monogamous, long-legged white birds with S-shaped necks feed in wetlands, nest in trees, and hang out in colonies that often include heron or other egret species.

Best place to see them: Throughout Everglades National Park, along Alligator Alley, and sometimes even on the fringes of Greater Fort Lauderdale.

❺ Greater Flamingo

Flocking together and using long legs and webbed feet to stir shallow waters and mud flats, color comes a couple of years after hatching from ingesting shrimplike crustaceans along with fish, fly larvae, and plankton.

Best place to see them: Try Snake Bight or Eco Pond, near Flamingo Marina.

❻ Osprey

Making a big comeback from chemical pollutant endangerment, ospreys (sometimes confused with bald eagles) are distinguished by black eyestripes down their faces. Gripping pads on feet with curved claws help them pluck fish from water.

Best place to see them: Look near water, where they're fishing for lunch in the shallow areas. Try the coasts, bays, and ponds of Everglades National Park. They also gravitate to trees You can usually spot them from the Gulf Coast Visitor Center, or you can observe them via boating in the Ten Thousand Islands.

❼ Roseate Spoonbill

These gregarious pink-and-white birds gravitate toward mangroves, feeding on fish, insects, amphibians, and some plants. They have long, spoon-like bills, and their feathers can have a touch of red and yellow. These birds appear in the Everglades year-round.

Best place to see them: Sandy Key, southwest of Flamingo, is a spoonbill nocturnal roosting spot, but at sunrise these colorful birds head out over Eco Pond to favored day hangouts throughout Everglades National Park.

❽ Wood Stork

Recognizable by featherless heads and prominent bills, these birds submerge in water to scoop up hapless fish. They are most common in the early spring and often easiest to spot in the morning.

Best place to see them: Amid the Ten Thousand Island areas, Nine Mile Pond, Mrazek Pond, and in the mangroves at Paurotis Pond.

● =Extremely Common ● =Very Common ● =Somewhat Common ● =Rare

THE STORY OF THE EVERGLADES

Dreams of draining southern Florida took hold in the early 1800s, expanding in the early 1900s to convert large tracts from wetlands to agricultural acreage. By the 1920s, towns like Fort Lauderdale and Miami boomed, and the sugar indus-try—which came to be known as "Big Sugar"—established its first sugar mills. In 1947 Ever-glades National Park opened as a refuge for wildlife.

Meanwhile, the sugar industry grew. In its infancy, about 175,000 tons of raw sugar per year was produced from fields totaling about 50,000 acres. But once the U.S. embargo stopped sugar imports from Cuba in 1960 and laws restricting acreage were lifted, Big Sugar took off. Less than five years later, the industry produced 572,000 tons of sugar and occupied nearly a quarter of a million acres.

Fast-forward to 2008, to what was hailed as the biggest conservation deal in U.S. history since the creation of the national parks. A trailblazing restoration strategy hinged on creating a water flow-way between Lake Okeechobee and the Everglades by buying up and flooding 187,000 acres of land. The country's largest producers of cane sugar agreed to sell the necessary 187,000 acres to the state of Florida for $1.75 billion. Environmentalists cheered.

But within months, news broke of a scaled-back land acquisition plan: $1.34 billion to buy 180,000 acres. By spring 2009, the restoration plan had shrunk to $536,000 to buy 73,000 acres. With the purchase still in limbo, critics claim the state might overpay for acreage appraised at pre-recession values and proponents fear dwindling revenues may derail the plan altogether.

The Big Sugar land deal is part of a larger effort to preserve the Everglades. In 2010, two separate lawsuits charged the state, along with the United States Environmental Protection Agency, with stalling Everglades cleanup that was supposed to begin in 2006. "Glacial delay" is how one judge put it. The state must reduce phosphorus levels in water that flows to the Everglades or face fines and sanctions for violating the federal Clean Water Act. The fate of the Everglades remains in the balance.

3

Updated by
Lynne Helm

More than 1.5 million acres of South Florida's 4.3 million acres of subtropical, watery wilderness were given national-park status and protection in 1947 with the creation of Everglades National Park. It's one of the country's largest national parks and is recognized by the world community as a Wetland of International Importance, an International Biosphere Reserve, and a World Heritage Site. Come here if you want to spend the day biking, hiking, or boating in deep, raw wilderness with lots of wildlife.

To the east of Everglades National Park, Biscayne National Park brings forth a pristine, magical, subtropical Florida. It's the nation's largest marine park and the largest national park within the continental United States boasting living coral reefs. A small portion of the park's 172,000 acres consists of mainland coast and outlying islands, but 95% remains submerged. Of particular interest are the mangroves and their tangled masses of stiltlike roots that thicken shorelines. These "walking trees," as some locals call them, have curved prop roots arching down from trunks, and aerial roots that drop from branches. The roots of these trees can filter salt from water and create a coastal nursery that sustains myriad types of marine life. You can see Miami's high-rise buildings from many of Biscayne's 44 islands, but the park is virtually undeveloped and large enough for escaping everything that Miami and the Upper Keys have become. To truly escape, grab scuba-diving or snorkeling gear and lose yourself in the wonders of the coral reefs.

On the northern edge of Everglades National Park lies Big Cypress National Preserve, one of South Florida's least developed watersheds. Established by Congress in 1974 to protect the Everglades, it comprises extensive tracts of prairie, marsh, pinelands, forested swamps, and sloughs. Hunting is allowed, as is off-road-vehicle use. Come here if you like alligators. Stop at the Oasis Visitor Center's boardwalk with alligators lounging underneath, and then drive Loop Road for a back-woods experience. If time and desire for watery adventure permits, kayak or canoe the Turner River.

Surrounding the parks and preserve are communities where you'll find useful outfitters: Everglades City, Florida City, and Homestead.

PLANNING

WHEN TO GO
Winter is the best, and busiest, time to visit the Everglades. Temperatures and mosquito activity are more tolerable, low water levels concentrate the resident wildlife, and migratory birds swell the avian population. In late spring the weather turns hot and rainy, and tours and facilities are less crowded. Migratory birds depart, and you must look harder to see wildlife. Summer brings intense sun and afternoon rainstorms. Water levels rise and mosquitoes descend, making outdoor activity virtually unbearable, unless you protect yourself with netting. Mosquito repellent is a necessity any time of year.

GETTING HERE AND AROUND
Miami International Airport (MIA) is 34 miles from Homestead and 47 miles from the eastern access to Everglades National Park. ⇨ *For MIA airline information, see the Travel Smart chapter.* Shuttles run between MIA and Homestead. Southwest Florida International Airport (RSW), in Fort Myers, a little over an hour's drive from Everglades City, is the closest major airport to the Everglades' western entrance. On-demand taxi transportation from the airport to Everglades City is available from MBA Airport Transportation and costs $150 for up to three passengers ($10 each for additional passengers).

Contacts MBA Airport Transportation. ☎ *239/225–0428*
⊕ *www.mbaairport.com.*

HOTELS
Accommodations near the parks range from inexpensive to moderate and offer off-season rates in summer, when rampant mosquito populations discourage spending time outdoors, especially at dusk. If you're devoting several days to exploring the east-coast Everglades, stay in park campgrounds; 11 miles away in Homestead–Florida City, where there are reasonably priced chain motels and RV parks; in the Florida Keys; or in the Greater Miami–Fort Lauderdale area. Lodgings and campgrounds are also plentiful on the Gulf Coast (in Everglades City, Marco Island, and Naples, the latter with the most upscale area accommodations).

RESTAURANTS
Dining in the Everglades area centers on mom-and-pop places serving hearty home-style food, and small eateries specializing in fresh local fare: alligator, fish, stone crab, frogs' legs, and Florida lobster from the Keys. American Indian restaurants serve local favorites as well as catfish, Indian fry bread (a flour-and-water flatbread), and pumpkin bread. A growing Hispanic population around Homestead means plenty of authentic, inexpensive Latin cuisine, with an emphasis on Cuban and

Mexican dishes. Restaurants in Everglades City, especially those along the river, specialize in fresh (often just hours out of the water) seafood including particularly succulent, sustainable stone crab. These mostly rustic places are ultracasual and often close in late summer or fall. For finer dining, head for Marco Island or Naples.

Hotel and restaurant reviews have been shortened. For full information, visit Fodors.com.

3

WHAT IT COSTS				
	$	$$	$$$	$$$$
Restaurants	under $15	$15–$20	$21–$30	over $30
Hotels	under $200	$200–$300	$301–$400	over $400

Restaurant prices are the average cost of a main course at dinner or, if dinner is not served, at lunch. Hotel prices are the lowest cost of a standard double room in high season.

ABOUT ACTIVITIES
While outfitters are listed with the parks and preserve, see our What's Nearby section later in this chapter for information about each town.

EVERGLADES NATIONAL PARK

45 miles southwest of Miami International Airport.

If you're heading across South Florida on U.S. 41 from Miami to Naples, you'll breeze right through the Everglades. Also known as Tamiami Trail, this mostly two-lane road skirts the edge of Everglades National Park and cuts across the Big Cypress National Preserve. You'll also be near the park if you're en route from Miami to the Florida Keys on U.S. 1, which cuts through Homestead and Florida City—communities east of the main park entrance. Basically, if you're in South Florida, you can't escape at least fringes of the Everglades. With tourist strongholds like Miami, Naples, and the Florida Keys so close, travelers from all over the world typically make day trips to the park.

Everglades National Park has three main entry points: the park headquarters at Ernest F. Coe Visitor Center, southwest of Homestead and Florida City; the Shark Valley area, accessed by Tamiami Trail (U.S. 41); and the Gulf Coast Visitor Center, south of Everglades City to the west and closest to Naples.

Explore on your own or participate in ranger-led hikes, bicycle or bird-watching tours, and canoe trips. The variety of these excursions is greatest from mid-December through Easter, and some adventures (canoe trips, for instance) typically aren't offered in sweltering summer. Among the more popular are the Anhinga Amble, a 50-minute walk around the Taylor Slough (departs from the Royal Palm Visitor Center), and the Early Bird Special, a 90-minute walk centered on birdlife (departs from Flamingo Visitor Center). Check with visitor centers for details.

CLOSE UP

War on Pythons

In 2013, Florida launched its first Python Challenge™ to put the kibosh on Burmese pythons, those deadly snakes literally squeezing the life out of Everglades wonders, from colorful birds to full-grown deer to gators.

The state-sponsored winter competition was a trailblazer, attracting amateurs and professionals alike from 38 states and Canada to help decimate this growing environmental threat. Sadly, only 68 pythons were captured of thousands estimated lurking in the Everglades.

Then the Challenge was scrapped, although the state continued its war with a python-removal program, issuing hunting permits to qualified applicants. In 2016, the Challenge made a comeback and now seems to be on again.

Even experienced Gladesmen with special permits to stalk these predators have trouble finding them—partly because tan, splotchy skin provides natural camouflage for slithering about and causing mayhem within the ecosystem. Unseasonably warm winter weather also leaves pythons, growing up to 26 feet long, without incentive to boldly expose themselves for sunning.

In 2012, the U.S. Department of the Interior—hailing a milestone in Everglades protection—announced a nationwide ban on the importation of Burmese pythons and other nonnative, large constrictor snakes, including African pythons and the yellow anaconda. The ban has stuck thus far and is helping with the problem.

No matter what the format for the state's effort to eradicate pythons, its war against invasive species and the efforts to protect Everglades wildlife continue unabated.

—Lynne Helm

PARK ESSENTIALS

Admission Fees The fee is $25 per vehicle; and $8 per pedestrian, bicycle, or motorcycle. Payable at gates, the admission is good for seven consecutive days at all park entrances. Annual passes are $40.

Admission Hours Open daily, year-round, both the main entrance near Florida City and Homestead, and the Gulf Coast entrance are open 24 hours a day. The Shark Valley entrance is open 8:30 am to 6 pm.

COE VISITOR CENTER TO FLAMINGO

About 30 miles southwest of Miami.

The most utilized access to Everglades National Park is via the park headquarters entrance southwest of Homestead and Florida City. If you're coming to the Everglades from Miami, take Route 836 West to Route 826/874 South to the Homestead Extension of Florida's Turnpike, U.S. 1, and Krome Avenue (Route 997/old U.S. 27). To reach the Ernest F. Coe Visitor Center from Homestead, go right (west) from U.S. 1 or Krome Avenue onto Route 9336 (Florida's only four-digit route) in Florida City and follow signage to the park entrance.

Route 9336 travels 38 miles from the Ernest F. Coe Visitor Center southwest to the Florida Bay at Flamingo. It crosses a section of the park's eight distinct ecosystems: hardwood hammock, freshwater prairie, pinelands, freshwater slough, cypress, coastal prairie, mangrove, and marine-estuarine. Route highlights include a dwarf cypress forest, the transition zone between saw grass and mangrove forest, and a wealth of wading birds at Mrazek and Coot Bay ponds—where in early morning or late afternoon you can observe them feeding. Be forewarned, however, that flamingo sightings are extremely rare. Boardwalks, looped trails, several short spurs, and observation platforms help you stay dry. You may want to stop along the way to walk several short trails (each takes about 30 minutes): the wheelchair-accessible Anhinga Trail, which cuts through saw-grass marsh and allows you to see lots of wildlife (be on the lookout for alligators and the trail's namesake waterbirds: anhingas); the junglelike—yet also wheelchair-accessible—Gumbo-Limbo Trail; the Pinelands Trail, where you can see the park's limestone bedrock; the Pahayokee Overlook Trail, ending at an observation tower; and the Mahogany Hammock Trail, with its dense growth. ■TIP➔ **Before heading out on the trails, inquire about insect and weather conditions to plan accordingly, stocking up on bug repellent, sunscreen, and water as necessary. Even on seemingly sunny days, it's smart to bring rain gear.**

EXPLORING

To explore this section of the park, follow Route 9336 from the park entrance to Flamingo; you'll find plenty of opportunities to stop along the way, and assorted activities to pursue in the Flamingo area. Other than campgrounds, there are no lodging options within the national park at this writing.

FAMILY **Ernest F. Coe Visitor Center.** Get your park map here, 365 days a year, but don't just grab and go; this visitor center's numerous interactive exhibits and films are well worth your time. The 15-minute film *River of Life,* updated frequently, provides a succinct park overview. A movie on hurricanes and a 35-minute wildlife film for children are available upon request. Learn about the Great Water Debate, detailing how the last century's gung ho draining of swampland for residential and agricultural development also cut off water-supply routes for precious wetlands in the Everglades ecosystem. You'll also find a schedule of daily ranger-led activities, mainly walks and talks; information on the popular Nike missile site tour (harking back to the Cuban missile crisis era); and details about canoe rentals and boat tours at Flamingo. The Everglades Discovery Shop stocks books, kids' stuff, plus insect repellent, sunscreen, and water. Coe Visitor Center, which has restrooms, is outside park gates, so you can stop in without paying park admission. ✉ *40001 State Rd. 9336, Homestead* ✛ *11 miles southwest of Homestead* ☎ *305/242–7700* 💲 *Free.*

FAMILY **Flamingo.** At the far end of the main road to the Flamingo community along Florida Bay, you'll find a marina (with beverages, snacks, and a gift shop), visitor center, and campground, with nearby hiking and nature trails. Despite the name, what you are unlikely to find here are flamingos. To improve your luck for glimpsing these flamboyant pink birds with toothpick legs, check out Snake Bight Trail, starting about 5 miles from the Flamingo outpost, but they are a rare sight indeed. Before

Hurricanes Katrina and Wilma hit in 2005, a lodge, cabins, and restaurant facilities in Flamingo provided Everglades National Park's only accommodations. Rebuilding of Flamingo Lodge, long projected, has yet to materialize. For now, you can still pitch tents or bring RVs to the campground, where improvements include solar-heated showers and electricity for RV sites. A houseboat rental concession offers a pair of 35-footers each sleeping six and equipped with shower, toilet, bedding, kitchenware, stereo, and depth finder. The houseboats (thankfully air-conditioned) have 60-horsepower outboards and rent for $350 per night, plus a $200 fuel deposit. ⊠ *Flamingo ⊕ www.nps.gov/ever/planyourvisit/flamdirections.*

NEED A BREAK

Worthwhile spots to pull over for a picnic are **Paurotis Pond**, about 10 miles north of Florida Bay, or **Nine Mile Pond**, less than 30 miles from the main visitor center. Another option is along **Bear Lake**, 2 miles north of the Flamingo Visitor Center.

FAMILY **Flamingo Visitor Center.** Check the schedule here for ranger-led activities, such as naturalist talks, trail hikes, and evening programs in the 100-seat campground amphitheater, replacing the old gathering spot destroyed by 2005 hurricanes. Mosquito repellent will be your favorite take-along here. If you're famished and haven't packed your own picnic, the center's Buttonwood Cafe (closed in summer) serves sandwiches, salads, and such. There's no other option for miles. You'll find natural history exhibits and pamphlets on canoe, hiking, and biking trails in the second-floor Florida Bay Flamingo Museum, accessible only by stairway and a steep ramp. You can get drinks and snacks at the marina store when the café is closed. ⊠ *1 Flamingo Lodge Hwy., Flamingo* 🕾 *239/695–2945, 239/695–3101 marina* 🎟 *Free.*

FAMILY **Royal Palm Visitor Center.** Ideal for when there's limited time to experience the Everglades, this small center with a bookstore and vending machines permits access to the popular, paved **Anhinga Trail boardwalk,** where in winter spotting alligators congregating in watering holes is virtually guaranteed. Neighboring **Gumbo Limbo Trail** takes you through a hardwood hammock. Combining these short strolls (½ mile or so) allows you to experience two Everglades ecosystems. Rangers conduct Anhinga Ambles in season (call ahead for times). A Glades Glimpse program takes place afternoons in season, as do starlight walks and bike tours. As always, arm yourself with insect repellent. If you have a mind for history, ask about narrated Nike missile site tours, stemming from the '60s-era Cuban missile crisis. ⊠ *Rte. 9336, Everglades National Park ⊹ 4 miles west of Ernest F. Coe Visitor Center* 🕾 *305/242–7700.*

SPORTS AND THE OUTDOORS

BIRD-WATCHING

Some of the park's best birding is in the Flamingo area.

BOATING

The 99-mile inland **Wilderness Trail** between Flamingo and Everglades City is open to motorboats as well as canoes, although, depending on water levels, powerboats may have trouble navigating above White-water Bay. Flat-water canoeing and kayaking are best in winter, when temperatures are moderate, rainfall diminishes, and mosquitoes back off—a little, anyway. You don't need a permit for day trips, although there's a seven-day, $5 launch fee for all motorized boats brought into the park. The Flamingo area has well-marked canoe trails, but be sure to tell someone where you're going and when you expect to return. Getting lost is easy, and spending the night without proper gear can be unpleasant, if not dangerous.

EVERGLADES BIRDING

Where birds of a feather flock, birders often do, too. Each January on the weekend before Martin Luther King Jr. Day, the Everglades Birding Festival, which began in the mid-aughts, attracts enthusiasts from far and wide. Field workshops cover "birding by ear," habitat, behavior, advanced skills, photography, and other topics. Target species range from the peregrine falcon to the purple swamp hen and plenty of feathered wonders in between. For info, check out ⊕ www.evergladesbird-ingfestival.com.

FAMILY **Flamingo Lodge, Marina, and Everglades National Park Tours.** Everglades National Park's official concessionaire operates a marina, runs tours, and rents canoes, kayaks, and skiffs, secured by credit cards. A one-hour, 45-minute backcountry cruise aboard the 50-passenger *Pelican* winds under a heavy canopy of mangroves, revealing abundant wildlife—from alligators, crocodiles, and turtles to herons, hawks, and egrets. You can rent a 17-foot, 40-hp skiff starting at 7 am for a full day (returning by 4 pm), a half day, or for as little as two hours; there is a $100 credit card deposit required. Canoes for up to three paddlers can be rented for two hours (minimum), four hours, eight hours, or overnight. Family canoes for up to four are available, and the concessionaire also rents bikes, binoculars, rods, reels, and other equipment for up to a full day. Feeling sticky after a day in the Glades? Hot showers are available ($). Flamingo Lodge, a victim of massive hurricane damage in 2005, remains closed pending a long-delayed fresh start. ■TIP→ **An experimental Eco Tent of canvas and wood, unveiled in winter 2012–13, was booked solid for the season. Built by University of Miami architecture students, Eco Tent sleeps four, has a table and chairs, and wins rave reviews from designers, park officials, and campers. It's a prototype for up to 40 more units, once funding is secured.** ⊠ *1 Flamingo Lodge Hwy., on Buttonwood Canal, Flamingo* ☎ *239/695–3101, 239/695–0124 Eco Tent reservations* ⊕ *www.evergladesnationalparkboattoursflamingo.com* ✉ *Pelican cruise from $37.63; skiff rentals from $80 (2 hrs); 3-person canoe rentals from $20.*

GULF COAST ENTRANCE

To reach the park's western gateway, take U.S. 41 west from Miami for 77 miles, turn left (south) onto Route 29, and travel another 3 miles through Everglades City to the Gulf Coast Ranger Station. From Naples on the Gulf Coast, take U.S. 41 east for 35 miles, and turn right onto Route 29.

FAMILY **Gulf Coast Visitor Center.** The best place to bone up on Everglades National Park's watery western side is at this center just south of Everglades City (5 miles south of Tamiami Trail) where rangers can give you the park lowdown and address your inquiries. In winter, backcountry campers purchase permits here and canoeists check in for trips to the Ten Thousand Islands and 99-mile Wilderness Waterway Trail. Nature lovers view interpretive exhibits on local flora and fauna while waiting for naturalist-led boat trips. In season (Christmas through Easter), rangers lead bike tours and canoe trips. A selection of about 30 nature presentations and orientation films are available by request for view on a TV screen. Admission is free only to this section, since no direct roads from here link to other parts of the park. ⊠ *815 Oyster Bar La., off Rte. 29, Everglades City* ☎ *239/695–3311.*

SPORTS AND THE OUTDOORS

BOATING AND KAYAKING

FAMILY **Everglades National Park Boat Tours.** In conjunction with boat tours at Flamingo, this operation runs 1½-hour trips through the Ten Thousand Islands National Wildlife Refuge. Adventure-seekers often see dolphins, manatees, bald eagles, and roseate spoonbills. In peak season (November–April), 49-passenger boats run on the hour and half hour daily. Mangrove wilderness tours on smaller boats are for up to six passengers. These one-hour, 45-minute trips are the best option to see alligators. The outfitter also rents canoes and kayaks. Ask about group discounts. ⊠ *Gulf Coast Visitor Center, 815 Oyster Bar La., Everglades City* ☎ *239/695–2591, 866/628–7275* ⊕ *www.evergladesnationalpark-boattoursgulfcoast.com/index.php* ⊟ *Tours from $40.*

Fodor'sChoice **Everglades Rentals & Eco Adventures.** Ivey House Inn houses this estab-
★ lished, year-round source for guided Everglades paddling tours and rentals for canoes and kayaks. Shuttles can deliver you to major launching areas such as Turner River. Highlights include bird and gator sightings, mangrove forests, no-man's-land beaches, and spectacular sunsets. Longer adventures include equipment rental, guide, and meals. ⊠ *Ivey House, 107 Camellia St., Everglades City* ☎ *877/567–0679, 239/695–3299* ⊕ *www.evergladesadventures.com* ⊟ *Rentals from $35.*

SHARK VALLEY

23½ miles west of Florida's Turnpike, off Tamiami Trail. Approximately 45 mins west of Miami.

You won't see sharks at Shark Valley. The name comes from the Shark River, also called the River of Grass, flowing through the area. Several species of shark swim up this river from the coast (about 45 miles south of Shark Valley) to give birth, though not at this particular spot.

Much skill is required to navigate boats through the shallow, muddy waters of the Everglades.

Young sharks (called pups), vulnerable to being eaten by adult sharks and other predators, gain strength in waters of the slough before heading out to sea.

The Shark Valley entrance to the national park is on U.S. 41 (Tamiami Trail), 25 miles west of Florida's Turnpike (SR 821) or 39 miles east of SR 29. Some GPS units don't recognize it. If asked for a cross street, use U.S. 41.

EXPLORING

Although Shark Valley is the national park's north entrance, no roads here lead directly to other parts of the park. However, it's still worth stopping to take the two-hour narrated bio-diesel tram tour from Shark Valley Tram Tours. Stop at the halfway point and ascend the Shark Valley Observation Tower via the ramp.

Prefer to do the trail on foot? It takes nerve to walk the paved 15-mile loop in Shark Valley, because in the winter months alligators lie alongside the road, basking in the sun—most, however, do move out of the way.

You also can ride a bicycle (the folks who operate the tram tours also rent one-speed, well-used bikes daily from 8:30 to 4 for $9 per hour with helmets available). Near the bike-rental area a short boardwalk trail meanders through saw grass, and another passes through a tropical hardwood hammock.

FAMILY **Shark Valley Observation Tower.** At the Shark Valley trail's end (really, the halfway point of the 15-mile loop), you can pause to navigate this tower, first built in 1984, spiraling nearly 50 feet upward. Once on top, you'll find the River of Grass gloriously spreads out as far as you can see.

Observe waterbirds as well as alligators, and maybe even river otters crossing the road. The tower has a wheelchair-accessible ramp to the top. If you don't want to take the tram from the Shark Valley Visitor Center, you can either hike or bike in, but private cars are not allowed. ⊠ *Shark Valley Loop Rd., Miami* ⊕ *www.sharkvalleytramtours.com.*

FAMILY **Shark Valley Visitor Center.** The old ramshackle outpost has been razed altogether to make room for a nice picnic area, and a new, white, concrete-block building nearby is now in place with the bike-rental concession and a bookstore (run by the Everglades Association) with hats, sunscreen, insect repellent, postcards, and other souvenirs. Park rangers are still here, ready for your questions. ⊠ *36000 S.W. 8th St., Miami* ✛ *23½ miles west of Florida's Tpke., off Tamiami Trail* ☎ *305/221–8776.*

> **THE EVERGLADES WITH KIDS**
>
> Although kids of all ages can enjoy the park, those six and older typically get the most out of the experience. Predators including alligators abound. Consider how much you as a supervising adult will enjoy keeping tabs on tiny ones around so much water and so many teeth. Some children are frightened by sheer wilderness.

SPORTS AND THE OUTDOORS

BIKING

FAMILY **Shark Valley Bicycle Rentals.** You can gaze at gators while getting your exercise, too, by renting a bike at the Shark Valley Visitor Center from the same outfitter that operates the tram tours. Pedal along 15 miles of paved, level roadway (no hills or dales) to the observation tower and back while keeping an eye on plentiful roadside reptiles. Bikes are single gear, coaster-style two-wheelers with baskets and helmets available, along with some child seats for kids under 35 pounds. The well-used fleet also includes a few 20-inch junior models. You'll need a driver's license or other ID for a deposit. Arm yourself with water, insect repellent, and sunscreen. ⊠ *Shark Valley Visitor Center, Shark Valley Loop Rd., Shark Valley* ☎ *305/221–8776* ⊕ *www.sharkvalleytramtours.com/biking* ⊠ *Rentals from $9 per hr.*

BOATING

Many Everglades-area tours operate only in season, roughly November through April.

FAMILY **Buffalo Tiger's Airboat Tours.** A former chief of Florida's Miccosukee tribe—Buffalo Tiger, who died in January 2015 at the age of 94—founded this Shark Valley–area tour operation, and his spirit carries on. Savvy guides narrate the trip to an old Indian camp on the north side of Tamiami Trail from the Native American perspective. Don't worry about airboat noise, since engines are shut down during informative talks. The 45-minute tours go 10–5 Saturday through Thursday, with longer private tours available. Look online for discount coupons. Reservations are not required, and credit cards are now accepted at this outpost. ⊠ *29708 S.W. 8th St., 5 miles east of Shark Valley, 25 miles west of Florida's Tpke., Miami* ☎ *305/559–5250* ⊕ *www.buffalotigersairboattours.com* ⊠ *From $24.75.*

GUIDED TOURS

FAMILY **Shark Valley Tram Tours.** Starting at the Shark Valley Visitor Center, these popular two-hour, narrated tours ($24) on bio-diesel trams follow a 15-mile loop road—great for viewing gators—into the interior, stopping at a wheelchair-accessible observation tower. Bring your own water. Reservations are strongly recommended December through April. ⊠ *Shark Valley Visitor Center, Shark Valley Loop Rd., Miami* ☎ *305/221–8455* ⊕ *www.sharkvalleytramtours.com* ⊠ *$24.*

BIG CYPRESS NATIONAL PRESERVE

Through the early 1960s the world's largest cypress-logging industry prospered in Big Cypress Swamp until nearly all the trees were cut down. With the demise of the industry, government entities began buying parcels. Now more than 729,000 acres, or nearly half of the swamp, form this national preserve. "Big" refers not to the new-growth trees but to the swamp, jutting into the north edge of Everglades National Park like a jigsaw-puzzle piece. Size and strategic location make Big Cypress an important link in the region's hydrological system, where rainwater first flows through the preserve, then south into the park, and eventually into Florida Bay. Its variegated pattern of wet prairies, ponds, marshes, sloughs, and strands provides a wildlife sanctuary, and thanks to a policy of balanced land use—"use without abuse"—the watery wilderness is devoted to recreation as well as to research and preservation. Bald cypress trees that may look dead are actually dormant, with green needles springing to life in spring. The preserve allows—in limited areas—hiking, hunting, and off-road-vehicle use (airboat, swamp buggy, four-wheel drive) by permit. Compared with Everglades National Park, the preserve is less developed and hosts fewer visitors. That makes it ideal for naturalists, birders, and hikers preferring to see more wildlife than people.

Several scenic drives link from Tamiami Trail, some requiring four-wheel-drive vehicles, especially in wet summer months. A few lead to camping areas and roadside picnic spots. Apart from the Oasis Visitor Center, popular as a springboard for viewing alligators, the newer Big Cypress Swamp Welcome Center features a platform for watching manatees. Both centers, along Tamiami Trail between Miami and Naples, feature a top-notch 25-minute film on Big Cypress.

PARK ESSENTIALS

Admission Fees There's no admission fee to visit the preserve.

Admission Hours The park is open 24 hours daily, year-round. Accessible only by boat, Adams Key is for day use only.

Contacts Big Cypress National Preserve. ☎ *239/695–1201* ⊕ *www.nps.gov/bicy.*

EXPLORING

FAMILY   **Big Cypress Swamp Welcome Center.** As a sister to the Oasis Visitor Center, the newer Big Cypress Swamp Welcome Center on the preserve's western side has abundant information, as well as restrooms, picnic facilities, and a 70-seat auditorium. An outdoor breezeway showcases an interactive Big Cypress watershed exhibit, illustrating Florida water flow. It's a convenient place to stop when crossing from either coast. ■TIP→ Love manatees? A platform allows for viewing these intriguing mammals, attracted to warm water. (They were possibly once mistaken for mermaids by thirsty or love-starved ancient sailors.) ⊠ *33000 Tamiami Trail E, 5 miles east of SR29, Ochopee* ☎ *239/695–4758* ⊕ *www.nps.gov/bicy/planyourvisit/visitorcenters.htm* ⊠ *Free.*

FAMILY   **Clyde Butcher's Big Cypress Gallery.** For taking home swamp memories in stark black and white, you can't do better than picking up a postcard, calendar, or more serious pieces of artwork by photographer Clyde Butcher at his namesake trailside gallery. Butcher, a big guy with an even bigger beard, is an affable personality renowned for his knowledge of the Glades and his ability to capture its magnetism through a large-format lens. Even if you can't afford his big stuff, you're warmly invited to gaze. Out back, Butcher and his wife, Niki, also rent a bungalow ($225 per night, October–April) and a cottage ($350 per night, year-round). ■TIP→ Ask about Clyde's private photography Swamp Walk Tours, bookable in advance, September through March. You'll need a hat, long pants, old sneakers, and—because you *will* get wet—spare, dry clothing. ⊠ *MM 54.5, 52388 Tamiami Trail, Ochopee* ☎ *239/695–2428* ⊕ *www.clydebutchersbigcypressgallery.com.*

FAMILY   **Oasis Visitor Center.** The big attraction at Oasis Visitor Center, on the east side of Big Cypress Preserve, is the observation deck for viewing fish, birds, and other wildlife. A small butterfly garden's native plants seasonally attract winged wonders. Inside, you'll find an exhibit area, bookshop, and a theater showing an informative 25-minute film on Big Cypress Preserve swamplands. Get your gator watch on at the center's observation deck where big alligators congregate. Leashed pets are allowed, but not on the boardwalk deck. Here's where you also can get off-road-vehicle permits. ⊠ *52105 Tamiami Trail, Ochopee* ✚ *24 miles east of Everglades City, 50 miles west of Miami, 20 miles west of Shark Valley* ☎ *239/695–1201* ⊕ *www.nps.gov/bicy/planyourvisit/ visitorcenters* ⊠ *Free.*

FAMILY   **Ochopee Post Office.** North America's smallest post office is a former irrigation pipe shed on the Tamiami Trail's south side. Blink and you'll risk missing it. To support this picturesque outpost during an era of postal service cutbacks, why not buy a postcard of this one-room shack with a U.S. flag outside for mailing to whomever would appreciate it? Mail packages or buy money orders here, too. ⊠ *38000 E. Tamiami Trail, 4 miles east of Rte. 29, Ochopee* ☎ *239/695–2099.*

WHERE TO EAT

$ ✕ **Joanie's Blue Crab Cafe.** West of the nation's tiniest post office by a
SEAFOOD   quarter mile or so, you'll find this red barn of a place dishing out
catfish, frogs' legs, gator, grouper, burgers, salads, and (no surprise
here) an abundance of soft-shell crabs, crab cakes, and she-crab soup.
Entrées are reasonably priced, and peanut butter pie makes for a solid
finish. **Known for:** beer and wine only; indoor/outdoor seating; early
closing (5 pm). ⑤ *Average main: $13* ✉ *39395 Tamiami Trail, Ochopee*
✢ *About 3½ miles east of Hwy. 29, less than a mile west of Ochopee
post office* ☎ *239/695–2682* ⊕ *www.joaniesbluecrabcafe.com* ☾ *Closed
Mon. (varies seasonally; call to confirm).*

SPORTS AND THE OUTDOORS

There are three types of trails—walking (including part of the extensive
Florida National Scenic Trail), canoeing, and bicycling. All three trail
types are easily accessed from the Tamiami Trail near the preserve visitor center, and one boardwalk trail departs from the center. Canoe and
bike equipment can be rented from outfitters in Everglades City, 24
miles west, and Naples, 40 miles west.

Hikers can tackle the Florida National Scenic Trail, which begins in
the preserve and is divided into segments of 6½ to 28 miles each. Two
5-mile trails, Concho Billy and Fire Prairie, can be accessed off Turner
River Road, a few miles east. Turner River Road and Birdon Road
form a 17-mile gravel loop drive that's excellent for birding. Bear Island
has about 32 miles of scenic, flat, looped trails that are ideal for bicycling. Most trails are hard-packed lime rock, but a few miles are gravel.
Cyclists share the road with off-road vehicles, most plentiful from mid-
November through December.

To see the best variety of wildlife from your vehicle, follow 26-mile
Loop Road, south of U.S. 41 and west of Shark Valley, where alligators,
raccoons, and soft-shell turtles crawl around beside the gravel road,
often swooped upon by swallowtail kites and brown-shouldered hawks.
Stop at H. P. Williams Roadside Park, west of the Oasis, and walk along
the boardwalk to spy gators, turtles, and garfish in the river waters.

RANGER PROGRAMS

From the Oasis Visitor Center you can get in on the seasonal ranger-
led or self-guided activities, such as campfire and wildlife talks, hikes,
slough slogs, and canoe excursions. The 8-mile Turner River Canoe
Trail begins nearby and crosses through Everglades National Park
before ending in Chokoloskee Bay, near Everglades City. Rangers lead
four-hour canoe trips and two-hour swamp walks in season; call for
days and times. Bring shoes and long pants for swamp walks and be
prepared to wade at least knee-deep in water. Ranger program reservations are accepted up to 14 days in advance.

BISCAYNE NATIONAL PARK

Occupying 172,000 acres along the southern portion of Biscayne Bay, south of Miami and north of the Florida Keys, Biscayne National Park is 95% submerged, its terrain ranging from 4 feet above sea level to 60 feet below. Contained within are four distinct zones: Biscayne Bay, undeveloped upper Florida Keys, coral reefs, and coastal mangrove forest. Mangroves line mainland shores much as they do elsewhere along South Florida's protected waters. Biscayne Bay serves as a lobster sanctuary and a nursery for fish, sponges, crabs, and other sea life. Manatees and sea turtles frequent its warm, shallow waters. The park hosts legions of boaters and landlubbers gazing in awe over the bay.

GETTING HERE

To reach Biscayne National Park from Homestead, take Krome Avenue to Route 9336 (Palm Drive) and turn east. Follow Palm Drive about 8 miles until it becomes Southwest 344th Street, and follow signs to park headquarters in Convoy Point. The entry is 9 miles east of Homestead and 9 miles south and east of Exit 6 (Speedway Boulevard/Southwest 137th Avenue) off Florida's Turnpike.

PARK ESSENTIALS

Admission Fees There's no fee to enter Biscayne National Park, and you don't pay a fee to access the islands, but there's a $25 overnight camping fee that includes a $5 dock charge to berth vessels at some island docks. The park concession charges for trips to the coral reefs and islands.

Admission Hours The park is open daily, year-round.

Contacts Biscayne National Park. ⊠ *Dante Fascell Visitor Center, 9700 S.W. 328th St., Homestead* ☎ *305/230–7275* ⊕ *www.nps.gov/bisc.*

EXPLORING

Biscayne is a magnet for diving, snorkeling, canoeing, birding, and, to some extent (if you have a private boat), camping. Elliott Key is the best place to hike.

Biscayne's corals range from soft, flagellant fans, plumes, and whips found chiefly in shallow patch reefs to the hard brain corals, elkhorn, and staghorn forms that can withstand depths and heavier shoreline wave action.

To the east, about 8 miles off the coast, 44 tiny keys stretch 18 nautical miles north to south, and are reached only by boat. No mainland commercial transportation operates to the islands, and only a handful are accessible: Elliott, Boca Chita, Adams, and Sands Keys, lying between Elliott and Boca Chita. The rest are wildlife refuges or have rocky shores or waters too shallow for boats. December through April, when the mosquito population is less aggressive, is the best time to explore. Bring repellent, sunscreen, and water.

Adams Key. A stone's throw from the western tip of Elliott Key and 9 miles southeast of Convoy Point, the island is open for day use. It was the onetime site of the Cocolobo Club, a yachting retreat known for hosting Presidents Harding, Hoover, Johnson, and Nixon as well as other famous and infamous luminaries. Hurricane Andrew blew away what remained of club facilities in 1992. Adams Key has picnic areas with grills, restrooms, dockage, and a short trail running along the shore and through a hardwood hammock. Rangers live on-island. Access is by private boat, with no pets or overnight docking allowed. ⊠ *Biscayne National Park* ⊕ *www.nps.gov/bisc.*

Boca Chita Key. Ten miles northeast of Convoy Point and about 12 miles south of the Cape Florida Lighthouse on Key Biscayne, this key once was owned by the late

BISCAYNE IN ONE DAY

Most visitors come to snorkel or dive. Divers should plan to spend the morning on the water and the afternoon exploring the visitor center. The opposite is true for snorkelers, as snorkel trips (and one-tank shallow-dive trips) depart in the afternoon. If you want to hike as well, turn to the trails at Elliott Key—just be sure to apply insect repellent (and sunscreen, too, no matter what time of year).

Mark C. Honeywell, former president of Honeywell Company, and is on the National Register of Historic Places for its 10 historic structures. A half-mile hiking trail curves around the island's south side. Climb the 65-foot-high ornamental lighthouse (by ranger tour only) for a panoramic view of Miami or check out the cannon from the HMS *Fowey*. There's no freshwater, access is by private boat only, and no pets are allowed. Only portable toilets are on-site, with no sinks or showers. A $25 fee for overnight docking (6 pm to 6 am) covers a campsite; pay at the harbor's automated kiosk. ⊠ *Biscayne National Park.*

FAMILY
Fodor's Choice
★
Dante Fascell Visitor Center. Go outside on the wide veranda to soak up views across mangroves and Biscayne Bay at this Convoy Point visitor center, which opened in 2002. Inside the museum, artistic vignettes and on-request videos including the 11-minute *Spectrum of Life* explore the park's four ecosystems, while the Touch Table gives both kids and adults a feel for bones, feathers, and coral. Facilities include the park's canoe and tour concession, restrooms with showers, a ranger information area, gift shop with books, and vending machines. Various ranger programs take place daily during busy fall and winter seasons. Rangers give informal tours on Boca Chita key, but these must be arranged in advance. A short trail and boardwalk lead to a jetty, and there are picnic tables and grills. This is the only area of the park accessible without a boat. You can snorkel from shore, but the water is shallow, with sea grass and a mud bottom. ⊠ *9700 S.W. 328th St., Homestead* ☎ *305/230–7275* ⊕ *www.nps.gov/bisc* ⊠ *Free.*

FAMILY
Elliott Key. The largest of the islands, 9 miles east of Convoy Point, Elliott Key has a mile-long loop trail on the bay side at the north end of the campground. Boaters may dock at any of 36 slips; the fee for staying overnight includes use of a tent area for up to six people in two tents. Head out on your own to hike the 6-mile trail along so-called Spite Highway, a 225-foot-wide swath of green that developers mowed down in hopes of linking this key to the mainland. Luckily the federal government stepped in, and now it's a hiking trail through tropical hardwood hammock. Facilities include restrooms, picnic tables, fresh

drinking water, cold (occasionally lukewarm) showers, grills, and a campground. Leashed pets are allowed in developed areas only, not on trails. A 30-foot-wide sandy shoreline about a mile north of the harbor on the west (bay) side of the key is the only one in the national park, and boaters like to anchor off here to swim. You can fish (check on license requirements) from the maintenance dock south of the harbor. The beach, fun for families, is for day use only; it has picnic areas and a short trail that cuts through the hammock. ⊠ *Biscayne National Park* 🚢 *$25 docking fee for campers.*

SPORTS AND THE OUTDOORS

BIRD-WATCHING

More than 170 species of birds have been identified in and around the park. Expect to see flocks of brown pelicans patrolling the bay—suddenly rising, then plunging beak first to capture prey in their baggy pouches. White ibis probe exposed mudflats for small fish and crustaceans. Although all the keys are excellent for birding, Jones Lagoon (south of Adams Key, between Old Rhodes Key and Totten Key) is outstanding. It's approachable only by nonmotorized craft.

DIVING AND SNORKELING

Diving is great year-around but best in summer, when calmer winds and smaller seas result in clearer waters. Ocean waters, 3 miles east of the Keys, showcase the park's main attraction—the northernmost section of Florida's living tropical coral reefs. Some are the size of an office desk, others as large as a football field. Glass-bottom-boat rides, when operating, showcase this underwater wonderland, but you really should snorkel or scuba dive to fully appreciate it.

A diverse population of colorful fish—angelfish, gobies, grunts, parrot fish, pork fish, wrasses, and many more—flits through the reefs. Shipwrecks from the 18th century are evidence of the area's international maritime heritage, and a Maritime Heritage Trail has been developed to link six of the major shipwreck and underwater cultural sites including the Fowey Rocks Lighthouse, built in 1878. Sites, including a 19th-century wooden sailing vessel, have been plotted with GPS coordinates and marked with mooring buoys.

WHAT'S NEARBY

EVERGLADES CITY

35 miles southeast of Naples and 83 miles west of Miami.

Aside from a chain gas station or two, Everglades City retains its Old Florida authenticity. No high-rises (other than an observation tower named for pioneer Ernest Hamilton) mar the landscape at this western gateway to Everglades National Park, just off the Tamiami Trail. Everglades City was developed in the late 19th century by Barron Collier, a wealthy advertising entrepreneur, who built it as a company town to house workers for his numerous projects, including construction of the

Tamiami Trail. It grew and prospered until the Depression and World War II. Today this ramshackle town draws adventure seekers heading to the park for canoeing, fishing, and bird-watching excursions. Airboat tours, though popular, are banned within the park because of the environmental damage they cause to the mangroves. The Everglades Seafood Festival, launched in 1970 and held the first full weekend of February, draws huge crowds for delights from the sea, music, and craft displays. At quieter times, dining choices center on a handful of rustic eateries big on seafood. The town is small, fishing-oriented, and unhurried, making it excellent for boating, bicycling, or just strolling around. You can pedal along the waterfront on a 2-mile strand out to Chokoloskee Island.

VISITOR INFORMATION

Everglades Area Chamber of Commerce Welcome Center. Pick up brochures, flyers and pamphlets for area lodging, restaurants, and attractions here, and ask for additional information from friendly staffers. Open daily 9 to 4. ⊠ *32016 E. Tamiami Trail, at Rte. 29* ☎ *239/695–3941* ⊕ *www. evergladeschamber.net.*

EXPLORING

Collier-Seminole State Park. Opportunity to try biking, hiking, camping, and canoeing in Everglades territory makes this 7,000-plus-acre park a prime introduction to this often forbidding mangrove swampland. Of historical interest, a Seminole War blockhouse has been re-created to hold the interpretative center, and one of the "walking dredges"—a towering black machine invented to carve the Tamiami Trail out of the muck—stands silent on grounds amid tropical hardwood forest. Kayaks and canoes can be launched into the Blackwater River here. Bring your own, or rent a canoe from the park by the hour or day. After a lengthy campground closure, upgraded campsites for tents to motor homes now include three restrooms and a laundry room. ⊠ *20200 E. Tamiami Trail, Naples* ☎ *239/394–3397* ⊕ *www.floridastateparks.org/ park/Collier-Seminole* ⊇ *$5 per car, $4 with lone driver, $2 for pedestrians or bikers; canoe rentals from $5 per hr.*

OFF THE BEATEN PATH

Fakahatchee Strand Preserve State Park. The half-mile Big Cypress Bend boardwalk through this linear swamp forest provides opportunity to see rare plants, nesting eagles, and Florida's largest stand of native royal palms coexisting—unique to Fakahatchee Strand—with bald cypress under the forest canopy. Fakahatchee Strand, about 20 miles long and 5 miles wide, is also the orchid and bromeliad capital of the continent with 44 native orchids and 14 native bromeliads, many blooming most extravagantly in hotter months. It's particularly famed for its ghost orchids (as featured in Susan Orlean's novel *The Orchid Thief*), visible on guided hikes. In your quest for ghost orchids, keep alert for white-tailed deer, black bears, bobcats, and the Florida panther. For park nature on parade, take the 12-mile-long (one-way) W. J. Janes Memorial Scenic Drive (deposit your admission fee at the honor box; have exact change). Hike its spur trails if you have time. Rangers lead swamp walks and canoe trips November through April. ⊠ *Boardwalk on north side of Tamiami Trail, 7 miles west of Rte. 29; W. J. Janes Scenic Dr., ¾ mile north of Tamiami Trail on Rte. 29; ranger station on W. J. Janes Scenic Dr., 137 Coastline Dr., Copeland* ☎ *239/695–4593*

OFF THE BEATEN PATH

Native plants hem paddlers in on both sides, and alligators lurk nearby.

⊕ *www.floridastateparks.org/fakahatcheestrand* ✉ *Free; W. J. Janes Memorial Scenic Drive $3 per car, $2 per motorcycle or pedestrian.*

FAMILY **Museum of the Everglades.** Through artifacts and photographs you can meet American Indians, pioneers, entrepreneurs, and anglers playing pivotal roles in southwest Florida development. Exhibits and a short film chronicle the tremendous feat of building the Tamiami Trail across mosquito-ridden, gator-infested Everglades wetlands. Permanent displays and monthly exhibits rotate works of local artists. The small museum is housed in the Laundry Building, completed in 1927 and once used for washing linens from Everglades City's Rod and Gun Club and Everglades Inn. ✉ *105 W. Broadway* ☎ *239/695–0008* ✉ *Free.*

WHERE TO EAT

$$ ✕ **City Seafood.** Owner Richard Wahrenberger serves up gems from the
SEAFOOD   sea delivered fresh from his own boats. Enjoy breakfast, lunch, or dinner inside this rustic haven, or sit outdoors to watch pelicans, gulls, tarpon, manatees, and the occasional gator play off the dock in the Barron River. **Known for:** serving sustainable stone crab in season; full bar open on weekends; wrapping and/or shipping fresh seafood. ⑤ *Average main: $15* ✉ *702 Begonia St.* ☎ *239/695–4700* ⊕ *www.cityseafood1.com.*

$$ ✕ **Everglades Adventure Center and Taste of the Everglades Restaurant.** For-
SEAFOOD   merly Everglades Seafood Depot, this restaurant still offers tasty, affordable meals in a scenic setting in a storied 1928 Spanish-style stucco structure fronting Lake Placid. Seafood, steaks, burgers, and dogs are the stars here. **Known for:** simple, affordable fare; views from tables on the back porch or by the windows; historic setting. ⑤ *Average main: $20* ✉ *102 Collier Ave.* ☎ *239/695–0075.*

$$ X **Havana Cafe.** Cuban specialties are a welcome alternative from the
CUBAN   typical seafood houses of Everglades City. This cheery eatery—3 miles south of Everglades City on Chokoloskee Island—has a dozen or so tables inside, and more seating on the porch amid plenty of greenery. **Known for:** good café con leche in the mornings; cash only when Internet is down; house-made hot sauce that you can take home in a bottle. $ *Average main: $15* ⌧ *191 Smallwood Dr., Chokoloskee* ☎ *239/695–2214* ⊕ *www.myhavanacafe.com* ☼ *No dinner Apr.–Oct.; no dinner Sun.–Thurs. Nov.–Mar.*

$$ X **Oyster House Restaurant.** One of the town's oldest fish houses, Oyster
SEAFOOD   House serves, along with the requisite oysters, all the local staples—
FAMILY   shrimp, gator tail, frogs' legs, stone crab, and grouper—in a lodge-like setting with mounted wild game on walls and rafters. Deep-frying remains an art in these parts, so if you're going to indulge, do it here where you can create your own fried platter for under $30. **Known for:** fried everything; will do you-catch-we-cook; nice views at sunset. $ *Average main: $20* ⌧ *901 S. Copeland Ave.* ☎ *239/695–2073* ⊕ *www.oysterhouserestaurant.com.*

$$$ X **Rod and Gun Club.** Striking, polished pecky-cypress woodwork in this
SEAFOOD   historic building dates from the 1920s, when wealthy hunters, anglers, and yachting parties arrived for the winter season. Fresh seafood dominates, from stone crab in season (October 15–May 15) to a surf-and-turf combo of steak and grouper or a swamp-and-turf duet of frogs' legs and steak, or pasta pairings. **Known for:** languorous service; will do you-catch-we cook; cash only. $ *Average main: $25* ⌧ *200 Riverside Dr.* ☎ *239/695–2101* ⊕ *www.everglades-rodandgun.com* ▭ *No credit cards* ☼ *Sometimes shuts down in summer. Call ahead.*

$$ X **Triad Seafood.** Along the Barron River, seafood houses, fishing boats,
SEAFOOD   and crab traps populate one shoreline; mangroves the other. Selling fresh
FAMILY   off the boat, some seafood houses added picnic tables and eventually grew into restaurants, like this one. **Known for:** best grouper sandwich in the area; screened porch for dining; expensive all-you-can-eat stone crab in season. $ *Average main: $15* ⌧ *401 School Dr.* ☎ *239/695–0722* ⊕ *www.triadseafoodmarketcafe.com* ☼ *Closed May 16–Oct. 15.*

WHERE TO STAY

$ ⌂ **Glades Haven Cozy Cabins.** Bob Miller wanted to build a Holiday Inn
HOTEL   next to his Oyster House Restaurant on marina-channel shores, but when that didn't fly, he sent for cabin kits and set up mobile-home-size units around a pool on his property as part of "Miller's World." Rent a cabin (no two are alike), and you get free boat docking. **Pros:** great nearby food options; convenient to ENP boating; free docking. **Cons:** trailer-park, crowded feel with a noisy bar nearby; no phones; no pets. $ *Rooms from: $99* ⌧ *801 Copeland Ave.* ☎ *239/695–2746, 888/956–6251* ⊕ *www.gladeshaven.com* ⌥ *24 cabins, 2 3-bedroom houses* ¶O¶ *No meals.*

$ ⌂ **Ivey House.** A remodeled 1928 boardinghouse built for crews working
B&B/INN   on the Tamiami Trail, Ivey House (originally operated by Mr. and Mrs.
Fodor'sChoice   Ivey) now fits adventurers on assorted budgets. **Pros:** historic; pleasant;
★   affordable. **Cons:** not on water; some small rooms. $ *Rooms from: $169* ⌧ *107 Camellia St.* ☎ *877/567–0679, 239/695–3299* ⊕ *www.iveyhouse.com* ⌥ *30 rooms, 18 with bath; 1 2-bedroom cottage* ¶O¶ *Breakfast.*

SPORTS AND THE OUTDOORS
AIR TOURS

Wings Ten Thousand Islands Aero Tours. These 20-minute to nearly two-hour flightseeing tours of the Ten Thousand Islands National Wildlife Refuge, Big Cypress National Preserve, Everglades National Park, and Gulf of Mexico operate November through April. Aboard an Alaskan Bush plane, you can see saw-grass prairies, American Indian shell mounds, alligators, and wading birds. Flights also can be booked to the Keys, connecting to the Dry Tortugas. ⊠ *Everglades Airpark, 650 Everglades City Airpark Rd.* ☎ *239/695–3296* 🛪 *From $50 per person (based on group of 3 or 4).*

BOATING AND CANOEING

On the Gulf Coast explore the nooks, crannies, and mangrove islands of Chokoloskee Bay and Ten Thousand Islands National Wildlife Refuge, as well as rivers near Everglades City. The Turner River Canoe Trail, popular and populated even on Christmas as a pleasant day trip with almost guaranteed bird and alligator sightings, passes through mangrove tunnels, dwarf cypress, coastal prairie, and freshwater slough ecosystems of Everglades National Park and Big Cypress National Preserve.

Glades Haven Marina. Access Ten Thousand Islands waters in a 19-foot Sundance or a 17-foot Flicker fishing boat. Basic rates are per day, but there are half-day and hourly options. The full-service marina outfitter also rents kayaks and canoes and has a 24-hour boat ramp and dockage for up to 24-foot vessels, where you can launch for a fee. ⊠ *801 Copeland Ave. S* ☎ *239/695–2628* ⊕ *www.gladeshaven.com* 🛪 *Boat rentals from $200 per day.*

FLORIDA CITY

3 miles southwest of Homestead on U.S. 1.

Florida's Turnpike ends in Florida City, the southernmost town on the Miami-Dade County mainland, spilling thousands of vehicles onto U.S. 1 and eventually west to Everglades National Park, east to Biscayne National Park, or south to the Florida Keys. Although Florida City begins immediately south of Homestead, the difference in towns couldn't be more noticeable. As the last outpost before 18 miles of mangroves and water, this stretch of U.S. 1 is lined with fast-food eateries, service stations, hotels, bars, dive shops, and restaurants. Hotel rates increase significantly during NASCAR races at the nearby Homestead-Miami Speedway. Like Homestead, Florida City is rooted in agriculture, with expanses of farmland west of Krome Avenue and a huge farmers' market that ships produce nationwide.

GETTING HERE AND AROUND

SuperShuttle. This 24-hour service runs air-conditioned vans between MIA and PortMiami or wherever else you'd like to go in the Miami-Dade County area; pickup is outside baggage claim. The shared van between MIA and PortMiami is $17 per person. ⊠ *Miami* ☎ *305/871–2000* ⊕ *www.supershuttle.com.*

EXPLORING

Tropical Everglades Visitor Center. Run by the nonprofit Tropical Everglades Visitor Association, this pastel-pink center with teal signage offers abundant printed material plus tips from volunteer experts on exploring South Florida, especially Homestead, Florida City, and the Florida Keys. ⊠ *160 U.S. 1* ☎ *305/245–9180, 800/388–9669* ⊕ *www. tropicaleverglades.com.*

WHERE TO EAT

$

SEAFOOD

✕ **Farmers' Market Restaurant.** Although this eatery is within the farmers' market on the edge of town and is big on serving fresh vegetables, seafood figures prominently on the menu. A family of anglers runs the place, so fish and shellfish are only hours from the sea, and there's a fish fry on Friday nights. **Known for:** early opening for breakfast; seafood-centric menu; using fresh produce from the market. ⑤ *Average main: $13* ⊠ *300 N. Krome Ave.* ☎ *305/242–0008.*

$$

SEAFOOD

✕ **Mutineer Restaurant.** Families and older couples flock to this kitschy roadside outpost that is shaped like a ship. Florida lobster tails, stuffed grouper, shrimp, and snapper top the menu, along with another half dozen daily seafood specials. **Known for:** family-friendly atmosphere; kitschy decor; the Wharf Lounge, with live entertainment on weekends. ⑤ *Average main: $20* ⊠ *11 S.E. 1st Ave. (U.S. 1), at Palm Dr.* ☎ *305/245–3377* ⊕ *www.mutineerrestaurant.com.*

WHERE TO STAY

$

HOTEL

▥ **Best Western Gateway to the Keys.** For easy access to Everglades and Biscayne National Parks as well as the Keys, you'll be well situated at this sprawling, two-story motel two blocks off Florida's Turnpike. **Pros:** convenient to parks, outlet shopping, and dining; free Wi-Fi and breakfast; attractive pool area. **Cons:** traffic noise; fills up fast in high season. ⑤ *Rooms from: $135* ⊠ *411 S. Krome Ave.* ☎ *305/246–5100, 888/981–5100* ⊕ *www.bestwestern.com/gatewaytothekeys* ⇆ *114 rooms* ⦿❘ *Breakfast.*

$

HOTEL

▥ **Fairway Inn.** With a waterfall pool, this two-story motel with exterior room entry has some of the area's lowest chain rates, and it's next to the Chamber of Commerce visitor center so you'll have easy access to tourism brochures and other information. **Pros:** affordable; convenient to restaurants, parks, and raceway. **Cons:** plain, small rooms; no-pet policy. ⑤ *Rooms from: $89* ⊠ *100 S.E. 1st Ave.* ☎ *305/248–4202, 888/340–4734* ⇆ *160 rooms* ⦿❘ *Breakfast.*

$

HOTEL

▥ **Ramada Inn.** If you're seeking an uptick from other chains, this kid-friendly property offers more amenities and comfort, such as 32-inch flat-screen TVs, free Wi-Fi, duvet-covered beds, closed closets, and stylish furnishings. **Pros:** extra room amenities; convenient location; guest laundry facilities. **Cons:** chain anonymity. ⑤ *Rooms from: $99* ⊠ *124 E. Palm Dr.* ☎ *305/247–8833* ⊕ *www.wyndhamhotels.com* ⇆ *118 rooms* ⦿❘ *Breakfast.*

$

HOTEL

▥ **Travelodge.** This bargain motor lodge is close to Florida's Turnpike, Everglades and Biscayne National Parks, and Homestead-Miami Speedway. **Pros:** convenience to track and U.S. 1; nice pool; complimentary breakfast. **Cons:** busy location; some small rooms; no pets. ⑤ *Rooms from: $89* ⊠ *409 S.E. 1st Ave.* ☎ *305/248–9777, 800/758–0618* ⊕ *www. tlflcity.com* ⇆ *88 rooms* ⦿❘ *Breakfast.*

SHOPPING

FAMILY **Robert Is Here.** Want take-home gifts? This historic fruit stand sells more than 100 types of jams, jellies, honeys, and salad dressings along with its vegetables, juices, fabulous fresh-fruit milk shakes (try the papaya key lime or guanabana, under $6), and some 30 kinds of tropical fruits, including (in season) carambola, lychee, egg fruit, monstera, sapodilla, dragonfruit, genipa, sugar apple, and tamarind. Back in 1960, the stand got started when pint-sized Robert sat at this spot hawking his father's bumper cucumber crop. Now with his own book (*Robert Is Here: Looking East for a Lifetime*), Robert remains on the scene daily with wife and kids, ships nationwide, and donates seconds to needy families. An assortment of animals out back—goats to iguanas and emus, along with a splash pool—adds to the fun. Picnic tables, benches, and a waterfall with a koi pond provide serenity. It's on the way to Everglades National Park, and Robert opens at 8 am, operating until at least 7, shutting down from Labor Day until November. ⊠ *19200 S.W. 344th St.* ☎ *305/246–1592.*

3

HOMESTEAD

30 miles southwest of Miami.

Since recovering from Hurricane Andrew in 1992, Homestead has redefined itself as a destination for tropical agro- and ecotourism. At a crossroads between Miami and the Keys as well as Everglades and Biscayne National Parks, the area has the added dimension of shopping centers, residential development, hotel chains, and the Homestead-Miami Speedway—when car races are scheduled, hotels hike rates and require minimum stays. The historic downtown has become a preservation-driven Main Street. Krome Avenue, where it cuts through the city's heart, is lined with restaurants, an arts complex, antiques shops, and low-budget, sometimes undesirable, accommodations. West of north–south Krome Avenue, miles of fields grow fresh fruits and vegetables. Some are harvested commercially, and others beckon with "U-pick" signs. Stands selling farm-fresh produce and nurseries that grow and sell orchids and tropical plants abound. In addition to its agricultural legacy, the town has an eclectic flavor, attributable to its population mix: descendants of pioneer Crackers, Hispanic growers and farm workers, professionals escaping the Miami hubbub, and latter-day northern retirees.

EXPLORING

FAMILY
Fodor's Choice
★
Fruit & Spice Park. Because it officially qualifies for tropical status, this 37-acre park in Homestead's Redland historic agricultural district is the only public botanical garden of its type in the United States. More than 500 varieties of fruit, nuts, and spices typically grow here, and there are 75 varieties of bananas alone, plus 160 of mango. Tram tours (included in admission) run three times daily, and you can sample fresh fruit at the gift shop, which also stocks canned and dried fruits plus cookbooks. The Mango Café, open daily from 11:30 am to 4:30 pm, serves mango salsa, smoothies, and shakes along with salads, wraps, sandwiches, and a yummy Mango Passion Cheesecake. Picnic in the garden at provided

Are baby alligators more to your liking than their daddies? You can pet one at Gator Park.

tables or on your own blankets. Annual park events include January's Redland Heritage Festival and June's Summer Fruit Festival. Kids age six and under are free. ✉ *24801 S.W. 187th Ave.* ☎ *305/247–5727* ⊕ *www.fruitandspicepark.com* ✉ *$8.*

Schnebly Redland's Winery. Homestead's fruity bounty comes in liquid form at this growing enterprise that began producing wines of lychee, mango, guava, and other fruits as a way to avoid waste from family groves each year—bounty not perfect enough for shipping. Over the years, this grape-free winery (now with a beer brewery, too) has expanded with a reception-tasting indoor area serving snacks and a lush plaza picnic area landscaped in coral rock, tropical plants, and waterfalls—topped with an Indian thatched chickee roof. Tours and tastings are offered daily. The Ultimate Tasting includes five wines and an etched Schnebly glass you can keep. Redlander Restaurant operates daily with an ever-changing menu. On Sunday, and on other occasions, there's yoga on the lawn. Count on a cover charge at the restaurant after 6 pm on Friday and Saturday nights. ✉ *30205 S.W. 217th Ave.* ☎ *305/242–1224, 888/717–9463 (WINE)* ⊕ *www.schneblywinery.com* ✉ *Winery tours (weekends only) $7; tastings $11.95.*

WHERE TO EAT

$ ✕ **Royal Palm Grill.** You may have a déjà vu moment if you drive down
AMERICAN Krome Avenue, where two Royal Palm Grills are just a hop-skip away from each other. This popular "breakfast all day, every day" enterprise has two locations, only a few blocks apart, to accommodate a steady stream of customers for the aforementioned breakfast fare from omelets and pancakes to biscuits and gravy, plus salads, steaks, and seafood. **Known**

for: early open, early close; popular for breakfast; nostalgic setup at the original location. ⑤ *Average main: $10* ✉ *Royal Palm Pharmacy, 806 N. Krome Ave.* ☎ *305/246–5701* ⊕ *royalpalmgrillfl.com* ⊗ *No dinner.*

$$ ✕ **Shiver's BBQ.** Piggin' out since the 1960s, Shiver's ranks as a lip-
BARBECUE smackin' must for lovers of hickory-smoked barbecued pork, beef, and
FAMILY chicken in assorted forms from baby back ribs to briskets. Longtime owners Martha and Perry Curtis are typically on hand attending to traditions with original recipes, although Martha does offer her new, alternative "secret recipe" sauce. **Known for:** corn-bread soufflé; picnic table seating; popular for takeout. ⑤ *Average main: $15* ✉ *28001 S. Dixie Hwy.* ☎ *305/248–2272* ⊕ *www.shiversbbq.com.*

$$ ✕ **White Lion Cafe.** Although the antique shop space within the bunga-
ITALIAN low-style café is now history, this 45-seat comfort-food haven, with full bar, remains embellished with reminders of the past, from a 1950s-era wooden wall phone to a metal icebox and a Coca-Cola machine. A mounted jackalope oversees a wide menu of blue-plate specials (Homestead crab cakes, burgers, fried chicken, meat loaf). **Known for:** comfort food galore; lots of potato options; kitschy decor. ⑤ *Average main: $18* ✉ *146 N.W. 7th St.* ☎ *305/248–1076* ⊕ *www.whitelioncafe.com* ⊗ *Closed. Sun. and Mon.*

WHERE TO STAY

$ 🛏 **Hotel Redland.** Of downtown Homestead's smattering of mom-and-
HOTEL pop lodging options, this historic inn is by far the most desirable with its Victorian-style rooms done up in pastels and reproduction antique furniture. **Pros:** historic character; convenient to downtown and near antiques shops; free Wi-Fi. **Cons:** traffic noise; small rooms. ⑤ *Rooms from: $120* ✉ *5 S. Flagler Ave.* ☎ *305/246–1904, 800/595–1904* ⊕ *www.hotelredland.com* ⇆ *13 rooms* ◯ *No meals.*

SPORTS AND THE OUTDOORS

AUTO RACING

Homestead-Miami Speedway. Buzzing more than 280 days each year, the 600-acre speedway hosts racing, manufacturer testing, car-club events, driving schools, and ride-along programs. The facility has 65,000 grandstand seats, club seating eight stories above racing action, and two tracks—a 2.21-mile continuous road course and a 1.5-mile oval. A packed schedule includes GRAND-AM and NASCAR events. Two tunnels on the grounds are below sea level. Parking includes space for 30,000 vehicles. ✉ *1 Speedway Blvd.* ☎ *866/409–7223* ⊕ *www.homesteadmiamispeedway.com.*

WATER SPORTS

Homestead Bayfront Park. Boaters, anglers, and beachgoers give high ratings to facilities at this recreational area adjacent to Biscayne National Park. The 174-slip Herbert Hoover Marina, accommodating up to 50-foot vessels, has a ramp, dock, bait-and-tackle shop, fuel station, ice, and dry storage. The park also has a snack bar, tidal swimming area, a beach with lifeguards, playground, ramps for people with disabilities, and a picnic pavilion with grills, showers, and restrooms. ✉ *9698 S.W. 328th St.* ☎ *305/230–3033* ⇆ *$7 per passenger vehicle on weekends; $12 per vehicle with boat Mon.–Thurs., $15 Fri.–Sun.; $15 per RV or bus.*

TAMIAMI TRAIL

U.S. 41, between Naples and Miami.

An 80-mile stretch of U.S. 41 (known as the Tamiami Trail) traverses the Everglades, Big Cypress National Preserve, and Fakahatchee Strand Preserve State Park. The road was conceived in 1915 to link Miami to Fort Myers and Tampa. When it finally became a reality in 1928, it cut through the Everglades and altered the natural flow of water as well as the lives of the Miccosukee Indians who were trying mightily to eke out a living fishing, hunting, farming, and frogging here. The landscape is surprisingly varied, changing from hardwood hammocks to pinelands, then abruptly to tall cypress trees dripping with Spanish moss and back to saw-grass marsh. Slow down to take in the scenery and you'll likely be rewarded with glimpses of alligators sunning themselves along the banks of roadside canals and hundreds of waterbirds, especially in the dry winter season. The man-made landscape includes Native American villages, chickee huts, and airboats parked at roadside enterprises. Between Miami and Naples the road goes by several names, including Tamiami Trail, U.S. 41, 9th Street in Naples, and, at the Miami end, Southwest 8th Street. ■TIP→ Businesses along the trail give their addresses based on either their distance from Krome Avenue, Florida's Turnpike, or Miami on the east coast or Naples on the west coast.

EXPLORING

FAMILY **Everglades Safari Park.** A perennial favorite with tour-bus operators, this family-run park open 365 days has an arena, seating up to 300 for shows with alligator wrestling. Before and after, get a closer look at both alligators and crocodiles on Gator Island, follow a jungle trail, walk through a small wildlife museum, or board an airboat for a 35-minute ride on the River of Grass (included in admission). There's also a restaurant, gift shop, and an observation platform overlooking the Glades. Smaller, private airboats can be chartered for tours lasting 40 minutes to two hours. Check online for coupons and count on free parking. ✉ *26700 S.W. 8th St., Miami* ✛ *15 miles west of Florida's Tpke.* ☎ *305/226–6923, 305/223–3804* ⊕ *www.evergladessafaripark.com* 🖃 *$25.*

FAMILY **Gator Park.** Here you can get face-to-face with and even touch an alligator—albeit a baby one—during the park's Wildlife Show. You also can squirm in a "reptilium" of some 30 different venomous and nonpoisonous native snakes or learn about American Indians of the Everglades through a reproduction of a Miccosukee village. The park, open rain or shine, also has 35-minute airboat tours as well as a gift shop and restaurant serving fare from burgers to gator tail and sausage. Admission includes the wildlife show and an airboat ride. ✉ *24050 Tamiami Trail, Miami* ✛ *12 miles west of Florida's Tpke.* ☎ *305/559–2255, 800/559–2205* ⊕ *www.gatorpark.com* 🖃 *$19.99.*

FAMILY **Miccosukee Indian Village and Gift Shop.** Showcasing the skills and lifestyle of the Miccosukee Tribe of Florida, this cultural center offers craft demonstrations and insight into interaction with alligators. Narrated 30-minute airboat rides take you into the wilderness where natives hid after the Seminole Wars and Indian Removal Act of the mid-1800s. In modern times, many of the Miccosukee have relocated to this village along Tamiami Trail, but most still maintain their hammock farming and hunting camps. The museum shows two films on tribal culture and displays chickee structures and artifacts. Guided tours run throughout the day, and a gift shop stocks dolls, apparel, silver jewelry, beadwork, and other handcrafts. The Miccosukee Everglades Music and Craft Festival, going strong for four decades, falls on a July weekend, and the 10-day Miccosukee Indian Arts Festival is in late December. ✉ *U.S. 41, just west of Shark Valley entrance, 25 miles west of Florida's Tpke., Miami* ☎ *305/552-8365* ⊕ *www.miccosukee.com* ☞ *Village $10, airboat rides $16.*

> ### CROCS OR GATORS?
>
> You can tell you're looking at a crocodile, not an alligator, if you can see its lower teeth protruding when those powerful jaws are shut. Gators are much darker in color—a grayish black—compared with the lighter tan shades of crocodiles. Alligator snouts—sort of U-shape—are also much broader than their long, thin A-shape crocodilian counterparts. South Florida is the world's only place where the two coexist in the wild. Alligators are primarily found in freshwater habitats, whereas crocodiles (better at expelling salt from water) are typically in coastal estuaries.

WHERE TO EAT

$$
SOUTHWESTERN
FAMILY

✕ **Miccosukee Restaurant.** For breakfast or lunch (or dinner until 9 pm, November–April), this roadside cafeteria a quarter mile from the Miccosukee Indian Village provides the best menu variety along Tamiami Trail in Everglades territory. Atmosphere comes from the view overlooking the River of Grass, friendly servers wearing traditional Miccosukee patchwork vests, and a mural depicting American Indian women cooking while men powwow. **Known for:** catfish and frogs' legs; Indian fry bread; basic diner staples. ⑤ *Average main: $15* ✉ *U.S. 41, 18 miles west of Miccosukee Resort & Gaming; 25 miles west of Florida's Tpke., Miami* ☎ *305/894-2374* ☉ *No dinner May–Oct.*

$
BARBECUE
FAMILY

✕ **Pit Bar-B-Q.** This old-fashioned roadside eatery along Tamiami Trail near Krome Avenue was launched in 1965 by the late Tommy Little, who wanted to provide easy access to cold drinks and rib-sticking fare for folks heading into or out of the Everglades. Now spiffed up, this backwoods heritage vision remains a popular, affordable family option. **Known for:** double-decker barbecue sandwiches; a few Latin specialties; family-friendly atmosphere (with weekend pony rides). ⑤ *Average main: $12* ✉ *16400 S.W. 8th St., 5 miles west of Florida's Tpke., Miami* ☎ *305/226-2272* ⊕ *www.thepitbarbq.com.*

WHERE TO STAY

$
RESORT

🛏 **Miccosukee Resort & Gaming.** Like an oasis on the horizon of endless saw grass, this nine-story resort at the southeastern edge of the Everglades can't help but attract attention, even if you're not on the lookout for 24-hour gaming action. **Pros:** casino; most modern resort in these parts; golf. **Cons:** smoky lobby; hotel guests find parking lot fills with gamblers; feels incompatible with the Everglades. ⑤ *Rooms from: $149* ✉ *500 S.W. 177th Ave., Miami* ✛ *6 miles west of Florida's Tpke.* ☎ *305/925-2555, 877/242-6464* ⊕ *www.miccosukee.com* ⇝ *256 rooms, 46 suites* ❍| *No meals.*

SPORTS AND THE OUTDOORS

BOAT TOURS

Many Everglades-area tours operate only in season, roughly November through April.

Coopertown Airboats. In business since 1945, the oldest airboat operator in the Everglades offers 35- to 40-minute tours that take you 9 miles to hammocks and alligator holes to see red-shouldered hawks or turtles. You also can book longer private charters. ⊠ *22700 S.W. 8th St., Miami* ✛ *11 miles west of Florida's Tpke.* ☎ *305/226–6048* ⊕ *www.coopertownairboats.com.* ⧉ *From $23.*

Everglades Alligator Farm. Open daily near the entrance to Everglades National Park, this working farm—home of the late 14-foot "Grandpa" gator (now mounted for display)—runs a 4-mile, 30-minute airboat tour with departures 25 minutes after the hour. The tour includes free hourly alligator, snake, and wildlife shows; or see only the gator farm and show. Alligator feedings are at noon and 3 pm. Look for online coupons. ⊠ *40351 S.W. 192nd Ave., Homestead* ☎ *305/247–2628* ⊕ *www. everglades.com.* ⧉ *From $19.50.*

FAMILY **Wooten's Everglades Airboat Tours.** This classic Florida roadside attraction, with a change of ownership a few seasons back, runs airboat tours through the Everglades for up to 22 people and swamp-buggy rides through the Big Cypress Swamp for up to 25. Each lasts approximately 30 minutes. (Swamp-buggies are giant tractorlike vehicles with huge rubber wheels.) More personalized airboat tours on smaller boats, seating six to eight, last about an hour. An on-site animal sanctuary with a live gator show shelters the typical Everglades array of alligators, snakes, and other creatures. Some packages include an airboat ride, swamp-buggy adventure, and sanctuary access. Rates change frequently, but check website for combo packages. ⊠ *32330 Tamiami Trail E, Ochopee* ✛ *1½ miles east of Rte. 29* ☎ *239/695–2781, 800/282–2781* ⊕ *www. wootensineverglades.com* ⧉ *Tours from $24; gator show $8.*

THE FLORIDA KEYS

WELCOME TO THE FLORIDA KEYS

TOP REASONS TO GO

★ **John Pennekamp Coral Reef State Park:** A perfect introduction to the Florida Keys, this nature reserve offers snorkeling, diving, camping, and kayaking. An underwater highlight is the massive *Christ of the Deep* statue.

★ **Viewing the Underwater World:** Whether you scuba dive, snorkel, or ride a glass-bottom boat, don't miss gazing at the coral reef and its colorful denizens.

★ **Sunset at Mallory Square:** Sure, it's touristy, but just once while you're here, you've got to witness the circuslike atmosphere of this nightly celebration.

★ **Duval crawl:** Shop, eat, drink, repeat. Key West's Duval Street and the nearby streets make a good day's worth of window-shopping and people-watching.

★ **Getting on the water:** From angling for trophy-size fish to zipping out to the Dry Tortugas, a boat trip is in your future. It's really the whole point of the Keys.

1 The Upper Keys. As the doorstep to the islands' coral reefs and blithe spirit, the Upper Keys introduce all that's sporting and sea-oriented about the Keys. They stretch from Key Largo to the Long Key Channel (MM 105–65).

2 The Middle Keys. Centered on the town of Marathon, the Middle Keys hold most of the chain's historic and natural attractions outside of Key West. They go from Conch (pronounced *konk*) Key through Marathon to the south side of the Seven Mile Bridge, including Pigeon Key (MM 65–40).

3 The Lower Keys. Pressure drops another notch in this laid-back part of the region, where key-deer viewing and fishing reign supreme. The Lower Keys go from Little Duck Key west through Big Coppitt Key (MM 40–9).

THE LOWER KEYS

Key West
Key West
International
Airport

4 Key West. The ultimate in Florida Keys craziness, this party town isn't for the closed-minded or those seeking a quiet retreat. The Key West area encompasses MM 9–0.

4

Homestead

TO MIAMI

905A

U.S. 1

Card Sound Bridge

905

Everglades National Park

9336

Barnes Sound

Whitewater Bay

CAPE SABLE

Flamingo

Florida Bay

Key Largo

Key Largo

1

THE UPPER KEYS

Tavernier

John Pennekamp Coral Reef State Park

Windley Key

Plantation Key

Islamorada

Upper Matecumbe Key

2

THE MIDDLE KEYS

Layton

Long Key

Lower Matecumbe Key

Craig Key

Long Key Channel

Conch Key

Duck Key

Grassy Key

Marathon Airport

Pigeon Key

Marathon

Vaca Key

Flat Deer Key

Seven Mile Bridge

Straits of Florida

Mexico

ATLANTIC OCEAN

GETTING ORIENTED

The Florida Keys are the dribble of islands off the peninsula's southern tip. From Miami International Airport, Key Largo is a 56-mile drive via the Florida Turnpike and U.S. 1. The rest of the Keys—Islamorada, Marathon, Bahia Honda Key, and Big Pine Key—fall in succession for the 85 miles between Key Largo and Key West along the Overseas Highway. At their north end, the Florida Keys front Florida Bay, part of Everglades National Park. The Middle and Lower keys front the Gulf of Mexico; the Atlantic Ocean borders the length of the chain on its eastern shores.

SEAFOOD IN THE FLORIDA KEYS

Fish. It's what's for dinner in the Florida Keys. The Keys' runway between the Gulf of Mexico or Florida Bay and Atlantic warm waters means fish of many fin. Restaurants take full advantage by serving it fresh, whether you caught it or a local fisherman did.

Menus at a number of colorful waterfront shacks such as **Snapper's** (⊠ *139 Seaside Ave., Key Largo* ☏ *305/852–5956*) in Key Largo and **Half Shell Raw Bar** (⊠ *231 Margaret St., Key West* ☏ *305/294–7496*) range from basic raw, steamed, broiled, grilled, or blackened fish to some Bahamian and New Orleans–style interpretations. Other seafood houses dress up their fish in creative haute cuisine styles, such as **Pierre's** (⊠ *MM 81.5 BS, Islamorada* ☏ *305/664–3225* ⊕ *www.pierres-restaurant.com*) hogfish meunière, or yellowtail snapper with pear-ricotta pasta purses with caponata and red pepper coulis at **Café Marquesa** (⊠ *600 Fleming St., Key West* ☏ *305/292–1244* ⊕ *www.marquesa.com*). Try a Keys-style breakfast of "grits and grunts"—fried fish and grits—at the **Stuffed Pig** (⊠ *3520 Overseas Hwy., Marathon* ☏ *305/743–4059*).

BUILT-IN FISH

You know it's fresh when you see a fish market as soon as you open the door to the restaurant where you're dining. It happens frequently in the Keys. You can even peruse the seafood showcases and pick the fish fillet or lobster tail you want.

Many of the Keys' best restaurants are found in marina complexes, where the commercial fishermen bring their catches straight from the sea. Those in **Stock Island** (one island north of Key West) and at **Keys Fisheries Market & Marina** (⊠ *MM 49 BS, end of 35th St., Marathon* ☏ *305/743-4353, 866/743-4353*) take some finding.

CONCH

One of the tastiest legacies of the Keys' Bahamian heritage (and most mispronounced), conch (pronounced *konk*) shows up on nearly every menu in some shape or form. It's so prevalent in local diets that natives refer to themselves as Conchs. Conch fritters are the most popular culinary manifestations, followed by cracked (pounded, breaded, and fried) conch, and conch salad, a ceviche-style refresher. Since the harvesting of queen conch is now illegal, most of the islands' conch comes from the Bahamas.

4

FLORIDA LOBSTER

Where are the claws? Stop looking for them: Florida spiny lobsters don't have 'em, never did. The sweet tail meat, however, makes up for the loss. Commercial and sport divers harvest these glorious crustaceans from late July through March. Check with local dive shops on restrictions, and then get ready for a fresh feast. Restaurants serve them broiled with drawn butter or in creative dishes such as lobster Benedict, lobster spring rolls, lobster Reuben, and lobster tacos.

GROUPER

Once central to Florida's trademark seafood dish—fried grouper sandwich—its populations have been overfished in recent years, meaning that the state has exerted more control over bag regulations and occasionally closes grouper fishing on a temporary basis during the winter season. Some restaurants have gone antigrouper to try to bring back the abundance, but most grab it when they can. Black grouper is the most highly prized of the several varieties.

STONE CRAB

In season October 15 through May 15, it gets its name from its rock-hard shell. Fishermen take only one claw, which can regenerate in a sustainable manner. Connoisseurs prefer them chilled with tangy mustard sauce. Some restaurants give you a choice of hot claws and drawn butter, but this means the meat will be cooked twice, because it's usually boiled or steamed as soon as it's taken from its crab trap.

YELLOWTAIL SNAPPER

The preferred species of snappers, it's more plentiful in the Keys than in any other Florida waters. As pretty as it is tasty, it's a favorite of divers and snorkelers. Mild, sweet, and delicate, its meat lends itself to any number of preparations. It's available pretty much year-round, and many restaurants will give you a choice of broiled, baked, fried, or blackened. Chefs top it with everything from key lime beurre blanc to mango chutney. **Ballyhoo's** in Key Largo (✉ *MM 97.8, in median* ☎ *305/852–0822*) serves it 10 different ways.

Updated by
Jill Martin

Your Keys experience begins on your 18-mile drive south on "The Stretch," a portion of U.S. 1 with a specially colored blue median that takes you from Florida City to Key Largo. The real magic begins at mile marker 113, where the Florida Keys Scenic Highway begins. As the only All-American Road in Florida, it is a destination unto itself, one that crosses 42 bridges over water, including the Seven Mile Bridge—with its stunning vistas—and ends in Key West. Look for crocodiles, alligators, and bald eagles along the way.

Key West has a Mardi Gras mood with Fantasy Festival, a Hemingway look-alike contest, and the occasional threat to secede from the Union. It's an island whose eclectic natives, known as "Conchs," mingle well with visitors (of the spring-break variety as well as those seeking to escape reality for a while) on this scenic, sometimes raucous 4x2-mile island paradise.

Although life elsewhere in the island chain isn't near as offbeat, it is as diverse. Overflowing bursts of bougainvillea, shimmering waters, and mangrove-lined islands can be admired throughout. The one thing most visitors don't admire much in the Keys are their beaches. They're not many, and they're not what you'd expect. The reason? The coral reef. It breaks up the waves and prevents sand from being dumped on the shores. That's why the beaches are mostly rough sand, as it's crushed coral. Think of it as a trade-off: the Keys have the only living coral reef in the United States, but that reef prevents miles of shimmering sands from ever arriving.

In season, a river of traffic gushes southwest on this highway. But that doesn't mean you can't enjoy the ride as you cruise along the islands. Gaze over the silvery blue-and-green Atlantic and its living coral reef, with Florida Bay, the Gulf of Mexico, and the backcountry on your right (the Keys extend southwest from the mainland). At a few points the ocean and gulf are as much as 10 miles apart; in most places, however, they're from 1 to 4 miles apart, and on the narrowest landfill islands they're separated only by the road.

While the views can be mesmerizing, to appreciate the Keys you need to get off the highway, especially in more developed regions like Key Largo, Islamorada, and Marathon. Once you do, rent a boat, anchor, and then fish, swim, or marvel at the sun, sea, and sky. Or visit one of the many sandbars, which are popular places to float the day away. Ocean side, dive or snorkel spectacular coral reefs or pursue grouper, blue marlin, mahimahi, and other deepwater game fish. Along Florida Bay's coastline, kayak to secluded islands through mangrove forests, or seek out the bonefish, snapper, snook, and tarpon that lurk in the shallow grass flats and mangrove roots of the backcountry.

4

PLANNING

WHEN TO GO
In high season, from mid-December through mid-April, traffic is inevitably heavy. From November to mid-December, crowds are thinner, the weather is superlative, and hotels and shops drastically reduce their prices. Summer is a second high season, especially among families, Europeans, bargain-seekers, and lobster divers.

Florida is rightly called the Sunshine State, but it could also be dubbed the "Humidity State." From June through September, 90% humidity levels are not uncommon. Thankfully, the weather in the Keys is more moderate than in mainland Florida. Temperatures can be 10°F cooler during the summer and up to 10°F warmer during the winter. The Keys also get substantially less rain than mainland Florida, mostly in quick downpours on summer afternoons. In hurricane season, June through November, the Keys get their fair share of warnings; pay heed, and evacuate earlier rather than later, when flights and automobile traffic get backed up.

GETTING HERE AND AROUND
AIR TRAVEL
About 450,000 passengers use Key West International Airport (EYW) each year; its most recent renovation includes a beach where travelers can catch their last blast of rays after clearing security. Because direct flights to Key West are few, many prefer flying into Miami International Airport (MIA) and driving the 110-mile Overseas Highway (aka U.S. 1).

BOAT AND FERRY TRAVEL
Key West Express operates air-conditioned ferries between the Key West Terminal (Caroline and Grinnell streets) and Marco Island and Fort Myers Beach. The trip takes at least four hours each way and costs $95 one way, from $125 round-trip (a $3 convenience fee is added to all online bookings). Ferries depart from Fort Myers Beach at 8:30 am and from Key West at 6 pm. The Marco Island ferry departs at 8:30 am (the return trip leaves Key West at 5 pm). A photo ID is required for each passenger. Advance reservations are recommended.

Boaters can travel to and through the Keys either along the Intracoastal Waterway (5-foot draft limitation) through Card, Barnes, and Blackwater sounds and into Florida Bay, or along the deeper Atlantic Ocean route through Hawk Channel, a buoyed passage. Refer to NOAA Nautical Charts Nos. 11451, 11445, and 11441. The Keys are full of marinas that welcome transient visitors, but they don't have enough slips for everyone. Make reservations in advance, and ask about channel and dockage depth—many marinas are quite shallow.

Contact Key West Express. ⊠ *100 Grinnell St., Key West* ☎ *239/463–5733 in Key West, 239/463–5733 in Fort Myers Beach, 239/463–5733 in Marco Island* ⊕ *www.seakeywestexpress.net.*

BUS TRAVEL

Keys Transportation provides private airport transfers to any destination in the Keys from either MIA or FLL. Prices start at $49 per person for transportation to Key Largo and get more expensive as you move south. Call or email for a price quote.

Greyhound Lines runs a special Keys shuttle twice a day (times depend on the day of the week) from Miami International Airport (departing from Concourse E, lower level) and stops throughout the Keys. Fares run from around $25 for Key Largo (⊠ *MM 99.6*) or Islamorada (⊠ *Burger King, MM 82*) to around $45 for Key West (⊠ *3535 S. Roosevelt, Key West International Airport*).

Keys Shuttle runs scheduled service six times a day in 15-passenger vans (9 passengers maximum) between Miami and Fort Lauderdale airports and Key West with stops throughout the Keys for $60 to $90 per person sharing rides.

SuperShuttle charges $191 for up to two passengers for trips to the Upper Keys; to go farther, you must book an entire 11-person van, which costs $402. For a trip to the airport, place your request 24 hours in advance.

Contacts Greyhound. ☎ *800/231–2222* ⊕ *www.greyhound.com.* **Keys Shuttle.** ⊠ *1333 Overseas Hwy., Marathon* ☎ *888/765–9997* ⊕ *www.keysshuttle.com.* **Keys Transportation.** ☎ *305/395–0299* ⊕ *www.keystransportation.com.* **SuperShuttle.** ☎ *800/258–3826* ⊕ *www.supershuttle.com.*

CAR TRAVEL

By car, from Miami International Airport, follow signs to Coral Gables and Key West, which puts you on LeJeune Road, then Route 836 west. Take the Homestead Extension of Florida's Turnpike south (toll road), which ends at Florida City and connects to the Overseas Highway (U.S. 1). Tolls from the airport run approximately $3. Payment is collected via SunPass, a prepaid toll program, or with Toll-By-Plate, a system that photographs each vehicle's license plate and mails a monthly bill for tolls, plus a $2.50 administrative fee, to the vehicle's registered owner.

Vacationers traveling in their own cars can obtain a mini-SunPass sticker via mail before their trip for $4.99 and receive the cost back in toll credits and discounts. The pass also is available at many major Florida retailers and turnpike service plazas. It works on all Florida toll roads and many bridges. For details on purchasing a mini-SunPass, call or visit the website.

For visitors renting cars in Florida, most major rental companies have programs allowing customers to use the Toll-By-Plate system. Tolls, plus varying service fees, are automatically charged to the credit card used to rent the vehicle (along with a hefty service charge in most cases). For details, including pricing options at participating rental-car agencies, check the program website. Under no circumstances should motorists attempt to stop in high-speed electronic tolling lanes. Travelers can contact Florida's Turnpike Enterprise for more information about the all-electronic tolling on Florida's Turnpike.

The alternative from Florida City is Card Sound Road (Route 905A), which has a (cash-only) bridge toll of $1. SunPass isn't accepted. Continue to the only stop sign and turn right on Route 905, which rejoins the Overseas Highway 31 miles south of Florida City.

Except in Key West, a car is essential for visiting the Keys.

Contacts Florida's Turnpike Enterprise. ☎ 800/749–7453 ⊕ www.floridas-turnpike.com. **SunPass.** ☎ 888/865–5352 ⊕ www.sunpass.com.

THE MILE MARKER SYSTEM

Getting lost in the Keys is almost impossible once you understand the unique address system. Many addresses are simply given as a mile marker (MM) number. The markers are small, green, rectangular signs along the side of the Overseas Highway (U.S. 1). They begin with MM 126, 1 mile south of Florida City, and end with MM 0, in Key West. Keys residents use the abbreviation BS for the bay side of Overseas Highway and OS for the ocean side. From Marathon to Key West, residents may refer to the bay side as the gulf side.

HOTELS

Throughout the Keys, the types of accommodations are remarkably varied, from 1950s-style motels to cozy inns to luxurious resorts. Most are on or near the ocean, so water sports are popular. Key West's lodging portfolio includes historic cottages, restored Conch houses, and large resorts. Some larger properties throughout the Keys charge a mandatory daily resort fee, which can cover equipment rental, fitness-center use, and other services. You can expect another 12.5% (or more) in state and county taxes. Some guesthouses and inns don't welcome children, and many don't permit smoking.

RESTAURANTS

Seafood rules in the Keys, which is full of chef-owned restaurants with not-too-fancy food. Many restaurants serve cuisine that reflects the proximity of the Bahamas and Caribbean (you'll see the term "Floribbean" on many menus). Tropical fruits figure prominently—especially on the beverage side of the menu. Florida spiny lobster should be local and fresh from August to March, and stone crabs from mid-October to mid-May. And don't dare leave the islands without sampling conch, be it in a fritter or in ceviche. Keep an eye out for authentic key lime pie—yellow custard in a graham-cracker crust. If it's green, just say "no." Note: Particularly in Key West and particularly during spring break, the more affordable and casual restaurants can get loud and downright rowdy, with young visitors often more interested in drinking than eating. Live music contributes to the decibel levels. If you're more of the quiet, intimate-dining type, avoid such overly exuberant scenes by eating early or choosing a restaurant where the bar isn't the main focus.

Hotel and restaurant reviews have been shortened. For full information, visit Fodors.com.

WHAT IT COSTS				
	$	**$$**	**$$$**	**$$$$**
Restaurants	under $15	$15–$20	$21–$30	over $30
Hotels	under $200	$200–$300	$301–$400	over $400

Restaurant prices are the average cost of a main course at dinner or, if dinner is not served, at lunch. Hotel prices are the lowest cost of a standard double room in high season.

VISITOR INFORMATION

There are several separate tourism offices in the Florida Keys, and you can use Visit Florida's website (⊕ *www.visitflorida.com*) for general information and referrals to local agencies. *See individual chapters for local visitor information centers.*

In addition to traditional tourist information, many divers will be interested in the Florida Keys National Marine Sanctuary, which has its headquarters in Key West and has another office in Key Largo.

Contact Florida Keys National Marine Sanctuary. ☏ *305/809–4700* ⊕ *floridakeys.noaa.gov.*

THE UPPER KEYS

Diving and snorkeling rule in the Upper Keys, thanks to North America's only living coral barrier reef that runs a few miles off the Atlantic coast. Divers of all skill levels benefit from accessible dive sites and an established tourism infrastructure. Fishing is another huge draw, especially around Islamorada, known for its sportfishing in both deep offshore waters and in the backcountry. Offshore islands accessible only by boat are popular destinations for kayakers. In short, if you don't like the water you might get bored here.

But true nature lovers won't feel shortchanged. Within 1½ miles of the bay coast lie the mangrove trees and sandy shores of Everglades National Park, where naturalists lead tours of one of the world's few saltwater forests. Here you'll see endangered manatees, curious dolphins, and other marine creatures. Although the number of birds has dwindled since John James Audubon captured their beauty on canvas, bird-watchers will find plenty to see, including the rare Everglades snail kite, bald eagles, ospreys, and a colorful array of egrets and herons. At sunset flocks take flight as they gather to find their night's roost, adding a swirl of activity to an otherwise quiet time of day.

GETTING HERE AND AROUND

Keys Transportation provides private airport transfers to any destination in the Keys from either MIA or FLL. Prices start at $49 per person for transportation to Key Largo and get more expensive as you move south. Call or email for a price quote. SuperShuttle charges $165 to $185 for two passengers for trips from Miami International Airport to Key Largo; reservations are required. For a trip to the airport, place your request 24 hours in advance. *For more information, see Getting Here and Around: Bus Travel.*

KEY LARGO

56 miles south of Miami International Airport.

The first of the Upper Keys reachable by car, 30-mile-long Key Largo is the largest island in the chain. Key Largo—named Cayo Largo ("Long Key") by the Spanish—makes a great introduction to the region. This is the gateway to the Keys, and an evening of fresh seafood and views of the sunset on the water will get you in the right state of mind.

The history of Largo reads much like that of the rest of the Keys: a succession of native people, pirates, wreckers, and developers. The first settlement on Key Largo was named Planter, back in the days of pineapple, and later, key lime plantations. For a time it was a convenient shipping port, but when the railroad arrived Planter died on the vine. Today three communities—North Key Largo and Key Largo as well as the separately incorporated city of Tavernier—make up the whole of Key Largo.

What's there to do on Key Largo besides gaze at the sunset? Not much if you're not into diving or snorkeling. Nobody comes to Key Largo without visiting John Pennekamp Coral Reef State Park, one of the jewels of the state park system. Water-sports enthusiasts head to the adjacent Key Largo National Marine Sanctuary, which encompasses about 190 square miles of coral reefs, sea-grass beds, and mangrove estuaries. If you've never tried diving, Key Largo is the perfect place to learn. Dozens of companies will be more than happy to show you the ropes.

Fishing is the other big draw, and world records are broken regularly in the waters around the Upper Keys. There are plenty of charter companies to help you find the big ones and teach you how to hook the elusive bonefish, sometimes known as the ghost fish.

On land, Key Largo provides all the conveniences of a major resort town, including restaurants that will cook your catch or prepare their own creations with inimitable style. You'll notice that some unusual specialties pop up on the menu, such as cracked conch, spiny lobster, and stone crab. Don't pass up a chance to try the local delicacies, especially the key lime pie.

Most businesses are lined up along U.S. 1, the four-lane highway that runs down the middle of the island. Cars whiz past at all hours—something to remember when you're booking a room. Most lodgings are on the highway, so you'll want to be as far back as possible. At MM 95, look for the mural painted in 2011 to commemorate the 100th anniversary of the railroad to the Keys.

GETTING HERE AND AROUND

Key Largo is 56 miles south of Miami International Airport, with its mile markers ranging from 106 to 91. The island runs northeast–southwest, with the Overseas Highway, divided by a median most of the way, running down the center. If the highway is your only glimpse of the island, you're likely to feel barraged by its tacky commercial side. Make a point of driving Route 905 in North Key Largo and down side streets to get a better feel for it.

VISITOR INFORMATION

In addition to traditional tourist information, many divers will be interested in the Florida Keys National Marine Sanctuary, which has an office in Key Largo.

Contacts Florida Keys National Marine Sanctuary. ☎ *305/809–4700* ⊕ *floridakeys.noaa.gov.* **Key Largo Chamber of Commerce.** ⊠ *MM 106 BS, 10600 Overseas Hwy.* ☎ *305/451–4747, 800/822–1088* ⊕ *www.keylargochamber.org.*

EXPLORING

TOP ATTRACTIONS

FAMILY **Dagny Johnson Key Largo Hammock Botanical State Park.** American crocodiles, mangrove cuckoos, white-crowned pigeons, Schaus swallowtail butterflies, mahogany mistletoe, wild cotton, and 100 other rare critters and plants inhabit these 2,400 acres, sandwiched between Crocodile Lake National Wildlife Refuge and the waters of Pennekamp Coral Reef State Park. The park is also a user-friendly place to explore the largest remaining stand of the vast West Indian tropical hardwood hammock and mangrove wetland that once covered most of the Keys. Interpretive signs describe many of the tropical tree species along a wide, 1-mile, paved road (2 miles round-trip) that invites walking and biking. A new, unpaved, extended loop trail can add 1–2 miles to your walk. There are also more than 6 additional miles of nature trails, most of which are accessible to both bikes and wheelchairs with a permit, easily obtainable from John Pennekamp State Park. Pets are welcome if on a leash no longer than 6 feet. You'll also find restrooms, information kiosks, and picnic tables. ■TIP→ **Rangers recommend not visiting when it's raining as the trees can drip poisonous sap.** ⊠ *Rte. 905 OS, ½ mile north of Overseas Hwy., North Key Largo* ☎ *305/451–1202* ⊕ *www.floridastateparks.org/keylargohammock* 🖅 *$2.50 (exact change needed).*

FAMILY **Dolphins Plus Bayside.** This educational program begins at the facility's bay-side lagoon with a get-acquainted session from a platform. After that, you slip into the water for some frolicking with your new dolphin pals. Options range from a shallow-water swim to a hands-on structured swim with a dolphin. You can also spend the day shadowing a trainer for a hefty $695 fee. ⊠ *MM 101.9 BS, 101900 Overseas Hwy.* ☎ *305/451–4060, 877/365–2683* ⊕ *www.dolphinsplus.com* 🖅 *$10 admission only; interactive programs from $150.*

FAMILY **Dolphins Plus Oceanside.** A sister property to Dolphins Plus Bayside, this Dolphins Plus offers some of the same programs, and the age requirement is lower. The cheapest option, a shallow-water program, begins with a one-hour briefing, after which you enter the water up to your waist to interact with the dolphins. You only get to see them: partici-pants can snorkel but are not allowed to touch the dolphins. Prefer to stay mostly dry? Opt to paint with a dolphin, or get a dolphin "kiss." For tactile interaction (fin tows, for example), sign up for the structured swim program, which is more expensive. ⊠ *MM 99, 31 Corrine Pl.* ☎ *305/451–1993, 866/860–7946* ⊕ *www.dolphinsplus.com* ✉ *Programs from $165.*

FAMILY **Florida Keys Wild Bird Center.** Have a nose-to-beak encounter with ospreys, hawks, herons, and other unreleasable birds at this bird rehabilitation center. The birds live in spacious screened enclosures along a boardwalk running through some of the best waterfront real estate in the Keys. Rehabilitated birds are set free, but about 30 have become permanent residents. Free birds—especially pelicans and egrets—come to visit every day for a free lunch from the center's staff. A short nature trail runs into the mangrove forest (bring bug spray May to October). A new addition is the interactive education center, now open about 1½ miles south. ⊠ *MM 93.6 BS, 93600 Overseas Hwy., Tavernier* ☎ *305/852–4486* ⊕ *www.keepthemflying.org* ✉ *Free, donations accepted.*

FAMILY **Jacobs Aquatic Center.** Take the plunge at one of three swimming pools: an eight-lane, 25-meter lap pool with two diving boards; a 3- to 4-foot-deep pool accessible to people with mobility challenges; and an interactive children's play pool with a waterslide, pirate ship, waterfall, and sloping zero entry instead of steps. Because so few of the motels in Key Largo have pools, it remains a popular destination for visiting families. ⊠ *Key Largo Community Park, 320 Laguna Ave., at St. Croix Pl.* ☎ *305/453–7946* ⊕ *www.jacobsaquaticcenter.org* ✉ *$12 ($2 discount weekdays).*

BEACHES

FAMILY
Fodor's Choice
★

John Pennekamp Coral Reef State Park. This state park is on everyone's list for easy access to the best diving and snorkeling in Florida. The underwater treasure encompasses 78 nautical square miles of coral reefs and sea-grass beds. It lies adjacent to the Florida Keys National Marine Sanctuary, which contains 40 of the 52 species of coral in the Atlantic Reef System and nearly 600 varieties of fish, from the color-ful parrot fish to the demure cocoa damselfish. Whatever you do, get in the water. Snorkeling and diving trips ($30 and $75, respectively, equipment extra) and glass-bottom-boat rides to the reef ($24) are available, weather permitting. One of the most popular snorkel trips is to see *Christ of the Deep*, the 2-ton underwater statue of Jesus. The park also has nature trails, two man-made beaches, picnic shelters, a snack bar, and a campground. **Amenities:** food and drink; parking (fee); showers; toilets; water sports. **Best for:** snorkeling; swimming. ⊠ *MM 102.5 OS, 102601 Overseas Hwy.* ☎ *305/451–1202 for park, 305/451–6300 for excursions* ⊕ *www.pennekamppark.com, www. floridastateparks.org/pennekamp* ✉ *$4 for 1 person in vehicle, $8 for 2–8 people, $2 for pedestrians and cyclists or extra people (plus a 50¢ per-person county surcharge).*

WHERE TO EAT

$
SEAFOOD
✕**Alabama Jack's.** Calories be damned—the conch fritters here are heaven on a plate. Don't expect the traditional, golf-ball-size spheres of dough; these are an unusual, mountainous, free-form creation of fried, loaded-with-flavor perfection. **Known for:** heavenly conch fritters; unique setting; weekend afternoon jam sessions. ⑤ *Average main: $11* ✉ *58000 Card Sound Rd.* ☎ *305/248–8741.*

$$$
SEAFOOD
✕**Ballyhoo's.** Occupying a 1930s Conch house with outdoor seating right alongside U.S. 1 under the sea grape trees, this local favorite is all about the fish (including the nautical decor). Yellowtail snapper, one of the moistest, most flavorful local fish, is served 10 different ways on the all-day menu, including blackened, stuffed with crab, and Parmesan crusted. **Known for:** all-you-can-eat specials like Friday fish dinners and in-season stone crab; Harvey's fish sandwich. ⑤ *Average main: $21* ✉ *MM 97.8 median, 97800 Overseas Hwy.* ☎ *305/852–0822* ⊕ *www. ballyhoosrestaurant.com.*

$$$
SEAFOOD
Fodor's Choice
★
✕**Buzzard's Roost Grill and Pub.** The views are nice at this waterfront restaurant but the food is what gets your attention. Burgers, fish tacos, and seafood baskets are lunch faves. **Known for:** marina views; daily chef's specials. ⑤ *Average main: $21* ✉ *Garden Cove Marina, 21 Garden Cove Dr.* ☎ *305/453–3746* ⊕ *www.buzzardsroostkeylargo.com.*

$
AMERICAN
✕**Chad's Deli & Bakery.** It's a deli! It's a bakery! It's a pasta place! It's also where the locals go. **Known for:** homemade soups and chowders; eight varieties of supersized homemade cookies. ⑤ *Average main: $10* ✉ *MM 92.3 BS, 92330 Overseas Hwy., Tavernier* ☎ *305/853–5566* ⊕ *www.chadsdeli.com.*

$$$
SEAFOOD
✕**The Fish House.** Restaurants not on the water have to produce the highest quality food to survive in the Keys. That's how the Fish House has succeeded since the 1980s—so much so that it built the Fish House Encore (a fancier version) next door to accommodate fans. **Known for:** smoked fish appetizer; excellent key lime pie; fresh-as-can-be seafood. ⑤ *Average main: $21* ✉ *MM 102.4 OS, 102341 Overseas Hwy.* ☎ *305/451–4665* ⊕ *www.fishhouse.com* ☾ *Closed Sept.*

$$$
SEAFOOD
✕**The Fish House Encore.** To accommodate the crowds that gather at the Fish House, the owners opened this place with similar but more refined cuisine ranging from sushi to steak. It's come into its own as a more formal dining venue than its sister establishment. **Known for:** formal dining venue; off-season all-you-can-eat specials; live piano music Thursday–Sunday. ⑤ *Average main: $27* ✉ *MM 102.3 OS, 102341 Overseas Hwy.* ☎ *305/451–4665, 305/451–0650* ⊕ *www.fishhouse. com* ☾ *Closed Tues. and Oct. No lunch.*

$
AMERICAN
✕**Harriette's Restaurant.** If you're looking for comfort food—like melt-in-your-mouth biscuits the size of a salad plate—try this refreshing throwback. Since the early 1980s, owner Harriette Mattson has been here to personally greet guests who come for the to-die-for omelets and old-fashioned hotcakes with sausage or bacon. **Known for:** breakfast and lunch that's worth the wait; 13 muffin flavors. ⑤ *Average main: $8* ✉ *MM 95.7 BS, 95710 Overseas Hwy.* ☎ *305/852–8689* ☾ *No dinner* ☞ *American Express not accepted.*

4

$$
SEAFOOD

X **Jimmy Johnson's Big Chill.** Owned by former NFL coach Jimmy Johnson, this waterfront establishment offers three entertaining experiences, and all are big winners. You'll find the best sports bar in the Upper Keys, complete with the coach's Super Bowl trophies; a main restaurant with all-glass indoor seating and a waterfront deck; and an enormous outdoor tiki bar with entertainment seven nights a week. **Known for:** great sports bar; fantastic bay views; tuna nachos. $ *Average main: $19* ⊠ *MM 104 BS, 104000 Overseas Hwy.* ☎ *305/453–9066* ⊕ *www. jjsbigchill.com.*

$$
AMERICAN

X **Key Largo Conch House.** Tucked into the trees along the Overseas Highway, this Victorian-style home (family owned since 2004) and its true-to-the-Keys style of cooking is worth seeking out—at least the Food Network and the Travel Channel have thought so in the past. The Old South veranda and patio seating are ideal for winter dining, but indoors the seating is tighter. **Known for:** serving lionfish; all-season outside dining. $ *Average main: $16* ⊠ *MM 100.2, 100211 Overseas Hwy.* ☎ *305/453–4844* ⊕ *www.keylargoconchhouse.com.*

$$
SEAFOOD
FAMILY

X **Mrs. Mac's Kitchen.** Townies pack the counters and booths at this tiny eatery, where license plates are stuck on the walls and made into chandeliers, for everything from blackened prime rib to crab cakes. Every night is themed including Meatloaf Monday, Italian Wednesday, and Seafood Sensation (offered Friday and Saturday). **Known for:** Champagne breakfast; nightly themed dinners. $ *Average main: $17* ⊠ *MM 99.4 BS, 99336 Overseas Hwy.* ☎ *305/451–3722, 305/451–6227* ⊕ *www. mrsmacskitchen.com* ⊘ *Closed Sun.*

$$
SEAFOOD

X **Snapper's.** In a lively, mangrove-ringed, waterfront setting, Snapper's has live music, Sunday brunch (including a build-your-own Bloody Mary bar), killer rum drinks, and seating alongside the fishing dock. "You hook 'em, we cook 'em" is the motto here but you have to clean your own fish and dinner is $14 for a single diner, $15 per person family-style meal with a mix of preparations when you provide the fish. **Known for:** you hook, we cook; nightlife; fresh yellowtail. $ *Average main: $17* ⊠ *MM 94.5 OS, 139 Seaside Ave.* ☎ *305/852–5956* ⊕ *www. snapperskeylargo.com.*

$$$
AMERICAN

X **Sundowners.** If it's a clear night and you can snag a reservation, this restaurant will treat you to a sherbet-hue sunset over Florida Bay. The food is also excellent: try the key lime seafood, a happy combo of sautéed shrimp, lobster, and lump crabmeat swimming in a tangy sauce spiked with Tabasco served over penne or rice. **Known for:** great sunset viewing; Friday-night fish fry. $ *Average main: $22* ⊠ *MM 104 BS, 103900 Overseas Hwy.* ☎ *305/451–4502* ⊕ *sundownerskeylargo.com.*

WHERE TO STAY

$
RESORT

🏨 **Amy Slate's Amoray Dive Resort.** You can read this hotel's name either as "a moray" (referring to the moray eels you'll encounter on the reef) or "amore" (Italian for love, which calls to mind the place's romantic atmosphere), and you'll understand the place's dual charms. **Pros:** top-notch dive operation; free use of snorkel equipment. **Cons:** noise from highway; minimum stays during peak times. $ *Rooms from: $159* ⊠ *MM 104.2 BS, 104250 Overseas Hwy.* ☎ *305/451–3595, 800/426–6729* ⊕ *www.amoray.com* ⮑ *23 rooms, 8 apartments* ⊘⊙ *No meals.*

$$ **Azul del Mar.** The dock points the way to many beautiful sunsets
B&B/INN at this no-smoking, adults-only boutique hotel, which Karol Marsden (an ad exec) and her husband Dominic (a travel photographer) have transformed from a run-down mom-and-pop place into a waterfront gem. **Pros:** great garden; good location; sophisticated design. **Cons:** small beach; high priced; minimum stays during holidays. $ *Rooms from: $299 ⊠ MM 104.3 BS, 104300 Overseas Hwy. ☎ 305/451–0337, 888/253–2985 ⊕ www.azulkeylargo.com ⟿ 6 units* ⟒*No meals.*

$ **Coconut Bay Resort & Bay Harbor Lodge.** Some 200 feet of waterfront
RESORT is the main attraction at these side-by-side sister properties that offer a choice between smaller rooms and larger separate cottages. **Pros:** bay front; neatly kept gardens; walking distance to restaurants; free use of kayaks, paddleboat, and paddleboards. **Cons:** a bit dated; small sea-walled sand beach. $ *Rooms from: $195 ⊠ MM 97.7 BS, 97702 Overseas Hwy. ☎ 305/852–1625, 800/385–0986 ⊕ www.coconut-baykeylargo.com ⟿ 21 units* ⟒*Breakfast.*

$$ **Coconut Palm Inn.** You'd never find this waterfront haven unless some-
B&B/INN one told you it was there, as it's tucked into a residential neighborhood beneath towering palms and native gumbo limbos. **Pros:** secluded; quiet; sophisticated feel. **Cons:** front desk closes early each evening; no access to ice machine when staff leaves; breakfast is ho-hum. $ *Rooms from: $299 ⊠ MM 92 BS, 198 Harborview Dr., via Jo-Jean Way off Overseas Hwy., Tavernier ☎ 305/852–3017 ⊕ www.coconutpalminn.com ⟿ 20 rooms* ⟒*Breakfast.*

$$ **Dove Creek Lodge.** With its sherbet-hued rooms and plantation-style
B&B/INN furnishings, these tropical-style units (19 in all) range in size from simple lodge rooms to luxury two-bedroom suites. **Pros:** luxurious rooms; walk to Snapper's restaurant; complimentary kayaks and Wi-Fi. **Cons:** no beach; some find the music from next door bothersome. $ *Rooms from: $269 ⊠ MM 94.5 OS, 147 Seaside Ave. ☎ 305/852–6200, 800/401–0057 ⊕ www.dovecreeklodge.com ⟿ 19 rooms* ⟒*Breakfast.*

$$ **Hilton Key Largo Resort.** Nestled within a hardwood hammock (loca-
RESORT lese for uplands habitat where hardwood trees such as live oak grow)
Fodor's Choice near the southern border of Everglades National Park, this sprawling,
★ 13-acre resort underwent a $25 million renovation in 2017 without skipping a beat. **Pros:** nice nature trail on bay side; pretty pools with waterfalls; awesome trees; bicycles available for rent. **Cons:** some rooms overlook the parking lot; pools near the highway; expensive per-night resort fee. $ *Rooms from: $269 ⊠ MM 97 BS, 97000 Overseas Hwy. ☎ 305/852–5553, 888/871–3437 ⊕ www.keylargoresort.com ⟿ 205 rooms* ⟒*No meals.*

$$ **Island Bay Resort.** When Mike and Carol Shipley took over this off-
RENTAL the-beaten-path resort in 2000, they revamped the 10 bay-side cottages, improved the landscaping, and added touches such as hammocks and Adirondack chairs that make you feel like this is your own personal tropical playground. **Pros:** on the water; sunset views. **Cons:** most units are small; no pool; lacks on-site amenities. $ *Rooms from: $249 ⊠ 92530 Overseas Hwy. ☎ 305/852–4087 ⊕ www.islandbayresort.com ⟿ 10 units* ⟒*No meals.*

$$
RESORT
Fodor's Choice
★

Kona Kai Resort, Gallery & Botanic Gardens. Brilliantly colored bougainvillea, coconut palm, and guava trees—and a botanical garden of other rare species—make this 2-acre adult hideaway one of the prettiest places to stay in the Keys. **Pros:** free custom tours of botanical gardens for guests; free use of sports equipment; knowledgeable staff. **Cons:** expensive; some rooms are very close together. *$ Rooms from: $299* ✉ *MM 97.8 BS, 97802 Overseas Hwy.* ☎ *305/852–7200, 800/365–7829* ⊕ *www.konakairesort.com* ⇄ *13 rooms* ⦿ *No meals.*

$$$
RESORT
FAMILY

Marriott's Key Largo Bay Beach Resort. This 17-acre bay-side resort has plenty of diversions, from diving to parasailing to a day spa. **Pros:** lots of activities; free covered parking; dive shop on property; free Wi-Fi. **Cons:** rooms facing highway can be noisy; thin walls. *$ Rooms from: $359* ✉ *MM 103.8 BS, 103800 Overseas Hwy.* ☎ *305/453–0000, 866/849–3753* ⊕ *www.marriottkeylargo.com* ⇄ *153 rooms* ⦿ *No meals.*

$
HOTEL

The Pelican. This 1950s throwback is reminiscent of the days when parents packed the kids into the station wagon and headed to no-frills seaside motels, complete with old-fashioned fishing off the dock. **Pros:** free use of kayaks and a canoe; well-maintained dock; reasonable rates. **Cons:** some small rooms; basic accommodations and amenities. *$ Rooms from: $159* ✉ *MM 99.3, 99340 Overseas Hwy.* ☎ *305/451–3576, 877/451–3576* ⊕ *www.hungrypelican.com* ⇄ *17 rooms, 4 efficiencies* ⦿ *Breakfast.*

$$$
RESORT
Fodor's Choice
★

Playa Largo Resort and Spa, Autograph Collection. This luxurious retreat, the first new hotel in Key Largo in over 21 years, is nestled on 14½ bay-front acres. **Pros:** comfortable rooms, most with balconies; soft-sand beach; excellent service; Playa Largo Kids Club. **Cons:** $25 a day resort fee; pricey spa; $18 daily charge for valet parking. *$ Rooms from: $399* ✉ *97450 Overseas Hwy.* ☎ *305/853–1001* ⊕ *playalargoresort. com* ⇄ *178 units* ⦿ *No meals* ▭ *No credit cards.*

$
HOTEL

Popp's Motel. Stylized metal herons mark the entrance to this 50-year-old family-run motel. **Pros:** beach; intimate feel; discounts for multiple-night stays. **Cons:** limited amenities; worn, outdated interiors. *$ Rooms from: $149* ✉ *MM 95.5 BS, 95500 Overseas Hwy.* ☎ *305/852–5201, 877/852–5201* ⊕ *www.poppsmotel.com* ⇄ *9 units* ⦿ *No meals.*

$
HOTEL

Seafarer Resort and Beach. If you're looking for modern and updated, this very basic, budget lodging isn't it. **Pros:** sandy beach; complimentary kayak use; cheap rates. **Cons:** can hear road noise in some rooms; some complaints about cleanliness. *$ Rooms from: $139* ✉ *MM 97.6 BS, 97684 Overseas Hwy.* ☎ *305/852–5349* ⊕ *www.seafarerkeylargo. com* ⇄ *15 units* ⦿ *No meals.*

NIGHTLIFE

The semiweekly *Keynoter* (Wednesday and Saturday), weekly *Reporter* (Thursday), and Friday through Sunday editions of the *Miami Herald* are the best sources of information on entertainment and nightlife. Daiquiri bars, tiki huts, and seaside shacks pretty well summarize Key Largo's bar scene.

Breezers Tiki Bar & Grille. Since its total makeover in 2016, you can now mingle with locals over cocktails and catch amazing sunsets from the comfort of an enclosed, air-conditioned bar. Floor-to-ceiling doors can be opened on cool days and closed on hot days. It's located at

Marriott's Key Largo Bay Beach Resort. ✉ *Marriott's Key Largo Bay Beach Resort, 103800 Overseas Hwy.* ☎ *305/453–0000.*

Caribbean Club. Walls plastered with Bogart memorabilia remind customers that the classic 1948 Bogart–Bacall flick *Key Largo* has a connection with this worn watering hole. Although no food is served and the floors are bare concrete, this landmark draws boaters, curious visitors, and local barflies to its humble bar stools and pool tables. But the real magic is around back, where you can grab a seat on the deck and catch a postcard-perfect sunset. Live music draws revelers Thursday through Sunday. ✉ *MM 104 BS, 104080 Overseas Hwy.* ☎ *305/451–4466* ⊕ *caribbeanclubkl.com.*

SHOPPING

4

For the most part, shopping is sporadic in Key Largo, with a couple of shopping centers and fewer galleries than you find on the other big islands. If you're looking to buy scuba or snorkel equipment, you'll have plenty of choices.

Gallery at Kona Kai. Wander the gallery and get a peek of island life as you admire original works by local artists, as well as works from frequent guests who dabble in a variety of mediums. The exhibits are geared toward the environment and what you might experience while you're visiting—botanicals, wildlife, sunrises, and sunsets. ✉ *MM 97.8 BS, 97802 Overseas Hwy.* ☎ *305/852–7200* ⊕ *www.g-k-k.com.*

FAMILY
Fodor's Choice
★

Key Largo Chocolates. Specializing in key lime truffles made with quality Belgian chocolate, this is the only chocolate factory in the Florida Keys. But you'll find much more than just the finest white-, milk-, and dark-chocolate truffles; try the cupcakes, ice cream, and famous "chocodiles." The salted turtles, a fan favorite, are worth every calorie. Chocolate classes are also available for kids and adults, and a small gift area showcases local art, jewelry, hot sauces, and other goodies. Look for the bright-green-and-pink building. ✉ *MM 100 BS, 100471 Overseas Hwy.* ☎ *305/453–6613* ⊕ *www.keylargochocolates.com.*

Key Lime Products. Go into olfactory overload—you'll find yourself sniffing every single bar of soap and scented candle inside this key lime treasure trove. Take home some key lime juice (supereasy pie-making directions are right on the bottle), marmalade, candies, sauces, even key lime shampoo. Outside, you'll find a huge selection of wood carvings, pottery, unique patio furniture, and artwork. The fresh fish sandwiches and conch fritters served here are alone worth the stop. ✉ *MM 95.2 BS, 95231 Overseas Hwy.* ☎ *305/853–0378, 800/870–1780* ⊕ *www.keylimeproducts.com.*

Randy's Florida Keys Gift Co. Since 1989, Randy's has been *the* place for unique gifts. Owner Randy and his wife Lisa aren't only fantastic at stocking the store with a plethora of items, they're also well respected in the community for their generosity and dedication. Stop in and say hello, then browse the tight aisles and loaded shelves filled with key lime candles, books, wood carvings, jewelry, clothing, T-shirts, and eclectic, tropical decor items. This friendly shop prides itself on carrying wares from local craftsmen, and there's something for every budget. ✉ *102421 Overseas Hwy.* ⊹ *On U.S. 1, next to the Sandal Factory Outlet* ☎ *305/453–9229* ⊕ *www.keysmermaid.com.*

Shell World. You can find lots of shops in the Keys that sell cheesy souvenirs—snow globes, alligator hats, and shell-encrusted anything. This is the granddaddy of them all. But this sprawling building in the median of Overseas Highway contains much more than the usual tourist trinkets—you'll find high-end clothing, jewelry, housewares, artwork, and a wide selection of keepsakes, from delightfully tacky to tasteful. ⊠ *MM 97.5, 97600 Overseas Hwy.* ☎ *305/852–8245, 888/398–6233* ⊕ *www.shellworldflkeys.com.*

SPORTS AND THE OUTDOORS

BOATING

FAMILY **Everglades Eco-Tours.** For over 30 years, Captain Sterling has operated Everglades and Florida Bay ecology tours and more expensive sunset cruises. With his expert guidance, you can see dolphins, manatees, and birds from the casual comfort of his pontoon boat, equipped with PVC chairs. Bring your own food and drinks; each tour has a maximum of six people. ⊠ *Sundowners Restaurant, MM 104 BS, 103900 Overseas Hwy.* ☎ *305/853–5161, 888/224–6044* ⊕ *www.captainsterling.com* 🖃 *From $59.*

FAMILY **M.V. *Key Largo Princess*.** Two-hour glass-bottom-boat trips and more expensive sunset cruises on a luxury 70-foot motor yacht with a 280-square-foot glass viewing area depart from the Holiday Inn docks three times a day. ■**TIP→** Purchase tickets online to save big. ⊠ *Holiday Inn, MM 100 OS, 99701 Overseas Hwy.* ☎ *305/451–4655, 877/648–8129* ⊕ *www.keylargoprincess.com* 🖃 *$35.*

CANOEING AND KAYAKING

Sea kayaking continues to gain popularity in the Keys. You can paddle for a few hours or the whole day, on your own or with a guide. Some outfitters even offer overnight trips. The **Florida Keys Overseas Paddling Trail**, part of a statewide system, runs from Key Largo to Key West. You can paddle the entire distance, 110 miles on the Atlantic side, which takes 9 to 10 days. The trail also runs the chain's length on the bay side, which is a longer route.

Coral Reef Park Co. At John Pennekamp Coral Reef State Park, this operator has a fleet of canoes and kayaks for gliding around the 2½-mile mangrove trail or along the coast. Powerboat rentals are also available. ⊠ *MM 102.5 OS, 102601 Overseas Hwy.* ☎ *305/451–6300* ⊕ *www. pennekamppark.com* 🖃 *Rentals from $12 per hr.*

Florida Bay Outfitters. Rent canoes, sea kayaks, or Hobie Eclipses (the newest craze) from this company, which sets up self-guided trips on the Florida Keys Paddling Trail, helps with trip planning, and matches equipment to your skill level. It also runs myriad guided tours around Key Largo. Take a full-moon paddle or a one- to seven-day kayak tour to the Everglades, Lignumvitae Key, or Indian Key. ⊠ *MM 104 BS, 104050 Overseas Hwy.* ☎ *305/451–3018* ⊕ *www.paddlefloridakeys. com* 🖃 *From $15.*

FISHING

Private charters and big "head" boats (so named because they charge "by the head") are great for anglers who don't have their own vessel.

Sailors Choice. Fishing excursions depart twice daily (half-day trips are cash only), but the company also does private charters. The 65-foot boat leaves from the Holiday Inn docks. Rods, bait, and license are included. ⊠ *Holiday Inn Resort & Marina, MM 100 OS, 99701 Overseas Hwy.* ☎ *305/451–1802, 305/451–0041* ⊕ *www.sailorschoicefishingboat.com* ✉ *From $40.*

SCUBA DIVING AND SNORKELING

Much of what makes the Upper Keys a singular dive destination is variety. Places like Molasses Reef, which begins 3 feet below the surface and descends to 55 feet, have something for everyone from novice snorkelers to experienced divers. The *Spiegel Grove,* a 510-foot vessel, lies in 130 feet of water, but its upper regions are only 60 feet below the surface. On rough days, Key Largo Undersea Park's Emerald Lagoon is a popular spot. Expect to pay about $80 to $85 for a two-tank, two-site dive trip with tanks and weights, or $35 to $40 for a two-site snorkel outing. Get big discounts by booking multiple trips.

Amy Slate's Amoray Dive Resort. This outfit makes diving easy. Stroll down to the full-service dive shop (PADI, TDI, and BSAC certified), then onto a 45-foot catamaran. Certification courses are also offered. ⊠ *MM 104.2 BS, 104250 Overseas Hwy.* ☎ *305/451–3595, 800/426–6729* ⊕ *www.amoray.com* ✉ *From $85.*

Conch Republic Divers. Book diving instruction as well as scuba and snorkeling tours of all the wrecks and reefs of the Upper Keys. Two-location dives are the standard, and you'll pay an extra $15 for tank and weights. ⊠ *MM 90.8 BS, 90800 Overseas Hwy.* ☎ *305/852–1655, 800/274–3483* ⊕ *www.conchrepublicdivers.com* ✉ *From $70.*

Coral Reef Park Co. At John Pennekamp Coral Reef State Park, this company gives 3½-hour scuba and 2½-hour snorkeling tours of the park. In addition to the great location and the dependability it's also suited for water adventurers of all levels. ⊠ *MM 102.5 OS, 102601 Overseas Hwy.* ☎ *305/451–6300* ⊕ *www.pennekamppark.com* ✉ *From $30.*

Horizon Divers. The company has customized diving and snorkeling trips that depart daily aboard a 45-foot catamaran. ⊠ *105800 Overseas Hwy* ☎ *305/453–3535, 800/984–3483* ⊕ *www.horizondivers.com* ✉ *From $50 for snorkeling, from $80 for diving.*

Island Ventures. If you like dry, British humor and no crowds, this is the operator for you. It specializes in small groups for snorkeling or dive trips, no more than 10 people per boat. Scuba trips are two tank, two locations, and include tanks and weights; ride-alongs pay just $35. Choose morning or afternoon. ⊠ *Jules Undersea Lodge, 51 Shoreland Dr.* ☎ *305/451–4957* ⊕ *www.islandventure.com* ✉ *Snorkel trips $50, diving $85.*

Ocean Divers. The PADI five-star facility has been around since 1975 and offers day and night dives, a range of courses, and dive-lodging packages. Two-tank reef dives include tank and weight rental. There are also organized snorkeling trips with equipment. ⊠ *MM 100 OS, 522 Caribbean Dr.* ☎ *305/451–1113, 800/451–1113* ⊕ *www.oceandivers.com* ✉ *Snorkel trips from $30, diving from $80.*

Fodor's Choice ★ **Quiescence Diving Services.** This operator sets itself apart in two ways: it limits groups to six to ensure personal attention and offers both two-dive day and night dives, as well as twilight dives when sea creatures are most active. There are also organized snorkeling excursions. ⊠ *MM 103.5 BS, 103680 Overseas Hwy.* ☎ *305/451–2440* ⊕ *www.quiescence.com* ✉ *Snorkel trips $49, diving from $69.*

ISLAMORADA

Islamorada is between MM 90.5 and 70.

Early settlers named this key after their schooner, *Island Home,* but to make it sound more romantic they translated it into Spanish: *Isla Morada.* The Chamber of Commerce prefers to use its literal translation, "Purple Island," which refers either to a purple-shelled snail that once inhabited these shores or to the brilliantly colored orchids and bougainvilleas.

Early maps show Islamorada as encompassing only Upper Matecumbe Key. But the incorporated "Village of Islands" is made up of a string of islands that the Overseas Highway crosses, including Plantation Key, Windley Key, Upper Matecumbe Key, Lower Matecumbe Key, Craig Key, and Fiesta Key. In addition, two state-park islands accessible only by boat—Indian Key and Lignumvitae Key—belong to the group.

Islamorada (locals pronounce it *"eye*-la-mor-*ah*-da") is one of the world's top fishing destinations. For nearly 100 years, seasoned anglers have fished these clear, warm waters teeming with trophy-worthy fish. There are numerous options for those in search of the big ones, including chartering a boat with its own crew or heading out on a vessel rented from one of the plethora of marinas along this 20-mile stretch of the Overseas Highway. More than 150 backcountry guides and 400 offshore captains are at your service.

GETTING HERE AND AROUND

Most visitors arrive in Islamorada by car. If you're flying in to Miami International Airport or Key West International Airport, you can easily rent a car (reserve in advance) to make the drive.

TOURS

Contact Florida Keys Food Tours. ☎ *305/393–9183* ⊕ *www.flkeysfoodtours.com.*

VISITOR INFORMATION

Contact Islamorada Chamber of Commerce & Visitors Center. ⊠ *MM 87.1 BS, 87100 Overseas Hwy.* ☎ *305/664–4503, 800/322–5397* ⊕ *www.islamorada-chamber.com.*

EXPLORING

TOP ATTRACTIONS

Florida Keys Memorial / Hurricane Monument. On Monday, September 2, 1935, more than 400 people perished when the most intense hurricane to make landfall in the United States swept through this area of the Keys. Two years later, the Florida Keys Memorial was dedicated in their honor. Native coral rock, known as keystone, covers the 18-foot obelisk monument that marks the remains of more than 300 storm

Islamorada's warm waters attract large fish and the anglers and charter captains who want to catch them.

victims. A sculpted plaque of bending palms and waves graces the front (although many are bothered that the palms are bending in the wrong direction). In 1995, the memorial was placed on the National Register of Historic Places. ⊠ *MM 81.8, in front of the public library, 81831 Old State Hwy. 4A, Upper Matecumbe Key* ✛ *Just south of the Cheeca Lodge entrance* ⌨ *Free.*

History of Diving Museum. Adding to the region's reputation for world-class diving, this museum plunges into the history of man's thirst for undersea exploration. Among its 13 galleries of interactive and other interesting displays are a submarine and helmet re-created from the film *20,000 Leagues Under the Sea.* Vintage U.S. Navy equipment, diving helmets from around the world, and early scuba gear explore 4,000 years of diving history. For the grand finale, spend $3 for a mouthpiece and sing your favorite tune at the helium bar. There are extended hours (until 7 pm) on the third Wednesday of every month. ⊠ *MM 83 BS, 82990 Overseas Hwy., Upper Matecumbe Key* ☎ *305/664–9737* ⊕ *www.divingmuseum.org* ⌨ *$12.*

FAMILY **Robbie's Marina.** Huge, prehistoric-looking denizens of the not-so-deep, silver-sided tarpon congregate around the docks at this marina on Lower Matecumbe Key. Children—and lots of adults—pay $3 for a bucket of sardines to feed them and $1 each for dock admission. Spend some time hanging out at this authentic Keys community, where you can grab a bite to eat indoors or out, shop at a slew of artisans' booths, or charter a boat, kayak, or other watercraft. ⊠ *MM 77.5 BS, 77522 Overseas Hwy., Lower Matecumbe Key* ☎ *305/664–9814, 877/664–8498* ⊕ *www.robbies.com* ⌨ *Dock access $1.*

FAMILY   **Theater of the Sea.** The second-oldest marine-mammal center in the world doesn't attempt to compete with more modern, more expensive parks. Even so, it's among the better attractions north of Key West, especially if you have kids in tow. In addition to marine-life exhibits and shows, you can make reservations for up-close-and-personal encounters like a swim with a dolphin or sea lion, or stingray and turtle feedings (which include general admission; reservations required). These are popular, so reserve in advance. Ride a "bottomless" boat to see what's below the waves and take a guided tour of the marine-life exhibits. Nonstop animal shows highlight conservation issues. You can stop for lunch at the grill, shop in the extensive gift shop, or sunbathe and swim at the private beach. This easily could be an all-day attraction. ⊠ *MM 84.5 OS, 84721 Overseas Hwy., Windley Key* ☎ *305/664–2431* ⊕ *www.theaterofthesea.com* ✉ *$31.95; interaction programs $45–$195.*

BEACHES

FAMILY   **Anne's Beach Park.** On Lower Matecumbe Key this popular village park is named for a local environmental activist. Its "beach" (really a typical Keys-style sand flat with a gentle slope) is best enjoyed at low tide. The nicest feature here is an elevated, wooden half-mile boardwalk that meanders through a natural wetland hammock. Covered picnic areas along the way give you places to linger and enjoy the view. Restrooms are at the north end. Weekends are packed with Miami day-trippers as it's the only public beach until you reach Marathon. **Amenities:** parking (no fee); toilets. **Best for:** partiers; snorkeling; swimming; windsurfing. ⊠ *MM 73.5 OS, Lower Matecumbe Key* ☎ *305/853–1685.*

WHERE TO EAT

$$$ ✕ **Chef Michael's.** This local favorite whose motto is "Peace. Love.
SEAFOOD   Hogfish." has been making big waves since its opening in 2011 with
Fodor'sChoice   chef Michael Ledwith at the helm. Seafood is selected fresh daily, then
★   elegantly prepared with a splash of tropical flair. **Known for:** fresh seafood daily; gluten-free and vegetarian options; melt-in-your-mouth steaks. ⑤ *Average main: $30* ⊠ *MM 81.7, 81671 Overseas Hwy., Upper Matecumbe Key* ☎ *305/664–0640* ⊕ *www.foodtotalkabout.com* ☉ *No lunch Mon.–Sat.*

$$$ ✕ **Green Turtle Inn.** This circa-1947 landmark inn and its vintage neon
SEAFOOD   sign is a slice of Florida Keys history. Period photographs decorate the wood-paneled walls. **Known for:** turtle chowder; a piece of Florida Keys history. ⑤ *Average main: $24* ⊠ *MM 81.2 OS, 81219 Overseas Hwy., Upper Matecumbe Key* ☎ *305/664–2006* ⊕ *www.greenturtlekeys.com* ☉ *Closed Mon.*

$$ ✕ **Hungry Tarpon.** As part of the colorful, bustling Old Florida scene
SEAFOOD   at Robbie's Marina, you know that the seafood here is fresh and top quality. The extensive menu seems as if it's bigger than the dining space, which consists of a few tables and counter seating indoors, plus tables out back under the mangrove trees, close to where tourists pay to feed the tarpon in the marina. **Known for:** extensive menu; heart-of-the-action location. ⑤ *Average main: $19* ⊠ *MM 77.5 BS, 77522 Overseas Hwy., Lower Matecumbe Key* ☎ *305/664–0535* ⊕ *www.hungrytarpon.com.*

$$ ✕ **Islamorada Fish Company.** When a restaurant is owned by Bass Pro
SEAFOOD   Shops, you know the seafood should be as fresh as you can get it. The
FAMILY   restaurant is housed in an open-air, oversized tiki hut right on Florida
Bay, making this the quintessential Keys experience. **Known for:** tour-
ist hot spot; great views; seafood baskets. $ *Average main: $18* ✉ *MM
81.5 BS, 81532 Overseas Hwy., Windley Key* ☎ *305/664–9271* ⊕ *res-
taurants.basspro.com/fishcompany/Islamorada/.*

$ ✕ **Island Grill at Snake Creek.** Don't be fooled by appearances; this shack
SEAFOOD   on the waterfront takes island breakfast, lunch, and dinner up a notch.
The eclectic menu tempts you with such dishes as its famed "original
tuna nachos," lobster rolls, and a nice selection of seafood and sand-
wiches. **Known for:** eclectic seafood options; slow service; nice views.
$ *Average main: $14* ✉ *MM 85.5 OS, 85501 Overseas Hwy., Windley
Key* ☎ *305/664–8400* ⊕ *www.keysislandgrill.com.*

$$$ ✕ **Kaiyo Grill & Sushi.** The decor—an inviting setting that includes col-
JAPANESE   orful abstract mosaics, polished wood floors, and upholstered ban-
quettes—almost steals the show at Kaiyo, but the food is equally
interesting. The menu, a fusion of East and West, offers sushi rolls that
combine local ingredients with traditional Japanese tastes. **Known for:**
excellent wine and sake pairings; show-stopping decor; East-meets-
West menu. $ *Average main: $28* ✉ *MM 81.5 OS, 81701 Overseas
Hwy., Upper Matecumbe Key* ☎ *305/664–5556* ⊕ *www.kaiyogrill.
com* ☽ *No lunch.*

$$ ✕ **Lorelei Restaurant & Cabana Bar.** While local anglers gather here for
AMERICAN   breakfast, lunch and dinner bring a mix of islanders and visitors for
straightforward food and front-row seats to the sunset. Live music
seven nights a week ensures a lively nighttime scene, and the menu
staves off inebriation with burgers, barbecued baby back ribs, and
Parmesan-crusted snapper. **Known for:** amazing sunset views; nightly
live music. $ *Average main: $15* ✉ *MM 82 BS, 81924 Overseas Hwy.,
Upper Matecumbe Key* ☎ *305/664–2692* ⊕ *www.loreleicabanabar.com.*

$$$$ ✕ **Marker 88.** A few yards from Florida Bay, this popular seafood res-
SEAFOOD   taurant has large picture windows that offer great sunset views. The
bay is lovely no matter what time of day you visit, though, and most
diners opt to sit outdoors. **Known for:** great outdoor seating; key lime
baked Alaska; extensive wine list. $ *Average main: $34* ✉ *MM 88
BS, 88000 Overseas Hwy., Plantation Key* ☎ *305/852–9315* ⊕ *www.
marker88.info.*

$$$ ✕ **Morada Bay Beach Café.** This bay-front restaurant wins high marks
ECLECTIC   for its surprisingly stellar cuisine, tables planted in the sand, and tiki
FAMILY   torches that bathe the evening in romance. Entrées feature alluring
combinations like fresh fish of the day sautéed with Meyer lemon butter and whole fried snapper with coconut rice. **Known for:** feet-in-
the-sand dining; full-moon parties. $ *Average main: $27* ✉ *MM 81
BS, 81600 Overseas Hwy., Upper Matecumbe Key* ☎ *305/664–0604*
⊕ *www.moradabay.com.*

$$$$ ✕ **Pierre's.** One of the Keys' most elegant restaurants, Pierre's marries
FRENCH   colonial style with modern food trends. Full of interesting architec-
Fodor's Choice   tural artifacts, the place oozes style, especially the wicker-chair-strewn
★   veranda overlooking the bay. **Known for:** romantic spot for that special

night out; seasonally changing menu; full-moon parties. ⑤ *Average main: $43* ✉ *MM 81.5 BS, 81600 Overseas Hwy., Upper Matecumbe Key* ☎ *305/664–3225* ⊕ *www.moradabay.com* ☾ *No lunch.*

WHERE TO STAY

$$
RESORT

⬚ **Amara Cay Resort.** Simple yet chic, Islamorada's newest resort is an oceanfront gem. **Pros:** free shuttle to local attractions; on-site dive shop; large heated pool. **Cons:** pricey $28 a day resort fee; expensive restaurant; living area of rooms lack seating. ⑤ *Rooms from: $299* ✉ *MM 80 OS, 80001 Overseas Hwy.* ☎ *305/664–0073* ⊕ *www.amaracayresort. com* ⇴ *110 rooms* ⑩ *No meals.*

$$$
B&B/INN
Fodor'sChoice
★

⬚ **Casa Morada.** This relic from the 1950s has been restyled into a suave, design-forward, all-suites property with outdoor showers and Jacuzzis in some of the suites. **Pros:** cool design; complimentary snacks and bottled water; complimentary use of bikes, kayaks, and snorkel gear. **Cons:** trailer park across the street; beach is small and inconsequential. ⑤ *Rooms from: $309* ✉ *MM 82 BS, 136 Madeira Rd., Upper Matecumbe Key* ☎ *305/664–0044, 888/881–3030* ⊕ *www.casamorada.com* ⇴ *16 suites* ⑩ *Breakfast.*

$$$$
RESORT
Fodor'sChoice
★

⬚ **Cheeca Lodge & Spa.** At 27 acres, this may be the largest resort in the Keys, and it's also big on included amenities. **Pros:** beautifully landscaped grounds; new designer rooms; water-sports center on property. **Cons:** expensive rates; expensive resort fee; very busy. ⑤ *Rooms from: $499* ✉ *MM 82 OS, 81801 Overseas Hwy., Upper Matecumbe Key* ☎ *305/664–4651, 800/327–2888* ⊕ *www.cheeca.com* ⇴ *123 rooms* ⑩ *No meals.*

$
HOTEL

⬚ **Drop Anchor Resort and Marina.** Immaculately maintained, this place has the feel of an old friend's beach house. **Pros:** bright and colorful; attention to detail; laid-back charm. **Cons:** noise from the highway; beach is better for fishing than swimming. ⑤ *Rooms from: $159* ✉ *MM 85 OS, 84959 Overseas Hwy., Windley Key* ☎ *305/664–4863, 888/664–4863* ⊕ *www.dropanchorresort.com* ⇴ *18 suites* ⑩ *No meals.*

$$
RESORT

⬚ **The Islander Resort, A Guy Harvey Outpost.** Guests here get to choose between a self-sufficient townhome on the bay side or an oceanfront resort with on-site restaurants and oodles of amenities. **Pros:** spacious rooms; nice kitchens; eye-popping views. **Cons:** pricey for what you get; beach has rough sand. ⑤ *Rooms from: $249* ✉ *MM 82.1 OS, 82200 Overseas Hwy., Upper Matecumbe Key* ☎ *305/664–2031, 800/753–6002* ⊕ *www.guyharveyoutpostislamorada.com* ⇴ *122 rooms, 24 townhomes* ⑩ *Breakfast.*

$$$$
HOTEL
Fodor'sChoice
★

⬚ **The Moorings Village.** This tropical retreat is everything you imagine when you envision the laid-back Keys—from hammocks swaying between towering trees to manicured sand lapped by aqua-green waves. **Pros:** romantic setting; good dining options with room-charging privileges; beautiful views. **Cons:** no room service; $25 daily resort fee for activities. ⑤ *Rooms from: $529* ✉ *MM 81.6 OS, 123 Beach Rd., Upper Matecumbe Key* ☎ *305/664–4708* ⊕ *www.themooringsvillage. com* ⇴ *18 cottages* ⑩ *No meals.*

$$$
HOTEL
Fodor'sChoice
★

⬚ **Ocean House.** This adults-only boutique hotel is situated right on the Atlantic, yet it's hidden from passersby amid lush gardens. **Pros:** complimentary use of kayaks, snorkel equipment, and bicycles; luxurious facilities and amenities. **Cons:** limited number of units means it's often booked solid; luxury comes at a price. $ *Rooms from: $319* ✉ *MM 82 OS, 82885 Old Hwy., Windley Key* ☎ *866/540–5520* ⊕ *www.ocean-housefloridakeys.com* ⇆ *8 suites* ¶⊙¶ *Some meals.*

$$
RESORT
🖼 **Postcard Inn Beach Resort & Marina at Holiday Isle.** After an $11 million renovation that encompassed updating everything from the rooms to the public spaces, this iconic property (formerly known as the Holiday Isle Beach Resort) has found new life. **Pros:** large private beach; heated pools; on-site restaurants including Ciao Hound Italian Kitchen. **Cons:** rooms near tiki bar are noisy; minimum stay required during peak times; rooms without an oceanfront view overlook a parking lot. $ *Rooms from: $267* ✉ *MM 84 OS, 84001 Overseas Hwy., Plantation Key* ☎ *305/664–2321* ⊕ *www.holidayisle.com* ⇆ *143 rooms* ¶⊙¶ *No meals.*

$
HOTEL
FAMILY
🖼 **Ragged Edge Resort.** Nicely tucked away in a residential area at the ocean's edge, this family-owned hotel draws returning guests who'd rather fish off the dock and grill up dinner than loll around in Egyptian cotton sheets. **Pros:** oceanfront; boat docks and ramp; cheap rates. **Cons:** dated decor; off the beaten path. $ *Rooms from: $169* ✉ *MM 86.5 OS, 243 Treasure Harbor Rd., Plantation Key* ☎ *305/852–5389, 800/436–2023* ⊕ *www.ragged-edge.com* ⇆ *10 units* ¶⊙¶ *No meals.*

SHOPPING

Art galleries, upscale gift shops, and the mammoth World Wide Sportsman (if you want to look the part of a local fisherman, you must wear a shirt from here) make up the variety and superior style of Islamorada shopping.

Banyan Tree. Stroll and shop among the colorful orchids and lush plants at this outdoor garden and indoor boutique known for its tropical splendor, unique gifts, and free-spirited clothing. There is nothing quite like it in the area. ✉ *MM 81.2 OS, 81197 Overseas Hwy., Upper Matecumbe Key* ☎ *305/664–3433* ⊕ *www.banyantreegarden.com* ☽ *Closed Sun.*

Casa Mar Village. Change is good, and in this case, it's fantastic. What was once a row of worn-down buildings is now a merry blend of gift shops and galleries with the added bonus of a place selling fresh-roasted coffee. By day, these colorful shops glisten at their canal-front location; by nightfall, they're lit up like a lovely Christmas town. The offerings include What The Fish Rolls & More restaurant; Casa Mar Seafood fish market; and Paddle The Florida Keys, where you can rent paddleboards and kayaks. ✉ *MM 90 OS, 90775 Old Hwy., Upper Matecumbe Key* ⊕ *www.casamarvillage.com.*

Gallery Morada. This gallery is a go-to destination for one-of-a-kind gifts, beautifully displayed blown glass, original sculptures, paintings, and jewelry by 200 artists. Its location, front and center, makes it the gateway to the Morada Way Arts and Cultural District, an area with artist galleries, shops, potters, gardens, and culinary classes. ✉ *MM 81.6 OS, 81611 Old Hwy., Upper Matecumbe Key* ☎ *305/664–3650* ⊕ *www.gallerymorada.com.*

Rain Barrel Artisan Village. This is a natural and unhurried shopping showplace. Set in a tropical garden of shady trees, native shrubs, and orchids, the crafts village has shops selling the work of local and national artists as well as resident artists who sell work from their own studios. Take a selfie with "Betsy," the giant Florida lobster, roadside. ⊠ *MM 86.7 BS, 86700 Overseas Hwy., Plantation Key* ☎ *305/852–3084* ⊕ *www. seefloridaonline.com/rainbarrel/index.html.*

Redbone Gallery. This gallery stocks hand-stitched clothing, giftware, and jewelry, in addition to works of art by watercolorists C.D. Clarke, Christine Black, and Julie Joyce; and painters David Hall, Steven Left, Tim Borski, and Jorge Martinez. Proceeds benefit cystic fibrosis research. Find them in the Morada Way Arts & Cultural District. ⊠ *MM 81.5 OS, 200 Morada Way, Upper Matecumbe Key* ☎ *305/664–2002* ⊕ *www.redbone.org.*

World Wide Sportsman. This two-level retail center sells upscale and everyday fishing equipment, resort clothing, sportfishing art, and other gifts. When you're tired of shopping, relax at the Zane Grey Long Key Lounge, located on the second level—but not before you step up and into *Pilar,* a replica of Hemingway's boat. ⊠ *MM 81.5 BS, 81576 Overseas Hwy., Upper Matecumbe Key* ☎ *305/664–4615, 800/327–2880.*

SPORTS AND THE OUTDOORS

BOATING

Bump & Jump. You can rent both fishing and deck boats here (from 15 to 29 feet) by the day or the week. Free local delivery with seven-day rentals from each of their locations is available. ⊠ *MM 85.9 BS and 99.7 OS, 85920 Overseas Hwy., Upper Matecumbe Key* ☎ *305/664–9404, 877/453–9463* ⊕ *www.keysboatrental.com* ▱ *Rentals from $185 per day.*

Early Bird Fishing Charters. Captain Ross knows these waters well and he'll hook you up with whatever is in season—mahimahi, sailfish, tuna, and wahoo, to name a few—while you cruise on a comfy and stylish 43-foot custom Willis charter boat. The salon is air-conditioned for those hot summer days, and everything but booze and food is included. ⊠ *Postcard Inn Marina, MM 84.5 OS, 84001 Overseas Hwy.* ☎ *305/942–3618* ⊕ *www.fishearlybird.com* ▱ *4 hrs $800; 6 hrs $1,000; 8 hrs $1,200.*

Nauti-Limo. Captain Joe Fox has converted the design of a 1983 pink Caddy stretch limo into a less-than-luxurious but certainly curious watercraft. The seaworthy hybrid—complete with wheels—can sail with the top down if you're in the mood. Only in the Keys! One-hour and longer tours are available. ⊠ *Lorelei Restaurant & Yacht Club, MM 82 BS, 96 Madeira Rd., Upper Matecumbe Key* ☎ *305/942–3793* ⊕ *www.nautilimo.com* ▱ *From $60.*

Robbie's Boat Rentals & Charters. This full-service company will even give you a crash course on how not to crash your boat. The rental fleet includes an 18-foot skiff with a 90-horsepower outboard to a 21-foot deck boat with a 130-horsepower engine. Robbie's also rents snorkeling gear (there's good snorkeling nearby) and sells bait, drinks, and snacks. Want to hire a guide who knows the local waters and where the fish lurk? Robbie's offers offshore-fishing trips, patch-reef trips, and party-boat fishing. Backcountry flats trips are a specialty. ⊠ *MM 77.5 BS, 77522 Overseas Hwy., Lower Matecumbe Key* ☎ *305/664–9814, 877/664–8498* ⊕ *www.robbies.com* ▱ *From $185 per day.*

Kayak ready to be used on the beach in the Florida Keys

FISHING

Here in the self-proclaimed "Sportfishing Capital of the World," sailfish is the prime catch in the winter and mahimahi in the summer. Buchanan Bank just south of Islamorada is a good spot to try for tarpon in the spring. Blackfin tuna and amberjack are generally plentiful in the area, too. ■TIP→ **The Hump at Islamorada ranks highest among anglers' favorite fishing spots in Florida (declared Florida Monthly magazine's best for seven years in a row) due to the incredible offshore marine life.**

Captain Ted Wilson. Go into the backcountry for bonefish, tarpon, redfish, snook, and shark aboard a 17-foot boat that accommodates up to three anglers. Choose half-day (four hours), three-quarter-day (six hours), or full-day (eight hours) trips, or evening tarpon fishing excursions. Rates are for one or two anglers. There's a $75 charge for an additional person. ⊠ *MM 79.9 OS, 79851 Overseas Hwy., Upper Matecumbe Key* ☎ *305/942–5224, 305/664–9463* ⊕ *www.captaintedwilson.com* 🖃 *Half-day and evening trips from $450.*

Florida Keys Fly Fish. Like other top fly-fishing and light-tackle guides, Captain Geoff Colmes helps his clients land trophy fish in the waters around the Keys, from Islamorada to Flamingo in the Everglades. ⊠ *105 Palm La., Upper Matecumbe Key* ☎ *305/853–0741* ⊕ *www.florida-keysflyfish.com* 🖃 *From $550.*

Florida Keys Outfitters. Long before fly-fishing became popular, Sandy Moret was fishing the Keys for bonefish, tarpon, and redfish. Now he attracts anglers from around the world on a quest for the big catch. His weekend fly-fishing classes include classroom instruction, equipment, and daily lunch. Guided fishing trips can be done for a half day or

DID YOU KNOW?

The coral making up the Barrier Reef is living and provides an ecosystem for small marine creatures. Bumping against or touching the coral can kill these creatures as well as damage the reef itself.

full day. Packages combining fishing and accommodations at Islander Resort are available. ✉ *Green Turtle, MM 81.2, 81219 Overseas Hwy., Upper Matecumbe Key* ☎ *305/664–5423* ⊕ *www.floridakeysoutfitters. com* 🖘 *Half-day trips from $495.*

Hubba Hubba Charters. Captain Ken Knudsen has fished the Keys waters since the 1950s. A licensed backcountry guide, he's ranked among Florida's top 10 by national fishing magazines. He offers four-hour sunset trips for tarpon and two-hour sunset trips for bonefish, as well as half- and full-day outings. Prices are for one or two anglers, and tackle and bait are included. ✉ *Bud n' Mary's Marina, MM 79.8 OS, Upper Matecumbe Key* ☎ *305/664–9281* 🖘 *From $250.*

Miss Islamorada. This 65-foot party boat offers full-day trips. Bring your lunch or buy one from the dockside deli. ✉ *Bud n' Mary's Marina, MM 79.8 OS, 79851 Overseas Hwy., Upper Matecumbe Key* ☎ *305/664–2461, 800/742–7945* ⊕ *www.budnmarys.com* 🖘 *$65.*

SCUBA DIVING AND SNORKELING

San Pedro Underwater Archaeological Preserve State Park. About 1¼ nautical miles south of Indian Key is the San Pedro Underwater Archaeological Preserve State Park, which includes the remains of a Spanish treasure-fleet ship that sank in 1733. The state of Florida protects the site for divers; no spearfishing or souvenir collecting is allowed. Seven replica cannons and a plaque enhance what basically amounts to a 90-foot-long pile of ballast stones. Resting in only 18 feet of water, its ruins are visible to snorkelers as well as divers and attract a colorful array of fish. ✉ *MM 85.5 OS* ☎ *305/664–2540* ⊕ *www.floridastateparks.org/sanpedro.*

Florida Keys Dive Center. Dive from John Pennekamp Coral Reef State Park to Alligator Reef with this outfitter. The center has two 46-foot Coast Guard–approved dive boats, offers scuba training, and is one of the few Keys dive centers to offer Nitrox and Trimix (mixed gas) diving. ✉ *MM 90.5 OS, 90451 Overseas Hwy., Plantation Key* ☎ *305/852–4599, 800/433–8946* ⊕ *www.floridakeysdivectr.com* 🖘 *Snorkeling from $38, diving from $65.*

Islamorada Dive Center. This one-stop dive shop has a resort, pool, restaurant, lessons, and twice-daily dive and snorkel trips and the newest fleet in the Keys. You can take a day trip with a two-tank dive or a one-tank night trip with their equipment or yours. Snorkel and spearfishing trips are also available. ✉ *MM 84 OS, 84001 Overseas Hwy., Windley Key* ☎ *305/664–3483, 800/327–7070* ⊕ *www.islamoradadivecenter. com* 🖘 *Snorkel trips from $45, diving from $85.*

WATER SPORTS

The Kayak Shack. You can rent kayaks for trips to Indian (about 20 minutes one way) and Lignumvitae (about 45 minutes one way) keys, two favorite destinations for paddlers. Kayaks can be rented for a half day (and you'll need plenty of time to explore those mangrove canopies). The company also offers guided two-hour tours, including a snorkel trip to Indian Key or backcountry ecotours. It also rents stand-up paddleboards, including instruction, and canoes. ✉ *Robbie's Marina, MM 77.5 BS, 77522 Overseas Hwy., Lower Matecumbe Key* ☎ *305/664–4878* ⊕ *www.kayaktheflorida-keys.com* 🖘 *From $40 for single, $55 for double; guided trips from $45.*

THE MIDDLE KEYS

Most of the activity in the Middle Keys revolves around the town of Marathon, the region's third-largest metropolitan area. On either end of it, smaller keys hold resorts, wildlife research and rehab facilities, a historic village, and a state park. The Middle Keys make a fitting transition from the Upper Keys to the Lower Keys not only geographically but also mentally. Crossing Seven Mile Bridge prepares you for the slow pace and don't-give-a-damn attitude you'll find a little farther down the highway. Fishing is one of the main attractions—in fact, the region's commercial fishing industry was founded here in the early 1800s. Diving is another popular pastime. There are also beaches and natural areas to enjoy in the Middle Keys, where mainland stress becomes an ever more distant memory.

DUCK KEY

MM 61.

Duck Key holds one of the region's nicest marina resorts, Hawks Cay, plus a boating-oriented residential community.

WHERE TO EAT

$$$ ✕ **Alma.** A refreshing escape from the Middle Keys' same-old menus,
LATIN AMERICAN Alma serves expertly prepared Florida and Latin-Caribbean dishes in an elegant setting. Nightly changing menus might include a trio of dishes that could include ceviche, ahi tuna with a wonderful garbanzo bean tomato sauce, gnocchi and exotic mushroom ragout, or pan-seared Wagyu steak. **Known for:** seafood and steaks with a Latin influence; nightly changing menu; high prices. ⑤ *Average main: $28 ⊠ Hawks Cay Resort, 61 Hawks Cay Blvd. ☎ 305/743–7000, 888/432–2242 ⊕ www. hawkscay.com ☺ No lunch.*

WHERE TO STAY

$$$ ⛱ **Hawks Cay Resort.** The 60-acre, Caribbean-style retreat with a full-ser-
RESORT vice spa and restaurants has plenty to keep the kids occupied (and adults
FAMILY happy). **Pros:** huge rooms; restful spa; full-service marina and dive
Fodor'sChoice shop. **Cons:** no real beach; far from Marathon's attractions. ⑤ *Rooms*
★ *from: $315 ⊠ MM 61 OS, 61 Hawks Cay Blvd. ☎ 305/743–7000, 888/432–2242 ⊕ www.hawkscay.com ☞ 161 rooms, 16 suites, 254 2- and 3-bedroom villas* ⍾ *No meals.*

GRASSY KEY

MM 60–57.

Local lore has it that this sleepy little key was named not for its vegetation—mostly native trees and shrubs—but for an early settler by the name of Grassy. A few families operating small fishing camps and roadside motels primarily inhabit the key. There's no marked definition between it and Marathon, so it feels sort of like a suburb of its much larger neighbor to the south. Grassy Key's sights tend toward the natural, including a worthwhile dolphin attraction and a small state park.

DID YOU KNOW?

Dolphins in Florida are predominantly of the Atlantic bottlenose variety. These playful and smart creatures love to leap out of the water and synchronize their movements with others. By swimming next to boats, dolphins can conserve energy.

GETTING HERE AND AROUND

Most visitors arriving by air drive to this destination either from Miami International Airport or Key West International Airport. Rental cars are readily available at both, and in the long run, are the most convenient means of transportation for getting here and touring around the Keys.

EXPLORING

TOP ATTRACTIONS

Curry Hammock State Park. Looking for a slice of the Keys that's far removed from tiki bars? On the ocean and bay sides of Overseas Highway are 260 acres of upland hammock, wetlands, and mangroves. On the bay side, there's a trail through thick hardwoods to a rocky shoreline. The ocean side is more developed, with a sandy beach, a clean bathhouse, picnic tables, a playground, grills, and a 28-site campground, each with electric and water. Locals consider the paddling trails under canopies of arching mangroves one of the best kayaking spots in the Keys. Manatees frequent the area, and it's a great spot for bird-watching. Herons, egrets, ibis, plovers, and sanderlings are commonly spotted. Raptors are often seen in the park, especially during migration periods. ⊠ *MM 57 OS, 56200 Overseas Hwy., Little Crawl Key* ☎ *305/289–2690* ⊕ *www. floridastateparks.org/curryhammock* 🖾 *$4.50 for 1 person, $6 for 2, 50¢ per additional person* ☞ *Campsites are $43 per night.*

FAMILY **Dolphin Research Center.** The 1963 movie *Flipper* popularized the notion of humans interacting with dolphins, and Milton Santini, the film's creator, also opened this center, which is home to a colony of dolphins and sea lions. The nonprofit center has educational sessions and programs that allow you to greet the dolphins from dry land or play with them in their watery habitat. You can even paint a T-shirt with a dolphin—you pick the paint, the dolphin "designs" your shirt. The center also offers five-day programs for children and adults with disabilities. ⊠ *MM 59 BS, 58901 Overseas Hwy.* ☎ *305/289–1121 information, 305/289–0002 reservations* ⊕ *www.dolphins.org* 🖾 *$28.*

WHERE TO EAT

$$$ ✕ **Hideaway Café.** The name says it all. Tucked between Grassy Key
AMERICAN and Marathon, it's easy to miss if you're mindlessly driving through the middle islands. **Known for:** seclusion and quiet; amazing escargot; hand-cut steaks and fresh fish. ⑤ *Average main: $30* ⊠ *Rainbow Bend Resort, MM 58 OS, 57784 Overseas Hwy.* ☎ *305/289–1554* ⊕ *www. hideawaycafe.com* ☾ *No lunch.*

MARATHON

MM 53–47.5.

New Englanders founded this former fishing village in the early 1800s. The community on Vaca Key subsequently served as a base for pirates, salvagers (also known as "wreckers"), spongers, and, later, Bahamian farmers who eked out a living growing cotton and other crops. More Bahamians arrived in the hope of finding work building the railroad. According to local lore, Marathon was renamed when a worker commented that it was a marathon task to position the tracks across the 6-mile-long island.

During the building of the railroad, Marathon developed a reputation for lawlessness that rivaled that of the Old West. It is said that to keep the rowdy workers from descending on Key West for their off-hours endeavors, residents would send boatloads of liquor up to Marathon. Needless to say, things have quieted down considerably since then.

Still, Marathon is a bustling town, at least compared to other communities in the Keys. As it leaves something to be desired in the charm department, Marathon may not be your first choice of places to stay, but water-sports types will find plenty to enjoy, and its historic and natural attractions merit a visit. Surprisingly good dining options abound, so you'll definitely want to stop for a bite even if you're just passing through on the way to Key West.

Throughout the year, Marathon hosts fishing tournaments (practically monthly), a huge seafood festival in March, and lighted boat parades around the holidays.

GETTING HERE AND AROUND

SuperShuttle charges $102 per passenger for trips from Miami International Airport to the Upper Keys. To go farther into the Keys, you must book an entire 11-person van, which costs about $280 to Marathon. For a trip to the airport, place your request 24 hours in advance. *See Getting Here and Around: Bus Travel.*

VISITOR INFORMATION

Contact Greater Marathon Chamber of Commerce and Visitor Center.
✉ MM 53.5 BS, 12222 Overseas Hwy. ☎ 305/743–5417, 800/262–7284 ⊕ www.floridakeysmarathon.com.

EXPLORING

TOP ATTRACTIONS

FAMILY **Crane Point Museum, Nature Center, and Historic Site.** Tucked away from the highway behind a stand of trees, Crane Point—part of a 63-acre tract that contains the last-known undisturbed thatch-palm hammock—is delightfully undeveloped. This multiuse facility includes the **Museum of Natural History of the Florida Keys,** which has displays about local wildlife, a seashell exhibit, and a marine-life display that makes you feel you're at the bottom of the sea. Kids love the replica 17th-century galleon and pirate dress-up room where they can play, and the re-created **Cracker House** filled with insects, sea-turtle exhibits, and children's activities. On the 1-mile indigenous loop trail, visit the **Laura Quinn Wild Bird Center** and the remnants of a Bahamian village, site of the restored **George Adderly House.** It is the oldest surviving example of Bahamian tabby (a concretelike material created from sand and seashells) construction outside of Key West. A boardwalk crosses wetlands, rivers, and mangroves before ending at Adderly Village. From November to Easter, docent-led tours are available; bring good walking shoes and bug repellent during warm weather. ✉ MM 50.5 BS, 5550 Overseas Hwy. ☎ 305/743–9100 ⊕ www.cranepoint.net ⌨ $14.95.

FAMILY **Florida Keys Aquarium Encounters.** This isn't your typical large-city aquarium. It's more hands-on and personal, and it's all outdoors with several tiki huts to house the encounters and provide shade as you explore, rain or shine; plan to spend at least two to three hours here. You'll find a 200,000-gallon aquarium and plenty of marine encounters (extra cost), as well as guided tours, viewing areas, and a predator tank. The Coral Reef encounter ($95 snorkel, $130 scuba) lets you dive in a reef environment without hearing the theme from *Jaws* in your head (although you can see several sharks on the other side of the glass). Touch tanks are great for all ages and even have unique critters like slipper lobsters. Hungry? The on-site Eagle Ray Cafe serves up wings, fish tacos, salads, burgers, and more. Note that general admission is required, even if you're signed up for a marine encounter. ✉ *MM 53 BS, 11710 Overseas Hwy.* ☎ *305/407–3262* ⊕ *www.floridakeysaquariumencounters.com* ✉ *$20.*

Pigeon Key. There's much to like about this 5-acre island under the Old Seven Mile Bridge. You might even recognize it from a season finale of the TV show *The Amazing Race.* You can reach it via a ferry that departs from behind the visitor center (look for the old red railroad car on Knight's Key, MM 47 OS). Once there, tour the island on your own or join a guided tour to explore the buildings that formed the early-20th-century work camp for the Overseas Railroad that linked the mainland to Key West in 1912. Later the island became a fish camp, a state park, and then government-administration headquarters. Exhibits in a small museum recall the history of the Keys, the railroad, and railroad baron Henry M. Flagler. The ferry ride with tour lasts two hours; visitors can self-tour and catch the ferry back in a half hour. ■ TIP→ Bring your own snorkel gear and dive flag and you can snorkel right from the shore. ✉ *MM 45 OS, 1 Knights Key Blvd., Pigeon Key* ☎ *305/743–5999* ⊕ *pigeonkey.net* ✉ *$12.*

Seven Mile Bridge. This is one of the most photographed images in the Keys. Actually measuring slightly less than 7 miles, it connects the Middle and Lower keys and is believed to be the world's longest segmental bridge. It has 39 expansion joints separating its various concrete sections. Each April runners gather in Marathon for the annual Seven Mile Bridge Run. The expanse running parallel to Seven Mile Bridge is what remains of the **Old Seven Mile Bridge,** an engineering and architectural marvel in its day that's now on the National Register of Historic Places. Once proclaimed the Eighth Wonder of the World, it rested on a record 546 concrete piers. No cars are allowed on the old bridge today. ✉ *Marathon.*

FAMILY **The Turtle Hospital.** More than 100 injured sea turtles check in here every year. The 90-minute guided tours take you into recovery and surgical areas at the world's only state-certified veterinary hospital for sea turtles. In the "hospital bed" tanks, you can see recovering patients and others that are permanent residents due to their injuries. After the tour, you can feed some of the "residents." Call ahead—space is limited and tours are sometimes canceled due to medical emergencies. The turtle ambulance out front makes for a memorable souvenir photo. ✉ *MM 48.5 BS, 2396 Overseas Hwy.* ☎ *305/743–2552* ⊕ *www.turtlehospital.org* ✉ *$22.*

BEACHES

FAMILY   **Sombrero Beach.** No doubt one of the best beaches in the Keys, here you'll find pleasant, shaded picnic areas that overlook a coconut palm–lined grassy stretch and the Atlantic Ocean. Roped-off areas allow swimmers, boaters, and windsurfers to share the narrow cove. Facilities include barbecue grills, a large playground, a pier, a volleyball court, and a paved, lighted bike path off Overseas Highway. Sunday afternoons draw lots of local families toting coolers. The park is accessible for those with disabilities and allows leashed pets. Turn east at the traffic light in Marathon and follow signs to the end. **Amenities:** showers; toilets. **Best for:** swimming; windsurfing. ⊠ *MM 50 OS, Sombrero Beach Rd.* ☎ *305/743–0033* ⚏ *Free.*

WHERE TO EAT

$ ✕**Fish Tales Market and Eatery.** This no-frills, roadside eatery has a loyal
SEAFOOD   local following, an unfussy ambience, a couple of outside picnic tables, and friendly service. Signature dishes include snapper on grilled rye with coleslaw and melted Muenster cheese, a fried fish burrito, and lobster bisque or tomato-based conch chowder. **Known for:** luscious lobster bisque; fresh and affordable seafood market; closing early. ⑤ *Average main: $9* ⊠ *MM 52.5 OS, 11711 Overseas Hwy.* ☎ *305/743–9196, 888/662–4822* ⊕ *www.floridalobster.com* ⊘ *Closed Sun. No dinner Sat.*

$$ ✕**Key Colony Inn.** The inviting aroma of an Italian kitchen pervades this
ITALIAN   family-owned favorite known for its Sunday brunch, served November through April. For lunch there are fish and steak entrées served with fries, salad, and bread in addition to Italian specialties. **Known for:** friendly and attentive service; Italian specialties; Sunday brunch. ⑤ *Average main: $20* ⊠ *MM 54 OS, 700 W. Ocean Dr., Key Colony Beach* ☎ *305/743–0100* ⊕ *www.kcinn.com.*

$$ ✕**Keys Fisheries Market & Marina.** From the parking lot, you can't miss
SEAFOOD   the enormous tiki bar on stilts, but the walk-up window on the ground
FAMILY   floor is the heart of this warehouse-turned-restaurant. Order at the window, pick up your food, then dine at one of the waterfront tables outfitted with rolls of paper towels. **Known for:** huge lobster Reuben; walk-up takeout window; adults-only upstairs tiki bar. ⑤ *Average main: $16* ⊠ *MM 49 BS, 3390 Gulfview Ave., at the end of 35th St.* ✛ *Turn onto 35th St. from Overseas Hwy.* ☎ *305/743–4353, 866/743–4353* ⊕ *www.keysfisheries.com.*

$$$ ✕**Lazy Days South.** Tucked into Marathon Marina a half mile north of the
SEAFOOD   Seven Mile Bridge, this restaurant offers views just as spectacular as its
Fodor'sChoice   highly lauded food. A spin-off of an Islamorada favorite, here you'll find
★   a wide range of daily offerings from fried or sautéed conch and a coconut-fried fish du jour sandwich to seafood pastas and beef tips over rice. **Known for:** water views; delicious seafood entrées. ⑤ *Average main: $22* ⊠ *MM 47.3 OS, 725 11th St.* ☎ *305/289–0839* ⊕ *www.lazydayssouth.com.*

$ ✕**The Stuffed Pig.** With only nine tables and a counter inside, this break-
DINER   fast-and-lunch place is always hopping. When the weather's right, grab a table out back. **Known for:** famous "pig's" breakfast; daily lunch specials; large portions. ⑤ *Average main: $9* ⊠ *MM 49 BS, 3520 Overseas Hwy.* ☎ *305/743–4059* ⊕ *www.thestuffedpig.com* ▭ *No credit cards* ⊘ *No dinner.*

$$$
SEAFOOD

✕ **Sunset Grille & Raw Bar.** After a walk or bike ride along the Old Seven Mile Bridge, treat yourself to a seafood lunch or dinner at this vaulted tiki hut by the bridge. For lunch, start with the conch chowder or fritters, and then move on to the Voodoo grouper sandwich topped with mango-guava mayo, and finish with a tasty key lime pie. **Known for:** weekend pool parties and barbecues; creative dinner specials. ⑤ *Average main: $22 ⊠ MM 47 OS, 7 Knights Key Blvd.* ☎ *305/396–7235* ⊕ *www.sunsetgrille7milebridge.com.*

WHERE TO STAY

$$
RENTAL

⌂ **Glunz Ocean Beach Hotel & Resort.** The Glunz family got it right when they purchased this former time-share property and put a whole lot of love into renovating it to its full oceanfront potential. **Pros:** oceanfront; helpful service; excellent free Wi-Fi. **Cons:** neighbor noise; small elevator; no interior corridors; not cheap. ⑤ *Rooms from: $280 ⊠ MM 53.5 OS, 351 E. Ocean Dr., Key Colony Beach* ☎ *305/289–0525* ⊕ *www. GlunzOceanBeachHotel.com* ⊃ *38 rooms, 8 villas* ⌶⌶ *No meals.*

$$$$
RESORT
FAMILY
Fodor's Choice
★

⌂ **Tranquility Bay.** Ralph Lauren could have designed the rooms at this stylish, luxurious resort on a nice beach. **Pros:** secluded setting; gorgeous design; lovely crescent beach. **Cons:** a bit sterile; no real Keys atmosphere; cramped building layout. ⑤ *Rooms from: $425 ⊠ MM 48.5 BS, 2600 Overseas Hwy.* ☎ *305/289–0888, 866/643–5397* ⊕ *www.tranquilitybay.com* ⊃ *102 rooms* ⌶⌶ *No meals.*

SPORTS AND THE OUTDOORS
BIKING

Tooling around on two wheels is a good way to see Marathon. There's easy cycling on a 1-mile off-road path that connects to the 2 miles of the Old Seven Mile Bridge leading to Pigeon Key.

Bike Marathon Bike Rentals. "Have bikes, will deliver" could be the motto of this company, which gets beach cruisers to your hotel door, including a helmet and basket. They also rent kayaks. Note that there's no physical location, but services are available Monday through Saturday 9–4 and Sunday 9–2. ⊠ *Marathon* ☎ *305/743–3204* ⊕ *www.bikemarathonbikerentals.com* ▭ *$45 per wk.*

Overseas Outfitters. Aluminum cruisers and hybrid bikes are available for rent at this outfitter. It's open weekdays 9–5:30 and Saturday 9–3. All rentals include a helmet and lock. ⊠ *MM 48 BS, 1700 Overseas Hwy.* ☎ *305/289–1670* ⊕ *www.overseasoutfitters.com* ▭ *Rentals from $15 per day.*

BOATING

Sail, motor, or paddle: whatever your choice of modes, boating is what the Keys is all about. Brave the Atlantic waves and reefs or explore the backcountry islands on the gulf side. If you don't have a lot of boating and chart-reading experience, it's a good idea to tap into local knowledge on a charter.

Captain Pip's. This operator rents 18- to 24-foot outboards as well as tackle and snorkeling gear. Fishing charters are also available with a captain and a mate (full-day charters are also available). Ask about multiday deals, or try one of their accommodation packages and walk right from your bay-front room to your boat. ⊠ *MM 47.5 BS, 1410 Overseas Hwy.* ☎ *305/743–4403, 800/707–1692* ⊕ *www. captainpips.com* ⌨ *Rentals from $195 per day; half-day charters from $650.*

Fish 'n Fun. Get out on the water on 19- to 26-foot powerboats. Rentals can be for a half or full day. The company also offers free delivery in the Middle Keys. ⊠ *Duck Key Marina, MM 61 OS, 1149 Greenbriar Rd.* ☎ *305/743–2275, 800/471–3440* ⊕ *www.fishnfunrentals.com* ⌨ *From $175.*

FISHING

For recreational anglers, the deepwater fishing is superb in both bay and ocean. Marathon West Hump, one good spot, has depths ranging from 500 to more than 1,000 feet. Locals fish from a half dozen bridges, including Long Key Bridge, the Old Seven Mile Bridge, and both ends of Tom's Harbor. Barracuda, bonefish, and tarpon all frequent local waters. Party boats and private charters are available.

Marathon Lady. Morning, afternoon, and night, fish for mahimahi, grouper, and other tasty catch aboard this 73-footer, which departs on half-day excursions from the Vaca Cut Bridge (MM 53), north of Marathon. Join the crew for night fishing ($55) from 6:30 to midnight from Memorial Day to Labor Day; it's especially beautiful on a full-moon night. ⊠ *MM 53 OS, 11711 Overseas Hwy., at 117th St.* ☎ *305/743–5580* ⊕ *www.marathonlady.net* ⌨ *From $50.*

Sea Dog Charters. Captain Jim Purcell, a deep-sea specialist for ESPN's *The American Outdoorsman,* provides one of the best values in Keys fishing. Next to the Seven Mile Grill, his company offers half- and full-day offshore, reef and wreck, and backcountry fishing trips, as well as fishing and snorkeling trips aboard 30- to 37-foot boats. The per-person for a half-day trip is the same regardless of whether your group fills the boat, and includes bait, light tackle, ice, coolers, and fishing licenses. If you prefer an all-day private charter on a 37-foot boat, he offers those, too, for up to six people. A fuel surcharge may apply. ⊠ *MM 47.5 BS, 1248 Overseas Hwy.* ☎ *305/743–8255* ⊕ *www. seadogcharters.net* ⌨ *From $60.*

SCUBA DIVING AND SNORKELING

Local dive operations take you to Sombrero Reef and Lighthouse, the most popular down-under destination in these parts. For a shallow dive and some lobster nabbing, Coffins Patch, off Key Colony Beach, is a good choice. A number of wrecks such as *Thunderbolt* serve as artificial reefs. Many operations out of this area will also take you to Looe Key Reef.

Hall's Diving Center & Career Institute. The institute has been training divers for more than 40 years. Along with conventional twice-a-day snorkel and two-tank dive trips to the reefs at Sombrero Lighthouse and wrecks like the *Thunderbolt,* the company has more unusual offerings like rebreather, photography, and Nitrox courses. ⊠ *MM 48.5 BS, 1994 Overseas Hwy.* ☎ *305/743–5929, 800/331–4255* ⊕ *www.hallsdiving. com* ⌨ *From $45.*

Spirit Snorkeling. Join regularly scheduled snorkeling excursions to Sombrero Reef and Lighthouse Reef on this company's comfortable catamaran. They also offer sunset cruises and private charters. ⊠ *MM 47.5 BS, 1410 Overseas Hwy., Slip No. 1* ☎ *305/289–0614* ⊕ *www. captainpips.com* ➳ *From $30.*

Tildens Scuba Center. Since the mid-1980s, Tildens Scuba Center has been providing lessons, tours, gear rental, and daily snorkel, scuba, and Snuba adventures. Look for the huge, colorful angelfish sculpture outside the building. ⊠ *MM 49.5 BS, 4650 Overseas Hwy.* ☎ *305/743–7255, 888/728–2235* ➳ *From $60 for snorkel trips; from $70 for dive trips.*

THE LOWER KEYS

Beginning at Bahia Honda Key, the islands of the Florida Keys become smaller, more clustered, and more numerous, a result of ancient tidal water flowing between the Florida Straits and the gulf. Here you're likely to see more birds and mangroves than other tourists, and more refuges, beaches, and campgrounds than museums, restaurants, and hotels. The islands are made up of two types of limestone, both denser than the highly permeable Key Largo limestone of the Upper Keys. As a result, freshwater forms in pools rather than percolating through the rock, creating watering holes that support alligators, snakes, deer, rabbits, raccoons, and migratory ducks. (Many of these animals can be seen in the National Key Deer Refuge on Big Pine Key.) Nature was generous with her beauty in the Lower Keys, which have both Looe Key Reef, arguably the Keys' most beautiful tract of coral, and Bahia Honda State Park, considered one of the best beaches in the world for its fine sand dunes, clear warm waters, and panoramic vista of bridges, hammocks, and azure sky and sea. Big Pine Key is fishing headquarters for a laid-back community that swells with retirees in the winter. South of it, the dribble of islands can flash by in a blink of an eye if you don't take the time to stop at a roadside eatery or check out tours and charters at the little marinas. They include Little Torch Key, Middle Torch Key, Ramrod Key, Summerland Key, Cudjoe Key, Sugarloaf Keys, and Saddlebunch Key. Lying offshore of Little Torch Key, Little Palm Island once welcomed U.S. presidents and other notables to its secluded fishing camp. It was also the location for the movie *PT 109* about John F. Kennedy's celebrated World War II heroism. Today it still offers respite to the upper class in the form of an exclusive getaway resort accessible only by boat or seaplane.

GETTING HERE AND AROUND

To get to the Lower Keys, fly into either Miami International Airport or Key West International Airport. Key West is considerably closer, but there are far fewer flights coming in and going out. Rental cars are available at both airports. In addition, there is bus service from the Key West airport; $4 one way with Key West Transit. *See Getting Here and Around: Bus Travel in Key West, below.*

BAHIA HONDA KEY

MM 38.5–36.

All of Bahia Honda Key is devoted to its eponymous state park, which keeps it in a pristine state. Besides the park's outdoor activities, it offers an up-close view of the original railroad bridge.

EXPLORING

TOP ATTRACTIONS

FAMILY **Bahia Honda State Park.** Most first-time visitors to the region are dis-
Fodor's Choice mayed by the lack of beaches—but then they discover Bahia Honda
★ Key. The 524-acre park sprawls across both sides of the highway, giving it 2½ miles of fabulous sandy coastline. The snorkeling isn't bad, either; there's underwater life (soft coral, queen conchs, random little fish) just a few hundred feet offshore. Although swimming, kayaking, fishing, and boating are the main reasons to visit, you shouldn't miss biking along the 2½ miles of flat roads or hiking the Silver Palm Trail, with rare West Indies plants and several species found nowhere else in the nation. Along the way you'll be treated to a variety of butterflies. Seasonal ranger-led nature programs take place at or depart from the Sand and Sea Nature Center. There are rental cabins, a campground, snack bar, gift shop, 19-slip marina, nature center, and facilities for renting kayaks and arranging snorkeling tours. Get a panoramic view of the island from what's left of the railroad—the Bahia Honda Bridge. ⊠ *MM 37 OS, 36850 Overseas Hwy.* ☎ *305/872-2353* ⊕ *www.floridastate-parks.org/park/Bahia-Honda* ⊴ *$4.50 for single occupant vehicle, $8 for vehicle with 2–8 people, plus $0.50 per person up to 8.*

BEACHES

Sandspur Beach. Bahia Honda Key State Beach contains three beaches in all—on both the Atlantic Ocean and the Gulf of Mexico. Sandspur Beach, the largest, is regularly declared the best beach in the Florida Keys, and you'll be hard-pressed to argue. The sand is baby-powder soft, and the aqua water is warm, clear, and shallow. With their mild currents, the beaches are great for swimming, even with small fry. **Amenities:** food and drink; showers; toilets; water sports. **Best for:** snorkeling; swimming. ⊠ *MM 37 OS, 36850 Overseas Hwy.* ☎ *305/872-2353* ⊕ *www.floridastateparks.org/park/Bahia-Honda* ⊴ *$4.50 for single-occupant vehicle, $9 for vehicle with 2–8 people.*

WHERE TO STAY

$ ⬚ **Bahia Honda State Park Cabins.** Elsewhere you'd pay big bucks for the
RENTAL wonderful water views available at these cabins on Florida Bay. Each of three cabins have two, two-bedroom units with a full kitchen and bath and air-conditioning (but no television, radio, or phone). **Pros:** great bay-front views; beachfront camping; affordable rates. **Cons:** books up fast; area can be buggy. $ *Rooms from: $163* ⊠ *MM 37 OS, 36850 Overseas Hwy.* ☎ *305/872-2353, 800/326-3521* ⊕ *www.reserveamerica.com* ⊃ *6 cabins* ⊚ *No meals.*

DID YOU KNOW?

An old railroad bridge connected Bahia Honda Key with Key West until a hurricane destroyed it in 1935. The bridge is no longer in operation, yet it's standing, barely. Falling debris prevents snorkeling below or exploring, but it makes for pretty photos, especially at sunrise and sunset.

SPORTS AND THE OUTDOORS

SCUBA DIVING AND SNORKELING

Bahia Honda Dive Shop. The concessionaire at Bahia Honda State Park manages a 19-slip marina; rents wet suits, snorkel equipment, and corrective masks; and operates twice-a-day offshore-reef snorkel trips. Park visitors looking for other fun can rent kayaks and beach chairs. ⊠ *MM 37 OS, 36850 Overseas Hwy.* ☎ *305/872-3210* ⊕ *www.bahiahondapark. com* ⊗ *Kayak rentals from $10 per hr.; snorkel tours from $30.*

BIG PINE KEY

MM 32–30.

Welcome to the Keys' most natural holdout, where wildlife refuges protect rare and endangered animals. Here you have left behind the commercialism of the Upper Keys for an authentic backcountry atmosphere. How could things get more casual than Key Largo, you might wonder? Find out by exiting U.S. 1 to explore the habitat of the charmingly diminutive Key deer or cast a line from No Name Bridge. Tours explore the expansive waters of National Key Deer Refuge and Great White Heron National Wildlife Refuge, one of the first such refuges in the country. Along with Key West National Wildlife Refuge, it encompasses more than 200,000 acres of water and more than 8,000 acres of land on 49 small islands. Besides its namesake bird, the Great White Heron National Wildlife Refuge provides habitat for uncounted species of birds and three species of sea turtles. It is the only U.S. breeding site for the endangered hawksbill turtle.

GETTING HERE AND AROUND

Most people rent a car to get to Big Pine Key so they can also explore Key West and other parts of the chain.

VISITOR INFORMATION

Contact Big Pine and the Lower Keys Chamber of Commerce. ☎ *305/872-2411, 800/872-3722* ⊕ *www.lowerkeyschamber.com.*

EXPLORING

TOP ATTRACTIONS

National Key Deer Refuge. This 84,824-acre refuge was established in 1957 to protect the dwindling population of the Key deer, one of more than 22 animals and plants federally classified as endangered or threatened, including 5 that are found nowhere else on Earth. The Key deer, which stands about 30 inches at the shoulders and is a subspecies of the Virginia white-tailed deer, once roamed throughout the Lower and Middle keys, but hunting, destruction of their habitat, and a growing human population caused their numbers to decline to 27 by 1957. The deer have made a comeback, increasing their numbers to approximately 750. The best place to see Key deer in the refuge is at the end of Key Deer Boulevard and on No Name Key, a sparsely populated island just east of Big Pine Key. Mornings and evenings are the best time to spot them. Deer may turn up along the road at any time of day, so drive slowly. They wander into nearby yards to nibble tender grass and bougainvillea blossom, but locals do not appreciate tourists driving into their neighborhoods after them. Feeding them is against the law and puts them in danger.

A quarry left over from railroad days, the **Blue Hole** is the largest body of freshwater in the Keys. From the observation platform and nearby walking trail, you might see the resident alligator, turtles, and other wildlife. There are two well-marked trails, recently revamped: the Jack Watson Nature Trail (0.6 mile), named after an environmentalist and the refuge's first warden; and the Fred Mannillo Nature Trail (0.2 mile), one of the most wheelchair-accessible places to see an unspoiled pine-rockland forest and wetlands. The visitor center has exhibits on Keys biology and ecology. The refuge also provides information on the Key West National Wildlife Refuge and the Great White Heron National Wildlife Refuge. Accessible only by water, both are popular with kayak outfitters. ⊠ *Visitor Center–Headquarters, Big Pine Shopping Center, MM 30.5 BS, 28950 Watson Blvd.* ☎ *305/872–2239* ⊕ *www.fws.gov/ nationalkeydeer* 🔒 *Free.*

WHERE TO EAT

$ ✕ **Good Food Conspiracy.** Like good wine, this small natural-foods eatery
VEGETARIAN and market surrenders its pleasures a little at a time. Step inside to the aroma of brewing coffee, and then pick up the scent of fresh strawberries or carrots blending into a smoothie, the green aroma of wheatgrass juice, followed by the earthy odor of hummus. **Known for:** vegetarian and vegan dishes; sandwiches and smoothies; organic items. $ *Average main: $10* ⊠ *MM 30.2 OS, 30150 Overseas Hwy.* ☎ *305/872–3945* ⊕ *www.goodfoodconspiracy.com* ⊗ *No dinner Sun.*

$$ ✕ **No Name Pub.** This no-frills honky-tonk has been around since 1936,
AMERICAN delighting inveterate locals and intrepid vacationers who come for the excellent pizza, cold beer, and *interesting* companionship. The decor, such as it is, amounts to the autographed dollar bills that cover every inch of the place. **Known for:** shrimp pizza and fish sandwich; local and tourist favorite; decor of dollar bills. $ *Average main: $15* ⊠ *MM 30 BS, 30813 Watson Blvd.* ✛ *From U.S. 1, turn west on Wilder Rd., left on South St., right on Ave. B, right on Watson Blvd.* ☎ *305/872–9115* ⊕ *www.nonamepub.com.*

WHERE TO STAY

$ 🏠 **Big Pine Key Fishing Lodge.** There's a congenial atmosphere at this
HOTEL lively, family-owned lodge-campground-marina—a happy mix of tent campers (who have the fabulous waterfront real estate), RVers (who look pretty permanent), and motel dwellers who like to mingle at the rooftop pool and challenge each other to a game of poker. **Pros:** local fishing crowd; nice pool; great price. **Cons:** RV park is too close to motel; deer will eat your food if you're camping. $ *Rooms from: $134* ⊠ *MM 33 OS, 33000 Overseas Hwy.* ☎ *305/872–2351* ⊕ *www.bpkfl. com* ➵ *16 rooms* ⦿| *No meals* ⌒ *To protect Key deer, no dogs allowed.*

$$$ 🏠 **Deer Run Bed & Breakfast.** Innkeepers Jen DeMaria and Harry Appel
B&B/INN were way ahead of the green-lodging game when they opened in 2004, and guests love how Key deer wander the grounds of this beachfront B&B on a residential street lined with mangroves. **Pros:** quiet location; vegan, organic breakfasts; complimentary bikes, kayaks, and state park passes. **Cons:** price is a bit high; hard to find. $ *Rooms from: $375* ⊠ *MM 33 OS, 1997 Long Beach Dr.* ☎ *305/872–2015* ⊕ *www.deerrunfloridabb.com* ➵ *4 rooms* ⦿| *Breakfast.*

SPORTS AND THE OUTDOORS
BIKING

A good 10 miles of paved roads run from MM 30.3 BS, along Wilder Road, across the bridge to No Name Key, and along Key Deer Boulevard into the National Key Deer Refuge. Along the way you might see some Key deer. Stay off the trails that lead into wetlands, where fat tires can damage the environment.

Big Pine Bicycle Center. Owner Marty Baird is an avid cyclist and enjoys sharing his knowledge of great places to ride. He's also skilled at selecting the right bike for the journey, and he knows his repairs, too. His old-fashioned single-speed, fat-tire cruisers rent by the half or full day. Helmets, baskets, and locks are included. ⊠ *MM 30.9 BS, 31 County Rd.* ☎ *305/872–0130* ⊕ *www.bigpinebikes.com* ◱ *From $10.*

FISHING

Cast from No Name Key Bridge or hire a charter to take you into backcountry or deep waters for fishing year-round.

Strike Zone Charters. Glass-bottom-boat excursions venture into the backcountry and Atlantic Ocean. The five-hour Island Excursion emphasizes nature and Keys history; besides close encounters with birds, sea life, and vegetation, there's a fish cookout on an island. Snorkel and fishing equipment, food, and drinks are included. This is one of the few nature outings in the Keys with wheelchair access. Deep-sea charter rates for up to six people can be arranged for a half or full day. It also offers flats fishing in the Gulf of Mexico. Dive excursions head to the wreck of the 110-foot *Adolphus Busch*, and scuba and snorkel trips to Looe Key Reef, prime scuba and snorkeling territory, aboard glass-bottom boats. ⊠ *MM 29.6 BS, 29675 Overseas Hwy.* ☎ *305/872–9863, 800/654–9560* ⊕ *www.strikezonecharter.com* ◱ *From $38.*

KAYAKING

There's nothing like the vast expanse of pristine waters and mangrove islands preserved by national refuges from here to Key West. The maze-like terrain can be confusing, so it's wise to hire a guide at least the first time out.

Big Pine Kayak Adventures. There's no excuse to skip a water adventure with this convenient kayak rental service, which delivers them to your lodging or anywhere between Seven Mile Bridge and Stock Island. The company, headed by *The Florida Keys Paddling Guide* author Bill Keogh, will rent you a kayak and then ferry you—called taxi-yakking—to remote islands with clear instructions on how to paddle back on your own. Rentals are by the half day or full day. Three-hour group kayak tours are the cheapest option and explore the mangrove forests of Great White Heron and Key Deer National Wildlife Refuges. More expensive four-hour custom tours transport you to exquisite backcountry areas teeming with wildlife. Kayak fishing charters are also popular. Paddleboard ecotours, rentals, and yoga are available. ⊠ *Old Wooden Bridge Fishing Camp, 1791 Bogie Dr.* ✛ *From MM 30, turn right at traffic light, continue on Wilder Rd. toward No Name Key; the fishing camp is just before the bridge with a big yellow kayak on the sign out front* ☎ *305/872–7474* ⊕ *www.keyskayaktours.com* ◱ *From $50.*

LITTLE TORCH KEY

MM 29–10.

Little Torch Key and its neighbor islands, Ramrod Key and Summerland Key, are good jumping-off points for divers headed for Looe Key Reef. The islands also serve as a refuge for those who want to make forays into Key West but not stay in the thick of things.

The undeveloped backcountry at your door makes Little Torch Key an ideal location for fishing and kayaking. Nearby **Ramrod Key,** which also caters to divers bound for Looe Key, derives its name from a ship that wrecked on nearby reefs in the early 1800s.

WHERE TO EAT

$
AMERICAN
✕ **Baby's Coffee.** The aroma of rich, roasting coffee beans arrests you at the door of "the Southernmost Coffee Roaster in America." Buy beans by the pound or coffee by the cup, along with sandwiches and sweets. **Known for:** best coffee in the Keys; gluten-free, vegan, and vegetarian specialty foods. ⑤ *Average main: $8* ⊠ *MM 15 OS, 3180 Overseas Hwy.* ☎ *305/744–9866, 800/523–2326* ⊕ *www.babyscoffee.com.*

$$
AMERICAN
✕ **Geiger Key Smokehouse Bar & Grill.** There's a strong hint of the Old Keys at this ocean-side marina restaurant, where local fisherman stop for breakfast before heading out to catch the big one, and everyone shows up on Sunday for the barbecue from 4 to 9. "On the backside of paradise," as the sign says, its tiki structures overlook quiet mangroves at an RV park marina. **Known for:** Sunday barbecue. ⑤ *Average main: $16* ⊠ *MM 10, 5 Geiger Key Rd., off Boca Chica Rd., Bay Point* ☎ *305/296–3553, 305/294–1230* ⊕ *www.geigerkeymarina.com.*

$$$$
ECLECTIC
✕ **Little Palm Island Restaurant.** The restaurant at the exclusive Little Palm Island Resort—its dining room and adjacent outdoor terrace lit by candles and warmed by live music—is one of the most romantic spots in the Keys. However, it's only open to nonguests on a reservations-only basis and no one under 16 is allowed on the island. **Known for:** oceanfront tables in the sand; Key deer meandering by your table; Sunday brunch buffet. ⑤ *Average main: $65* ⊠ *MM 28.5 OS, 28500 Overseas Hwy.* ☎ *305/872–2551* ⊕ *www.littlepalmisland.com.*

$$
SEAFOOD
✕ **Mangrove Mama's Restaurant.** This could be the prototype for a Keys restaurant, given its shanty appearance, lattice trim, and roving sort of indoor-outdoor floor plan. Then there's the seafood, from the ubiquitous fish sandwich (fried, grilled, broiled, or blackened) to lobster Reubens, crab cakes, and coconut shrimp. **Known for:** pizza; award-winning conch chowder; all kinds of seafood dishes. ⑤ *Average main: $20* ⊠ *MM 20 BS, Sugarloaf Key* ☎ *305/745–3030* ⊕ *www.mangrovemamasrestaurant.com.*

$$$
SEAFOOD
Fodor's Choice
★
✕ **Square Grouper.** In an unassuming warehouse-looking building right off U.S. 1, chef and owner Lynn Bell is creating seafood magic. Just ask the locals, who wait in line for a table along with visitors in the know. But don't let the exterior fool you: the dining room is surprisingly suave, with butcher paper–lined tables, mandarin-colored walls, and textural components throughout. **Known for:** everything made fresh, in-house; long lines in season. ⑤ *Average main: $25* ⊠ *MM 22.5 OS, Cudjoe Key* ☎ *305/745–8880* ⊕ *www.squaregrouperbarandgrill.com* ☉ *Closed Sun.; Mon. May–Dec.; and Sept.*

WHERE TO STAY

$$$$
RESORT
Fodor's Choice
★

⬚ **Little Palm Island Resort & Spa.** *Haute tropicale* best describes this luxury retreat, and "second mortgage" might explain how some can afford the extravagant prices. **Pros:** secluded setting; heavenly spa; easy wildlife viewing. **Cons:** expensive; might be too quiet for some; only accessible by boat or seaplane. ⓢ *Rooms from: $1590* ✉ *MM 28.5 OS, 28500 Overseas Hwy.* ☎ *305/872–2524, 800/343–8567* ⊕ *www. littlepalmisland.com* ↝ *30 suites* |◯| *Some meals* ↜ *No one under 16 allowed on island.*

$
HOTEL

⬚ **Looe Key Reef Resort & Center.** If your Keys vacation is all about diving, you won't mind the no-frills, basic motel rooms with dated furniture at this scuba-obsessed operation because it's the closest place to stay to the stellar reef. **Pros:** guests get discounts on dive and snorkel trips; inexpensive rates. **Cons:** some reports of uncleanliness; unheated pool; close to the road. ⓢ *Rooms from: $115* ✉ *MM 27.5 OS, 27340 Overseas Hwy., Ramrod Key* ☎ *305/872–2215, 877/816–3483* ⊕ *www.diveflakeys.com* ↝ *23 rooms, 1 suite* |◯| *No meals.*

$
HOTEL

⬚ **Parmer's Resort.** Almost every room at this budget-friendly option has a view of South Pine Channel, with the lovely curl of Big Pine Key in the foreground. **Pros:** bright rooms; pretty setting; good value. **Cons:** a bit out of the way; housekeeping costs extra; little shade around the pool. ⓢ *Rooms from: $159* ✉ *MM 28.7 BS, 565 Barry Ave.* ☎ *305/872–2157* ⊕ *www.parmersresort.com* ↝ *47 units* |◯| *Breakfast.*

SPORTS AND THE OUTDOORS

BOATING

Dolphin Marina. Dolphin Marina rents 19- and 22-foot boats with 150 horsepower for up to eight people by the half day and full day. An onsite marina store has all the supplies you'll need for a day on the water. ✉ *28530 Overseas Hwy.* ☎ *305/872–2685* ⊕ *www.dolphinmarina.net* ▱ *From $200 half day; from $250 full day.*

SCUBA DIVING AND SNORKELING

This is the closest you can get on land to Looe Key Reef, and that's where local dive operators love to head.

In 1744 the HMS *Looe*, a British warship, ran aground and sank on one of the most beautiful coral reefs in the Keys. Today the key owes its name to the ill-fated ship. The 5.3-square-nautical-mile reef, part of the **Florida Keys National Marine Sanctuary,** has strands of elkhorn coral on its eastern margin, purple sea fans, and abundant sponges and sea urchins. On its seaward side, it drops almost vertically 50 to 90 feet. In its midst, **Shipwreck Trail** plots the location of nine historic wreck sites in 14 to 120 feet of water. Buoys mark the sites, and underwater signs tell the history of each site and what marine life to expect. Snorkelers and divers will find the sanctuary a quiet place to observe reef life—except in July, when the annual Underwater Music Festival pays homage to Looe Key's beauty and promotes reef awareness with six hours of music broadcast via underwater speakers. Dive shops, charters, and private boats transport about 500 divers and snorkelers to hear the spectacle, which includes classical, jazz, New Age, and Caribbean music, as well as a little Jimmy Buffett. There are even underwater Elvis impersonators.

Looe Key Reef Resort & Dive Center. This center, the closest dive shop to Looe Key Reef, offers two affordable trips daily, 7:30 am or 12:15 pm (for divers, snorkelers, or bubble watchers). The maximum depth is 30 feet, so snorkelers and divers go on the same boat. Call to check for availability for wreck and night dives. The dive boat, a 45-foot catamaran, is docked at the full-service Looe Key Reef Resort. ✉ *Looe Key Reef Resort, MM 27.5 OS, 27340 Overseas Hwy., Ramrod Key* 🕾 *305/872–2215, 877/816–3483* ⊕ *www.diveflakeys.com* 🖛 *From $40.*

WATER SPORTS

Reelax Charters. For a guided kayak tour, join Captain Andrea Paulson of Reelax Charters, who takes you to remote locations. Charters carry up to three people and can include snorkeling and beaching on a secluded island in the Keys backcountry. ✉ *Sugarloaf Marina, MM 17 BS, 17015 Overseas Hwy., Sugarloaf Key* 🕾 *305/304–1392* ⊕ *www.keyskayaking. com* 🖛 *From $240.*

Sugarloaf Marina. Rates for one-person kayaks are based on an hourly or daily rental. Two-person kayaks are also available. Delivery is free for rentals of three days or more. The folks at the marina can also hook you up with an outfitter for a day of offshore or backcountry fishing. There's also a well-stocked ship store. ✉ *MM 17 BS, 17015 Overseas Hwy., Sugarloaf Key* 🕾 *305/745–3135* ⊕ *www.sugarloafkeymarina. com* 🖛 *From $15 per hr.*

KEY WEST

Situated 150 miles from Miami, 90 miles from Havana, and an immeasurable distance from sanity, this end-of-the-line community has never been like anywhere else. Even after it was connected to the rest of the country—by the railroad in 1912 and by the highway in 1938—it maintained a strong sense of detachment. The United States acquired Key West from Spain in 1821, along with the rest of Florida. The Spanish had named the island Cayo Hueso, or Bone Key, after the Native American skeletons they found on its shores. In 1823, President James Monroe sent Commodore David S. Porter to chase pirates away. For three decades, the primary industry in Key West was wrecking—rescuing people and salvaging cargo from ships that foundered on the nearby reefs. According to some reports, when pickings were lean the wreckers hung out lights to lure ships aground. Their business declined after 1849, when the federal government began building lighthouses.

In 1845, the army began construction on Ft. Taylor, which kept Key West on the Union side during the Civil War. After the fighting ended, an influx of Cubans unhappy with Spain's rule brought the cigar industry here. Fishing, shrimping, and sponge gathering became important industries, as did pineapple canning. Throughout much of the 19th century and into the 20th, Key West was Florida's wealthiest city in per-capita terms. But in 1929, the local economy began to unravel. Cigar making moved to Tampa, Hawaii dominated the pineapple industry, and the sponges succumbed to blight. Then the Depression hit, and within a few years half the population was on relief.

Tourism began to revive Key West, but that came to a halt when a hurricane knocked out the railroad bridge in 1935. To help the tourism industry recover from that crushing blow, the government offered incentives for islanders to turn their charming homes—many of them built by shipwrights—into guesthouses and inns. That wise foresight has left the town with more than 100 such lodgings, a hallmark of Key West vacationing today. In the 1950s, the discovery of "pink gold" in the Dry Tortugas boosted the economy of the entire region. Catching Key West shrimp required a fleet of up to 500 boats and flooded local restaurants with some of the sweetest shrimp alive. The town's artistic community found inspiration in the colorful fishing boats.

Key West reflects a diverse population: Conchs (natives, many of whom trace their ancestry to the Bahamas), freshwater Conchs (longtime residents who migrated from somewhere else years ago), Hispanics (primarily Cuban immigrants), recent refugees from the urban sprawl of mainland Florida, military personnel, and an assortment of vagabonds, drifters, and dropouts in search of refuge. The island was once a gay vacation hot spot, and it remains a decidedly gay-friendly destination. Some of the once-renowned gay guesthouses, however, no longer cater to an exclusively gay clientele. Key Westers pride themselves on their tolerance of all peoples, all sexual orientations, and even all animals. Most restaurants allow pets, and it's not surprising to see stray cats, dogs, and even chickens roaming freely through the dining rooms. The chicken issue is one that government officials periodically try to bring to an end, but the colorful fowl continue to strut and crow, particularly in the vicinity of Old Town's Bahamian Village.

As a tourist destination, Key West has a lot to sell—an average temperature of 79°F, 19th-century architecture, and a laid-back lifestyle. Yet much has been lost to those eager for a buck. Duval Street is starting to resemble a shopping mall with name-brand storefronts, garish T-shirt shops, and tattoo shops with sidewalk views of the inked action. Cruise ships dwarf the town's skyline and fill the streets with day-trippers gawking at the hippies with dogs in their bike baskets, gay couples walking down the street holding hands, and the oddball lot of locals, some of whom bark louder than the dogs.

GETTING HERE AND AROUND

AIR TRAVEL

You can fly directly to Key West on a limited number of flights, most of which connect at other Florida airports. But a lot of folks fly into Miami or Fort Lauderdale and drive down or take the bus.

BOAT TRAVEL

Key West Express operates air-conditioned ferries between the Key West Terminal (Caroline and Grinnell streets) and Marco Island, and Fort Myers Beach. The trip from Fort Myers Beach takes at least four hours each way and costs $95 one way, $155 round-trip. Ferries depart from Fort Myers Beach at 8:30 am and from Key West at 6 pm. The Miami and Marco Island ferry costs $95 one way and $155 round-trip, and departs at 8:30 am. A photo ID is required for each passenger. Advance reservations are recommended and can save money.

BUS AND SHUTTLE TRAVEL TO KEY WEST

Greyhound Lines runs a special Keys Shuttle up to twice a day (depending on the day of the week) from Miami International Airport (departing from Concourse E, lower level) that stops throughout the Keys. Fares run about $45 (Web fare) to $57 for Key West. Keys Shuttle runs scheduled service three times a day in 15-passenger vans between Miami Airport and Key West with stops throughout the Keys for $70 to $90 per person. SuperShuttle charges $102 per passenger for trips from Miami International Airport to the Upper Keys. To go farther into the Keys, you must book an entire 11-person van, which costs about $350 to Key West. You need to place your request for transportation back to the airport 24 hours in advance. Uber is also available throughout the Keys and from the airport, but you must download the company's smartphone app and register a credit card in order to use the service. *For detailed information on these services, see Getting Here and Around: Bus Travel*

BUS TRAVEL AROUND KEY WEST

Between mile markers 4 and 0, Key West is the one place in the Keys where you could conceivably do without a car, especially if you plan on staying around Old Town. If you've driven the 106 miles down the chain, you're probably ready to abandon your car in the hotel parking lot anyway. Trolleys, buses, bikes, scooters, and feet are more suitable alternatives. When your feet tire, catch a rickshaw-style pedicab ride, which will run you about $1.50 a minute. But to explore the beaches, New Town, and Stock Island, you'll need a car or taxi.

The City of Key West Department of Transportation has six color-coded bus routes traversing the island from 5:30 am to 11:30 pm. Stops have signs with the international bus symbol. Schedules are available on buses and at hotels, visitor centers, shops, and online. The fare is $2 one way. Its Lower Keys Shuttle bus runs between Marathon to Key West ($4 one way), with scheduled stops along the way.

VISITOR INFORMATION

Contacts Gay & Lesbian Community Center. ✉ *513 Truman Ave.* ☎ *305/292–3223* ⊕ *www.lgbtcenter.com.* **Greater Key West Chamber of Commerce.** ☎ *305/294–2587, 800/527–8539* ⊕ *www.keywestchamber.org.*

TOURS

BIKE TOURS

Lloyd's Original Tropical Bike Tour. Explore the natural, noncommercial side of Key West at a leisurely pace, stopping on backstreets and in backyards of private homes to sample native fruits and view indigenous plants and trees with a 30-year Key West veteran. The behind-the-scenes tours run two hours and include a bike rental. ✉ *Truman Ave. and Simonton St.* ☎ *305/304–4700* ⊕ *www.lloydstropicalbiketour.com* 🖃 *$39.*

BUS TOURS

City View Trolley Tours. In 2010, City View Trolley Tours began service, offering a little competition to the Conch Train and Old Town Trolley, which are owned by the same company. Purchase your tickets online or with your smartphone, and save $5 per person. Tours depart every 30 minutes from 9:30 to 4:30. Passengers can board and disembark at any of nine stops, and can reboard at will. ⊠ *Key West* ☎ *305/294–0644* ⊕ *www.cityviewtrolleys.com* ✉ *From $19.*

Conch Tour Train. The Conch Tour Train is a 90-minute narrated tour of Key West, traveling 14 miles through Old Town and around the island. Board at Mallory Square or Angela Street and Duval Street depot every half hour (9–4:30 from Mallory Square). Discount tickets are available online. ⊠ *Key West* ☎ *305/294–5161, 888/916–8687* ⊕ *www.conchtourtrain.com* ✉ *$30.45.*

Gay & Lesbian Trolley Tour. Decorated with a rainbow, the Gay and Lesbian Trolley Tour rumbles around the town beginning at 11 am every Saturday morning. The 70-minute tour highlights Key West's influential gay history. ⊠ *513 Truman Ave.* ☎ *305/294–4603* ⊕ *www.keywestsites.com* ✉ *$20.*

Old Town Trolley. Old Town Trolley operates trolley-style buses, departing from Mallory Square every 30 minutes from 9 to 4:30, for 90-minute narrated tours of Key West. The smaller trolleys go places the larger Conch Tour Train won't fit and you can ride a second consecutive day for free. You may disembark at any of 13 stops and reboard a later trolley. You can save $3 by booking online. It also offers package deals with Old Town attractions. ⊠ *201 Front St.* ☎ *305/296–6688, 888/910–8687* ⊕ *www.trolleytours.com* ✉ *$30.45.*

WALKING TOURS

Historic Florida Keys Foundation. In addition to publishing several good guides on Key West, the foundation conducts tours of the City Cemetery on Tuesday and Thursday at 9:30 am. ⊠ *Old City Hall, 510 Greene St.* ☎ *305/292–6718* ⊕ *www.historicfloridakeys.org* ✉ *$15.*

Key West Promotions. If you're not entirely a do-it-yourselfer, Key West Promotions offers a variety of guided tours, including the famous pub crawl, a historic homes and gardens walking tour, a southernmost bike tour, a chilling ghost tour, and a palate-pleasing, Taste of Key West restaurant experience. ⊠ *218 Whitehead St.* ☎ *305/294–7170* ⊕ *www.keywestwalkingtours.com.*

EXPLORING

OLD TOWN

The heart of Key West, the historic Old Town area runs from White Street to the waterfront. Beginning in 1822, wharves, warehouses, chandleries, ship-repair facilities, and eventually, in 1891, the U.S. Custom House, sprang up around the deep harbor to accommodate the navy's large ships and other sailing vessels. Wreckers, merchants, and sea captains built lavish houses near the bustling waterfront. A remarkable number of these fine Victorian and pre-Victorian structures have been restored to their original grandeur and now serve as homes, guesthouses, shops, restaurants, and museums. These, along with the dwellings of famous writers, artists, and politicians who've come to Key West over the past 175 years, are among the area's approximately 3,000 historic structures. Old Town also has the city's finest restaurants and hotels, lively street life, and popular nightspots.

TOP ATTRACTIONS

Audubon House and Tropical Gardens. If you've ever seen an engraving by ornithologist John James Audubon, you'll understand why his name is synonymous with birds. See his works in this three-story house, which was built in the 1840s for Captain John Geiger and filled with period furniture. It now commemorates Audubon's 1832 stop in Key West while he was traveling through Florida to study birds. After an introduction by a docent, you can do a self-guided tour of the house and gardens. An art gallery sells lithographs of the artist's famed portraits. ⊠ *205 Whitehead St.* ☎ *305/294–2116, 877/294–2470* ⊕ *www.audubonhouse.com* ▭ *$12.*

Fodor's Choice
★

Custom House. When Key West was designated a U.S. port of entry in the early 1820s, a customhouse was established. Salvaged cargoes from ships wrecked on the reefs were brought here, setting the stage for Key West to become—for a time—the richest city in Florida. The imposing redbrick-and-terra-cotta Richardsonian Romanesque–style building reopened as a museum and art gallery in 1999. Smaller galleries have long-term and changing exhibits about the history of Key West, including a Hemingway room and a permanent Henry Flagler exhibit that commemorates the arrival of Flagler's railroad to Key West in 1912. ⊠ *281 Front St.* ☎ *305/295–6616* ⊕ *www.kwahs.com* ▭ *$10.*

Dry Tortugas National Park and Historic Key West Bight Museum. If you can't see Ft. Jefferson in the Dry Tortugas in person, this is the next best thing. Opened in 2013 by the national park's official ferry commissioner, this free attraction located in Key West's historic seaport has an impressive (1:87) scale model of the fort; life-size figures including the fort's most famous prisoner, Dr. Samuel Mudd; and even a junior ranger station for the little ones with hands-on educational fun. The exhibits are housed in a historic site as well, the old Thompson Fish House, where local fisherman would bring their daily catch for processing. History lingers on within these walls, but to get a whiff of the sea and days gone past, you'll have to walk the docks out front. ⊠ *240 Margaret St.* ☎ *305/294–7009* ⊕ *www.drytortugas.com* ▭ *Free.*

Fodor's Choice
★

The Ernest Hemingway Home and Museum. Amusing anecdotes spice up the guided tours of Ernest Hemingway's home, built in 1801 by the town's most successful wrecker. While living here between 1931 and 1942, Hemingway wrote about 70% of his life's work, including classics like *For Whom the Bell Tolls.* Few of his belongings remain aside from some books, and there's little about his actual work, but photographs help you visualize his day-to-day life. The famous six-toed descendants of Hemingway's cats—many named for actors, artists, authors, and even a hurricane—have free rein of the property. Tours begin every 10 minutes and take 30 minutes; then you're free to explore on your own. Be sure to find out why there is a urinal in the garden! ⊠ *907 Whitehead St.* ☎ *305/294–1136* ⊕ *www.hemingwayhome.com* ▭ *$13.*

Fort Zachary Taylor Historic State Park. Construction of the fort began in 1845 but was halted during the Civil War. Even though Florida seceded from the Union, Yankee forces used the fort as a base to block Confederate shipping. More than 1,500 Confederate vessels were detained in Key West's harbor. The fort, finally completed in 1866, was also used in the Spanish-American War. Take a 30-minute guided walking tour

Key West

WISTERIA ISLAND

SUNSET KEY

FLEMING KEY

DREDGERS KEY

Key West Bight

Garrison Bight

Key West Municipal Beach

Key West International Airport

ATLANTIC OCEAN

C.B. Harvey Memorial Rest Beach

Smathers Beach

Key West Municipal Beach

South Roosevelt Blvd.

North Roosevelt Blvd.

Northside Dr.

Duck Ave.

Flagler Ave.

Kennedy Dr.

14th

12th

10th

7th Ave.

6th Ave.

Macmillan

Patterson

2nd St.

1st St.

George St.

Thompson St.

Bertha St.

Patricia St.

Atlantic Blvd.

Leon St.

Flagler Ave.

Laird St.

Casa Marina Ct.

West Martello Tower

Higgs Beach-Astro City Playground

South Beach

Dog Beach

Vernon

Simonton St.

Duval St.

Whitehead St.

William St.

Margaret

Reynolds

Grinnell St.

Frances St.

White St.

Palm Ave.

Virginia St.

Duncan St.

United St.

Varela St.

Verela St.

Windsor Ln.

Truman Ave.

Petronia St.

Olivia St.

Julia St.

Virginia St.

Amelia St.

Covington

Thomas St.

Whitehead St.

Angela St.

Southard St.

Fleming St.

Eaton St.

Caroline St.

Greene St.

Front St.

See inset at left

0 — 1/2 mile
0 — 1/2 km

KEY

▶ **1** Sights

1 Restaurants & Hotels

Sights ▶

The Ernest Hemingway
Home and Museum **1**

Fort East Martello
Museum & Gardens **13**

Fort Zachary Taylor
Historic State Park **8**

Audubon House
and Tropical Gardens **3**

Custom House **5**

Dry Tortugas National Park
and Historic Key West
Bight Museum **12**

Harry S Truman
Little White House
Museum **4**

Historic Seaport
at Key West Bight **7**

The Key West Butterfly and
Nature Conservatory **9**

Key West Library **11**

Key West Lighthouse
Museum and Keeper's
Quarters **2**

Key West Tropical Forest
& Botanical Garden **14**

Mallory Square and Pier **6**

The Southernmost
Point **10**

Restaurants ▶

Hogfish Bar & Grill **4**

Tavern N Town **3**

Hotels ▶

Best Western Key
Ambassador Resort Inn **5**

Key West Marriott
Beachside Hotel **2**

Parrot Key Resort **1**

(inset map)

Elizabeth St.

Southard St.

Eaton St.

Free School La.

Simonton St.

Olivia St.

Duval St.

Whitehead St.

Thomas St.

Front St.

Greene St.

Caroline St.

Eaton St.

Fleming St.

Angela St.

Petronia St.

Truman Ave.

7

6

5

3

4

2

1

See the typewriter Hemingway used at his home office in Key West. He lived here from 1931 to 1942.

of the redbrick fort, a National Historic Landmark, at noon and 2, or self-guided tour anytime between 8 and 5. In February a celebration called Civil War Heritage Days includes costumed reenactments and demonstrations. From mid-January to mid-April the park serves as an open-air gallery for pieces created for Sculpture Key West. One of its most popular features is its man-made beach, a rest stop for migrating birds in the spring and fall; there are also picnic areas, hiking and biking trails, and a kayak launch. ⊠ *Southard St., at end of street, through Truman Annex* ☎ *305/292–6713* ⊕ *www.floridastateparks.org/park/ Fort-Taylor* 🖃 *$4 for single-occupant vehicles, $6 for 2–8 people in a vehicle, plus a 50¢ per person county surcharge.*

Harry S Truman Little White House Museum. Renovations to this circa-1890 landmark have restored the home and gardens to the Truman era, down to the wallpaper pattern. A free photographic review of visiting dignitaries and presidents—John F. Kennedy, Jimmy Carter, and Bill Clinton are among the chief executives who passed through here—is on display in the back of the gift shop. Engaging 45-minute tours begin every 20 minutes until 4:30. They start with an excellent 10-minute video on the history of the property and Truman's visits. On the grounds of **Truman Annex,** a 103-acre former military parade grounds and barracks, the home served as a winter White House for presidents Truman, Eisenhower, and Kennedy. Entry is cheaper when purchased in advance online; tickets bought on-site add sales tax. ■ **TIP→ The house tour does require climbing steps. Visitors can do a free self-guided botanical tour of the grounds with a brochure from the museum store.** ⊠ *111 Front St.* ☎ *305/294–9911* ⊕ *www.trumanlittlewhitehouse.com* 🖃 *$16.13.*

CLOSE UP

Hemingway Was Here

In a town where Pulitzer Prize–winning writers are almost as common as coconuts, Ernest Hemingway stands out. Many bars and restaurants around the island claim that he ate or drank there.

Hemingway came to Key West in 1928 at the urging of writer John Dos Passos and rented a house with his second wife, Pauline Pfeiffer. They spent winters in the Keys and summers in Europe and Wyoming, occasionally taking African safaris. Along the way, they had two sons, Patrick and Gregory. In 1931, Pauline's wealthy uncle Gus gave the couple the house at 907 Whitehead Street. Now known as the Ernest Hemingway Home & Museum, it's Key West's number one tourist attraction. Renovations included the addition of a pool and a tropical garden.

In 1935, when the visitor bureau included the house in a tourist brochure, Hemingway promptly built the brick wall that surrounds it today. He wrote of the visitor bureau's offense in a 1935 essay for *Esquire,* saying, "The house at present occupied by your correspondent is listed as number eighteen in a compilation of the forty-eight things for a tourist to see in Key West. So there will be no difficulty in a tourist finding it or any other of the sights

of the city, a map has been prepared by the local F.E.R.A. authorities to be presented to each arriving visitor. This is all very flattering to the easily bloated ego of your correspondent but very hard on production."

During his time in Key West, Hemingway penned some of his most important works, including *A Farewell to Arms, To Have and Have Not, Green Hills of Africa,* and *Death in the Afternoon.* His rigorous schedule consisted of writing almost every morning in his second-story studio above the pool, then promptly descending the stairs at midday. By afternoon and evening he was ready for drinking, fishing, swimming, boxing, and hanging around with the boys.

One close friend was Joe Russell, a craggy fisherman and owner of the rugged bar Sloppy Joe's, originally at 428 Greene Street but now at 201 Duval Street. Russell was the only one in town who would cash Hemingway's $1,000 royalty check. Russell and Charles Thompson introduced Hemingway to deep-sea fishing, which became fodder for his writing.

Hemingway stayed in Key West for 11 years before leaving Pauline for his third wife. Pauline and the boys stayed on in the house, which sold in 1951 for $80,000, 10 times its original cost.

4

Historic Seaport at Key West Bight. What was once a funky—in some places even seedy—part of town is now an 8½-acre historic restoration of 100 businesses, including waterfront restaurants, open-air bars, museums, clothing stores, bait shops, dive shops, docks, a marina, and watersports concessions. It's all linked by the 2-mile waterfront **Harborwalk,** which runs between Front and Grinnell streets, passing big ships, schooners, sunset cruises, fishing charters, and glass-bottom boats. ✉ *100 Grinnell St.* ⊕ *www.keywestseaport.com.*

Coffee Plantation. Get your morning (or afternoon) buzz, and hook up to the Internet in the comfort of a homelike setting in a circa-1890 Conch house. Munch on sandwiches, wraps, and pastries, and sip a hot or cold espresso beverage. ⊠ *713 Caroline St.* ☎ *305/295–9808* ⊕ *www.coffee-plantationkeywest.com.*

FAMILY **The Key West Butterfly and Nature Conservatory.** This air-conditioned refuge for butterflies, birds, and the human spirit gladdens the soul with hundreds of colorful wings—more than 45 species of butterflies alone—in a lovely glass-encased bubble. Waterfalls, artistic benches, paved pathways, birds, and lush, flowering vegetation elevate this above most butterfly attractions. The gift shop and gallery are worth a visit on their own. ⊠ *1316 Duval St.* ☎ *305/296–2988, 800/839–4647* ⊕ *www.keywestbutterfly.com* ⌨ *$12.*

Key West Library. Check out the pretty palm garden next to the Key West Library at 700 Fleming Street, just off Duval. This leafy, outdoor reading area, with shaded benches, is the perfect place to escape the frenzy and crowds of downtown Key West. There's free Internet access in the library, too. ⊠ *700 Fleming St.* ☎ *305/292–3595* ⊕ *www.keyslibraries.org.*

Key West Lighthouse Museum and Keeper's Quarters. For the best view in town, climb the 88 steps to the top of this 1847 lighthouse. The 92-foot structure has a Fresnel lens, which was installed in the 1860s at a cost of $1 million. The keeper lived in the adjacent 1887 clapboard house, which now exhibits vintage photographs, ship models, nautical charts, and lighthouse artifacts from all along the Key reefs. A kids' room is stocked with books and toys. ⊠ *938 Whitehead St.* ☎ *305/295–6616* ⊕ *www.kwahs.com* ⌨ *$10.*

Mallory Square and Pier. For cruise-ship passengers, this is the disembarkation point for an attack on Key West. For practically every visitor, it's the requisite venue for a nightly sunset celebration that includes street performers—human statues, sword swallowers, tightrope walkers, musicians, and more—plus craft vendors, conch fritter fryers, and other regulars who defy classification. With all the activity, don't forget to watch the main show: a dazzling tropical sunset. ⊠ *Mallory Sq.*

The Southernmost Point. Possibly the most photographed site in Key West (even though the actual geographic southernmost point in the continental United States lies across the bay on a naval base, where you see a satellite dish), this is a must-see. Who wouldn't want his picture taken next to the big striped buoy that marks the southernmost point in the continental United States? A plaque next to it honors Cubans who lost their lives trying to escape to America and other signs tell Key West history. ⊠ *Whitehead and South Sts.*

NEW TOWN

The Overseas Highway splits as it enters Key West, the two forks rejoining to encircle New Town, the area east of White Street to Cow Key Channel. The southern fork runs along the shore as South Roosevelt Boulevard (Route A1A) and skirts Key West International Airport, while the northern fork runs along the north shore as North Roosevelt

Divers examine the intentionally scuttled 327-foot former U.S. Coast Guard cutter *Duane* in 120 feet of water off Key Largo.

Boulevard and turns into Truman Avenue once it hits Old Town. Part of New Town was created with dredged fill. The island would have continued growing this way had the Army Corps of Engineers not determined in the early 1970s that it was detrimental to the nearby reef.

TOP ATTRACTIONS

Fort East Martello Museum & Gardens. This redbrick Civil War fort never saw a lick of action during the war. Today it serves as a museum, with historical exhibits about the 19th and 20th centuries. Among the latter are relics of the USS *Maine*, cigar factory and shipwrecking exhibits, and the citadel tower you can climb to the top. The museum, operated by the Key West Art and Historical Society, also has a collection of Stanley Papio's "junk art" sculptures inside and out, and a gallery of Cuban folk artist Mario Sanchez's chiseled and painted wooden carvings of historic Key West street scenes. ⊠ *3501 S. Roosevelt Blvd.* ☎ *305/296–3913* ⊕ *www.kwahs.com* 🖃 *$9.*

Key West Tropical Forest & Botanical Garden. Established in 1935, this unique habitat is the only frost-free botanical garden in the continental United States. You won't see fancy topiaries and exotic plants, but you'll see a unique ecosystem that naturally occurs in this area and the Caribbean. There are paved walkways that take you past butterfly gardens, mangroves, Cuban palms, lots of birds like herons and ibis, and ponds where you can spy turtles and fish. It's a nice respite from the sidewalks and shops, and offers a natural slice of Keys paradise. ⊠ *5210 College Rd.* ☎ *305/296–1504* ⊕ *www.kwbgs.org* 🖃 *$7.*

THE CONCH REPUBLIC

Beginning in the 1970s, pot smuggling became a source of income for islanders who knew how to dodge detection in the maze of waterways in the Keys. In 1982, the U.S. Border Patrol threw a roadblock across the Overseas Highway just south of Florida City to catch drug runners and undocumented aliens. Traffic backed up for miles as Border Patrol agents searched vehicles and demanded that the occupants prove U.S. citizenship. Officials in Key West, outraged at being treated like foreigners by the federal government, staged a protest and formed their own "nation," the so-called Conch Republic. They hoisted a flag and distributed mock border passes, visas, and Conch currency. The embarrassed Border Patrol dismantled its roadblock, and now an annual festival recalls the city's victory.

BEACHES

OLD TOWN

Dog Beach. Next to Louie's Backyard restaurant, this tiny beach—the only one in Key West where dogs are allowed unleashed—has a shore that's a mix of sand and rocks. **Amenities:** none. **Best for:** walking. ⊠ *Vernon and Waddell Sts.* 🎫 *Free.*

FAMILY **Fort Zachary Taylor Beach.** The park's beach is the best and safest place to swim in Key West. There's an adjoining picnic area with barbecue grills and shade trees, a snack bar, and rental equipment, including snorkeling gear. A café serves sandwiches and other munchies. Water shoes are recommended since the bottom is rocky here. **Amenities:** food and drink; showers; toilets; water sports. **Best for:** swimming; snorkeling. ⊠ *Southard St., at end of street, through Truman Annex* 📞 *305/292–6713* ⊕ *www.floridastateparks.org/forttaylor* 🎫 *$4 for 1-occupant vehicles, $6 for 2–8 people in a vehicle, plus 50¢ per person county surcharge.*

FAMILY **Higgs Beach–Astro City Playground.** This Monroe County park with its groomed pebbly sand is a popular sunbathing spot. A nearby grove of Australian pines provides shade, and the West Martello Tower provides shelter should a storm suddenly sweep in. Kayak and beach-chair rentals are available, as is a volleyball net. The beach also has the largest AIDS memorial in the country and a cultural exhibit commemorating the grave site of 295 enslaved Africans who died after being rescued from three South America–bound slave ships in 1860. An athletic trail with 10 fitness stations is a new addition. Hungry? Grab a bite to eat at the on-site restaurant, Salute. Across the street, **Astro City Playground** is popular with young children. **Amenities:** parking; toilets; water sports. **Best for:** swimming; snorkeling. ⊠ *Atlantic Blvd., between White and Reynolds Sts.* 🎫 *Free.*

NEW TOWN

C.B. Harvey Memorial Rest Beach. This beach and park were named after Cornelius Bradford Harvey, former Key West mayor and commissioner. Adjacent to Higgs Beach, it has half a dozen picnic areas

across the street, dunes, a pier, and a wheelchair and bike path. **Amenities:** none. **Best for:** walking. ⊠ *Atlantic Blvd., east side of White St. Pier* ⊠ *Free.*

Smathers Beach. This wide beach has nearly 1 mile of nice white sand, plus beautiful coconut palms, picnic areas, and volleyball courts, all of which make it popular with the spring-break crowd. Trucks along the road rent rafts, Windsurfers, and other beach "toys." **Amenities:** food and drink; parking; toilets; water sports. **Best for:** partiers. ⊠ *S. Roosevelt Blvd.* ⊠ *Free.*

WHERE TO EAT

Bring your appetite, a sense of daring, and a lack of preconceived notions about propriety. A meal in Key West can mean overlooking the crazies along Duval Street, watching roosters and pigeons battle for a chunk of food that may have escaped your fork, relishing the finest in what used to be the dining room of a 19th-century Victorian home, or gazing out at boats jockeying for position in the marina. And that's just the diversity of the setting. Seafood dominates local menus, but the treatment afforded that fish or crustacean can range from Cuban and New World to Asian and Continental.

OLD TOWN

$$
JAPANESE
✕ **Ambrosia.** Ask any savvy local where to get the best sushi on the island and you'll undoubtedly be pointed to this bright and airy dining room with a modern indoor waterfall literally steps from the Atlantic. Grab a seat at the sleek bar, where the back wall glows from purple to blue, or sit at the sushi bar and watch owner and head sushi chef Masa (albeit not the famous chef from New York and Las Vegas) prepare an impressive array of superfresh sashimi delicacies. **Known for:** consistently good fish; great tempura and teriyaki bento lunch specials; the Ambrosia special, with a mix of sashimi, sushi, and rolls. $ *Average main: $20* ⊠ *Santa Maria Resort, 1401 Simonton St.* ☎ *305/293–0304* ⊕ *www.ambrosiasushi.com* ☉ *Closed 2 wks after Labor Day. No lunch weekends.*

$$$
ECLECTIC
✕ **Azur Restaurant.** Fuel up on the finest fare at this former gas station, now part of the Eden House complex. In a contemporary setting with indoor and outdoor seating, welcoming staff serves original, eclectic dishes for breakfast, lunch, and dinner that stand out from those at the hordes of Key West restaurants. **Known for:** four varieties of gnocchi; medium plates; Sunday brunch. $ *Average main: $26* ⊠ *425 Grinnell St.* ☎ *305/292–2987* ⊕ *www.azurkeywest.com.*

$$$
CARIBBEAN
✕ **Blue Heaven.** The outdoor dining area here is often referred to as "the quintessential Keys experience," and it's hard to argue. There's much to like about this historic Caribbean-style restaurant where Hemingway refereed boxing matches and customers cheered for cockfights. **Known for:** house-made desserts and breads; lobster Benedict with key lime hollandaise; the wait for a table. $ *Average main: $24* ⊠ *729 Thomas St.* ☎ *305/296–8666* ⊕ *www.blueheavenkw.com* ☉ *Closed after Labor Day for 6 wks.*

$$
SEAFOOD
Fodor's Choice
★

✗ B.O.'s Fish Wagon. What started out as a fish house on wheels appears to have broken down on the corner of Caroline and William streets and is today the cornerstone for one of Key West's junkyard-chic dining institutions. Step up to the wood-plank counter window and order the specialty: a grouper sandwich fried or grilled and topped with key lime sauce. **Known for:** lots of Key West charm; self-service; all seating on picnic tables in the yard. $ *Average main: $18* ⊠ *801 Caroline St.* ☎ *305/294–9272.*

$
VEGETARIAN

✗ The Café. You don't have to be a vegetarian to love this new-age café decorated with bright artwork and a corrugated-tin-fronted counter. Local favorites include homemade soup, veggie sandwiches and burgers (order them with a side of sweet-potato fries), grilled portobello mushroom salad, seafood, vegan specialties, stir-fry dinners, and grilled Gorgonzola pizza with caramelized onions, walnuts, and spinach. **Known for:** vegan options; wine and beer only; some seafood served. $ *Average main: $11* ⊠ *509 Southard St.* ☎ *305/296–5515* ⊕ *www.thecafekw.com.*

$$$
EUROPEAN
Fodor's Choice
★

✗ Café Marquesa. Chef Susan Ferry presents seven or more inspired entrées on her changing menu each night. Delicious dishes can include anything from yellowtail snapper to Australian rack of lamb. **Known for:** relaxed but elegant setting; good wine and martini lists; desserts worth ordering. $ *Average main: $29* ⊠ *600 Fleming St.* ☎ *305/292–1244* ⊕ *www.marquesa.com* ☾ *No lunch.*

$$$
FRENCH

✗ Café Solé. This little corner of France hides behind a high wall in a residential neighborhood. Inside, French training intertwines with local ingredients, creating delicious takes on classics, including a must-try conch carpaccio, yellowtail snapper with mango salsa, and some of the best bouillabaisse that you'll find outside of Marseilles. **Known for:** hogfish in several different preparations; intimate, romantic atmosphere; worthy desserts. $ *Average main: $27* ⊠ *1029 Southard St.* ☎ *305/294–0230* ⊕ *www.cafesole.com.*

$$$
MODERN
AMERICAN

✗ Camille's Restaurant. Break out the stretchy pants because everything on the menu at this affordable hot spot not only sounds scrumptious, it is. Locals have tried to keep this place a secret for over 20 years, but the word is out for great breakfast, lunch, and dinner. **Known for:** popularity with both locals and tourists; great grilled stone-crab cakes; unique Barbie doll collection. $ *Average main: $21* ⊠ *1202 Simonton St., at Catherine St.* ☎ *305/296–4811* ⊕ *www.camilleskeywest.com.*

$$$
SEAFOOD

✗ Conch Republic Seafood Company. Because of its location where the fast ferry docks, Conch Republic does a brisk business. It's huge, open-air, and on the water, so the place is hard to miss. **Known for:** ambitious menu of Caribbean-inspired seafood; no reservations; live music most nights. $ *Average main: $25* ⊠ *631 Greene St., at Elizabeth St.* ☎ *305/294–4403* ⊕ *www.conchrepublicseafood.com.*

$
FRENCH

✗ Croissants de France. Pop into the bakery for something sinfully sweet or spend some time people-watching at the sidewalk café next door. You can get breakfast or lunch at the café, and the bakery is open late. **Known for:** gluten-free buckwheat crepes; popularity with both locals and visitors; great coffee and croissants. $ *Average main: $14* ⊠ *816 Duval St.* ☎ *305/294–2624* ⊕ *www.croissantsdefrance.com.*

$$
SEAFOOD
Ｘ Dante's Key West Restaurant and Pool Bar. With the motto "Come be an aquaholic," Dante's is as unique as Key West itself. Sun loungers, tiki bars, and tables with umbrellas and chairs surround a large free-form swimming pool. **Known for:** menu of typical bar food and snacks with a few entrées; popular happy hour; raucous weekend pool parties. $⑤ Average main: $18 ⊠ Conch Harbor Marina, 951 Caroline St. ☎ 305/423–2001 ⊕ www.danteskeywest.com.*

$$$
MODERN
AMERICAN
Ｘ Deuce's Off the Hook Grill. It's a tight fit with only six tables (and six counter seats), but if you don't mind sitting close to fellow diners, you will be rewarded with a made-from-scratch meal almost anytime of day. A specials board lists plenty of tempting options, but be sure to ask the price—seafood risotto might *sound* great, but when the reality hits your bill, your wallet won't be happy. **Known for:** excellent fresh seafood; small and can be busy; popular brunch spot. $⑤ Average main: $21 ⊠ 728 Simonton St. ☎ 305/414–8428 ⊕ www.offthehookkeywest. com ⊘ Closed Tues.*

$$
CUBAN
Ｘ El Meson de Pepe. If you want to get a taste of the island's Cuban heritage, this is the place. After watching a Mallory Square sunset, you can dine alfresco or in the dining room on refined versions of Cuban classics. **Known for:** oversized mojitos; Latin band during the nightly sunset celebration; touristy atmosphere. $⑤ Average main: $19 ⊠ Mallory Sq., 410 Wall St. ☎ 305/295–2620 ⊕ www.elmesondepepe.com.*

$
CUBAN
Ｘ El Siboney. Dining at this family-style restaurant is like going to Mom's for Sunday dinner—if your mother is Cuban. The dining room is noisy, and the food is traditional *cubano*. To make a good thing even better, the prices are very reasonable and the homemade sangria is *muy bueno*. **Known for:** memorable paella and traditional dishes; wine and beer only; cheaper than more touristy options close to Duval. $⑤ Average main: $11 ⊠ 900 Catherine St. ☎ 305/296–4184 ⊕ www. elsiboneyrestaurant.com.*

$$
SEAFOOD
FAMILY
Ｘ Half Shell Raw Bar. Smack-dab on the docks, this legendary institution gets its name from the oysters, clams, and peel-and-eat shrimp that are a departure point for its seafood-based diet. It's not clever recipes or fine dining (or even air-conditioning) that packs 'em in; it's fried fish, po'boy sandwiches, and seafood combos. **Known for:** cheap oysters for happy hour; few non-seafood options; good people-watching spot. $⑤ Average main: $16 ⊠ Lands End Village at Historic Seaport, 231 Margaret St. ☎ 305/294–7496 ⊕ www.halfshellrawbar.com.*

$$
AMERICAN
Ｘ Jimmy Buffett's Margaritaville Cafe. If you must have your cheeseburger in paradise, it may as well be here, where you can chew along with the songs playing on the sound system, TV monitors, and movie screen. The first of Buffett's line of chain eateries, it belongs here more than anywhere else, but quite frankly it's more about the name, music, and attitude (and margaritas) than the food. **Known for:** typical Caribbean bar food; live music at night; raucous party atmosphere almost all the time. $⑤ Average main: $16 ⊠ 500 Duval St. ☎ 305/292–1435 ⊕ www. margaritaville.com.*

$$$
ECLECTIC
Ｘ Latitudes. For a special treat, take the short boat ride to lovely Sunset Key for lunch or dinner on the beach. Creativity and quality ingredients combine for dishes that are bound to impress as much as the setting.

Known for: seating both inside and outside on the patio; sophisticated atmosphere and expensive food; free 10-minute ferry ride (and reservations) required. $ *Average main: $28* ⊠ *Sunset Key Guest Cottages, 245 Front St.* ☎ *305/292–5300, 888/477–7786* ⊕ *www.sunsetkeycottages. com/latitudes-key-west.*

$$$$
ECLECTIC
✕ **Louie's Backyard.** Feast your eyes on a steal-your-breath-away view and beautifully presented dishes prepared by executive chef Doug Shook. Once you get over sticker shock on the seasonally changing menu, settle in on the outside deck and enjoy dishes like cracked conch with mango chutney, lamb chops with sun-dried tomato relish, and tamarind-glazed duck breast. **Known for:** the more affordable Cafe at Louie's, upstairs for dinner only; cheaper versions of the same food at lunch; drinks at Afterdeck Bar, directly on the water. $ *Average main: $36* ⊠ *700 Waddell Ave.* ☎ *305/294–1061* ⊕ *www.louiesbackyard.com* ☉ *Closed Labor Day–mid-Sept. Cafe closed Sun. and Mon.*

$$
ITALIAN
✕ **Mangia Mangia.** This longtime favorite serves large portions of home-made pastas that can be matched with any of their homemade sauces. Tables are arranged in a brick garden hung with twinkling lights and in a cozy, casual dining room in an old house. **Known for:** extensive wine list with many old and rare vintages; wine and beer only; nice garden for outdoor seating. $ *Average main: $16* ⊠ *900 Southard St.* ☎ *305/294–2469* ⊕ *www.mangia-mangia.com* ☉ *No lunch.*

$$$$
AMERICAN
✕ **Michaels Restaurant.** White tablecloths, subdued lighting, and romantic music give Michaels the feel of an urban eatery, while garden seating reminds you that you are in the Keys. Chef-owner Michael Wilson flies in prime rib, cowboy steaks, and rib eyes from Allen Brothers in Chicago, which has supplied top-ranked steak houses for more than a century. **Known for:** elegant, romantic atmosphere; small plates available until 7:30 Sunday–Thursday; steak and seafood, which dominate the menu. $ *Average main: $32* ⊠ *532 Margaret St.* ☎ *305/295–1300* ⊕ *www.michaelskeywest.com* ☉ *No lunch.*

$$$$
ECLECTIC
✕ **Nine One Five.** Twinkling lights draped along the lower- and upper-level outdoor porches of a 100-year-old Victorian home set an unstuffy and comfortable stage here. If you like to sample and sip, you'll appreciate the variety of smaller-plate selections and wines by the glass. **Known for:** signature "tuna dome" with fresh crab wrapped in ahi-tuna sashimi; intimate and inviting atmosphere; outdoor dining overlooks upper Duval. $ *Average main: $32* ⊠ *915 Duval St.* ☎ *305/296–0669* ⊕ *www.915duval.com* ☉ *No lunch.*

$$$$
EUROPEAN
✕ **Pisces.** In a circa-1892 former store and home, chef William Arnel and staff create a contemporary setting with a stylish granite bar, Andy Warhol originals, and glass oil lamps. Favorites include "lobster tango mango," flambéed in cognac and served with saffron butter sauce and sliced mangoes. **Known for:** dressy, upscale setting; excellent wine list; gracious service. $ *Average main: $35* ⊠ *1007 Simonton St.* ☎ *305/294–7100* ⊕ *www.pisceskeywest.com* ☉ *Closed summer. No lunch.*

$$$
ITALIAN
✕ **Salute on the Beach.** Sister restaurant to Blue Heaven, this colorful establishment sits on Higgs Beach, giving it one of the island's best lunch views—and a bit of sand and salt spray on a windy day. The intriguing menu is Italian with a Caribbean flair and will not disappoint. **Known**

4

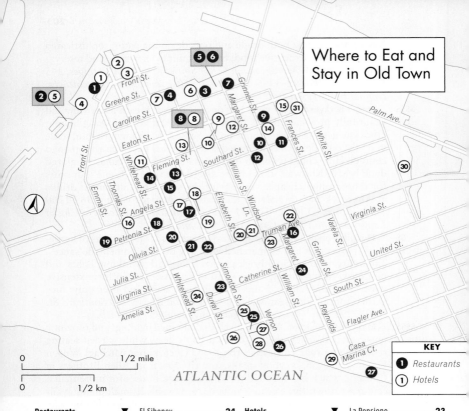

Where to Eat and Stay in Old Town

for: amazing water views; casual, inviting atmosphere; popular with locals as well as visitors. ⑤ *Average main: $22* ⊠ *Higgs Beach, 1000 Atlantic Blvd.* ☎ *305/292–1117* ⊕ *www.saluteonthebeach.com.*

$ ✕ **Santiago's Bodega.** If you've ever wondered where chefs go for a great
TAPAS   meal in the Lower Keys, this is their secret spot. Picky palates will be
Fodor'sChoice   satisfied at this funky, dark, and sensuous corner house, which is well
★   off the main drag. **Known for:** only small plates served, so great for sharing; outdoor dining on the front porch; desserts as good as everything else. ⑤ *Average main: $13* ⊠ *Bahama Village, 207 Petronia St.* ☎ *305/296–7691* ⊕ *www.santiagosbodega.com.*

$$ ✕ **Sarabeth's.** Named for the award-winning jam-maker and pastry chef
AMERICAN   Sarabeth Levine, who runs the kitchen, it naturally is proclaimed for its all-morning, all-afternoon breakfast, best enjoyed in the picket-fenced front yard of this circa-1870 synagogue. Lemon ricotta pancakes, pumpkin waffles, omelets, and homemade jams make the meal. **Known for:** breakfast and brunch specialties, including famous lemon-ricotta pancakes; daily specials; good desserts. ⑤ *Average main: $20* ⊠ *530 Simonton St., at Souhard St.* ☎ *305/293–8181* ⊕ *www.sarabethskeywest.com* ⊘ *Closed Mon. Christmas through Easter, and Tues.*

$$$ ✕ **Seven Fish.** This local hot spot has relocated to a new, easy-to-find
SEAFOOD   location that exudes a casual Key West vibe, but you'll still find the same eclectic mix of dishes. Their specialty, however, will always be the local fish of the day (like snapper with creamy Thai curry). **Known for:** fresh seafood; busy spot requiring reservations; casual, inviting atmosphere. ⑤ *Average main: $26* ⊠ *921 Truman Ave.* ☎ *305/296–2777* ⊕ *www.7fish.com* ⊘ *Closed Tues. No lunch.*

$$ ✕ **Turtle Kraals.** Named for the kraals, or corrals, where sea turtles were
SEAFOOD   once kept until they went to the cannery, this place calls to mind the
FAMILY   island's history. The lunch–dinner menu offers an assortment of marine cuisine that includes seafood enchiladas, mesquite-grilled fish of the day, and mango crab cakes. **Known for:** wood-smoked entrées as good as the fish; happy-hour turtle races; location overlooking the Historic Seaport. ⑤ *Average main: $16* ⊠ *231 Margaret St.* ☎ *305/294–2640* ⊕ *www.turtlekraals.com.*

NEW TOWN

$ ✕ **Hogfish Bar & Grill.** It's worth a drive to Stock Island, one of Florida's
SEAFOOD   last surviving working waterfronts, just outside Key West, to indulge in the freshness you'll witness at this down-to-earth spot. Hogfish is the specialty, of course. **Known for:** "Killer Hogfish Sandwich" on Cuban bread; a spot to watch the shrimpers and fishermen unload their catch; ultracasual atmosphere with picnic tables outside. ⑤ *Average main: $13* ⊠ *6810 Front St., Stock Island* ☎ *305/293–4041* ⊕ *www.hogfishbar.com.*

$$$ ✕ **Tavern N Town.** This handsome and warm restaurant has an open
ECLECTIC   kitchen that adds lovely aromas from the wood-fired oven. The dinner menu offers a variety of options, including small plates and full entrées. **Known for:** upscale atmosphere (and prices); popular happy hour; winning the Master Chef's Classic at Key West Food & Wine Festival. ⑤ *Average main: $26* ⊠ *Key West Marriott Beachside Resort, 3841 N. Roosevelt Blvd.* ☎ *305/296–8100, 800/546–0885* ⊕ *www.beachsidekeywest.com* ⊘ *No lunch.*

WHERE TO STAY

Historic cottages, restored century-old Conch houses, and large resorts are among the offerings in Key West, the majority charging between $100 and $300 a night. In high season, Christmas through Easter, you'll be hard-pressed to find a decent room for less than $200, and most places raise prices considerably during holidays and festivals. Many guesthouses and inns do not welcome children under 16, and most do not permit smoking indoors. Most tariffs include an expanded Continental breakfast and, often, an afternoon glass of wine or snack.

LODGING ALTERNATIVES

The Key West Lodging Association is an umbrella organization for dozens of local properties. Vacation Rentals Key West lists historic cottages, homes, and condominiums for rent. Rent Key West Vacations specializes in renting vacation homes and condos for a week or longer. Vacation Key West lists all kinds of properties throughout Key West. In addition to these local agencies, ⊕ *airbnb.com* and ⊕ *vrbo.com* have many offerings in Key West.

Contacts Key West Lodging Association. ☏ 800/492–1911 ⊕ www.keywestinns.com. **Key West Vacations.** ☏ 888/775–3993 ⊕ www. keywestvacations.com. **Rent Key West Vacations.** ✉ 1075 Duval St., Suite C11 ☏ 305/294–0990, 800/833–7368 ⊕ www.rentkeywest.com. **Vacation Key West.** ✉ 100 Grinnell St., Key West Ferry Terminal ☏ 305/295–9500, 800/595–5397 ⊕ www.vacationkw.com.

OLD TOWN

$$$
B&B/INN
Ambrosia Key West. If you desire personal attention, a casual atmosphere, and a dollop of style, stay at these twin inns spread out on nearly 2 acres. **Pros:** spacious rooms; poolside breakfast; friendly staff. **Cons:** on-street parking can be tough to come by; a little too spread out. ⑤ *Rooms from: $325* ✉ *615, 618, 622 Fleming St.* ☏ *305/296–9838, 800/535–9838* ⊕ *www.ambrosiakeywest.com* ⤳ *16 rooms, 3 town houses, 1 cottage* ⑩ *Breakfast.*

$
B&B/INN
Angelina Guest House. In the heart of Old Town, this home away from home offers simple, clean, attractively priced accommodations. **Pros:** good value; nice garden; friendly staff. **Cons:** thin walls; basic rooms; shared balcony. ⑤ *Rooms from: $134* ✉ *302 Angela St.* ☏ *305/294–4480, 888/303–4480* ⊕ *www.angelinaguesthouse.com* ⤳ *13 rooms* ⑩ *Breakfast.*

$$
B&B/INN
Azul Key West. The ultramodern—nearly minimalistic—redo of this classic circa-1903 Queen Anne mansion is a break from the sensory overload of Key West's other abundant Victorian guesthouses. **Pros:** lovely building; marble-floored baths; luxurious linens. **Cons:** on a busy street. ⑤ *Rooms from: $269* ✉ *907 Truman Ave.* ☏ *305/296–5152, 888/253–2985* ⊕ *www.azulhotels.us* ⤳ *11 rooms* ⑩ *Breakfast.*

$$$
RESORT
FAMILY
Casa Marina, A Waldorf-Astoria Resort. At any moment, you expect the landed gentry to walk across the oceanfront lawn of this luxurious resort, just as they did when this 6½-acre resort opened on New Year's Eve in 1920. **Pros:** nice beach; historic setting; away from the crowds. **Cons:** long walk to central Old Town; expensive resort fee. ⑤ *Rooms from: $399* ✉ *1500 Reynolds St.* ☏ *305/296–3535, 866/203–6392* ⊕ *www.casamarinaresort.com* ⤳ *311 rooms* ⑩ *No meals.*

$$
B&B/INN
Courtney's Place. If you like kids, cats, and dogs, you'll feel right at home in this collection of accommodations ranging from cigar-maker cottages to shotgun houses. **Pros:** near Duval Street; fairly priced. **Cons:** small parking lot; small pool; minimum-stay requirements. *$ Rooms from: $249 ⊠ 720 Whitmarsh La., off Petronia St. ☎ 305/294–3480, 800/869–4639 ⊕ www.courtneysplacekeywest.com ➷ 10 rooms, 8 cottages ❐ Breakfast.*

$$$
HOTEL
Crowne Plaza Key West–La Concha. History and franchises can mix, as this 1920s-vintage hotel proves with its handsome atrium lobby and sleep-conducive rooms. **Pros:** restaurant and Starbucks in-house; close to downtown attractions; free Wi-Fi. **Cons:** high-traffic area; confusing layout; expensive valet-only parking. *$ Rooms from: $339 ⊠ 430 Duval St. ☎ 305/296–2991 ⊕ www.laconchakeywest.com ➷ 178 rooms ❐ No meals.*

$$
HOTEL
Eden House. From the vintage metal rockers on the street-side porch to the old neon hotel sign in the lobby, this 1920s rambling Key West mainstay hotel is high on character, low on gloss. **Pros:** free parking; hot tub is actually hot; daily happy hour around the pool. **Cons:** pricey; a bit of a musty smell in some rooms; no TV in some rooms. *$ Rooms from: $200 ⊠ 1015 Fleming St. ☎ 305/296–6868, 800/533–5397 ⊕ www.edenhouse.com ➷ 44 rooms ❐ No meals.*

$$$$
HOTEL
Fodor'sChoice
★
The Gardens Hotel. Built in 1875, this gloriously shaded, well-loved property was a labor of love from the get-go, and it covers a third of a city block in Old Town. **Pros:** luxurious bathrooms; secluded garden seating; free Wi-Fi. **Cons:** hard to get reservations; expensive; nightly secure parking fee. *$ Rooms from: $415 ⊠ 526 Angela St. ☎ 305/294–2661, 800/526–2664 ⊕ www.gardenshotel.com ➷ 23 rooms ❐ Breakfast.*

$
HOTEL
Harborside Motel & Marina. This little motel neatly packages three appealing characteristics—affordability, safety, and a pleasant location between Old Town and New Town at Garrison Bight. **Pros:** grills for cookouts; friendly fishing atmosphere; boat slips. **Cons:** more than a mile from Duval Street; cash deposit for keys required. *$ Rooms from: $189 ⊠ 903 Eisenhower Dr. ☎ 305/294–2780, 800/501–7823 ⊕ www.keywestharborside.com ➷ 12 rooms, 4 houseboats ❐ No meals.*

$$
B&B/INN
Heron House. Conch-style architecture harks back to this property's circa-1900 origins as a boardinghouse and cigar-maker cottages. **Pros:** charming; fluffy bathrobes. **Cons:** faces noisy Eaton Street; owner's suite smells musty. *$ Rooms from: $229 ⊠ 412 Frances St. ☎ 305/296–4719, 888/265–2395 ⊕ www.heronhousecourt.com ➷ 15 rooms ❐ Breakfast.*

$$$$
RESORT
FAMILY
Hyatt Centric Key West Resort and Spa. With its own man-made beach, the Hyatt Key West is one of few resorts where you can dig your toes in the sand, then walk a short distance away to the streets of Old Town. **Pros:** a little bit away from the bustle of Old Town; plenty of activities; Wi-Fi and bottled water included in resort fee. **Cons:** beach is small; cramped-feeling property; $15 a night self-parking fee, $20 valet. *$ Rooms from: $419 ⊠ 601 Front St. ☎ 305/809–1234 ⊕ www.keywest.hyatt.com ➷ 118 rooms ❐ No meals.*

4

$$$
B&B/INN
⊡ **Island City House Hotel.** A private garden with brick walkways, tropical plants, and a canopy of palms sets this convivial guesthouse apart from the pack. **Pros:** lush gardens; knowledgeable staff. **Cons:** spotty Wi-Fi service; no front-desk staff at night; some rooms are small. ⓢ *Rooms from: $320* ✉ *411 William St.* ☎ *305/294–5702, 800/634–8230* ⊕ *www.islandcityhouse.com* ⤥ *24 suites* ⓧ *No meals.*

$$$$
HOTEL
⊡ **Island House.** Geared specifically toward gay men, this hotel features a health club, a video lounge, a café and bar, and rooms in historic digs. **Pros:** lots of privacy; just the place to get that all-over tan; free happy hour for guests. **Cons:** no women allowed; three rooms share a bath. ⓢ *Rooms from: $459* ✉ *1129 Fleming St.* ☎ *305/294–6284, 800/890–6284* ⊕ *www.islandhousekeywest.com* ⤥ *34 rooms, 31 with bath* ⓧ *No meals.*

$$
B&B/INN
⊡ **Key Lime Inn.** This 1854 Grand Bahama–style house on the National Register of Historic Places succeeds by offering amiable service, a great location, and simple rooms with natural-wood furnishings. **Pros:** walking distance to clubs/bars; some rooms have private outdoor spaces; free Wi-Fi. **Cons:** standard rooms are pricey; pool faces a busy street; mulch-covered paths. ⓢ *Rooms from: $259* ✉ *725 Truman Ave.* ☎ *305/294–5229, 800/549–4430* ⊕ *www.keylimeinn.com* ⤥ *37 rooms* ⓧ *Breakfast.*

$
B&B/INN
⊡ **Key West Bed and Breakfast/The Popular House.** There are accommodations for every budget here, but the owners reason that budget travelers deserve as pleasant an experience (and lavish a tropical Continental breakfast) as their well-heeled counterparts. **Pros:** lots of art; tiled outdoor shower; hot tub and sauna area is a welcome hangout. **Cons:** some rooms are small; four rooms have shared baths. ⓢ *Rooms from: $135* ✉ *415 William St.* ☎ *305/296–7274, 800/438–6155* ⊕ *www.keywest-bandb.com* ⤥ *10 rooms, 6 with bath* ⓧ *Breakfast.*

$$
B&B/INN
⊡ **La Pensione.** Hospitality and period furnishings make this 1891 home, once owned by a cigar executive, a wonderful glimpse into Key West life in the late 19th century. **Pros:** pine-paneled walls; off-street parking; some rooms have wraparound porches. **Cons:** street-facing rooms are noisy; rooms do not have TVs; rooms can only accommodate two people. ⓢ *Rooms from: $258* ✉ *809 Truman Ave.* ☎ *305/292–9923, 800/893–1193* ⊕ *www.lapensione.com* ⤥ *9 rooms* ⓧ *Breakfast.*

$$$$
RESORT
⊡ **Margaritaville Key West Resort & Marina.** This elegant waterfront resort's two three-story, Keys-style buildings huddle around its 37-slip marina in the middle of Old Town overlooking Mallory Square. **Pros:** rooms are large by Key West standards; access to Sunset Key; free Wi-Fi. **Cons:** feels too big for Key West; often crowded; heavy on conference clientele. ⓢ *Rooms from: $409* ✉ *245 Front St.* ☎ *305/294–4000* ⊕ *www.margaritavillekeywest.com* ⤥ *210 rooms* ⓧ *No meals.*

$$$
RESORT
⊡ **The Marker.** As the first new hotel to open in Key West since the early 1990s, The Marker is a welcome and luxurious addition to the waterfront in Old Town, with Conch-style architecture and an authentic Keys aesthetic. **Pros:** convenient Old Town location; on-site restaurant Cero Bodega; three saltwater pools. **Cons:** $30 per night resort fee; underground parking $30 a night; lots of walking if your room isn't near the

amenities. ⑤ *Rooms from: $400* ✉ *200 William St.* ☎ *305/501–5193*
⊕ *www.themarkerkeywest.com* ⤴ *96 rooms* ⑩ *No meals.*

$$$
HOTEL
Fodor's Choice
★

☷ **Marquesa Hotel.** In a town that prides itself on its laid-back luxury,
this complex of four restored 1884 houses stands out. **Pros:** room ser-
vice; romantic atmosphere; turndown service. **Cons:** street-facing rooms
can be noisy; expensive rates. ⑤ *Rooms from: $395* ✉ *600 Fleming St.*
☎ *305/292–1919, 800/869–4631* ⊕ *www.marquesa.com* ⤴ *27 rooms*
⑩ *No meals.*

$$
B&B/INN

☷ **Merlin Guesthouse.** Key West guesthouses don't usually welcome families, but this laid-back jumble of rooms and suites is an exception. **Pros:**
good location near Duval Street; good rates. **Cons:** neighbor noise,
especially in the front rooms; street parking or $10 nightly for their
private lot. ⑤ *Rooms from: $279* ✉ *811 Simonton St.* ☎ *305/296–3336,*
800/642–4753 ⊕ *www.historickeywestinns.com* ⤴ *16 rooms, 4 cottages* ⑩ *Breakfast.*

$$
B&B/INN

☷ **Mermaid & the Alligator.** An enchanting combination of flora and
fauna makes this 1904 Victorian house a welcoming retreat. **Pros:** hot
plunge pool; massage pavilion; island-getaway feel. **Cons:** minimum
stay required (length depends on season); dark public areas; plastic lawn
chairs. ⑤ *Rooms from: $278* ✉ *729 Truman Ave.* ☎ *305/294–1894,*
800/773–1894 ⊕ *www.kwmermaid.com* ⤴ *9 rooms* ⑩ *Breakfast.*

$$$
B&B/INN

☷ **NYAH: Not Your Average Hotel.** From its charming white picket
fence, it may look similar to other Victorian-style, Key West B&Bs,
but that's where the similarities end. **Pros:** central location; expert
staff; free daily happy hour. **Cons:** small rooms; even smaller clos-
ets; no toiletries provided. ⑤ *Rooms from: $349* ✉ *420 Margaret St.*
☎ *305/296–2131* ⊕ *www.nyahotels.com* ⤴ *36 rooms* ⑩ *Breakfast*
⚲ *Age 18 and over only.*

$$$$
RESORT
Fodor's Choice
★

☷ **Ocean Key Resort & Spa.** This full resort—relatively rare in Key West—
has large, tropical-look rooms with private balconies and excellent
amenities, including a pool and bar overlooking Sunset Pier and a Thai-
inspired spa. **Pros:** well-trained staff; lively pool scene; best spa on the
island. **Cons:** $20 per night valet parking; too bustling for some; pricey.
⑤ *Rooms from: $495* ✉ *Zero Duval St.* ☎ *305/296–7701, 800/328–*
9815 ⊕ *www.oceankey.com* ⤴ *100 rooms* ⑩ *No meals.*

$$$$
RESORT

☷ **Pier House Resort and Spa.** This upscale resort is near Mallory Square
in the heart of Old Town, offering a wide range of amenities, including
a beach, and comfortable, traditionally furnished rooms. **Pros:** beautiful beach; free Wi-Fi; nice spa. **Cons:** lots of conventions; poolside
rooms are small; not really suitable for children under 16. ⑤ *Rooms
from: $470* ✉ *1 Duval St.* ☎ *305/296–4600, 800/327–8340* ⊕ *www.
pierhouse.com* ⤴ *145 rooms* ⑩ *No meals.*

$$$
RESORT

☷ **The Reach, A Waldorf Astoria Resort.** Embracing Key West's only natu-
ral beach, this full-service, luxury resort offers sleek rooms, all with
balconies and modern amenities as well as reciprocal privileges to its
sister Casa Marina resort nearby. **Pros:** removed from Duval hubbub;
great sunrise views; pullout sofas in most rooms. **Cons:** expensive
resort fee; high rates; some say it lacks the grandeur you'd expect
of a Waldorf property. ⑤ *Rooms from: $399* ✉ *1435 Simonton St.*

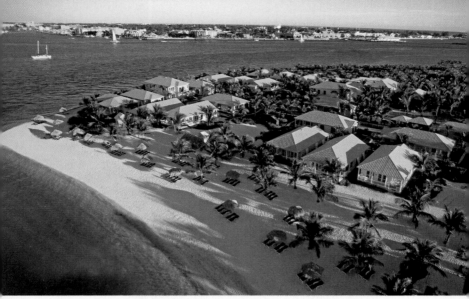

Sunset Key cottages are right on the water's edge, far away from the action of Old Town.

☎ 305/296–5000, 888/318–4316 ⊕ www.reachresort.com ⇆ 72 rooms, 78 suites ⎟◎⎟ No meals.

$$$$
RENTAL
Fodor's Choice
★

🏨 **Santa Maria Suites.** It's odd to call this a hidden gem when it sits on a prominent corner just one block off Duval, but you'd never know what luxury awaits behind its concrete facade, which creates total seclusion from the outside world. **Pros:** amenities galore; front desk concierge services; private parking lot. **Cons:** daily resort fee; beds low to the ground; only two-bedroom units available. ⑤ *Rooms from: $549* ✉ *1401 Simonton St.* ☎ 866/726–8259, 305/296–5678 ⊕ *www. santamariasuites.com* ⇆ *35 suites* ⎟◎⎟ *No meals.*

$$$
B&B/INN

🏨 **Simonton Court.** A small world all its own, this adults-only B&B makes you feel deliciously sequestered from Key West's crasser side but keeps you close enough to get there on foot. **Pros:** lots of privacy; well-appointed accommodations; friendly staff. **Cons:** minimum stays required in high season; $25 a night off-street parking; some street noise in basic rooms. ⑤ *Rooms from: $310* ✉ *320 Simonton St.* ☎ 305/294–6386, 800/944–2687 ⊕ *www.simontoncourt.com* ⇆ *23 rooms, 6 cottages* ⎟◎⎟ *Breakfast.*

$$$
HOTEL

🏨 **Southernmost Beach Resort.** Rooms at this hotel on the quiet end of Duval—a 20-minute walk from downtown—are modern and sophisticated, far enough from the hubub that you can relax but close enough that you can participate if you wish. **Pros:** pool attracts a lively crowd; access to nearby properties and beach; free parking and Wi-Fi. **Cons:** can get crowded around the pool and public areas; expensive nightly resort fee; beach is across the street. ⑤ *Rooms from: $359* ✉ *1319 Duval St.* ☎ 305/296–6577, 800/354–4455 ⊕ *www.southernmost-beachresort.com* ⇆ *118 rooms* ⎟◎⎟ *No meals.*

$$
B&B/INN

Southwinds. Operated by the same company as the ultra-high-end Santa Maria Suites, this motel-style property, though still pretty basic, has been modestly upgraded and is a good value-oriented option in pricey Key West. **Pros:** early (2 pm) check-in may be available; clean and spacious rooms; free parking and Wi-Fi. **Cons:** bland decor; small pools. $ *Rooms from: $200* ✉ *1321 Simonton St.* ☎ *305/296–2829, 877/879–2362* ⊕ *www.keywestsouthwinds.com* ⇆ *58 rooms* ❢⊘ *Breakfast.*

$
B&B/INN

Speakeasy Inn. During Prohibition, Raul Vasquez made this place popular by smuggling in rum from Cuba; today its reputation is for having reasonably priced rooms within walking distance of the beach. **Pros:** good location; all rooms have kitchenettes; free parking, first come first served. **Cons:** no pool; on busy Duval; rooms are fairly basic. $ *Rooms from: $189* ✉ *1117 Duval St.* ☎ *305/296–2680* ⊕ *www.speakeasyinn.com* ⇆ *7 suites* ❢⊘ *Breakfast.*

$$$$
RESORT
Fodor's Choice
★

Sunset Key. This luxurious private island retreat with its own sandy beach feels completely cut off from the world, yet you're just minutes away from the action: a 10-minute ride from Mallory Square on the 24-hour free ferry. **Pros:** all units have kitchens; roomy verandas; free Wi-Fi. **Cons:** luxury doesn't come cheap; beach shore is rocky; launch runs only every 30 minutes. $ *Rooms from: $780* ✉ *245 Front St.* ☎ *305/292–5300, 888/477–7786* ⊕ *www.westinsunsetkeycottages.com* ⇆ *40 cottages* ❢⊘ *Breakfast.*

NEW TOWN

$$
HOTEL

Best Western Key Ambassador Resort Inn. You know what to expect from this chain hotel: well-maintained rooms, predictable service, and competitive prices. **Pros:** big pool area; popular tiki bar; most rooms have screened-in balconies. **Cons:** airport noise; lacks personality. $ *Rooms from: $300* ✉ *3755 S. Roosevelt Blvd., New Town* ☎ *305/296–3500, 800/432–4315* ⊕ *www.keyambassador.com* ⇆ *100 rooms* ❢⊘ *Breakfast.*

$$$$
HOTEL

Key West Marriott Beachside Hotel. This hotel vies for convention business with the biggest ballroom in Key West, but it also appeals to families with its spacious condo units decorated with impeccable good taste. **Pros:** private beach; poolside cabanas; complimentary shuttle to Old Town and airport. **Cons:** small beach; lots of conventions and conferences; cookie-cutter facade. $ *Rooms from: $409* ✉ *3841 N. Roosevelt Blvd., New Town* ☎ *305/296–8100, 800/546–0885* ⊕ *www.keywestmarriottbeachside.com* ⇆ *93 rooms, 93 1-bedroom suites, 10 2-bedroom suites, 26 3-bedroom suites* ❢⊘ *No meals.*

$$$
HOTEL

Parrot Key Resort. This revamped destination resort feels like an old-fashioned beach community with picket fences and rocking-chair porches. **Pros:** four pools; finely appointed units; access to marina and other facilities at three sister properties in Marathon. **Cons:** outside of walking distance to Old Town; no transportation provided; hefty resort fee. $ *Rooms from: $329* ✉ *2801 N. Roosevelt Blvd., New Town* ☎ *305/809–2200* ⊕ *www.parrotkeyresort.com* ⇆ *74 rooms, 74 suites, 74 3-bedroom villas* ❢⊘ *No meals.*

NIGHTLIFE

Rest up: much of what happens in Key West occurs after dark. Open your mind and take a stroll. Scruffy street performers strum next to dogs in sunglasses. Characters wearing parrots or iguanas try to sell you your photo with their pet. Brawls tumble out the doors of Sloppy Joe's. Drag queens strut across stages in Joan Rivers garb. Tattooed men lick whipped cream off women's body parts. And margaritas flow like a Jimmy Buffett tune.

BARS AND LOUNGES

Capt. Tony's Saloon. When it was the original Sloppy Joe's in the mid-1930s, Hemingway was a regular. Later, a young Jimmy Buffett sang here and made this watering hole famous in his song "Last Mango in Paris." Captain Tony was even voted mayor of Key West. Yes, this place is a beloved landmark. Stop in and take a look at the "hanging tree" that grows through the roof, listen to live music seven nights a week, and play some pool. ⊠ *428 Greene St.* ☎ *305/294–1838* ⊕ *www. capttonyssaloon.com.*

Cowboy Bill's Honky Tonk Saloon. Ride the mechanical bucking bull, listen to live bands croon cry-in-your-beer tunes, and grab some pretty decent chow at the indoor-outdoor spread known as Cowboy Bill's Honky Tonk Saloon. There's live music from Tuesday through Saturday. Wednesday brings—we kid you not—sexy bull riding. ⊠ *610½ Duval St.* ☎ *305/295–8219* ⊕ *www.cowboybillskw.com.*

Durty Harry's. This megasize entertainment complex is home to eight different bars and clubs, both indoor and outdoor. Their motto is, "Eight Famous Bars, One Awesome Night," and they're right. You'll find pizza, dancing, live music, Rick's Key West, and the infamous Red Garter strip club. ⊠ *208 Duval St.* ☎ *305/296–5513* ⊕ *www. ricksbarkeywest.com.*

The Garden of Eden. Perhaps one of Duval's more unusual and intriguing watering holes, The Garden of Eden sits atop the Bull & Whistle saloon and has a clothing-optional policy. Most drinkers are looky-lous, but some actually bare it all, including the barmaids. ⊠ *Bull & Whistle Bar, 224 Duval St.* ☎ *305/396–4565.*

Green Parrot Bar. Pause for a libation in the open air and breathe in the spirit of Key West. Built in 1890 as a grocery store, this property has been many things to many people over the years. It's touted as the oldest bar in Key West and the sometimes-rowdy saloon has locals outnumbering out-of-towners, especially on nights when bands play. ⊠ *601 Whitehead St., at Southard St.* ☎ *305/294–6133* ⊕ *www. greenparrot.com.*

Hog's Breath Saloon. Belly up to the bar for a cold mug of the signature Hog's Breath Lager at this infamous joint, a must-stop on the Key West bar crawl. Live bands play daily 1 pm–2 am (except when the game's on TV). You never know who'll stop by and perhaps even jump on stage for an impromptu concert (can you say Kenny Chesney?). ⊠ *400 Front St.* ☎ *305/296–4222* ⊕ *www.hogsbreath.com.*

THE HOLIDAYS KEY WEST STYLE

On New Year's Eve, Key West celebrates the turning of the calendar page with three separate ceremonies that parody New York's dropping-of-the-ball drama. Here they let fall a 6-foot conch shell from Sloppy Joe's Bar, a pirate wench from the towering mast of a tall ship at the Historic Seaport, and a drag queen (elegantly decked out in a ball gown and riding an oversize red high-heel shoe) at Bourbon Street Pub. You wouldn't expect any less from America's most outrageous city.

Key West is one of the nation's biggest party towns, so the celebrations here take on a colorful hue.

In keeping with Key West's rich maritime heritage, its monthlong Bight Before Christmas begins Thanksgiving Eve at Key West Bight. The Lighted Boat Parade creates a quintessential Florida spectacle with live music and decorated vessels of all shapes and sizes.

Some years, Tennessee Williams Theatre hosts a Key West version of the *Nutcracker*. In this unorthodox retelling, the heroine sails to a coral reef and is submerged in a diving bell. (What? No sugarplum fairies?) Between Christmas and New Year's Day, the Holiday House and Garden Tour is another yuletide tradition.

Margaritaville Café. A youngish, touristy crowd mixes with aging Parrot Heads. It's owned by former Key West resident and recording star Jimmy Buffett, who has been known to perform here. The drink of choice is, of course, a margarita, made with Jimmy's own brand of Margaritaville tequila. There's live music nightly, as well as lunch and dinner. ⊠ *500 Duval St.* ☎ *305/292–1435* ⊕ *www.margaritaville.com.*

Pier House. The party here begins at the Beach Bar with live entertainment daily to celebrate the sunset on the beach, then moves to the funky Chart Room. It's small and odd, but there are free hot dogs and peanuts, and its history is worth learning. ⊠ *1 Duval St.* ☎ *305/296–4600, 800/327–8340* ⊕ *www.pierhouse.com.*

Schooner Wharf Bar. This open-air waterfront bar and grill in the historic seaport district retains its funky Key West charm and hosts live entertainment daily. Its margaritas rank among Key West's best, as does the bar itself, voted Best Local's Bar six years in a row. For great views, head up to the second floor and be sure to order up some fresh seafood and fritters and Dark and Stormy cocktails. ⊠ *202 William St.* ☎ *305/292–3302* ⊕ *www.schoonerwharf.com.*

Sloppy Joe's. There's history and good times at the successor to a famous 1937 speakeasy named for its founder, Captain Joe Russell. Decorated with Hemingway memorabilia and marine flags, the bar is popular with travelers and is full and noisy all the time. A Sloppy Joe's T-shirt is a de rigueur Key West souvenir, and the gift shop sells them like crazy. Grab a seat (if you can) and be entertained by the bands and by the parade of people in constant motion. ⊠ *201 Duval St.* ☎ *305/294–5717* ⊕ *www.sloppyjoes.com.*

Sloppy Joe's is one must-stop on most Key West visitors' bar-hop stroll, also known as the Duval Crawl.

Two Friends Patio Lounge. Love karaoke? Get it out of your system at Two Friends Patio Lounge, where your performance gets a live Internet feed via the bar's Karaoke Cam. The singing starts at 8:30 pm most nights. The Bloody Marys are famous. ✉ *512 Front St.* ☎ *305/296–3124* ⊕ *www.twofriendskeywest.com.*

SHOPPING

On these streets, you'll find colorful local art of widely varying quality, key limes made into everything imaginable, and the raunchiest T-shirts in the civilized world. Browsing the boutiques—with frequent pub stops along the way—makes for an entertaining stroll down Duval Street. Cocktails certainly help the appreciation of some goods, such as the figurine of a naked man blowing bubbles out his backside or the swashbuckling pirate costumes that are no longer just for Halloween.

ARTS AND CRAFTS

Alan S. Maltz Gallery. The owner, declared the state's official wildlife photographer by the Wildlife Foundation of Florida, captures the state's nature and character in stunning portraits. Spend four figures for large-format images on canvas or save on small prints and closeouts. ✉ *1210 Duval St.* ☎ *305/294–0005* ⊕ *www.alanmaltz.com.*

Art@830. This inviting gallery carries a little bit of everything, from pottery to paintings and jewelry to sculptures. Most outstanding is its selection of glass art, particularly the jellyfish lamps. Take time to admire all that is here. ✉ *830 Caroline St., Historic Seaport* ☎ *305/295–9595* ⊕ *www.art830.com.*

Gallery on Greene. This is the largest gallery–exhibition space in Key West and it showcases 37 museum-quality artists. They pride themselves on being the leader in the field of representational fine art, painting, sculptures, and reproductions from the Florida Keys and Key West. You can see the love immediately from gallery curator Nancy Frank, who aims to please everyone, from the casual buyer to the established collector. ⊠ *606 Greene St.* ☎ *305/294–1669* ⊕ *www. galleryongreene.com.*

Gingerbread Square Gallery. The oldest private art gallery in Key West represents local and internationally acclaimed artists on an annually changing basis, in mediums ranging from paintings to art glass. ⊠ *1207 Duval St.* ☎ *305/296–8900* ⊕ *www.gingerbreadsquaregallery.com.*

Glass Reunions. Find a collection of wild and impressive fine-art glass here. It's worth a stop in just to see the imaginative and over-the-top glass chandeliers, jewelry, dishes, and platters. ⊠ *825 Duval St.* ☎ *305/294–1720* ⊕ *www.glassreunions.com.*

Key West Pottery. You won't find any painted coconuts here, but you will find a collection of contemporary tropical ceramics. Wife-and-husband owners Kelly Lever and Adam Russell take real pride in this working studio that, in addition to their own creations, features artists from around the country. This is one of the island's few specialty galleries. ⊠ *1203 Duval St.* ☎ *305/900–8303* ⊕ *www.keywestpottery.com.*

Lucky Street Gallery. High-end contemporary paintings are the focus at this gallery that has been in business for over 30 years. There are also a few pieces of jewelry by internationally recognized Key West–based artists. Changing exhibits, artist receptions, and special events make this a lively venue. Although the location has changed, the passionate staff remains the same. ⊠ *1204 White St.* ☎ *305/294–3973* ⊕ *www. luckystreetgallery.com.*

BOOKS

Key West Island Bookstore. This home away from home for the large Key West writers' community carries new, used, and rare titles. It specializes in Hemingway, Tennessee Williams, and South Florida mystery writers. ⊠ *513 Fleming St.* ☎ *305/294–2904* ⊕ *www.key-westislandbooks.com.*

CLOTHING AND FABRICS

Fairvilla Megastore. Don't leave town without a browse through the legendary shop. Although it's not really a clothing store, you'll find an astonishing array of fantasy wear, outlandish costumes (check out the pirate section), as well as other "adult" toys. (Some of the products may make you blush.) ⊠ *520 Front St.* ☎ *305/292–0448* ⊕ *www. fairvilla.com.*

Kino Sandals. A pair of Kino sandals was once a public declaration that you'd been to Key West. The attraction? You can watch these inexpensive items being made. The factory has been churning out several styles since 1966. Walk up to the counter, grab a pair, try them on, and lay down some cash. It's that simple. ⊠ *107 Fitzpatrick St.* ☎ *305/294–5044* ⊕ *www.kinosandalfactory.com.*

Seam Shoppe. Take home a shopping bag full of scarlet hibiscus, fuchsia heliconias, blue parrot fish, and even pink flamingo fabric, selected from the city's widest selection of tropical-print fabrics. ✉ *1113 Truman Ave.* ☎ *305/296–9830* ⊕ *www.tropicalfabricsonline.com.*

FOOD AND DRINK

Fausto's Food Palace. Since 1926 Fausto's has been the spot to catch up on the week's gossip and to chill out in summer—it has groceries, organic foods, marvelous wines, a sushi chef on duty 8 am–3 pm, and box lunches to go. There are two locations you can shop at in Key West (the other is at 1105 White Street) plus a recently opened online store. ✉ *522 Fleming St.* ☎ *305/296–5663* ⊕ *www.faustos.com.*

Fodor'sChoice
★
Kermit's Key West Lime Shoppe. You'll see Kermit himself standing on the corner every time a trolley passes, pie in hand. Besides pie, his shop carries a multitude of key lime products from barbecue sauce to jelly beans. His prefrozen pies, topped with a special long-lasting whipped cream instead of meringue, travels well. This is a must-stop shop while in Key West. The key lime pie is the best on the island; once you try it frozen on a stick, dipped in chocolate, you may consider quitting your job and moving here. Savor every bite on the outdoor patio/garden area. Heaven. ✉ *200 Elizabeth St., Historic Seaport* ☎ *305/296–0806, 800/376–0806* ⊕ *www.keylimeshop.com.*

Peppers of Key West. If you like it hot, you'll love this collection of hundreds of sauces, salsas, and sweets guaranteed to light your fire. Sampling encouraged. ✉ *602 Greene St.* ☎ *305/295–9333, 800/597–2823* ⊕ *www.peppersofkeywest.com.*

GIFTS AND SOUVENIRS

Cayo Hueso y Habana. Part museum, part shopping center, this circa-1879 warehouse includes a hand-rolled-cigar shop, one-of-a-kind souvenirs, a Cuban restaurant, and exhibits that tell of the island's Cuban heritage. Outside, a memorial garden pays homage to the island's Cuban ancestors. ✉ *410 Wall St., Mallory Sq.* ☎ *305/293–7260.*

Montage. For that unique (but slightly overpriced) souvenir of your trip to Key West head here, where you'll discover hundreds of handcrafted signs of popular Key West guesthouses, inns, hotels, restaurants, bars, and streets. If you can't find what you're looking for, they'll make it for you. ✉ *291 Front St.* ⊹ *Next to Margaritaville* ☎ *305/395–9101, 877/396–4278* ⊕ *www.montagekeywest.com.*

SHOPPING CENTERS

Bahama Village. Where to start your shopping adventure? This cluster of spruced-up shops, restaurants, and vendors is responsible for the restoration of the colorful historic district where Bahamians settled in the 19th century. The village lies roughly between Whitehead and Fort streets and Angela and Catherine streets. Hemingway frequented the bars, restaurants, and boxing rings in this part of town. ✉ *Between Whitehead and Fort Sts. and Angela and Catherine Sts.*

SPORTS AND THE OUTDOORS

Unlike the rest of the region, Key West isn't known primarily for outdoor pursuits. But everyone should devote at least half a day to relaxing on a boat tour, heading out on a fishing expedition, or pursuing some other adventure at sea. The ultimate excursion is a boat or seaplane trip to Dry Tortugas National Park for snorkeling and exploring Ft. Jefferson. Other excursions cater to nature lovers, scuba divers, and snorkelers, and folks who just want to get out in the water and enjoy the scenery and sunset. For those who prefer land-based recreation, biking is the way to go. Hiking is limited, but walking the streets of Old Town provides plenty of exercise.

BIKING

Key West was practically made for bicycles, but don't let that lull you into a false sense of security. Narrow and one-way streets along with car traffic result in several bike accidents a year. Some hotels rent or lend bikes to guests; others will refer you to a nearby shop and reserve a bike for you. Rentals usually start at about $12 a day, but some places also rent by the half day. ■ TIP→ Lock up; bikes—and porch chairs!—are favorite targets for local thieves.

A&M Rentals. Rent beach cruisers with large baskets, scooters, and electric mini-cars. Look for the huge American flag on the roof, or call for free airport, ferry, or cruise-ship pickup. ⊠ *523 Truman Ave.* ☎ *305/294–0399* ⊕ *www.amscooterskeywest.com* ⌨ *Bicycles from $15, scooters from $35, electric cars from $99.*

Eaton Bikes. Tandem, three-wheel, and children's bikes are available in addition to the standard beach cruisers and hybrid bikes. Delivery is free for all Key West rentals. ⊠ *830 Eaton St.* ☎ *305/294–8188* ⊕ *www. eatonbikes.com* ⌨ *From $18 per day.*

Moped Hospital. This outfit supplies balloon-tire bikes with yellow safety baskets for adults and kids, as well as scooters and even double-seater scooters. ⊠ *601 Truman Ave.* ☎ *305/296–3344, 866/296–1625* ⊕ *www.mopedhospital.com* ⌨ *Bicycles from $12 per day, scooters from $35 per day.*

BOATING

Key West is surrounded by marinas, so it's easy to find what you're looking for, whether it's sailing with dolphins or paddling in the mangroves. In addition to its popular kayaking trips, Key West Eco-Tours offers sunset sails and private charters *(see Kayaking).*

Classic Harbor Line. The *Schooner America 2.0* is refined and elegant, and her comfortable seating makes her a favorite when she sails Key West each November–April. Two-hour sunset Champagne cruises are an island highlight. ⊠ *202-R Williams St.* ☎ *305/293–7245* ⊕ *www. sail-keywest.com* ⌨ *From $55 day sail, from $85 sunset sail.*

Dancing Dolphin Spirit Charters. Victoria Impallomeni-Spencer, a wilderness guide and environmental marine science expert, invites up to six nature lovers—especially children—aboard the *Imp II,* a 25-foot Aquasport, for four- and seven-hour ecotours that frequently include encounters with wild dolphins. While island-hopping, you visit underwater gardens, natural shoreline, and mangrove habitats. For the "Dolphin Day for Humans" tour, you'll be pulled through the water, equipped with mask and snorkel, on a specially designed "dolphin water massage board" that simulates dolphin swimming motions. Sometimes dolphins follow the boat and swim among participants. All equipment is supplied. Captain Victoria is known around these parts as the dolphin whisperer as she's been guiding for over 40 years. ⊠ *MM 5 OS, Murray's Marina, 5710 Overseas Hwy.* ☎ *305/304–7562, 305/745–9901* ⊕ *www.dancingdolphinspirits.com* ⊒ *From $500.*

FISHING

Any number of local fishing guides can take you to where the big ones are biting, either in the backcountry for snapper and snook or to the deep water for the marlins and shark that lured Hemingway here.

Key West Bait & Tackle. Prepare to catch a big one with the live bait, frozen bait, and fishing equipment provided here. They even offer rod and reel rentals (starting at $15 for one day, $5 each additional day). Stop by their on-site Live Bait Lounge where you can sip $3.25 ice-cold beer while telling fish tales. ⊠ *241 Margaret St.* ☎ *305/292–1961* ⊕ *www. keywestbaitandtackle.com.*

Key West Pro Guides. This outfitter offers private charters, and you can choose four-, five-, six-, or eight-hour trips. Choose from flats, backcountry, reef, offshore fishing, and even specialty trips to the Dry Tortugas. Whatever your fishing (even spearfishing) pleasure, their captains will hook you up. ⊠ *G–31 Miriam St.* ☎ *866/259–4205* ⊕ *www.keywestproguides.com* ⊒ *From $450.*

GOLF

Key West Golf Club. Key West isn't a major golf destination, but there is one course on Stock Island designed by Rees Jones that will downright surprise you with its water challenges and tropical beauty. It's also the only "Caribbean" golf course in the United States, boasting 200 acres of unique Florida foliage and wildlife. Hole 8 is the famous "Mangrove Hole," which will give you stories to tell. It's a 143-yard, par 3 that is played completely over a mass of mangroves with their gnarly roots and branches completely intertwined. Bring extra balls and book your tee time early in season. Nike rental clubs available. ⊠ *6450 E. College Rd.* ☎ *305/294–5232* ⊕ *www.keywestgolf.com* ⊒ *$55–$99* ⅄ *18 holes, 6500 yards, par 70.*

KAYAKING

Key West Eco-Tours. Key West is surrounded by marinas, so it's easy to find a water-based activity or tour, whether it's sailing with dolphins or paddling in the mangroves. These sail-kayak-snorkel excursions take you into backcountry flats and mangrove forests without the crowds. The 4½-hour trip includes a light lunch, equipment, and even dry camera bags. Private sunset sails, kayak, and paddleboard tours are available, too. ⊠ *Historic Seaport, 100 Grinnell St.* ☎ *305/294–7245* ⊕ *www.keywestecotours.com* ⊒ *From $115.*

Lazy Dog. Take a two- or four-hour guided sea kayak–snorkel tour around the mangrove islands just east of Key West. Costs include transportation, bottled water, a snack, and supplies, including snorkeling gear. Paddleboard tours and PaddleYoga and PaddleFit classes are also available, as are rentals for self-touring. ⊠ *5114 Overseas Hwy.* ☎ *305/295–9898* ⊕ *www.lazydog.com* ☞ *From $40.*

SCUBA DIVING AND SNORKELING

The Florida Keys National Marine Sanctuary extends along Key West and beyond to the Dry Tortugas. Key West National Wildlife Refuge further protects the pristine waters. Most divers don't make it this far out in the Keys, but if you're looking for a day of diving as a break from the nonstop party in Old Town, expect to pay about $65 and upward for a two-tank dive. Serious divers can book dive trips to the Dry Tortugas. The USS *Vandenberg* is another popular dive spot, known for its world's-first underwater transformative art exhibit on an artificial reef.

Captain's Corner. This PADI-certified dive shop has classes in several languages and twice-daily snorkel and dive trips to reefs and wrecks aboard the 60-foot dive boat *Sea Eagle.* Use of weights, belts, masks, and fins is included. ⊠ *125 Ann St.* ☎ *305/296–8865* ⊕ *www.captainscorner.com* ☞ *From $45.*

Dive Key West. Operating over 40 years, Dive Key West is a full-service dive center that has charters, instruction, gear rental, sales, and repair. You can take either snorkel excursions or scuba trips with this outfit that is dedicated to coral reef education and preservation. ⊠ *3128 N. Roosevelt Blvd.* ☎ *305/296–3823* ⊕ *www.divekeywest.com* ☞ *Snorkeling from $69, scuba from $95.*

FAMILY **Snuba of Key West.** If you've always wanted to dive but never found the time to get certified, Snuba is for you. You can dive safely using a regulator tethered to a floating air tank with a simple orientation. Ride out to the reef on a catamaran, then follow your guide underwater for a one-hour tour of the coral reefs. It's easy and fun. No prior diving or snorkeling experience is necessary, but you must know how to swim and be at least eight years old. The price includes beverages. ⊠ *Garrison Bight Marina, Palm Ave., between Eaton St. and N. Roosevelt Blvd.* ☎ *305/292–4616* ⊕ *www.snubakeywest.com* ☞ *From $109.*

STAND-UP PADDLEBOARDING

SUP Key West. This ancient sport from Hawaii involves a surfboard and a paddle and has quickly become a favorite Florida water sport known as SUP (stand-up paddleboarding). SUP Key West gives lessons and morning, afternoon, or sunset tours of the estuaries. What's more, your tour guides are experts (one's even a PhD) in marine biology and ecology. Call ahead to make arrangements. ⊠ *110 Grinnell St.* ☎ *305/240–1426* ⊕ *www.supkeywest.com* ☞ *From $45.*

EXCURSION TO DRY TORTUGAS NATIONAL PARK

70 miles southwest of Key West.

The Dry Tortugas lie in the central time zone. Key West Seaplane pilots like to tell their passengers that they land 15 minutes before they take off. If you can't do the time-consuming and (by air, at least, expensive) trip, the national park operates an interpretive center in the Historic Seaport at Old Key West Bight.

GETTING HERE AND AROUND

For now, the ferryboat *Yankee Freedom III* departs from a marina in Old Town and does day trips to Garden Key. Key West Seaplane Adventures has half- and full-day trips to the Dry Tortugas, where you can explore Ft. Jefferson, built in 1846, and snorkel on the beautiful protected reef. Departing from the Key West airport, the flights include soft drinks and snorkel equipment for $265 half day, $465 full day, plus there's a $10 park fee (cash only). If you want to explore the park's other keys, look into renting a boat or hiring a private charter. The Dry Tortugas National Park and Historic Key West Bight Museum at 240 Margaret Street is a way to experience it for free. *See Exploring in Key West.*

Key West Seaplane Adventures. The 35- to 40-minute trip to the Dry Tortugas skims above the trademark windowpane-clear waters of the Florida Keys. The seaplane perspective provides an awesome experience that could result in a stiff neck from craning to look out the window and down from 500 feet above. In the flats that edge Key West, you can spot stingrays, sea turtles, and sharks in the shallow water. In the area dubbed The Quicksands, water plunges to 30-foot depths and sand undulates in dunelike formations. Shipwrecks also festoon these waters; here's where Mel Fisher harvested treasure from the *Atocha* and *Margarita*. His 70-foot work ship, the *Arbutus*, deteriorated and eventually sank at the northern edge of the treasure sites. With its mast poking out above water, it's easy to spot and fun to photograph. From there, the water deepens from emerald hues to shades of deep blue as depths reach 70 feet. Seaplanes of Key West's most popular trip is the half-day option, where you spend about 2½ hours on Garden Key. The seaplanes leave during your stay, so be prepared to carry all of your possessions with you. The morning trip beats the ferries to the island, so you'll have it to yourself until the others arrive. Snorkeling equipment, soft drinks, and birding lists are supplied. ⊠ *3471 S. Roosevelt Blvd., Key West* ☎ *305/293–9300* ⊕ *www.keywestseaplanecharters.com* ✉ *From $317.*

Yankee Freedom III. The fast, sleek, 110-foot catamaran *Yankee Freedom III* travels to the Dry Tortugas in 2¼ hours. The time passes quickly on the roomy vessel equipped with four restrooms, three warm freshwater showers, and two bars. Stretch out on two decks that are both air-conditioned, with cushioned seating. There is also an open sundeck with sunny and shaded seating. Continental breakfast and lunch are included. On arrival, a naturalist leads a 45-minute guided tour, which is followed by lunch and a free afternoon for swimming, snorkeling (gear included), and exploring. The vessel is

ADA certified for visitors using wheelchairs. The Dry Tortugas lies in the central time zone. ✉ *Lands End Marina, 240 Margaret St., Key West* ☎ *305/294–7009, 800/634–0939* ⊕ *www.yankeefreedom. com* 🖥 *$175; parking $13 in city garage.*

EXPLORING

Dry Tortugas National Park. This park, 70 miles off the shores of Key West, consists of seven small islands. Tour the fort; then lay out your blanket on the sunny beach for a picnic before you head out to snorkel on the protected reef. Many people like to camp here ($15 per site for one of eight sites, plus a group site and overflow area; first come, first served), but note that there's no freshwater supply and you must carry off whatever you bring onto the island.

The typical visitor from Key West, however, makes it no farther than the waters of Garden Key. Home to 19th-century Ft. Jefferson, it is the destination for seaplane and fast ferry tours out of Key West. With 2½ to 6½ hours to spend on the island, visitors have time to tour the mammoth fort-prison and then cool off with mask and snorkel along the fort's moat wall.

History buffs might remember long-deactivated Ft. Jefferson, the largest brick building in the western hemisphere, as the prison that held Dr. Samuel Mudd, who unwittingly set John Wilkes Booth's leg after the assassination of Abraham Lincoln. Three other men were also held there for complicity in the assassination. Original construction on the fort began in 1846 and continued for 30 years, but was never completed because the invention of the rifled cannon made it obsolete. That's when it became a Civil War prison and later a wildlife refuge. In 1935 President Franklin Roosevelt declared it a national monument for its historic and natural value.

The brick fort acts as a gigantic, almost 16-acre reef. Around its moat walls, coral grows and schools of snapper, grouper, and wrasses hang out. To reach the offshore coral heads requires about 15 minutes of swimming over sea-grass beds. The reef formations blaze with the color and majesty of brain coral, swaying sea fans, and flitting tropical fish. It takes a bit of energy to swim the distance, but the water depth pretty much measures under 7 feet all the way, allowing for sandy spots to stop and rest. (Standing in sea-grass meadows and on coral is detrimental to marine life.)

Serious snorkelers and divers head out farther offshore to epic formations, including Palmata Patch, one of the few surviving concentrations of elkhorn coral in the Keys. Day-trippers congregate on the sandy beach to relax in the sun and enjoy picnics. Overnight tent campers have use of restroom facilities and achieve a total getaway from noise, lights, and civilization in general. Remember that no matter how you get here, the park's $10 admission fee must be paid in cash.

The park has set up with signage a self-guided tour that takes about 45 minutes. You should budget more time if you're into photography, because the scenic shots are hard to pass up. Ranger-guided tours are also available at certain times. Check in at the visitor center for a schedule. The small office also shows an orientation video, sells books and other educational materials, and, most importantly, provides a blast of air-conditioning on hot days.

Birders in the know bring binoculars to watch some 100,000 nesting sooty terns at their only U.S. nesting site, Bush Key, adjacent to Garden Key. Noddy terns also nest in the spring. During winter migrations, birds fill the airspace so thickly they literally fall from the sky to make their pit stops, birders say. Nearly 300 species have been spotted in the park's seven islands, including frigate birds, boobies, cormorants, and broad-winged hawks. Bush Key is closed to foot traffic during nesting season, January through September. ⊠ *Key West* ⊕ *www.nps.gov/drto* ▧ *$10.*

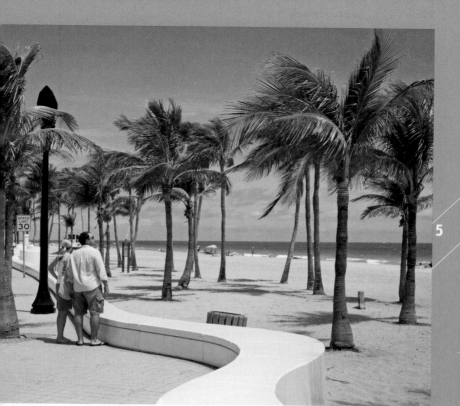

FORT LAUDERDALE

WELCOME TO FORT LAUDERDALE

TOP REASONS TO GO

★ **Blue waves:** The cerulean waters of the Atlantic Ocean hugging Broward County's entire coast form a 23-mile stretch of picturesque beaches between Miami-Dade and Palm Beach counties.

★ **Inland waterways:** More than 300 miles of inland waterways, including downtown Fort Lauderdale's historic New River and Intracoastal, create what's known as the "Venice of America."

★ **Everglades adventures:** The untamed landscape of the Everglades—home to alligators, crocodiles, colorful birds, and other elusive wildlife—is a short trip from beachfront luxury.

★ **Emerging arts scene:** Experience the local contemporary art scene as it grows into a major force in the region.

★ **Cruise gateway:** A dozen supermodern terminals serve about 4 million cruisers and ferry guests a year at Port Everglades, the busiest cruise port in the country.

1 Fort Lauderdale. Anchored by the New River and an eclectic downtown hub, Fort Lauderdale comprises high-rise condos along with single-family homes, museums, parks, and attractions. Las Olas Boulevard's boutiques, sidewalk cafés, and restaurants complement 23 miles of sparkling beaches.

2 Lauderdale-by-the-Sea. North of Fort Lauderdale on State Road A1A, old-school seaside charm draws families and cost-conscious travelers to a more low-rise, low-key beach alternative to Fort Lauderdale.

3 Hollywood. From the beachside Broadwalk to historic Young Circle (now ArtsPark), this South Broward destination provides grit and good times in a laid-back manner.

GETTING ORIENTED

Along Florida's Gold Coast, Fort Lauderdale and Broward County present a delightful middle ground between the posh Palm Beaches and the extravagance of Miami. From downtown Fort Lauderdale, it's about a four-hour drive to Orlando or Key West, but Broward's allure is undeniable. From ocean side to inland, the county's sprawling geography encompasses 31 communities with a resident population of nearly 1.8 million.

5

Deerfield Beach
Hillsboro Beach
Coconut Creek
Sample Rd.
Margate
Coconut Cr. Pkwy.
North Lauderdale
Atlantic Blvd.
Pompano Beach
Cypress Creek Rd.
Commercial Blvd.
Lauderdale-by-the-Sea
Oakland Park Blvd.
Lauderdale Lakes
Oakland Park
Wilton Manors
Sunrise Blvd.
Fort Lauderdale
Broward Blvd.
Las Olas Blvd.
Davie Blvd.
Melrose Park
S.E. 17th St. Causeway
Port Everglades
Fort Lauderdale-Hollywood International Airport
Griffin Rd.
Stirling Rd.
Dania Beach
Dania Beach Blvd.
Sheridan St.
Hollywood Blvd.
Hollywood
Pembroke Rd.
Hallandale
Hallandale Blvd.

ATLANTIC OCEAN

Powerline Rd.
Dixie Hwy.
Federal Hwy.
N. Andrews Ave.
S.W. 31st Ave.
Dixie Hwy.

0   3 mi
0   3 km

Updated
by Galena
Mosovich

It was only a matter of time before the sun-soaked streets of Fort Lauderdale faced an identity crisis. What was once a hotbed of dive bars, diners, and all-day beach parties is now a more upscale destination with a deeper focus on quality in the pursuit of leisure. The city's elevated personality has paved the way for creative organizations, notable eateries, and premium entertainment options to stake their claims and has attracted a menagerie of world-class hotel brands and condo developments. Fortunately, the upscaling is generally guided by an understated interpretation of luxury that doesn't follow Miami's over-the-top lead. Fort Lauderdale is still a place where flip-flops are acceptable, if not encouraged.

Along The Strip and west to the Intracoastal, many of the mid-century-modern boutique properties are trying to preserve the neighborhood's vintage design aesthetic. Somehow, Greater Fort Lauderdale gracefully melds disparate eras into nouveau nirvana, seasoned with a lot of sand. This could be the result of its massive territory: Broward County encompasses more than 1,100 square miles of land—ranging from dense residential enclaves to agricultural farms and subtropical wilds. But it's the county's beautiful beaches and some 3,000 hours of sunshine each year that make all this possible.

Fort Lauderdale was named for Major William Lauderdale, who built a fort in 1838 during the Second Seminole War. It was incorporated in 1911 with only 175 residents, but it grew quickly during the Florida boom of the 1920s, and it became a popular spring break destination in the 1960s. Today's population is more than 176,000, and the suburbs continue to grow. Of Broward County's 31 municipalities and unincorporated areas, Fort Lauderdale is the largest. And now, show-stopping hotels, a hot food scene, and a burgeoning cultural platform accompany the classic beach lifestyle.

PLANNING

WHEN TO GO

Peak season is Thanksgiving through April, when cultural events (performing arts, visual art, concerts, and other outdoor entertainment) go full throttle. Expect extreme heat and humidity along with rain in the summer. Hurricanes come most notably in August and September. Tee times are harder to get on weekends year-round. Regardless of season, remember that Fort Lauderdale sunshine will burn even on a cloudy day.

GETTING HERE AND AROUND

AIR TRAVEL

Fort Lauderdale–Hollywood International Airport (FLL) serves more than 26 million passengers a year. FLL is 3 miles south of downtown Fort Lauderdale—just off U.S. 1 (South Federal Highway) between Fort Lauderdale and Hollywood, and near Port Everglades and Fort Lauderdale Beach. Other options include **Miami International Airport (MIA)**, which is about 32 miles southwest, and the far less chaotic **Palm Beach International Airport (PBI)**, which is about 50 miles north.

Airport Information Fort Lauderdale–Hollywood International Airport (FLL). ☎ 866/435–9355 ⊕ www.broward.org/airport. **Miami International Airport (MIA).** ☎ 800/825–5642 ⊕ www.miami-airport.com. **Palm Beach International Airport (PBI).** ☎ 561/471–7420 ⊕ www.pbia.org.

BUS TRAVEL

Broward County Transit (BCT) operates Bus Route 1 between the airport and its main terminal at Broward Boulevard and Northwest First Avenue in downtown Fort Lauderdale. Service from the airport is every 20 to 30 minutes and begins at 5:29 am on weekdays, 6:04 am Saturday, and 6:44 am Sunday; the last bus leaves the airport at 11:36 pm on weekdays, 11:44 pm Saturday, and 9:44 pm Sunday. The one-way cash fare is $2 (exact change). ■TIP→ **The Northwest First Avenue stop is in a sketchy part of town. Exercise caution there, day or night. Better yet, take an Uber, Lyft, or taxi to and from the airport.** BCT also covers the county on fixed routes to four transfer terminals: Broward Central Terminal, West Regional Terminal, Lauderhill Mall Transfer Facility, and Northeast Transit Center. The fare for an all-day bus pass is $5 (exact change). Service starts around 4:30 am and continues to 12:40 am, except on Sunday.

Bus Contacts Broward County Transit. ☎ 954/357–8400 ⊕ www.broward.org/BCT.

CAR TRAVEL

Renting a car to get around Broward County is highly recommended. Traditional cabs are unreliable and expensive; ride-hailing apps such as Uber and Lyft are a cheaper, better option. Public transportation is not a realistic option for most travelers, but the Sun Trolley can be sufficient for some visitors who don't need or wish to explore beyond the downtown core and beaches.

By car, access to Broward County from north or south is via Florida's Turnpike, Interstate 95, U.S. 1, or U.S. 441. Interstate 75 (Alligator Alley, requiring a toll despite being part of the nation's interstate-highway system) connects Broward with Florida's west coast and runs parallel to State Road 84 within the county. East–west Interstate 595 runs from westernmost Broward County and connects Interstate 75 with Interstate 95 and U.S. 1, providing easy access to the airport and seaport. State Road A1A, designated a Florida Scenic Highway by the state's Department of Transportation, runs parallel to the beach.

TRAIN TRAVEL

Amtrak provides daily service to Fort Lauderdale and stops in Deerfield Beach and Hollywood.

All three of the region's airports link to Tri-Rail, a commuter train operating daily through Palm Beach, Broward, and Miami-Dade counties.

New, privately operated high-speed Brightline service began in summer 2017, connecting downtown Miami, Fort Lauderdale, and West Palm Beach. The trip from downtown Miami to Fort Lauderdale takes about 30 minutes; it's another 30 minutes to West Palm Beach.

Contacts Brightline. ⊕ *gobrightline.com.*

HOTELS

A collection of relatively young luxury beachfront hotels—the Atlantic Hotel & Spa, Hilton Fort Lauderdale Beach Resort, the Ritz-Carlton, the W, the Westin—that opened within the last decade are welcoming newcomers to the "Luxe Lauderdale" corridor. Seriously sophisticated places to stay include The Conrad, Four Seasons, and The Gale, while smaller retro spots are disappearing. You can also find hotel chains along the Intracoastal Waterway. If you want to be *on* the beach, be sure to ask when booking your room as many hotels on the inland waterways or on A1A advertise "waterfront" accommodations.

RESTAURANTS

Greater Fort Lauderdale offers one of the best and most diverse dining scenes of any U.S. city its size. There are more than 4,000 eateries in Broward offering everything from new American and South American to pan-Asian cuisines. Go beyond the basics, and you'll find an endless supply of hidden gems.

Hotel and restaurant reviews have been shortened. For full information, visit Fodors.com.

WHAT IT COSTS			
$	$$	$$$	$$$$
Restaurants under $15	$15–$20	$21–$30	over $30
Hotels under $200	$200–$300	$301–$400	over $400

Restaurant prices are the average cost of a main course at dinner or, if dinner is not served, at lunch. Hotel prices are the lowest cost of a standard double room in high season.

FORT LAUDERDALE

Like most of southeast Florida, Fort Lauderdale has long been revitalizing. Despite wariness of pretentious overdevelopment, city leaders have allowed a striking number of glittering high-rises and new hotels. Nostalgic locals and frequent visitors fret over the diminishing vision of sailboats bobbing in waters near downtown; however, Fort Lauderdale remains the yachting capital of the world, and the water toys don't seem to be going anywhere. Sharp demographic changes are also changing the face of Greater Fort Lauderdale with increasingly cosmopolitan communities, more minorities (including Hispanics and people of Caribbean descent), as well as gays and lesbians. Young professionals and families are settling into Fort Lauderdale proper, whereas longtime residents are heading north for more space. Downtown Fort Lauderdale's burgeoning arts district, cafés, and nightlife venues continue to the main drag of Las Olas Boulevard, where boutiques and restaurants dot the pedestrian-friendly street. Farther east is the sparkling shoreline. There are myriad neighborhoods to the north and south of Las Olas Boulevard that all offer their own brand of charm.

GETTING HERE AND AROUND

The Fort Lauderdale metro area is laid out in a grid system, and only a few waterways and bridges interrupt the relatively straight path of streets and roads. Nomenclature is important here: streets, roads, courts, and drives run east–west; avenues, terraces, and ways run north–south; boulevards can (and do) run any which way. For visitors, Las Olas Boulevard is one of the most important east–west passageways. It runs from the beach to downtown; whereas State Road A1A—dubbed Atlantic Boulevard, Ocean Boulevard, and Fort Lauderdale Beach—runs parallel to the north–south oceanfront. These names are confusing, and visitors can get mixed up with the streets called Atlantic and Ocean in both Hollywood and Pompano Beach, respectively.

The city's road system suffers from traffic overload. Interstate 595 connects the city and suburbs and provides a direct route to the Fort Lauderdale–Hollywood International Airport and Port Everglades, but lanes slow to a crawl during rush hours. The Intracoastal Waterway is the nautical equivalent of an interstate highway; it runs north–south through Fort Lauderdale and provides easy boating access to local hot spots as well as neighboring waterfront communities.

To bounce around Fort Lauderdale for free (with exceptions), catch a multicolored Sun Trolley. There are seven routes and each operates on its own schedule. Simply wave at the trolley driver: trolleys will stop for pickups anywhere along their route. Luggage is not allowed on the trolley, so this isn't a viable option for airport transportation. The most popular routes—Las Olas/Beaches—is $1 per ride or $3 for a day pass (cash only). It's best to review Sun Trolley's routes and schedules before trying this service.

Yellow Cab covers most of Broward County, but it's very expensive, and there's a $10 minimum for all trips originating from seaport or airport, and an additional $3 service charge when you start at the airport. You can book by phone, text, app, or website, and all Yellow Cab vehicles accept major credit cards. The Uber and Lyft apps are more concerned with the user experience and charge cheaper rates, hence their significant presence in the area.

Contacts Sun Trolley. ☎ 954/876–5539 ⊕ www.suntrolley.com. **Yellow Cab.** ☎ 954/777–7777 ⊕ yellowcabbroward.com.

TOURS

The labyrinthine waterways of Fort Lauderdale are home to thousands of privately owned vessels, but you don't need to be or know a boat owner to play on the water. To fully understand this city of canals (aka the "Venice of America"), you must see it from the water. Kick back on a boat tour or hop on a Water Taxi, Fort Lauderdale's floating trolley.

Carrie B Cruises. Board the *Carrie B*, a 112-foot paddle wheeler, for a 90-minute sightseeing tour of the New River, Intracoastal Waterway, and Port Everglades. Cruises depart at 11 am, 1 pm, and 3 pm daily from October through April; Thursday–Monday between May and September. The cost is $23.95 plus tax. Book ahead online for discounts. ⊠ *440 N. New River Dr. E, off Las Olas Blvd.* ☎ *888/238–9805* ⊕ *www.carriebcruises.com.*

FAMILY **Jungle Queen Riverboats.** The kitschy *Jungle Queen* and *River Queen* riverboats cruise through the heart of Fort Lauderdale on the New River. It's an old-school experience because this company launched its tours in 1935, and the touristy charm is just part of the fun. The daily morning sightseeing cruise at 11 am costs $23.50. The afternoon cruise and tour of Tropical Isle at 1:30 pm is $29.95. The daily afternoon and evening cruises at 4:30 and 7:30 pm are Thursday–Sunday and cost $23.50. The 6 pm all-you-can-eat barbecue dinner cruise runs Tuesday–Sunday and costs $52.95. ⊠ *Bahia Mar Yachting Center, 801 Seabreeze Blvd.* ☎ *954/462–5596* ⊕ *www.junglequeen.com.*

FAMILY
Fodor'sChoice
★
Water Taxi. At once a sightseeing tour and a mode of transportation, the Water Taxi is a smart way to experience most of Fort Lauderdale and Hollywood's waterways. The system has three connected routes: the Fort Lauderdale, the Margaritaville Express, and the Hollywood Local. The Fort Lauderdale route runs every 30 minutes from around 9:45 am to 11 pm; the other two routes have published schedules (check out the website). It's possible to cruise all day while taking in the sights. Captains and crew share fun facts and white lies about the city's history, as well as quirky tales about celebrity homes. A day pass is $26. ⊠ *Fort Lauderdale* ☎ *954/467–6677* ⊕ *www.watertaxi.com.*

VISITOR INFORMATION

Greater Fort Lauderdale Convention and Visitors Bureau. ⊠ *101 N.E. 3rd Ave., #100* ☎ *954/765–4466* ⊕ *www.sunny.org.*

EXPLORING

DOWNTOWN AND LAS OLAS

The jewel of downtown is the Arts and Entertainment District, where Broadway shows, ballet, and theater take place at the riverfront Broward Center for the Performing Arts. A cluster of cultural entities are within a five-minute walk: the Museum of Discovery and Science, the Fort Lauderdale Historical Society, and NSU's art museum. Restaurants, sidewalk cafés, bars, and dance clubs flourish along Las Olas's downtown extension, and its main presence brings a more upscale atmosphere. Riverwalk ties these two areas together with a 2-mile stretch along the New River's north and south banks, though the commercial success of this section has been tepid. Tropical gardens with benches and interpretive displays line the walk on the north, with boat landings on the south side.

TOP ATTRACTIONS

Fodor's Choice ★ **Flagler Arts and Technology Village (FATVillage).** Inspired by Miami's Wynwood Arts District, Flagler Arts & Technology Village (or FATVillage) encompasses several square blocks of a formerly blighted warehouse district in downtown Fort Lauderdale. It's now thriving with a slew of production studios, art studios, loft-style apartments, and a fabulous coffee shop. On the last Saturday of the month, FATVillage hosts an evening art walk, in which businesses display contemporary artworks by local talent, and where food trucks gather. There are libations, of course, and the village erupts into a giant, culture-infused street party. Many tourists come specifically for this monthly affair, but if you are visiting by day, check out one of Fort Lauderdale's coolest coffee shops, Next Door at C&I Studios. It's nestled inside a creative agency's lofty space, where the decor alone will keep you stimulated. Adorned with antique nods to the literary world, tufted couches, and an eerie 1972 Airstream trailer, Next Door serves the locally made Brew Urban Cafe. ⊠ 521 N.W. 1st Ave., Downtown ☎ 954/760–5900 ⊕ www.fatvillage.com.

Historic Stranahan House Museum. The city's oldest surviving structure was once home to businessman Frank Stranahan, who arrived from Ohio in 1892. With his wife, Ivy, the city's first schoolteacher, he befriended and traded with Seminole Indians. In 1901 he built a store that would later become his home after serving as a post office, a general store, and a restaurant. The couple's tale is filled with ups and downs. Their home remains Fort Lauderdale's principal link to its brief history and has been on the National Register of Historic Places since 1973. Self-guided tours of the museum are not allowed. ⊠ 335 S.E. 6th Ave., Downtown ✛ Just off Las Olas Blvd. on the New River ☎ 954/524–4736 ⊕ www.stranahanhouse.org ☎ $12.

Fodor's Choice ★ **Las Olas Boulevard.** What Lincoln Road is to South Beach, Las Olas Boulevard is to Fort Lauderdale. Regarded as the heart and soul of Broward County, Las Olas is the premier street for restaurants, art galleries, museums, shopping, dining, and people-watching. Lined with high-rises in the downtown area and original boutiques and ethnic eateries along 10 blocks of the main stretch, it's also home to beautiful mansions and traditional Florida homes along the Intracoastal Waterway to the east, which typify the modern-day aesthetic of Fort Lauderdale. The ocean appears beyond the residential swath, and that's where you see that the name "Las Olas" (Spanish for "The Waves") begins to make more sense. It's a pedestrian-friendly thoroughfare, but it's not closed to vehicular traffic at any point. ⊠ E. Las Olas Blvd., Downtown ⊕ www.lasolasboulevard.com.

FAMILY **Museum of Discovery and Science and AutoNation IMAX Theater.** There are
Fodor's Choice dozens of interactive exhibits here to entertain children—*and* adults—
★ through the wonders of science and Florida's delicate ecosystem. The
state-of-the-art "7-D" theater takes guests on a virtual tour of aviation
technology, while the Ecodiscovery Center comes with an Everglades
Airboat Adventure ride, resident otters, and an interactive Florida storm
center. The 300-seat AutoNation IMAX theater is part of the complex
and shows mainstream and educational films, some in 3-D, on the
biggest screen in South Florida with a rare high-tech laser projection
system. ⊠ *401 S.W. 2nd St., Downtown* ☎ *954/467–6637 museum,*
954/463–4629 IMAX ⊕ *www.mods.org* ⊠ *Museum $16, $21 with 1*
classic IMAX screening.

Fodor's Choice **NSU Museum of Art Fort Lauderdale.** Led by visionary director and chief
★ curator Bonnie Clearwater, the NSU Museum of Art's international
exhibition programming ignites downtown Fort Lauderdale. The interior of the 83,000-square-foot modernist building, designed by architect
Edward Larrabee Barnes in 1986, holds an impressive permanent collection of more than 7,000 works, including the country's largest collection of paintings by American realist William Glackens, and pivotal
works by female and multicultural artists, avant-garde CoBrA artists,
and a wide array of Latin American masters. ■TIP→ **The lobby-level**
Museum Café is a cool hangout with art-inspired gifts. ⊠ *1 E. Las Olas*
Blvd., Downtown ☎ *954/525–5500* ⊕ *www.nsuartmuseum.org* ⊠ *$12*
⊘ *Closed Mon.*

WORTH NOTING

FAMILY **Fort Lauderdale Antique Car Museum.** To preseve the history of the Pack-
ard, a long-vanished luxury American car company, Arthur O. Stone
and his wife, Shirley, set up a foundation and a showroom in downtown Fort Lauderdale. The collection includes about two dozen of the
buggy-style Packards (all in pristine and working condition) made in
the Midwest from 1909 to 1958. The collection includes everything
from grease caps, spark plugs, and gearshift knobs to Texaco Oil signage, plus an enlarged automotive library. There's also a gallery salut-
ing Franklin Delano Roosevelt and his family. ⊠ *1527 S.W. 1st Ave.,*
Downtown ☎ *954/779–7300* ⊕ *www.antiquecarmuseum.net* ⊠ *$10*
minimum donation ⊘ *Closed Sun.*

FAMILY **Fort Lauderdale Fire and Safety Museum.** The museum is housed inside
the historic building formerly known as Fire Station No. 3, which has
been restored to its original Mediterranean beauty (circa 1927). The
Sailboat Bend landmark was designed by architect Francis Abreu and
retired from active duty in 2004; it now functions on the weekends as
a historical, cultural, and educational facility with vintage equipment
including a 1942 Chevrolet "Parade" fire engine. Legend has it the fire
station is haunted by a young firefighter. ⊠ *1022 W. Las Olas Blvd., at*
S.W. 11th Ave., Downtown ☎ *954/763–1005* ⊕ *www.fortlauderdale-*
firemuseum.com ⊠ *Free; donations appreciated* ⊘ *Closed weekdays.*

DID YOU KNOW?

Sculptor Peter Wolf Toth fashioned this totem pole for Fort Lauderdale's D.C. Alexander Park on Seabreeze Boulevard near the New River Sound. Toth, who has sculpted works throughout the country, often creates art that represents the lives of early Native Americans.

ALONG THE BEACH

If you want to stop for a bite to eat or a drink before or after visiting Bonnet House, consider **Casablanca Café** (✉ *3049 Alhambra St.*) or **Steak 954** (✉ *W Fort Lauderdale, 401 N. Fort Lauderdale Beach Blvd.*)

FAMILY

Fodor'sChoice

★

Bonnet House Museum and Gardens. This 35-acre subtropical estate endures as a tribute to Old South Florida. Prior to its "modern" history, the grounds had already seen 4,000 years of activity when settler Hugh Taylor Birch purchased the site in 1895. Birch gave it to his daughter Helen as a wedding gift when she married Frederic Bartlett, and the newlyweds built a charming home for a winter residence in 1920. Years after Helen died, Frederic married his second wife, Evelyn, and the artistically gifted couple embarked on a mission to embellish the property with personal touches and surprises that are still evident today. This historic place is a must-see for its architecture, artwork, and horticulture. While admiring the fabulous gardens, look out for playful monkeys swinging from the trees. ✉ *900 N. Birch Rd., Beachfront* ☎ *954/563–5393* ⊕ *www.bonnethouse.org* ✉ *$20 for house tours, $10 for gardens only; $2 for tram tour* ⊙ *Closed Mon.*

WILTON MANORS AND OAKLAND PARK

North of Fort Lauderdale, Wilton Manors is the hub of gay life in the greater Fort Lauderdale area and has several popular restaurants and bars. Oakland Park, immediately to the north, also has several restaurants that are worth a visit.

WESTERN SUBURBS AND BEYOND

West of Fort Lauderdale is an ever-evolving suburbia, where most of Broward's gated communities, golf courses, shopping outlets, casinos, and chain restaurants exist. As you reach the county's western side, the terrain takes on more characteristics of the Everglades, and you can see alligators sunning on canal banks with other exotic reptiles and birds. Tourists flock to the actual Everglades for airboat rides, but the best way to experience the largest subtropical wilderness in the United States is to visit the Everglades National Park itself.

TOP ATTRACTIONS

FAMILY

Fodor'sChoice

★

Ah-Tah-Thi-Ki Museum. A couple of miles from Billie Swamp Safari is Ah-Tah-Thi-Ki Museum, which means "a place to learn, a place to remember" in the Seminole language. This Smithsonian Institution Affiliate documents the living history and culture of the Seminole Tribe of Florida through artifacts, exhibits, and experiential learning. There's a mile-long boardwalk above the swamplands (wheelchair-accessible) that leads you through the Big Cypress Reservation. At the midpoint of the boardwalk, you can take a break at the re-created ceremonial grounds. ✉ *30290 Josie Billie Hwy., Clewiston* ✛ *At corner of W. Boundary Rd.* ☎ *877/902–1113* ⊕ *www.ahtahthiki.com* ✉ *$10.*

FAMILY

Billie Swamp Safari. Four different ecosystems in the "River of Grass" are preserved by the Seminole Tribe of Florida, and these daily tours by airboat or swamp buggy can introduce you to the elusive wildlife that resides in each area. Sightings of deer, turtles, raccoons, wild hogs, hawks, eagles, and alligators are likely but certainly not guaranteed. Animal exhibits, a petting zoo, and snake/critter shows provide a solid contingency plan. For the rugged adventurer, overnight camping in a native-style chickee (thatched-roof dwelling) is available. If a sleepover is too much, Twilight Expeditions offer a campfire with storytelling followed by a nighttime tour. Head to the Swamp Water Café to try Native American dishes like Indian fry bread with honey, Indian tacos, and bison burgers. Check the website for showtimes and tour schedules. ⊠ *Big Cypress Seminole Indian Reservation, 30000 Gator Tail Trail, Clewiston* ☎ *863/983–6101* ⊕ *www.billieswamp.com* ✉ *Swamp Safari Day Package $50; Twilight Swamp Expedition $43.*

FAMILY **Butterfly World.** More than 80 native and international butterfly species live inside the first and largest butterfly house in the United States. The 3-acre site inside Tradewinds Park in Coconut Creek has aviaries, observation decks, waterfalls, ponds, and tunnels. There are lots of birds, too: kids love the lorikeet aviary, where birds alight on every limb. ⊠ *Tradewinds Park, 3600 W. Sample Rd., Coconut Creek* ☎ *954/977–4400* ⊕ *www.butterflyworld.com* ✉ *$26.95.*

FAMILY **Everglades Holiday Park.** Many episodes of Animal Planet's *Gator Boys* are filmed here, making this wetland "park" an extremely popular tourist attraction. Take an hour-long airboat tour, snap a selfie with a python, and catch the alligator wrestling in the pit. ⚠ **The airboats tend to be supersized, and the overall experience can feel very commercialized.** ⊠ *21940 Griffin Rd.* ☎ *954/434–8111* ⊕ *www.evergladesholiday-park.com* ✉ *$29.99 (includes group photo).*

FAMILY **Flamingo Gardens.** Wander through the aviary, arboretum wildlife sanctuary, and Everglades museum in the historic Wray Home. A half-hour guided tram ride winds through tropical fruit groves and wetlands, where the largest collection of native wildlife lives (flamingos, alligators, bobcats, otters, panthers, and more). ⊠ *3750 S. Flamingo Rd., Davie* ☎ *954/473–2955* ⊕ *www.flamingogardens.org* ✉ *$19.95.*

FAMILY **Sawgrass Recreation Park.** Catch a good glimpse of plants and wildlife—from ospreys and alligators to turtles, snakes, and fish—on a half-hour airboat ride through the Everglades. The fee covers admission to all nature exhibits as well as a visit to a model Seminole village. ■ TIP→ **Nature truly comes alive at night. Sawgrass Recreation Park offers nighttime airboat rides on Wednesday and Saturday at 8 pm, reservatons required.** ⊠ *1006 N. U.S. 27, Weston* ⊕ *GPS does not work with this address. Call for directions.* ☎ *888/424–7262, 954/389–0202 for directions* ⊕ *www.evergladestours.com* ✉ *$22.95; night tours $40.*

BEACHES

FAMILY
Fodor's Choice
★

Fort Lauderdale Beach. The same stretch of sand that once welcomed America's wild spring breakers is now miles of beachside sophistication. It remains gloriously open and uncluttered when compared to other major beaches along the Florida coastline; walkways line both sides of the road, and traffic is trimmed to two gently curving northbound lanes. Fort Lauderdale Beach unofficially begins between the B Ocean Resort (formerly the Sheraton Yankee Clipper) and the DoubleTree by Hilton Bahia Mar Resort, starting with the quiet **Fort Lauderdale Beach Park,** where picnic tables and palm trees rule. Going north, a younger crowd

Sights ▼

Ah-Tah-Thi-Ki
Museum **1**

Billie Swamp
Safari **2**

Butterfly
World **3**

Everglades
Holiday Park **5**

Flamingo
Gardens **6**

Sawgrass
Recreation
Park **4**

Restaurants ▼

Angelo Elia Pizza,
Wine Bar,
and Tapas **2**

Tropical Acres
Steakhouse **3**

Hotels ▼

Bonaventure
Resort and Spa ...**1**

gravitates toward the section near Las Olas Boulevard. The beach is actually most crowded from here to **Beach Place,** home of Marriott's vacation rentals and touristy places like Hooters and Fat Tuesday (and a beach-themed CVS Pharmacy). An LGBT crew soaks up the sun along **Sebastian Street Beach,** just north of the Ritz-Carlton. Families with children enjoy hanging out between Seville Street and Vistamar Street, between the Westin Fort Lauderdale Beach and the Atlantic Resort and Spa. High-spirited dive bars dot The Strip and epitomize its "anything goes" attitude. **Amenities:** food and drink; lifeguards; parking (fee). **Best for:** sunrise; swimming; windsurfing; walking; partiers. ⊠ *S.R. A1A, from Holiday Dr. to Sunrise Blvd., Beachfront.*

FAMILY **Harbor Beach.** The posh Harbor Beach community includes Fort Lauderdale's most opulent residences on the Intracoastal Waterway. Due east of this community, a stunning beach has adopted the name of its neighborhood. The Harbor Beach section has some of the few private beaches in Fort Lauderdale, most of which belong to hotels like the Marriott Harbor Beach Resort and the Lago Mar Resort & Club. (Only hotel guests have access.) Such status allows the hotels to provide guests with full-service amenities and dining options on their own slices of heaven. **Amenities:** water sports. **Best for:** solitude; swimming; walking. ⊠ *S. Ocean La. and Holiday Dr., Beachfront.*

FAMILY
Fodor'sChoice
★

Hugh Taylor Birch State Park. North of the bustling beachfront and Sunrise Boulevard, quieter sands run parallel to Hugh Taylor Birch State Park, an exquisite patch of Old Florida. The 180-acre subtropical oasis forms a barrier island between the Atlantic Ocean and the Intracoastal Waterway—surprisingly close to the urban core. Lush vegetation includes mangroves, and there are lovely nature trails through the hammock system. Visit the Birch House Museum, enjoy a picnic, play volleyball, or grab a canoe, kayak, or stand-up paddleboard. **Amenities:** toilets, water sports. **Best for:** solitude; walking. ✉ 3109 E. Sunrise Blvd., Intracoastal and Inland ☏ 954/564–4521 ⊕ www.floridastateparks. org/HughTaylorBirch 🎫 $4 for 1-person in vehicle; $6 for group in vehicle; $2 per pedestrian or bicyclist.

WHERE TO EAT

DOWNTOWN AND LAS OLAS

5

$$
MODERN
AMERICAN

✗ **American Social.** In the sports bar desert of South Florida, it's nice to know you can eat well while watching your team. American Social flaunts a seafood mac 'n' cheese skillet, shrimp-pesto flatbread, and a full spectrum of gourmet burgers with sides of Parmesan-truffle fries or sweet-potato fries. **Known for:** upscale bar food; live sports on TV; craft beers and good cocktails. ⑤ Average main: $20 ✉ 721 E. Las Olas Blvd., Downtown ☏ 954/764–7005 ⊕ www.americansocialbar.com.

$$$
MODERN
AMERICAN
FAMILY
Fodor'sChoice
★

✗ **Big City Tavern.** A must-visit Las Olas landmark, Big City Tavern mingles Asian entrées like shrimp pad thai, Italian four-cheese ravioli, and an American grilled chicken Cobb salad. The crispy flatbread changes every day. ■ TIP➡ Big City is open late for drinks, with a special late-night food menu. **Known for:** eclectic menu; weekend brunch; fun bar scene. ⑤ Average main: $26 ✉ 609 E. Las Olas Blvd., Downtown ☏ 954/727–0307 ⊕ www.bigcitylasolas.com.

$$
DINER
FAMILY

✗ **The Floridian.** This classic 24-hour diner serves up no-nonsense breakfast favorites (no matter the hour) like oversized omelets with biscuits, toast or English muffins, and a choice of grits or sliced tomatoes. Good hangover eats abound, but don't expect anything exceptional besides the location and the low prices. **Known for:** breakfast anytime; low prices; always open. ⑤ Average main: $15 ✉ 1410 E. Las Olas Blvd., Downtown ☏ 954/463–4041 ⊕ www.thefloridiandiner.com.

$
BAKERY
FAMILY

✗ **Gran Forno Bakery.** Most days, the Italian sandwiches, specialty breads, and pastries sell out before noon at this aptly named bakery ("large oven" in Italian). Customers line up in the morning to get Gran Forno's hot artisanal breads like ciabatta (800 loaves are made a day), returning later for the decadent desserts. **Known for:** great Italian-style breads; desserts; strong coffee. ⑤ Average main: $14 ✉ 1235 E. Las Olas Blvd., Downtown ☏ 954/467–2244 ⊕ www.granforno.com.

$$$$
MODERN
AMERICAN

✗ **Grille 401.** Grille 401's new American cuisine merges Osaka-style pressed sushi, classic filet mignon, and crispy crab fritters with stuffed pork chops. The house-made desserts include a white-chocolate brioche bread pudding and a carrot cake made with shredded carrots and toasted pecans. **Known for:** power lunchers by day, sophisticated diners by night; outdoor deck; good cocktails. ⑤ Average main: $33 ✉ 401 E. Las Olas Blvd., Downtown ☏ 954/767–0222 ⊕ www.grille401.com.

Where to Eat and Stay
in Fort Lauderdale

N.W. 13th St.
N.W. 12th St.
N.W. 11th St.
W. Sunrise Blvd.

N.W. 15th Ave.
N.W. 9th Ave.

845

95

N.W. 9th St.
N.W. 8th St.
N.W. 7th St.

N.W. 6th St.

N.W. 5th St.
N.W. 4th St.
N.W. 2nd St.

N.E. 7th Ave.

N. Andrews Ave.

N.E. 4th Ave.

Federal Hwy.

N.W. 6th St.

N.E. 14th Ave.

W. Broward Blvd.

S.W. 2nd St.

Las Olas Riverfront

Kilwin's Chocolates & Ice Cream

842

16
17
21 22
23
27
18 19 20

24
25
26

12

S.W. 6th St.

Federal Hwy.

(Davie Blvd.) 736

S.W. 12th St.
S.W. 13th St.
S.W. 14th St.

28

29

Oakland Park

E Oakland Park Blvd.

Coral Shores

5

NE 26th St.

Wilton Manors East

Coral Ridge

1

NE 18th St.

NE 17th St.

1

NE 31st St.

Lauderdale Beach

Intracoastal Waterway

Bayview Dr.

Middle River Dr.

Middle River

NE 32nd Ave.

NE 33rd Ave.

N-Ocean Blvd.

NE 21st St.

1A

1 4

Hugh Taylor Birch State Park

1

Federal Hwy.

1A

30

31

32

33

13

1A

811

13 - 15

Ne

Restaurants ▼

American Social **22**

Anthony's Coal Fired
Pizza **32**

Beauty and the Feast
Bar | Kitchen **7**

Big City Tavern **21**

Canyon Southwest Cafe **3**

Casablanca Cafe **9**

Casa D'Angelo
Ristorante **2**

Coco Asian
Bistro and Bar **31**

Eduardo de San Angel **13**

The Floridian **26**

Gran Forno Bakery **27**

Grille 401 ....**19**

Kitchenetta **5**

Lips **14**

Lobster Bar Sea Grille **20**

Luigi's Coal Oven Pizza **24**

Mai-Kai Restaurant and
Polynesian Show **15**

Market 17 ....**30**

Ocean 2000 Restaurant **4**

Old Fort Lauderdale
Breakfast House
(O-B House) **16**

Old Heidelberg
Restaurant **33**

Pelican Landing **10**

Rocco's Tacos and
Tequila Bar **25**

The Royal Pig Pub **18**

S3 ....**6**

Sea Level Restaurant
and Ocean Bar **11**

Southport Raw Bar **29**

Steak 954 ....**8**

Sublime Restaurant
and Bar **1**

3030 Ocean **12**

Timpano Italian
Chophouse **17**

Tom Jenkins' Bar-B-Q **28**

Wild Sea Oyster
Bar and Grille **23**

Hotels ▼

The Atlantic
Resort and Spa **2**

B Ocean Resort **7**

Bahia Mar Fort Lauderdale
Beach Hotel,
a DoubleTree by Hilton **6**

Bonaventure
Resort and Spa **13**

Fort Lauderdale Marriott
Harbor Beach
Resort and Spa **8**

Hilton Fort Lauderdale
Beach Resort **3**

Hilton Fort Lauderdale
Marina **11**

Hyatt Regency
Pier Sixty-Six **9**

Lago Mar
Resort and Club **10**

Pelican Grand
Beach Resort **1**

Pineapple Point **12**

The Ritz-Carlton,
Fort Lauderdale **5**

W Fort Lauderdale **4**

5

$$$$
SEAFOOD
Fodor'sChoice
★
✕**Lobster Bar Sea Grille.** Lobster Bar Sea Grille brought a much-needed infusion of sophisticated dining to the downtown food scene. The selection of seafood and fish is solid and ranges from Nova Scotian lobsters to Atlantic char from Iceland. **Known for:** fresh seafood and steaks; sophisticated atmosphere; separate lounge menu. ⑤ *Average main: $40* ✉ *450 E. Las Olas Blvd., Downtown* ☎ *954/772–2675* ⊕ *www.buck-headrestaurants.com/lobster-bar-sea-grille.*

$$
PIZZA
FAMILY
Fodor'sChoice
★
✕**Luigi's Coal Oven Pizza.** One of the best little pizza joints in South Florida, Luigi's Coal Oven Pizza has the full gamut of pizzas, phenomenal salads with fresh dressings, classics like eggplant parmigiana, and oven-baked chicken wings. For the Margherita Napoletana, the quality and flavors of the crust, cheese, and sauce are the result of Luigi's century-old recipe from Napoli. **Known for:** traditional Neopolitan pizza; petite dining room; coal-fired oven. ⑤ *Average main: $19* ✉ *1415 E. Las Olas Blvd., Downtown* ☎ *954/522–9888* ⊕ *www.luigiscoalovenpizza.com.*

$$$
AMERICAN
Fodor'sChoice
★
✕**Old Fort Lauderdale Breakfast House (O-B House).** Locals can't get enough of the O-B House's commitment to quality; you'll only find fresh and organic ingredients here. Try cheesy grits, mega-pancakes with real Vermont maple syrup, or the free-range-egg omelets with wild-caught mahimahi. **Known for:** organic ingredients; breakfast; unique renovation of an old post office. ⑤ *Average main: $21* ✉ *333 Himmarshee St., Downtown* ☎ *954/530–7520* ⊕ *www.o-bhouse.com* ↻ *No lunch Sun.*

$$
MODERN
MEXICAN
Fodor'sChoice
★
✕**Rocco's Tacos and Tequila Bar.** With pitchers of margaritas, Rocco's is more of a scene than a restaurant. In fact, Rocco's drink menu is even larger than its sizable food menu. **Known for:** cocktails over food; great guacamole; busy atmosphere. ⑤ *Average main: $19* ✉ *1313 E. Las Olas Blvd., Downtown* ☎ *954/524–9550* ⊕ *www.roccostacos.com.*

$$$
CAJUN
✕**The Royal Pig Pub.** This gastropub revels in doling out hefty portions of Cajun comfort food and potent cocktails. In fact, it's one of Fort Lauderdale's busiest watering holes. **Known for:** busy bar; barbecue shrimp; weekend brunch. ⑤ *Average main: $22* ✉ *350 E. Las Olas Blvd., Downtown* ☎ *954/617–7447* ⊕ *www.royalpigpub.com.*

$$$
ITALIAN
✕**Timpano Italian Chophouse.** Combine the likes of a high-end steak house with a typical Italian-American trattoria, and you've got yourself a successful recipe for an Italian chophouse. Timpano's Italian-centric offerings include fresh pastas, flatbreads, and the full gamut of Parmesans, marsalas, and fra diavolos. **Known for:** great salads; steakhouse favorites; live music in the Starlight Lounge. ⑤ *Average main: $21* ✉ *450 E. Las Olas Blvd., Downtown* ☎ *954/462–9119* ⊕ *www.timpanochophouse.net.*

$$$$
SEAFOOD
✕**Wild Sea Oyster Bar and Grille.** In the heart of Las Olas, this oyster bar and grill keeps things simple with a small menu focused on a beautiful raw bar and ever-changing preparations of diverse catches from Florida, Hawaiian, and New England waters. **Known for:** seafood galore; raw bar; extensive wine list. ⑤ *Average main: $43* ✉ *Riverside Hotel, 620 E. Las Olas Blvd., Downtown* ☎ *954/467–0671* ⊕ *www.WildSeaLasOlas.com.*

ALONG THE BEACH

$$$
MODERN AMERI-
CANSOUTHERN
FAMILY
Fodor'sChoice
★

✕**Beauty and the Feast Bar | Kitchen.** Feast on a creative array of small plates with a Southern twist. The oceanfront restaurant is ideal for hungry and adventurous eaters who don't mind mixing and matching flavor profiles. **Known for:** small-plates menu; casual atmosphere; weekend brunch. $ *Average main: $26* ⊠ *The Atlantic Hotel and Spa, 601 N. Fort Lauderdale Beach Blvd., Beachfront* ☏ *954/567–8070* ⊕ *www. atlantichotelfl.com.*

$$$
ECLECTIC
FAMILY

✕**Casablanca Cafe.** The menu at this piano bar and restaurant offers a global hodgepodge of American, Mediterranean, and Asian flavors, with a specific focus on eclectic preparations of Florida fish. The food isn't particularly good, but the ambience at this historic home is excellent. **Known for:** outdoor dining; historic setting in Jova House; popular piano bar. $ *Average main: $28* ⊠ *3049 Alhambra St., Beachfront* ☏ *954/764–3500* ⊕ *www.casablancacafeonline.com.*

$$$$
SEAFOOD
FAMILY
Fodor'sChoice
★

✕**Ocean2000 Restaurant.** Locals know where to go for inspired regional cooking. At Ocean2000, the ethos is guided by freshness, and the seafood is unrivaled. **Known for:** fresh seafood; beachfront location; elegant, romantic atmosphere. $ *Average main: $32* ⊠ *Pelican Grand Beach Resort, 2000 N. Ocean Blvd., Beachfront* ☏ *954/556–7667* ⊕ *www.pelicanbeach.com/ocean2000.aspx.*

$$$
FUSION

✕**S3.** S3 stands for the fabulous trio of sun, surf, and sand, paying homage to its prime beachfront location. The menu features a variety of Japanese-inspired raw dishes, sushi rolls, and small plates, and large plates with a new American focus. **Known for:** eclectic Asian and American flavors; solid selection of wine and cocktails; drawing both locals and visitors. $ *Average main: $29* ⊠ *Hilton Fort Lauderdale Beach Resort, 505 N. Fort Lauderdale Beach Blvd., Beachfront* ⊕ *www.s3restaurant.com.*

$$$
SEAFOOD
FAMILY

✕**Sea Level Restaurant and Ocean Bar.** You have to take the road less traveled to find Sea Level, a haven for fresh seafood. The indoor-outdoor restaurant literally overlooks the ocean from sea level at Marriott's Harbor Beach Resort and Spa and its seasonal menu wows with daily specials and cocktails featuring ingredients from the chef's organic garden. **Known for:** the freshest seafood; outdoor dining; good cocktail menu. $ *Average main: $25* ⊠ *Fort Lauderdale Marriott Harbor Beach Resort and Spa, 3030 Holiday Dr., Beachfront* ☏ *954/765–3041* ⊕ *www.marriott.com/hotel-restaurants/fllsb-fort-lauderdale-marriott-harbor-beach-resort-and-spa/sea-level/5152470/about.mi.*

$$$$
MODERN
AMERICAN
Fodor'sChoice
★

✕**Steak 954.** It's not just the steaks that impress at Stephen Starr's superstar spot inside the chic W Fort Lauderdale, the seafood selections shine, too. Order as many dishes as possible, like the lobster and crab-coconut ceviche, the red snapper tiradito, and the Colorado lamb chops. **Known for:** high-quality (and expensive) steaks and seafood; outdoor dining; Sunday brunch. $ *Average main: $55* ⊠ *W Fort Lauderdale, 401 N. Fort Lauderdale Beach Blvd., Beachfront* ☏ *954/414–8333* ⊕ *www.steak954.com.*

$$$$
SEAFOOD
Fodor'sChoice
★

✕**3030 Ocean.** 3030 Ocean's unpredictable menus are guided by award-winning chef Adrienne Grenier's perfectionist flair. Her interpretation of modern American seafood focuses on balancing complex flavors to enhance her fresh ingredients—without subtracting from their integrity. **Known for:** ever-changing menu; fresh seafood; consistently

Sand can sometimes be forgiving if you fall, and bicyclists also appreciate the ocean views.

good food. $ *Average main: $39* ✉ *Fort Lauderdale Marriott Harbor Beach Resort and Spa, 3030 Holiday Dr., Beachfront* ☎ *954/765–3030* ⊕ *www.3030ocean.com.*

INTRACOASTAL AND INLAND

$$ ✕ **Anthony's Coal Fired Pizza.** Before this legendary South Florida pizzeria
PIZZA spread to more than 50 outposts across six states, Anthony's original
FAMILY coal-fired oven was heating up Fort Lauderdale in a big way. Its flagship location still packs the house nightly, serving a simple menu of pizza made with fresh ingredients in an 800°F oven, chicken wings, and salads. **Known for:** approachable menu with pizza and Italian favorites; casual, fun atmosphere; coal-fired oven. $ *Average main: $17* ✉ *2203 S. Federal Hwy., Intracoastal and Inland* ☎ *954/462–5555* ⊕ *www.acfp.com.*

$$$$ ✕ **Canyon Southwest Cafe.** Inside this magical enclave, Southwestern
SOUTHWESTERN- fusion boasts Central and South American flavors and a twist of Asian
INTERNATIONAL influence. Pair the fresh seafood or wild game with a robust selection
Fodor'sChoice of tequilas, a few mezcals, and a decent wine list. **Known for:** local
★ ingredients; long waits; large slection of tequilas. $ *Average main: $31* ✉ *1818 E. Sunrise Blvd., Intracoastal and Inland* ⊹ *At N.E. 18th Ave.* ☎ *954/765–1950* ⊕ *www.canyonfl.com* ⊗ *No lunch.*

$$$$ ✕ **Casa D'Angelo Ristorante.** Casa D'Angelo is always packed. The Tus-
ITALIAN can-style fine-dining restaurant is beloved for its rustic and refined phi-
Fodor'sChoice losophy. **Known for:** everything made from scratch; grilled tiger prawns;
★ extensive wine list. $ *Average main: $38* ✉ *1201 N. Federal Hwy., Intracoastal and Inland* ☎ *954/564–1234* ⊕ *www.casa-d-angelo.com.*

$$$
ASIAN
Fodor's Choice
★
× **Coco Asian Bistro and Bar.** The best of Thailand and Japan unite in an unassuming Fort Lauderdale strip mall. Chef-owner Mike Ponluang's lobster pad thai and classic curries are the go-to for loyal locals, as are sushi rolls and more traditional Japanese selections. **Known for:** eclectic and extensive pan-Asian menu; soothing, elegant atmosphere; good desserts. $ *Average main: $27* ⊠ *Harbor Shops, 1841 Cordova Rd., Intracoastal and Inland* ☎ *954/525–3541* ⊕ *www.cocoasianbistro. com* ⊗ *No lunch weekends.*

$$
ITALIAN
FAMILY
Fodor's Choice
★
× **Kitchenetta.** Kitchenetta is a modern trattoria serving gourmet Italian-American favorites in an industrial-chic setting. The best things to come out of this family-owned kitchen include the spaghetti with Neopolitan-style stuffed artichokes (seasonal), gnocchi Gorgonzola, and the wood-fired mushroom pizza. **Known for:** family-sized portions; good pastas; special Sunday supper. $ *Average main: $19* ⊠ *2850 N. Federal Hwy., Intracoastal and Inland* ☎ *954/567–3333* ⊕ *www.kitchenetta. com* ⊗ *Closed Mon. No lunch.*

$$$$
AMERICANCON-
TEMPORARY
× **Market 17.** Market 17 sources ingredients exclusively from local farmers and fishermen and guests are able to see which farms and purveyors on the restaurant's website. As such, the menu changes daily. **Known for:** entirely locavore menu; constantly evolving offerings; house-made charcuterie. $ *Average main: $31* ⊠ *1850 S.E. 17th St., Intracoastal and Inland* ✛ *Next to the Convention Center* ☎ *954/835–5507* ⊕ *www. market17.net* ⊗ *Closed Mon. No lunch.*

$$$
GERMAN
FAMILY
× **Old Heidelberg Restaurant.** Old Heidelberg is like a Bavarian mirage on State Road 84 with a killer list of German specialties and beers on tap. Classics like bratwurst, knockwurst, kielbasa, and spaetzle dovetail nicely with four types of Wiener schnitzel. **Known for:** kitschy decor; large selection of German imports on tap; extensive menu of German favorites. $ *Average main: $25* ⊠ *900 W. S.R. 84, Intracoastal and Inland* ☎ *954/463–6747* ⊕ *www.heidelbergfl.com* ⊗ *No lunch weekends.*

$$
SEAFOOD
FAMILY
× **Pelican Landing.** Somehow Pelican Landing has managed to stay under the radar in spite of its high-quality seafood, burgers, and Caribbean dishes. The fish is caught daily, served simply blackened or grilled, and presented with sides. **Known for:** fresh seafood; casual atmosphere; sunset views. $ *Average main: $19* ⊠ *Hyatt Regency Pier Sixty Six, 2301 S.E. 17th St., Intracoastal and Inland* ✛ *At end of main dock* ☎ *954/525–6666* ⊕ *www.pier66.hyatt.com.*

$$
SEAFOOD
× **Southport Raw Bar.** You can't go wrong at this unpretentious dive where seafood reigns. Feast on raw or steamed clams, raw oysters, and peel-and-eat shrimp. **Known for:** low prices; fresh seafood; ample choices for meat lovers. $ *Average main: $19* ⊠ *1536 Cordova Rd., Intracoastal and Inland* ☎ *954/525–2526* ⊕ *www.southportrawbar.com.*

$$
VEGETARIAN
FAMILY
× **Sublime Restaurant and Bar.** Sublime's dishes are organic and free from any animal products. It's known for showing the world that veganism doesn't have to compromise flavor or creativity; innovative pizzas, pastas, and meat substitutes can satisfy any carnivore craving. **Known for:** strictly vegan cuisine; all-organic ingredients; elegant atmosphere. $ *Average main: $20* ⊠ *1431 N. Federal Hwy., Intracoastal and Inland* ☎ *954/615–1431* ⊕ *www.sublimerestaurant.com* ⊗ *Closed Mon.*

$ ✕ **Tom Jenkins' Bar-B-Q.** Big portions of dripping barbecue are dispensed
BARBECUE   at this chill spot for eat-in or takeout. Dinners come with two sides
FAMILY   like baked beans, collards, or mighty tasty mac 'n cheese. **Known for:**
ample portions; very reasonable prices; good sides. ⑤ *Average main:*
$12 ✉ *1236 S. Federal Hwy., Intracoastal and Inland* ☎ *954/522–5046*
⊕ *www.tomjenkinsbbq.com* ☉ *Closed Sun. and Mon.*

WESTERN SUBURBS AND BEYOND

$$ ✕ **Angelo Elia Pizza, Bar and Tapas.** This casual Weston outpost is one
PIZZA   of chef Angelo Elia's popular Tuscan-inspired restaurants in Bro-
FAMILY   ward County. Affordable small plates, salads, ceviches, and pizzas are
Fodor'sChoice   neighborhood favorites. **Known for:** moderate prices; family-friendly
★   atmosphere; house-made gelato. ⑤ *Average main: $20* ✉ *Country Isles*
Shopping Center, 1370 Weston Rd., Weston ☎ *954/306–0037* ⊕ *www.*
angeloeliapizza.com.

$$$ ✕ **Tropical Acres Steakhouse.** This old-school, family-owned steak house
STEAKHOUSE   hasn't changed much since it opened in 1949. Sizzling steaks are served
FAMILY   from a fiery grill, and there are dozens of other entrées to choose from
(like frogs' legs, rack of lamb, boneless New York strip). **Known for:**
nostalgia galore; family-friendly dining; popular happy hour. ⑤ *Average*
main: $24 ✉ *2500 Griffin Rd.* ☎ *954/989–2500* ⊕ *www.tropicalacres.*
com ☉ *Closed Sun. in July–Nov. No lunch.*

WILTON MANORS AND OAKLAND PARK

$$$ ✕ **Eduardo de San Angel.** Authentic chilies, spices, and herbs enhance
MEXICAN   classic seafood, meat, and poultry dishes at this inviting Mexican
enclave known for its hospitality. The restaurant has packed the house
for over 20 years, a testament to its popularity and excellent cuisine.
Known for: authentic upscale Mexican cuisine; sautéed beef tenderloin
tips with mushrooms and onions; cilantro soup. ⑤ *Average main: $30*
✉ *2822 E. Commercial Blvd., Oakland Park* ☎ *954/772–4731* ⊕ *www.*
eduardodesanangel.com ☉ *Closed Sun.*

$$ ✕ **Lips.** The 1990s are still alive and well at Lips. The hit restaurant and
AMERICAN   drag-show bar is a hot spot for groups celebrating birthdays, bachelor-
ette parties, and other milestones requiring glitz and glamour. **Known**
for: drag performances while you dine; Sunday brunch; raucous celebrations. ⑤ *Average main: $20* ✉ *1421 E. Oakland Park Blvd., Oakland*
Park ☎ *954/567–0987* ⊕ *www.fladragshow.com* ☉ *Closed Mon.*

$$$$ ✕ **Mai-Kai Restaurant and Polynesian Show.** Touristy to some yet downright
SOUTH PACIFIC   divine to others, Mai-Kai merges the South Pacific with South Florida.
FAMILY   This torch-lit landmark is undeniably gimmicky, but it's the only place
in town for tiki cocktails and Polynesian dance and fire shows. **Known**
for: Peking duck; good wine list; long waits—reservations are essential. ⑤ *Average main: $39* ✉ *3599 N. Federal Hwy., Oakland Park*
☎ *954/563–3272* ⊕ *www.maikai.com.*

WHERE TO STAY

DOWNTOWN AND LAS OLAS

$$
B&B/INN

🏨 **Pineapple Point.** Tucked a few blocks behind Las Olas Boulevard in the residential neighborhood of Victoria Park, clothing-optional Pineapple Point is a magnificent maze of posh tropical cottages and dense foliage catering to the gay community and is nationally renowned for its stellar service. **Pros:** superior service; tropical setting. **Cons:** difficult to find at first; need a vehicle for beach jaunts. $ *Rooms from: $298* ⊠ *315 N.E. 16th Terr., Downtown* ☎ *954/527–0094, 888/844–7295* ⊕ *www.pineapplepoint.com* ➔ *25 rooms* ⦿ *Breakfast.*

ALONG THE BEACH

$$$
HOTEL
FAMILY

🏨 **The Atlantic Resort and Spa.** This towering oceanfront beauty has fantastic views of the ocean from its beds (unless, of course, you select a city view). **Pros:** oceanfront property; en suite kitchenettes; member of the Preferred Hotels & Resorts portfolio. **Cons:** dated decor in the rooms; expensive parking. $ *Rooms from: $350* ⊠ *601 N. Fort Lauderdale Beach Blvd., Beachfront* ☎ *954/567–8020* ⊕ *www.atlantichotelfl.com* ➔ *124 rooms* ⦿ *No meals.*

$$
HOTEL

🏨 **B Ocean Resort.** Formerly the Sheraton Yankee Clipper Hotel, this classic riverboat-shaped landmark is chic yet functional, but it's the views and beach access that truly set it apart. **Pros:** retro mermaid show in swimming pool; proximity to beach; excellent gym. **Cons:** small rooms; low ceilings in lobby; faded exteriors. $ *Rooms from: $250* ⊠ *1140 Seabreeze Blvd., Beachfront* ☎ *954/564–1000* ⊕ *www.boceanfortlauderdale.com* ➔ *486 rooms* ⦿ *No meals.*

$$
HOTEL
FAMILY

🏨 **Bahia Mar Fort Lauderdale Beach Hotel, A DoubleTree by Hilton.** This nicely situated resort has identical rooms in both its marina building and its tower building; however, the latter offers superior views. **Pros:** crosswalk from hotel to beach; on-site yacht center; Water Taxi stop. **Cons:** dated exteriors; small bathrooms; snug rooms. $ *Rooms from: $215* ⊠ *801 Seabreeze Blvd., Beachfront* ☎ *954/764–2233* ⊕ *www.bahiamar-hotel.com* ➔ *296 rooms* ⦿ *No meals.*

$$$$
RESORT
FAMILY
Fodor's Choice
★

🏨 **Fort Lauderdale Marriott Harbor Beach Resort and Spa.** Bill Marriott's personal choice for his annual four-week family vacation, the Marriott Harbor Beach sits on a quarter-mile of private beach; it bursts with the luxe personality of a top-notch island resort. **Pros:** private beachfront; all rooms have balconies; great eateries; no resort fees. **Cons:** Wi-Fi isn't free; expensive parking; large resort feel. $ *Rooms from: $450* ⊠ *3030 Holiday Dr., Beachfront* ☎ *954/525–4000* ⊕ *www.marriott.com* ➔ *650 rooms* ⦿ *No meals.*

$$$
HOTEL
FAMILY
Fodor's Choice
★

🏨 **Hilton Fort Lauderdale Beach Resort.** This oceanfront sparkler features tasteful guest rooms and a fabulous sixth-floor pool deck. **Pros:** fun poolscape and adults-only lounge; most rooms have balconies; great spa. **Cons:** charge for Wi-Fi; expensive valet parking. $ *Rooms from: $329* ⊠ *505 N. Fort Lauderdale Beach Blvd., Beachfront* ☎ *954/414–2222* ⊕ *www.hilton.com* ➔ *374 rooms* ⦿ *No meals.*

$$$
RESORT
FAMILY

🏨 **Lago Mar Resort and Club.** The sprawling family-friendly Lago Mar retains its sparkle and authentic Florida feel thanks to frequent renovations and committed owners. **Pros:** secluded setting; fun activities;

upscale spa. **Cons:** not easy to find; far from restaurants and beach action. $ *Rooms from: $400* ⊠ *1700 S. Ocean La., Beachfront* ☎ *855/209–5677* ⊕ *www.lagomar.com* ⚓ *204 rooms* ⎮◎⎮ *No meals.*

$$
RESORT
FAMILY
Fodor's Choice
★

⛫ **Pelican Grand Beach Resort.** This bright yellow Key West–style Noble House property fuses a heritage seaside charm with understated luxury. **Pros:** incredible spa; directly on the beach; Ocean 2000 restaurant. **Cons:** small fitness center; slightly dated room decor; small property. $ *Rooms from: $270* ⊠ *2000 N. Atlantic Blvd., Beachfront* ☎ *954/568–9431* ⊕ *www.pelicanbeach.com* ⚓ *159 rooms* ⎮◎⎮ *No meals.*

$$$$
HOTEL
Fodor's Choice
★

⛫ **The Ritz-Carlton, Fort Lauderdale.** Twenty-four dramatically tiered, glass-walled stories rise from the sea, forming a sumptuous resort that is helping to revive a golden age of luxury travel. **Pros:** prime beach location; ultramodern elegance; organic spa treatments. **Cons:** expensive valet parking; limited dining options. $ *Rooms from: $750* ⊠ *1 N. Fort Lauderdale Beach Blvd., Beachfront* ☎ *954/465–2300* ⊕ *www.ritzcarlton.com/FortLauderdale* ⚓ *192 rooms* ⎮◎⎮ *No meals.*

$$$$
HOTEL

⛫ **W Fort Lauderdale.** Fort Lauderdale's trendiest hotel has a glamorous poolscape, übermodern rooms and suites, and dramatic views from every direction. **Pros:** amazing pool; very pet-friendly; complimentary Wi-Fi. **Cons:** party atmosphere not for everyone; hard to navigate the property; hectic valet. $ *Rooms from: $500* ⊠ *435 N. Fort Lauderdale Beach Blvd., Beachfront* ☎ *954/462–1633* ⊕ *www.wfortlauderdalehotel.com* ⚓ *465 rooms* ⎮◎⎮ *No meals.*

INTRACOASTAL AND INLAND

$
RESORT
FAMILY
Fodor's Choice
★

⛫ **Hilton Fort Lauderdale Marina.** Since its $72 million renovation in 2011, the mammoth, 589-room, 20-boat-slip Hilton Fort Lauderdale Marina has maintained its modern edge without compromising its charming, old-school Key West style. **Pros:** sexy fire pit; outdoor bar popular with locals; easy water-taxi access. **Cons:** no bathtubs in tower rooms; small fitness center. $ *Rooms from: $169* ⊠ *1881 S.E. 17th St., Intracoastal and Inland* ☎ *954/463–4000* ⊕ *www.fortlauderdalemarinahotel.com* ⚓ *589 rooms* ⎮◎⎮ *No meals.*

$$$
RESORT

⛫ **Hyatt Regency Pier Sixty-Six.** Don't let the 1970s exterior of the iconic waterfront tower fool you; this 22-acre resort is more contemporary than it seems, with conveniences and activities galore. **Pros:** great views; free beach shuttle and easy Water Taxi access; complimentary Wi-Fi. **Cons:** rooms need a refresh; rotating rooftop venue is exclusively for private events; dated exterior. $ *Rooms from: $380* ⊠ *2301 S.E. 17th St. Causeway, Intracoastal and Inland* ☎ *954/525–6666* ⊕ *www.pier66.hyatt.com* ⚓ *384 rooms* ⎮◎⎮ *No meals.*

WESTERN SUBURBS AND BEYOND

$$
RESORT
FAMILY

⛫ **Bonaventure Resort and Spa.** This suburban enclave targets conventions and business travelers as well as international vacationers who value golf, the Everglades, and shopping over beach proximity. **Pros:** lush landscaping; pampering spa. **Cons:** difficult to find; 30-minute drive from airport; poor views from some rooms; rental car necessary. $ *Rooms from: $284* ⊠ *250 Racquet Club Rd., Weston* ☎ *954/389–3300* ⊕ *www.bonaventureresortandspa.com* ⚓ *501 rooms* ⎮◎⎮ *No meals.*

Lago Mar Resort and Club in Fort Lauderdale has its own private beach on the Atlantic Ocean.

NIGHTLIFE AND PERFORMING ARTS

NIGHTLIFE

DOWNTOWN AND LAS OLAS

The majority of Fort Lauderdale nightlife takes place near downtown, beginning on Himmarshee Street (2nd Street) and continuing on to the Riverfront, and then to Las Olas Boulevard. The downtown Riverfront tends to draw a younger demographic somewhere between underage teens and late twenties. On Himmarshee Street, a dozen rowdy bars and clubs, ranging from the seedy to the sophisticated, entice a wide range of partygoers. Toward East Las Olas Boulevard, near the financial towers and boutique shops, bars cater to the yuppie crowd.

Fodor'sChoice
★

Laser Wolf. Far from the main drag of Fort Lauderdale's nightlife district, Laser Wolf celebrates the urban grit on the other side of the tracks as an artsy, hipster, craft-beer bar. It's located on the railroad tracks in a cool indoor-outdoor space and might be the most popular bar for locals because of its great drinks, music, and overall vibe. Motto: "No jerks. Yes beer." ■TIP➜ **Drive or Uber it here. It's best not to walk from other bars off Las Olas and Himmarshee due to distance and safety concerns.** ✉ *901 Progresso Dr., No. 101, Downtown* ☎ *954/667–9373* ⊕ *www. laserwolf.bar/home.html.*

Maguire's Hill 16. With the requisite lineup of libations and pub-style food, this classic Irish pub is good for no-frills fun, fried eats, and daily live music. It's famous locally as the oldest traditional Irish pub and restaurant in Fort Lauderdale. ✉ *535 N. Andrews Ave., Downtown* ☎ *954/764–4453* ⊕ *www.maguireshill16.com.*

ROK: BRG. Downtown Fort Lauderdale loves this personality-driven burger bar and gastropub as it gives the grown-ups something to enjoy in the teenage-infested nightlife district. The long and narrow venue, adorned with exposed-brick walls and flat-screen TVs, is great for watching sports and for mingling on weekends. Locals come here for the great cocktails and beer selection. The burgers are also locally famous. ✉ *208 S.W. 2nd St., Downtown* ☎ *954/525–7656* ⊕ *www.rokbrgr.com.*

Stache, 1920's Drinking Den. Inspired by the Roaring Twenties, this speak-easy-style drinking den and nightclub infuses party-hard downtown Fort Lauderdale with some class and pizzazz. Expect awesome craft cocktails, inclusive of bespoke ice cubes, especially for old-school drinks like man-hattans and sidecars. Late night on Friday and Saturday anticipate great house music and a fun, easy-on-the-eyes, young, sophisticated crowd. ✉ *109 S.W. 2nd Ave., Downtown* ☎ *954/449–1044* ⊕ *www.stacheftl.com.*

Fodor's Choice
★
Tap 42 Bar and Kitchen. With 42 rotating draft beers from around the United States, 50-plus bourbons, a few dozen original cocktails (including beer cocktails), and 66 bottled craft beers, good times await. The drafts adorn a stylish wall constructed of pennies, which creates an interesting trompe l'oeil. The venue attracts large crowds of young professionals for nights of heavy drinking and high-calorie bar eats. ✉ *1411 S. Andrews Ave., Downtown* ☎ *954/463–4900* ⊕ *www.tap42.com.*

Tarpon Bend. This casual two-story restaurant transforms into a hopping bar scene in the early evening. It's consistently busy, especially late night, and is one of the only places that's survived all the ups and downs of downtown Fort Lauderdale. ✉ *200 S.W. 2nd St., Downtown* ☎ *954/523–3233* ⊕ *www.tarponbend.com.*

ALONG THE BEACH

Given its roots as a beachside party town, it's hard to believe that Fort Lauderdale Beach offers very few options in terms of nightlife. A few dive bars are at opposite ends of the main strip, near Sunrise Boulevard and Route A1A, as well as Las Olas Boulevard and A1A. On the main thoroughfare between Las Olas and Sunrise, a few high-end bars at the beach's showstopping hotels have become popular, namely those at the W Fort Lauderdale.

Elbo Room. You can't go wrong wallowing in the past, lifting a drink, and exercising your elbow at the Elbo, a noisy, suds-drenched hot spot since 1938. It seems like nothing has changed here since Fort Lauderdale's spring break heyday. The watering hole phased out food (except for light nibbles) ages ago, but kept a hokey sense of humor: upstairs a sign proclaims "We don't serve women here. You have to bring your own." ✉ *241 S. Fort Lauderdale Blvd., Beachfront* ☎ *954/463–4615* ⊕ *www.elboroom.com.*

McSorley's Beach Pub. This modern take on a classic Irish pub offers standard pub fun—from a jukebox to 35 beers on tap—but remains wildly popular thanks to its location right across from Fort Lauderdale beach. Indeed it's one of the few places on the beach to get an affordable drink and attracts its fair share of tourists and locals. Upstairs, the pub has a second lounge that's far more clubby as well as a rooftop terrace. ✉ *837 N. Fort Lauderdale Beach Blvd., Beachfront* ☎ *954/565–4446* ⊕ *www.mcsorleysftl.com.*

FAMILY **The World Famous Parrot Lounge.** A venerable Fort Lauderdale hangout, this dive bar–sports bar is particularly popular with Philadelphia Eagles fans and folks reminiscing about the big hair and spray tans of 1980s Fort Lauderdale (i.e., its heyday). This place is stuck in the past, but it's got great bartenders, wings, chicken fingers, poppers, and skins. 'Nuff said. ✉ *911 Sunrise La., Beachfront* ☎ *954/563–1493* ⊕ *www. parrotlounge.com.*

The Wreck Bar. Travel back in time to the 1950s at this "under the sea" dive bar, where huge aquariums and a porthole show off live mermaids, who perform in the pool on Friday and Saturday. ✉ *B Ocean Resort, 1140 Seabreeze Blvd., Beachfront* ☎ *954/564–1000* ⊕ *www.bocean-fortlauderdale.com.*

INTRACOASTAL AND INLAND

Bars and pubs along Fort Lauderdale's Intracoastal cater to the city's large, transient boating community. Heading inland along Sunrise Boulevard, the bars around Galleria Mall target thirty- and forty-something singles.

WILTON MANORS AND OAKLAND PARK

The hub of Fort Lauderdale's gay nightlife is in Wilton Manors. Wilton Drive, aka "The Drive," has numerous bars, clubs, and lounges that cater to the LGBT community.

Georgie's Alibi Monkey Bar Ptown / FTL. An anchor for the Wilton Manors gay community fills to capacity for cheap Long Island Iced Teas and stands out as a kind of gay Cheers—a chill neighborhood drinking hole with darts, pool, and friendly people. ✉ *2266 Wilton Dr., Wilton Manors* ☎ *954/565–2526* ⊕ *www.alibiwiltonmanors.com.*

Rosie's Bar and Grill. Rosie's is very lively, pumping out pop tunes and award-winning burgers. It's the go-to gay-friendly place for affordable drinks and great times. Sunday brunch, with its cast of alternating DJs, is wildly popular. ✉ *2449 Wilton Dr., Wilton Manors* ☎ *954/563–0123* ⊕ *www.rosiesbng.com.*

Village Pub and Pub Grub. Arguably the most consistently busy spot on "The Drive" in Wilton Manors, this gay pub delivers good times and cheap drinks nightly. Regardless of where you start or end your gay pub crawl in Wilton Manors, you'll invariably end up here at some point—and you'll be dancing. ✉ *2283 Wilton Dr., Wilton Manors* ☎ *754/200–5244* ⊕ *www.villagepubwm.com.*

WESTERN SUBURBS AND BEYOND

Florida's cowboy country, Davie, offers country-western fun out in the 'burbs. In addition, South Florida's Native American tribes have long offered gambling on Indian Territory near Broward's western suburbs. With new laws, Broward's casinos offer Vegas-style slot machines and even blackjack. Hollywood's Seminole Hard Rock Hotel & Casino offers the most elegant of Broward's casino experiences. *See Nightlife in Hollywood.*

5

SHOPPING

FOOD

FAMILY   **Living Green Fresh Market.** Living Green Fresh Market is a fabulous alternative to overpriced behemoths for the health-conscious in Oakland Park. This green shop and café is bursting with colorful, local, fresh produce, wild-caught fish, prepared foods, and other goods. The quality is top-notch yet the prices are affordable. You can grab breakfast or lunch and cross things off your grocery list, while knowing that each item has a ton of integrity. Plus, there's Puro fair-trade coffee. ⊠ *1305 E. Commercial Blvd., Oakland Park* ☎ *954/771–9770* ⊕ *www.livinggreenfreshmarket.com.*

MALLS

FAMILY   **The Galleria at Fort Lauderdale.** Fort Lauderdale's most sophisticated mall is just west of the Intracoastal Waterway. The split-level emporium comprises Neiman Marcus, Apple, Cole Haan, Macy's, and 100 specialty shops. You can chow down at The Capital Grille, Truluck's, P.F. Chang's China Bistro, or Seasons 52. The mall itself is open Monday through Saturday 10–9, Sunday noon–6. The stand-alone restaurants and bars are open later. ⊠ *2414 E. Sunrise Blvd., Intracoastal and Inland* ☎ *954/564–1036* ⊕ *www.galleriamall-fl.com.*

FAMILY
Fodor'sChoice
★
Sawgrass Mills. This alligator-shaped megamall draws millions of shoppers a year to its collection of 350 outlet stores. According to the mall, it's the second largest attraction in Florida—second only to Walt Disney World. While this may be an exaggeration, prepare for insane crowds. ⊠ *12801 W. Sunrise Blvd., at Flamingo Rd., Sunrise* ⊕ *www.simon. com/mall/sawgrass-mills.*

SHOPPING DISTRICTS

FAMILY   **The Gallery at Beach Place.** Just north of Las Olas Boulevard on Route A1A, this shopping gallery is attached to the mammoth Marriot Beach Place time-share. Spaces are occupied by touristy shops that sell everything from sarongs to alligator heads, chain restaurants like Hooter's, bars serving frozen drinks, and a supersize CVS pharmacy, which sells everything you need for the beach. ■**TIP**➔ Beach Place has covered parking, and usually has plenty of spaces, but you can pinch pennies by using a nearby municipal lot. ⊠ *17 S. Fort Lauderdale Beach Blvd., Beachfront* ⊕ *www.galleryatbeachplace.com.*

FAMILY
Fodor'sChoice
★
Las Olas Boulevard. Las Olas Boulevard is the epicenter of Fort Lauderdale's lifestyle. Not only are 50 of the city's best boutiques, 30 top restaurants, and a dozen art galleries found along this landscaped street, but Las Olas links the growing downtown with its beautiful beaches. ⊠ *E. Las Olas Blvd., Downtown* ⊕ *www.lasolasboulevard.com.*

SPORTS AND THE OUTDOORS

BIKING

Among the most popular routes are Route A1A and Bayview Drive, especially in early morning before traffic builds, and a 7-mile bike path that parallels State Road 84 and New River and leads to Markham Park, which has mountain-bike trails. ■**TIP**➔ Alligator alert: Do not dangle your legs from seawalls.

FAMILY **Broward BCycle.** The big-city trend of "pay and ride" bicycles is alive and well in Broward County. With 40 station locations over 20 scenic miles, from as far south as Hallandale to as far north as Pompano Beach and Coconut Creek, bikes can be rented for as little as 30 minutes or as long as a week, and can be picked up and dropped off at any and all stations in Broward County. Most stations are found downtown and along the beach. This is an excellent green and health-conscious way to explore Fort Lauderdale. Please note, however, that helmets are not provided at the kiosks. ⊕ *broward.bcycle.com.*

FISHING

FAMILY **Bahia Mar Yachting Center.** If you're interested in a saltwater charter, check out the offerings at the marina of the Bahia Mar Fort Lauderdale. Sportfishing and drift fishing bookings can be arranged. Snorkeling and diving outfitter Sea Experience also leaves from here, as does the famous *Jungle Queen* steamboat. In addition, the Water Taxi makes regular stops here. ⊠ *Bahia Mar Fort Lauderdale Beach – A DoubleTree by Hilton Hotel, 801 Seabreeze Blvd., Beachfront* ☏ *954/627–6309.*

RODEOS

FAMILY **Davie Pro Rodeo.** South Florida has a surprisingly large cowboy scene, concentrated in the western suburb of Davie. And for decades, the Bergeron Rodeo Grounds (also known as the Davie Pro Rodeo Arena) has hosted the area's best riders and ropers. Throughout the year, the rodeo hosts national tours and festivals as well as the annual Southeaster Circuit Finals. Check the website for the exact dates of these rodeos. ⊠ *Bergeron Rodeo Grounds, 4271 Davie Rd., Davie* ☏ *954/680–8005* ⊕ *www.davieprorodeo.com.*

SCUBA DIVING AND SNORKELING

FAMILY **Lauderdale Diver.** This dive center facilitates daily trips on a bevy of hard-core dive boats up and down Broward's shoreline (they don't have their own boats, but they work with a handful of preferred outfitters). A variety of snorkeling, reef-diving, and wreck-diving trips are offered as well as scuba-diving lessons. ⊠ *1334 S.E. 17th St., Intracoastal and Inland* ☏ *954/467–2822* ⊕ *www.lauderdalediver.com.*

FAMILY
Fodor's Choice
★
Sea Experience. The *Sea Experience I* leaves daily at 10:15 am and 2:15 pm for two-hour glass-bottom-boat-and-snorkeling combination trips through offshore reefs. Beginner and advanced scuba-diving experiences are available. ⊠ *Bahia Mar Fort Lauderdale Beach – A DoubleTree by Hilton Hotel, 801 Seabreeze Blvd., Beachfront* ☏ *954/770–3483* ⊕ *www.seaxp.com.*

TENNIS

FAMILY **Jimmy Evert Tennis Center.** This grande dame of Fort Lauderdale's public tennis facilities is where legendary champ Chris Evert learned her two-handed backhand under the watchful eye of her now-retired father, Jimmy, the center's tennis pro for 37 years. There are 22 courts (18 lighted clay courts, three hard courts, and a low-compression "beach" court). ⊠ *Holiday Park, 701 N.E. 12th Ave., Intracoastal and Inland* ☏ *954/828–5378* ⊕ *www.fortlauderdale.gov/departments/parks-recreation/tennis-centers/jimmy-evert-tennis-center* 🖙 *$18 per day for nonresidents.*

5

LAUDERDALE-BY-THE-SEA

Lauderdale-by-the-Sea is 5 miles north of Fort Lauderdale.

North of Fort Lauderdale's Birch Recreation Area, Route A1A edges away from the beach through a stretch known as Galt Ocean Mile, and a succession of ocean-side communities line up against the sea. Traffic can line up, too, as it passes through a changing pattern of beach-blocking high-rises and modest family vacation towns and back again. As far as tourism goes, these communities, which include Pompano Beach and Deerfield Beach, tend to cater to a different demographic than Fort Lauderdale.

Just north of Fort Lauderdale proper, the low-rise family resort town of Lauderdale-by-the-Sea boasts shoreline access that's rapidly disappearing in neighboring beach towns. The closest and most convenient of the A1A cities to Fort Lauderdale proper embraces its quaint personality by welcoming guests to a different world, drawing a mix of Europeans and cost-conscious families who are looking for fewer frills and longer stays.

GETTING HERE AND AROUND

Lauderdale-by-the-Sea is just north of Fort Lauderdale. From Interstate 95, exit at Commercial Boulevard and head east past the Intracoastal Waterway. From U.S. 1 (Federal Highway), go east at Commercial Boulevard. If driving north on State Road A1A, simply continue north from Fort Lauderdale Beach.

ESSENTIALS

Visitor Information Lauderdale-by-the-Sea Chamber of Commerce.
⊠ *4201 N. Ocean Dr., Lauderdale-by-the-Sea* ☎ *954/776–1000* ⊕ *www.lbts.com.*

BEACHES

FAMILY   **Lauderdale-by-the-Sea Beach.** Preferred by divers and snorkelers, this laid-back beach is a gateway to magnificent coral reefs. When you're not underwater, look up and you'll likely see a pelican flying by. It's a super-relaxing retreat from the buzz of Fort Lauderdale's busy beaches. That said, the southern part of the beach is crowded near the restaurants at the intersection of A1A and Commercial Boulevard. The no-frills hotels and small inns for families and vacationers visiting for a longer stay are filled with Europeans. Look for metered parking around Commercial Boulevard and A1A. **Amenities:** food and drink; lifeguards; parking (fee). **Best for:** snorkeling; swimming. ⊠ *Commercial Blvd. at State Rd. A1A, Lauderdale-by-the-Sea.*

WHERE TO EAT

$$$ ✕ **Aruba Beach Café.** This casual beachfront eatery is arguably Lauder-
CARIBBEAN   dale-by-the-Sea's most famous restaurant. Aruba Beach serves Carib-
FAMILY   bean-American cuisine with standouts including Caribbean conch chowder and conch fritters. **Known for:** Bimini bread with Aruba glaze; live music; Sunday breakfast buffet. ⑤ *Average main: $21* ⊠ *1 Commercial Blvd., Lauderdale-by-the-Sea* ☎ *954/776–0001* ⊕ *www. arubabeachcafe.com.*

$ ✕**LaSpada's Original Hoagies.** The crew at this seaside hole-in-the-wall
AMERICAN puts on quite a show while assembling their sandwiches—locals rave
FAMILY that this Broward County chain has the best around. Fill up on the
Fodor'sChoice foot-long "Monster" (ham, turkey, roast beef, and cheese), "Mama"
★ (turkey and Genoa salami), or hot meatballs marinara. **Known for:**
the "Monster," a foot-long with ham, turkey, roast beef, cheese; fresh
bread; freshly sliced meats. $ *Average main: $12* ✉ *233 Commercial
Blvd., Lauderdale-by-the-Sea* ☎ *954/776–7893* ⊕ *www.laspadashoa-
gies.com* ↻ *There are 4 additional locations in Broward County.*

WHERE TO STAY

$ ▦ **Blue Seas Courtyard.** Husband-and-wife team Cristie and Marc Furth
B&B/INN have run this whimsical Mexican-themed motel in Lauderdale-by-the-
FAMILY Sea since 1971. **Pros:** south-of-the-border vibe; friendly owners; vintage
Fodor'sChoice stoves from 1972; across the street from the beach. **Cons:** no ocean
★ views; old bathtubs in some rooms. $ *Rooms from: $178* ✉ *4525 El
Mar Dr., Lauderdale-by-the-Sea* ☎ *954/772–3336* ⊕ *www.bluesea-
scourtyard.com* ↻ *12 rooms* ❖ *Breakfast.*

$$ ▦ **High Noon Beach Resort.** This family-run hotel sits on 300 feet of beachy
B&B/INN paradise with plenty of cozy spots, two heated pools, and an ambience
FAMILY that keeps visitors coming back for more. **Pros:** directly on the beach;
friendly vibe; great staff. **Cons:** dated room decor; no maid service on
Sunday; no guarantee for room type. $ *Rooms from: $226* ✉ *4424
El Mar Dr., Lauderdale-by-the-Sea* ☎ *954/776–1121, 800/382–1265*
⊕ *www.highnoonresort.com* ↻ *40 rooms, 1 beach house* ❖ *Breakfast.*

$ ▦ **Sea Lord Hotel and Suites.** This gem is one of the nicest in Lauderdale-
B&B/INN by-the-Sea. Many of the rooms have great ocean views, balconies,
Fodor'sChoice and full kitchens. **Pros:** gorgeous beach location; great staff; rooms
★ have balconies and full kitchens. **Cons:** limited parking; no restau-
rant. $ *Rooms from: $190* ✉ *4140 El Mar Dr., Lauderdale-by-the-
Sea* ☎ *954/776–1505, 800/344–4451* ⊕ *www.sealordhotel.com* ↻ *47
rooms* ❖ *Breakfast.*

SPORTS AND THE OUTDOORS

FAMILY **Anglins Fishing Pier.** A longtime favorite for 24-hour fishing, it's a spot
where you may catch snapper, snook, cobia, blue runner, and pom-
pano. The on-site bait-and-tackle shop can advise newbies to advanced
anglers. ✉ *2 Commercial Blvd., Lauderdale-by-the-Sea* ☎ *954/491–
9403* ⊕ *www.boatlessfishing.com/anglins.htm.*

HOLLYWOOD

Hollywood has had several face-lifts to shed its old-school image, but
there's still something delightfully retro about the city. Young Circle,
once down-at-heel, is now Broward's first ArtsPark. On Hollywood's
western outskirts, the flamboyant Seminole Hard Rock Hotel & Casino
has enlivened this previously downtrodden section of the State Road
7/U.S. 441 corridor, drawing local weekenders, architecture buffs, par-
tiers, and gamblers. But Hollywood's redevelopment efforts don't end

there: new shops, restaurants, and art galleries open at a persistent clip, and the city has continually spiffed up its boardwalk—a wide pedestrian walkway along the beach—where local joggers are as commonplace as sun-seeking snowbirds from the north. On the coast of Hallandale, the beach is backed by older, towering condominiums. Inland, Hallandale has been trying to get some business from neighboring Aventura and Sunny Isles in Dade County with the development of the high-end Village at Gulfstream Park, a luxury retail arcade anchored by a reinvented casino and racetrack.

GETTING HERE AND AROUND

From Interstate 95, exit east on Sheridan Street or Hollywood Boulevard for Hollywood, or Hallandale Beach Boulevard for either Hollywood or Hallandale.

ESSENTIALS

Visitor Information Hollywood Community Redevelopment Agency.
☎ 954/924–2980 ⊕ www.visithollywoodfl.org.

EXPLORING

FAMILY
Fodor'sChoice
★
Art and Culture Center/Hollywood. The Center, which is southeast of Young Circle, has a great reputation for presenting übercool contemporary art exhibitions and providing the community with educational programming for adults and children. Check online for the latest exhibition schedule. ⊠ 1650 Harrison St. ☎ 954/921–3274 ⊕ www.artandculturecenter.org ⊠ $7.

FAMILY
ArtsPark at Young Circle. In the center of downtown Hollywood, this 10-acre urban park has promenades and green spaces, public art, a huge playground for kids, a state-of-the-art amphitheater, and spaces for educational workshops like weekly glassblowing and jewelry making. ⊠ 1 N. Young Cir. ☎ 954/921–3500 ⊕ www.visithollywoodfl.org/artspark.aspx.

Design Center of the Americas (DCOTA). Though access is typically reserved strictly to those in the design biz, the Design Center of the Americas still permits visitors to browse the myriad showrooms, which parade the latest and greatest in home furnishings and interior design. Note, however, that this is purely for inspiration as direct consumer sales are not permitted. ⊠ 1855 Griffin Rd., Dania Beach ☎ 954/920–7997 Ext. 240 ⊕ www.dcota.com.

FAMILY
West Lake Park and Anne Kolb Nature Center. Grab a canoe or kayak, or take a 40-minute guided boat tour at this lakeside park on the Intracoastal Waterway. At 1,500 acres, it's one of Florida's largest urban nature facilities. Extensive boardwalks traverse mangrove wetlands that shelter endangered and threatened species. A 65-foot observation tower showcases the entire park. At the **Anne Kolb Nature Center,** there's a 3,500-gallon aquarium. The center's exhibit hall has interactive displays explaining the park's delicate ecosystem. ⊠ 1200 Sheridan St. ☎ 954/357–5161 ⊕ www.broward.org/parks/WestLakePark ⊠ Park: weekdays free, weekends and holidays $1.50. Exhibit hall: $2.

BEACHES

FAMILY
Fodor's Choice
★

Dr. Von D. Mizell-Eula Johnson State Park. Formerly known as John U. Lloyd Beach State Park, this 310-acre park was renamed Dr. Von D. Mizell-Eula Johnson State Park in honor of the duo who led efforts to change the "colored beach" into a state park in 1973 and create appropriate access for residents. Native sea grapes, gumbo-limbo trees, and other native plants offer shade. Nature trails and a marina are large draws; canoeing on Whiskey Creek is also popular. The beaches are excellent, but beware of mosquitoes in summer **Amenities:** parking (fee); toilets. **Best for:** solitude; sunrise. ⊠ *6503 N. Ocean Dr.* ☎ *954/923–2833* ⊕ *www.floridastateparks.org/park/Mizell-Johnson* 🅿 *$6 per vehicle for 2–8 passengers; $4 for lone driver.*

FAMILY
Fodor's Choice
★

Hollywood Beach and Broadwalk. The name might be Hollywood, but there's nothing hip or chic about **Hollywood North Beach Park,** which sits at the north end of Hollywood (State Road A1A and Sheridan Street), before the 2½-mile pedestrian Broadwalk begins. And this is a good thing. It's an easygoing place to enjoy the sun, sand, and sea. The year-round **Dog Beach of Hollywood,** between Pershing and Custer streets, allows canine companions to join the fun a few days a week. Walk along the **Broadwalk** for a throwback to the 1950s, with mom-and-pop stores and ice-cream parlors, where elderly couples go for long strolls, and families build sand castles. The popular stretch has spiffy features like a pristine pedestrian walkway, a concrete bike path, a crushed-shell jogging path, an 18-inch decorative wall separating the Broadwalk from the sand, and places to shower off after a dip. Expect to hear French spoken throughout Hollywood since its beaches are a getaway for Quebecois. **Amenities:** food and drink; lifeguards; showers; parking (fee); toilets. **Best for:** sunrise; swimming; walking. ⊠ *320 Johnson St.* ⊕ *www.visithollywoodfl.org* 🅿 *Parking in public lots $1.50 per hr weekdays, $2 per hr weekends.*

WHERE TO EAT

$$
AMERICAN
FAMILY
Fodor's Choice
★

✕ **Jaxson's Ice Cream Parlour and Restaurant.** This mid-century landmark whips up malts, shakes, and jumbo sundaes from ice cream that is made on-site daily. Owner Monroe Udell's trademarked Kitchen Sink—a small sink full of ice cream, topped by sparklers—is a real hoot for parties. **Known for:** license-plate decor; house-made ice cream; salads and sandwiches for those without a sweet tooth. $ *Average main: $15* ⊠ *128 S. Federal Hwy., Dania Beach* ☎ *954/923–4445* ⊕ *www.jaxsonsicecream.com.*

$$$
GREEK
FAMILY

✕ **Taverna Opa.** It's a Greek throwdown every night at this Hollywood institution. Expect a lively night of great eats (including amazing hot and cold meze, wood-fire-grilled meats and seafood), table-top dancing, and awkward moments (especially when suburban dads with two left feet decide to get in on the act), and lots of wine to make it all okay. **Known for:** location near Water Taxi stop; louder atmosphere as the night wears on; menu of Greek favorites. $ *Average main: $29* ⊠ *410 N. Ocean Dr.* ☎ *954/929–4010* ⊕ *www.tavernaopa.com.*

WHERE TO STAY

$$$
RESORT
FAMILY
Fodor's Choice
★

Margaritaville Beach Resort. The funky boardwalk of Hollywood Beach has a tropical destination inspired by Jimmy Buffett's lifelong search for paradise. **Pros:** oceanfront location; fun water activities; daily live entertainment. **Cons:** the surrounding area isn't very upscale; touristy vibe; must be a Jimmy Buffett fan. $ *Rooms from: $349* ✉ *1111 N. Ocean Dr.* ☎ *954/874–4444* ⊕ *www.margaritavillehollywoodbeachresort.com* 📞 *349 rooms* ○ *No meals.*

$$$
HOTEL

Seminole Hard Rock Hotel & Casino. On the industrial flatlands of western Hollywood, the Seminole Hard Rock Hotel & Casino is a magnet for folks looking for Las Vegas–style entertainment casinos that never close, clubbing, and hedonism. **Pros:** limitless entertainment; solid bars and restaurants. **Cons:** in an unsavory neighborhood; no tourist sights in close proximity; rental car necessary. $ *Rooms from: $399* ✉ *1 Seminole Way* ☎ *866/502–7529* ⊕ *www.seminolehardrockhollywood.com* 📞 *469 rooms* ○ *No meals.*

NIGHTLIFE

Hollywood may have a sleepy, small-town feel on the east side, but the Seminole Hard Rock Hotel & Casino brings a twist of Vegas to the west.

Fodor's Choice
★

Seminole Hard Rock Hotel & Casino. Seminole Hard Rock Hotel & Casino is a Vegas-inspired gaming and entertainment complex in a fairly forlorn area of Hollywood. Once inside the Hard Rock fortress, you'll feel the excitement immediately. In addition to the AAA Four Diamond hotel, there's a monster casino, a 5,500-seat concert venue (Hard Rock Live), plus dozens of restaurants, bars, and nightclubs. ■ TIP→ **The Seminole Hard Rock Hotel & Casino is not to be confused with its neighbor, the Seminole Classic Casino.** ✉ *1 Seminole Way* ☎ *866/502–7529* ⊕ *www. seminolehardrockhollywood.com.*

6

PALM BEACH AND THE TREASURE COAST

WELCOME TO PALM BEACH AND THE TREASURE COAST

TOP REASONS TO GO

★ **Exquisite resorts:** Two grandes dames, The Breakers and the Boca Raton Resort & Club, perpetually draw the rich, the famous, and anyone else who can afford the luxury. The Eau Palm Beach and Four Seasons sparkle with service fit for royalty.

★ **Beautiful beaches:** From Jupiter, where dogs run free, to Stuart's tubular waves, to the broad stretches of sand in Delray Beach and Boca Raton, swimmers, surfers, sunbathers—and sea turtles looking for a place to hatch their eggs—all find happiness.

★ **Top-notch golf:** The Champion Course and re-envisioned Fazio Course at PGA National Resort & Spa are world renowned; pros sharpen up at PGA Village.

★ **Horse around:** Wellington, with its popular polo season, is often called the winter equestrian capital of the world.

★ **Excellent fishing:** The Atlantic Ocean, teeming with kingfish, sailfish, and wahoo, is a treasure chest for anglers.

1 **Palm Beach.** With Gatsby-era architecture, stone-and-stucco estates, and extravagant dining, Palm Beach is a must-see for travelers to the area. Plan to spend time on Worth Avenue, a collection of more than 200 chic shops, and at Whitehall, the palatial retreat for Palm Beach's founder, Henry Flagler. West Palm Beach and its environs, including Lake Worth, are bustling with their own identities. Culture fans have plenty to cheer about with the Kravis Center and Norton Museum of Art; sports enthusiasts will have a ball golfing or boating or catching a spring-training game at the new stadium in West Palm Beach; and kids love Lion Country Safari.

2 **Delray Beach.** Its lively downtown, with galleries, independent boutiques, and trendy restaurants blocks from the ocean, is perfect for strolling. The Tennis Center draws the Love-Love crowds. To the west is the unique Morikami Museum and Japanese Gardens.

3 **Boca Raton.** An abundance of modern shopping plazas mix with historic buildings from the 1920s, masterpieces by renowned architect Addison Mizner. Parks line much of the oceanfront.

4 **North County.** Palm Beach Gardens, Jupiter, quaint Juno Beach, and Tequesta are more laid-back cousins to the areas south, with country clubs, newer malls, and family-oriented activities at the baseball stadium subbing for nightlife here. It's a golfer's paradise with PGA courses that make the pros.

GETTING ORIENTED

This diverse region extends 120 miles from laid-back Sebastian to tony Boca Raton. The area's glitzy epicenter, Palm Beach, attracts socialites, the well-heeled, and interested onlookers. The northernmost cities are only about 100 miles from Orlando, making that area an ideal choice for families wanting some beach time to go with their visit to Mickey Mouse. Delightfully funky Delray Beach is only an hour north of Miami. The Intracoastal Waterway runs parallel to the ocean and transforms from a canal to a tidal lagoon separating islands from the mainland, starting with Palm Beach and moving northward to Singer Island (Palm Beach Shores and Riviera Beach), Jupiter Island, Hutchinson Island (Stuart, Jensen Beach, and Fort Pierce), and Orchid Island (Vero Beach and Sebastian).

5 **Treasure Coast.** The area north of Palm Beach county—from Stuart and beyond—remains blissfully low-key, with fishing towns, spring-training stadiums, and ecotourism attractions until you hit the cosmopolitan— yet understated—Vero Beach.

6

ATLANTIC OCEAN

piter Island
be Sound

Tequesta
upiter
1A
Juno Beach
Singer Island
Palm Beach Gardens
Palm Beach Shores
Riviera Beach
1
Palm Beach
1
1A
Lake Worth
South Palm Beach
Manalapan
Boynton Beach
95
Gulf Stream
Delray Beach
Highland Beach
1A
Boca Raton
1

Updated by
Jan Norris

A golden stretch of the Atlantic shore, the Palm Beach area resists categorization, and for good reason: the territory stretching south to Boca Raton, appropriately coined the Gold Coast, defines old-world glamour and new-age sophistication.

To the north you'll uncover the comparatively undeveloped Treasure Coast—liberally sprinkled with seaside gems and wide-open spaces along the road awaiting your discovery. Speaking of discovery, its moniker came from the 1715 sinking of a Spanish fleet that dumped gold, jewels, and silver in the waters; today the *Urca de Lima*, one of the original 11 ships and now an undersea "museum," can be explored by scuba divers.

Altogether, there's a delightful disparity between Palm Beach, pulsing with old-money wealth, and under-the-radar Hutchinson Island. Seductive as the gorgeous beaches, eclectic dining, and leisurely pursuits can be, you should also take advantage of flourishing commitments to historic preservation and the arts, as town after town yields intriguing museums, galleries, theaters, and gardens.

Palm Beach, proud of its status as America's first luxe resort destination and still glimmering with its trademark Mediterranean-revival mansions, manicured hedges, and highbrow shops, can rule supreme as the focal point for your sojourn any time of year. From there, head off in one of two directions: south toward Delray Beach and Boca Raton along an especially scenic estate-dotted route known as A1A, or back north to the beautiful barrier islands of the Treasure Coast. For rustic inland activities such as bass fishing and biking atop the dike around Lake Okeechobee, head west.

PLANNING

WHEN TO GO

The weather is optimal from November through May, but the trade-off is that roads, hotels, and restaurants are more crowded and prices higher. If the scene is what you're after, try the early weeks of December when the "season" isn't yet in full swing. However, be warned that after Easter, the crowd relocates to the Hamptons, and Palm Beach feels like another universe. For some, that's a blessing—and a great time to take advantage of lower summer lodging rates and dining deals—but you'll need to bring your tolerance for heat, humidity, and afternoon downpours.

GETTING HERE AND AROUND

AIR TRAVEL

Palm Beach International Airport is in West Palm, but it's possible (and sometimes cheaper) to fly to Fort Lauderdale, Miami, or Orlando. Do rent a car if you plan on exploring. Scenic Route A1A, also called Ocean Boulevard or Ocean Drive, depending on where you are, ventures out onto the barrier islands. Interstate 95 runs parallel to U.S. 1, a main north–south thoroughfare in the region (also known as Federal Highway), but a few miles inland.

Airport **Palm Beach International Airport** (PBI). ⊠ 1000 Turnage Blvd., West Palm Beach ⊹ From I–95, use the airport flyover exit; from Florida's Tpke., use the Southern Blvd. exit and drive east to the airport exit ☎ 561/471–7420 ⊕ www.pbia.org.

Airport Transfers **SuperShuttle.** ☎ 800/258–3826 ⊕ www.supershuttle.com.

BUS TRAVEL

The county's bus service, Palm Tran, runs two routes (Nos. 44 and 40) that offer daily service connecting the airport, the Tri-Rail stop near it, and locations in central West Palm Beach. A network of 34 routes joins towns all across the area; it's $5 for a day pass. The free Downtown Trolley connects the West Palm Beach Amtrak station and the Tri-Rail stop in West Palm on its Green Line. Its Yellow Line makes continuous loops down Clematis Street, the city's main stretch of restaurants and watering holes interspersed with stores, and through CityPlace, a shopping-dining-theater district, and to the Kravis Center. Hop on and off at any of the stops. The trolley's Yellow Line runs Sunday to Wednesday 11–9 and Thursday to Saturday 11–11. The trolley's Green Line, which stretches farther east, west, and south, and connects to Tri-Rail and Amtrak, runs weekdays 7–7, Saturday 9–7, and Sunday 11–7. A seasonal Blue Line, operating from fall to spring, runs from downtown West Palm Beach to Northwood Village, and the Palm Beach Outlets mall. Times are Thursday–Saturday, 11–10.

Contacts **Downtown Trolley.** ☎ 561/833–8873 ⊕ www.downtownwpb.com/trolley/. **Palm Tran.** ☎ 561/841–4287 ⊕ www.pbcgov.com/palmtran.

TAXI TRAVEL

Several taxi companies serve the area, including the Southeastern Florida Transportation Group. Also available are limousine services to Palm Beach or out of county. The ride-sharing services Uber (⊕ *www.uber.com*) and Lyft (⊕ *www.lyft.com*) are accessible as apps from your phone.

Contacts AmeriCab. ☎ 561/337–7777 ⊕ *www.americabtaxi.com.* **Limos of Palm Beach.** ☎ 561/459–7128 ⊕ *www.limosofpb.com.* **Palm Beach Yellow Cab.** ☎ 561/721–2222 ⊕ *www.palmbeachyellowcab.com.* **Southeastern Florida Transportation Group.** ☎ 561/777–7777 ⊕ *www.yellowcabflorida.com.*

TRAIN TRAVEL

Amtrak stops daily in West Palm Beach. The station is at the same location as the Tri-Rail stop, so the same free shuttle, the Downtown Trolley, is available (via the trolley's Green Line).

Tri-Rail Commuter Service is a rail system with 18 stops altogether between West Palm Beach and Miami; tickets can be purchased at each stop, and a one-way trip from the first to the last point is $6.90 weekdays, $5 weekends. Three stations—West Palm Beach, Lake Worth, and Boca—have free shuttles to their downtowns, and taxis are on call at others.

A new high-speed train line, Brightline began running in late summer, 2017. It will connect downtown Miami to Fort Lauderdale and West Palm Beach in 30 and 60 minutes respectively.

Contacts Amtrak. ☎ 800/872–7245 ⊕ *www.amtrak.com.* **Brightline.** ⊕ *gobrightline.com.* **Tri-Rail.** ☎ 800/874–7245 ⊕ *www.tri-rail.com.*

HOTELS

Palm Beach has a number of smaller hotels in addition to the famous Breakers. Lower-priced hotels and bed-and-breakfasts can be found in West Palm Beach, Palm Beach Gardens, and Lake Worth. Heading south, the ocean-side town of Manalapan has the Eau Palm Beach Resort & Spa. The Seagate Hotel & Spa sparkles in Delray Beach, and the posh Boca Beach Club lines the superlative swath of shoreline in Boca Raton. In the opposite direction there's the PGA National Resort & Spa, and on the opposite side of town on the ocean is the Marriott on Singer Island, a well-kept secret for spacious, sleek suites. Even farther north, Vero Beach has a collection of luxury boutique hotels, as well as more modest options along the Treasure Coast. To the west, towns close to Lake Okeechobee offer country-inn accommodations geared to bass-fishing pros.

RESTAURANTS

Numerous elegant establishments offer upscale American, Continental, and international cuisine, but the area also is chock-full of casual waterfront spots serving affordable burgers and fresh seafood feasts. Snapper and grouper are especially popular here, along with the ubiquitous shrimp. Happy hours and early-bird menus, Florida hallmarks, typically entice the budget-minded with several dinner entrées at reduced prices offered during certain hours, usually before 5 or 6.

Hotel and restaurant reviews have been shortened. For full information, visit Fodors.com.

WHAT IT COSTS				
	$	$$	$$$	$$$$
Restaurants	under $15	$15–$20	$21–$30	over $30
Hotels	under $200	$200–$300	$301–$400	over $400

Restaurant prices are the average cost of a main course at dinner or, if dinner is not served, at lunch. Hotel prices are the lowest cost of a standard double room in high season.

VISITOR INFORMATION

Contacts Discover the Palm Beaches. ✉ *1555 Palm Beach Lakes Blvd., Suite 800, West Palm Beach* ☎ *561/233-3000* ⊕ *www.palmbeachfl.com.*

PALM BEACH

70 miles north of Miami, off I–95.

Long reigning as the place where the crème de la crème go to shake off winter's chill, Palm Beach, which is actually on a barrier island, continues to be a seasonal hotbed of platinum-grade consumption. The town celebrated its 100th birthday in 2011, and there's no competing with its historic social supremacy. It's been the winter address for heirs of the iconic Rockefeller, Vanderbilt, Colgate, Post, Kellogg, and Kennedy families. Even newer power brokers, with names like Kravis, Peltz, and Trump, are made to understand that strict laws govern everything from building to landscaping, and not so much as a pool awning gets added without a Town Council nod. Only three bridges allow entry, and huge tour buses are a no-no.

All this fabled ambience started with Henry Morrison Flagler, Florida's premier developer, and cofounder, along with John D. Rockefeller, of Standard Oil. No sooner did Flagler bring the railroad to Florida in the 1890s than he erected the famed Royal Poinciana and Breakers hotels. Rail access sent real-estate prices soaring, and ever since, princely sums have been forked over for personal stationery engraved with 33480, the zip code of Palm Beach (which didn't actually get its status as an independent municipality until 1911). Setting the tone in this town of unparalleled Florida opulence is the ornate architectural work of Addison Mizner, who began designing homes and public buildings here in the 1920s and whose Moorish-Gothic Mediterranean-revival style has influenced virtually all landmarks.

But the greater Palm Beach area is much larger and encompasses several communities on the mainland and to the north and south. To provide Palm Beach with servants and other workers, Flagler created an off-island community across the Intracoastal Waterway (also referred to as Lake Worth in these parts). West Palm Beach, now cosmopolitan and noteworthy in its own right, evolved into an economically vibrant business hub and a sprawling playground with some of the best nightlife and cultural attractions around, including the glittering Kravis Center for the Performing Arts, the region's principal entertainment venue. The mammoth Palm Beach County Judicial Center and Courthouse and the State Administrative Building underscore the breadth of the city's governmental and corporate activity.

The burgeoning equestrian development of Wellington, with its horse shows and polo matches, lies a little more than 10 miles west of downtown, and is the site of much of the county's growth.

Spreading southward from the Palm Beach/West Palm Beach nucleus set between the two bridges that flow from Royal Poinciana Way and Royal Palm Way into Flagler Drive on the mainland are small cities like Lake Worth, with its charming artsy center, Lantana, and Manalapan (home to the fabulous Eau Palm Beach resort, formerly the Ritz-Carlton Palm Beach). All three have turf that's technically on the same island as Palm Beach, and at its bottom edge across the inlet is Boynton Beach, a 20-minute drive from Worth Avenue.

GETTING HERE AND AROUND

Palm Beach is 70 miles north of Miami (a 90-minute trip with traffic). To access Palm Beach off Interstate 95, exit east at Southern Boulevard, Belvedere Road, or Okeechobee Boulevard. To drive from Palm Beach to Lake Worth, Lantana, Manalapan, and Boynton Beach, head south on Ocean Boulevard/Route A1A; Lake Worth is roughly 6 miles south, and Boynton is another 6. Similarly, to reach them from West Palm Beach, take U.S. 1 or Interstate 95. To travel between Palm Beach and Singer Island, you must cross over to West Palm before returning to the beach. Once there, go north on U.S. 1 and then cut over on Blue Heron Boulevard/Route 708. If coming straight from the airport or somewhere farther west, take Interstate 95 up to the same exit and proceed east. The main drag in Palm Beach Gardens is PGA Boulevard/Route 786, which is 4 miles north on U.S. 1 and Interstate 95; A1A merges with it as it exits the top part of Singer Island. Continue on A1A to reach Juno Beach and Jupiter.

TOURS

FAMILY **DivaDuck Amphibious Tours.** Running 75 minutes, these duck tours go in and out of the water on USCG-inspected amphibious vessels around West Palm Beach and Palm Beach. The tours depart two or three times most days for $29 per person (adults); there are discounts for seniors and kids. ⊠ *CityPlace, 600 S. Rosemary Ave., West Palm Beach* ⊹ *Corner of Hibiscus St. and Rosemary Ave.* ☎ *877/844–4188* ⊕ *www.divaduck.com.*

Island Living Tours. Book a private mansion-viewing excursion around Palm Beach, and hear the storied past of the island's upper crust. Owner Leslie Diver also hosts an Antique Row Tour and a Worth Avenue Shopping Tour. Vehicle tours are 90 minutes for the "Best of Palm Beach" and 2½ hours for a more extensive architecture and history tour. Costs are from $60 to $150 per person, depending on the vehicle used. Leslie also runs 90-minute bicycle tours through Palm Beach ($45, not including bike rental). One bicycle tour explores the Estate Section and historic Worth Avenue; another explores the island's lesser known North End. Call in advance for location and to reserve. ☎ *561/868–7944* ⊕ *www.islandlivingpb.com.*

Draped in European elegance, The Breakers in Palm Beach sits on 140 acres along the oceanfront.

EXPLORING

PALM BEACH

Most streets around major attractions and commercial zones have free parking as well as metered spaces. If you can stake out a place between a Rolls-Royce and a Bentley, do so, but beware of the "Parking by Permit Only" signs, as a $50 ticket might take the shine off your spot. Better yet, if you plan to spend an entire afternoon strolling Worth Avenue, park in the Apollo lot behind Tiffany's midway off Worth on Hibiscus; some stores will validate your parking ticket.

TOP ATTRACTIONS

Fodor's Choice
★

The Breakers. Built by Henry Flagler in 1896 and rebuilt by his descendants after a 1925 fire, this magnificent Italian Renaissance–style resort helped launch Florida tourism with its Gilded Age opulence, attracting influential wealthy Northerners to the state. The hotel, still owned by Flagler's heirs, is a must-see even if you aren't staying here. Walk through the 200-foot-long lobby, which has soaring arched ceilings painted by 72 Italian artisans and hung with crystal chandeliers. Meet for a drink at the HMF, one of the most beautiful bars in the state. ■TIP→ Book a pampering spa treatment or dine at the popular oceanfront Seafood Bar that was renovated in 2016. The $25 parking fee is waived if you spend at least $25 anywhere in the hotel (just have your ticket validated). ⊠ *1 S. County Rd.* ☎ *561/655–6611* ⊕ *www. thebreakers.com.*

Fodor's Choice
★

Henry Morrison Flagler Museum. The worldly sophistication of Florida's Gilded Age lives on at Whitehall, the plush 55-room "marble palace" Henry Flagler commissioned in 1901 for his third wife, Mary Lily

Kenan. Architects John Carrère and Thomas Hastings were instructed to create the finest home imaginable—and they outdid themselves. Whitehall rivals the grandeur of European palaces and has an entrance hall with a baroque ceiling similar to Louis XIV's Versailles. Here you'll see original furnishings; a hidden staircase Flagler used to sneak from his bedroom to the billiards room; an art collection; a 1,200-pipe organ; and Florida East Coast Railway exhibits, along with Flagler's personal railcar, No. 91, showcased in an 8,000-square-foot beaux arts–style pavilion behind the mansion. Docent-led tours and audio tours are included with admission. The museum's Café des Beaux-Arts, open from Thanksgiving through mid-April, offers a Gilded Age–style early afternoon tea for $40 (11:30 am–2:30 pm); the price includes museum admission. ⊠ *1 Whitehall Way* ☎ *561/655–2833* ⊕ *www.flaglermuseum.us* ⌥ *$18.*

Fodor'sChoice **Worth Avenue.** Called "the Avenue" by Palm Beachers, this half-mile-
★ long street is synonymous with exclusive shopping. Nostalgia lovers recall an era when faces or names served as charge cards, purchases were delivered home before customers returned from lunch, and bills were sent directly to private accountants. Times have changed, but a stroll amid the Spanish-accented buildings, many designed by Addison Mizner, offers a tantalizing taste of the island's ongoing commitment to elegant consumerism. Explore the labyrinth of nine pedestrian "vias" off of each side that wind past boutiques, tiny plazas, bubbling fountains, and bougainvillea-festooned balconies; this is where the smaller, unique shops are. The Worth Avenue Association holds historic walking tours on Wednesdays at 11 am during "season" (after Thanksgiving to late April). The $10 fee benefits local nonprofit organizations. ⊠ *Worth Ave., between Cocoanut Row and S. Ocean Blvd.* ☎ *561/659–6909* ⊕ *www.worth-avenue.com.*

WORTH NOTING

Bethesda-by-the-Sea. This Gothic-style Episcopal church had a claim to fame upon its creation in 1926: it was built by the first Protestant congregation in southeast Florida. Church lecture tours, covering Bethesda's history, architecture, and more, are offered at 12:15 on the second and fourth Sunday each month from September to mid-May (excluding December) and at 11:15 on the fourth Sunday each month from end of May to August. Also notable are the annual Boar's Head and Yule Log festivals in January. Adjacent is the formal, ornamental Cluett Memorial Garden. ⊠ *141 S. County Rd.* ☎ *561/655–4554* ⊕ *www.bbts.org* ⌥ *Free.*

El Solano. No Palm Beach mansion better represents the town's luminous legacy than the Spanish-style home built by Addison Mizner as his own residence in 1925. Mizner later sold El Solano to Harold Vanderbilt, and the property was long a favorite among socialites for parties and photo shoots. Vanderbilt held many a gala fund-raiser here. Beatle John Lennon and his wife, Yoko Ono, bought it less than a year before Lennon's death. It's still privately owned and not open to the public, but it's well worth a drive-by on any self-guided Palm Beach mansion tour. ⊠ *720 S. Ocean Blvd.*

Palm Beach and West Palm Beach

CLOSE UP

The Mansions of Palm Beach

Whether you aspire to be a former president (Kennedy), a current one (Trump), or a rock legend (John Lennon, Rod Stewart, Jimmy Buffett—all onetime or current Palm Beach residents)—no trip to the island is complete without gawking at the megamansions lining its perfectly manicured streets.

No one is more associated with how the island took shape than Addison Mizner, architect extraordinaire and society darling of the 1920s. But what people may not know is that a "fab four" was really the force behind the residential streets as they appear today: Mizner, of course, plus Maurice Fatio, Marion Sims Wyeth, and John Volk.

The four architects dabbled in different genres, some more so than others, but the unmissable style is Mediterranean revival, a Palm Beach hallmark mix of stucco walls, Spanish red-tile roofs, Italianate towers, Moorish-Gothic carvings, and the uniquely Floridian use of coquina, a grayish porous limestone made of coral rock with fossil-like imprints of shells. As for Mizner himself, he had quite the repertoire of signature elements, including using differently sized and shaped windows on one facade, blue tile work inside and out, and tiered roof lines (instead of one straight-sloping panel across, having several sections overlap like scales on a fish).

The majority of preserved estates are clustered in three sections: along Worth Avenue; the few blocks of South County Road after crossing Worth and the streets shooting off it; and the 5-mile stretch of South Ocean Boulevard from Barton Avenue to near Phipps Ocean Park, where the condos begin cropping up.

If 10 miles of riding on a bike while cars zip around you isn't intimidating, the two-wheeled trip may be the best way to fully take in the beauty of the mansions and surrounding scenery. Many hotels have bicycles for guest use. Another option is the dependable Palm Beach Bicycle Trail Shop (📠 561/659–4583 ⊕ www.palmbeach-bicycle.com). Otherwise, driving is a good alternative. Just be mindful that Ocean Boulevard is a one-lane road and the only route on the island to cities like Lake Worth and Manalapan, so you can't go too slowly, especially at peak travel times.

If gossip is more your speed, in-the-know concierges rely on Leslie Diver's "Island Living Tours" (📠 561/868–7944 ⊕ www.islandlivingpb.com); she's one of the town's leading experts on architecture *and* dish, both past and present.

Top 10 Self-Guided Stops: (1) Casa de Leoni (✉ 450 Worth Ave., Addison Mizner); (2) Villa des Cygnes (✉ 456 Worth Ave., Addison Mizner and Marion Sims Wyeth); (3) 17 Golfview Road (Marion Sims Wyeth); (4) 220 and 252 El Bravo Way (John Volk); (5) 126 South Ocean Boulevard (Marion Sims Wyeth); (6) El Solano (✉ 720 S. Ocean Blvd., Addison Mizner); (7) Casa Nana (✉ 780 S. Ocean Blvd., Addison Mizner); (8) 920 and 930 South Ocean Boulevard (Maurice Fatio); (9) Mar-a-Lago (✉ 1100 S. Ocean Blvd., Joseph Urban); (10) Il Palmetto (✉ 1500 S. Ocean Blvd., Maurice Fatio).

—Dorothea Hunter Sönne

Mar-a-Lago. Breakfast-food heiress Marjorie Merriweather Post commissioned a Hollywood set designer to create Ocean Boulevard's famed Mar-a-Lago, a 114-room, 110,000-square-foot Mediterranean-revival palace. Its 75-foot Italianate tower is visible from many areas of Palm Beach and from across the Intracoastal Waterway in West Palm Beach. Its notable owner, President Donald Trump, has turned it into a private membership club and has realized Marjorie Post's dream of turning the estate into a presidential retreat. Tourists have to enjoy the view from the car window or bicycle seat, but even the gates are impressive. ⊠ *1100 S. Ocean Blvd.* ☎ *561/832–2600* ⊕ *www.maralagoclub.com.*

FAMILY **Society of the Four Arts.** Despite widespread misconceptions of its members-only exclusivity, this privately endowed institution—founded in 1936 to encourage appreciation of art, music, drama, and literature—is funded for public enjoyment. The Esther B. O'Keeffe gallery building artfully melds an exhibition hall that houses traveling exhibits with a 700-seat theater. A library designed by prominent Mizner-peer Maurice Fatio, a children's library, a botanical garden, and the Philip Hulitar Sculpture Garden round out the facilities and are open daily. A complete schedule of programming is available on the society's website. ⊠ *2 Four Arts Plaza* ☎ *561/655–7227* ⊕ *www.fourarts.org* ✉ *$5 gallery; special program costs vary.*

WEST PALM BEACH

Long considered Palm Beach's less privileged stepsister, West Palm Beach has come into its own over the past 35 years, and just in this millennium the $30 million Centennial Square waterfront complex at the eastern end of Clematis Street, with piers, a pavilion, and an amphitheater, has transformed West Palm into an attractive, easy-to-walk downtown area—not to mention there's the Downtown Trolley that connects the shopping-and-entertainment mecca CityPlace with restaurant-and-lounge-lined Clematis Street. The recently opened Palm Beach Outlet Mall gives options to those looking for tony bargains. West Palm is especially well regarded for its arts scene, with unique museums and performance venues; a number of public art projects have appeared around the city. New attractions, such as the Manatee Lagoon, where the gentle sea creatures are visible up close in winter by the dozens, and a new stadium and sports complex for spring-training games, offer families many options while vacationing.

The city's outskirts, vast flat stretches with strip malls and car dealerships, may not inspire, but are worth driving through to reach attractions scattered around the southern and western reaches. Several sites are especially rewarding for children and other animal and nature lovers.

TOP ATTRACTIONS

Ann Norton Sculpture Gardens. This landmarked complex is a testament to the creative genius of the late American sculptor Ann Weaver Norton (1905–82), who was the second wife of Norton Museum founder, industrialist Ralph H. Norton. A set of art galleries in the studio and main house where she lived is surrounded by 2 acres of gardens with 300 species of rare palm trees, eight brick megaliths, a monumental

The Armory Art Center in West Palm Beach helps students of all ages create works of art in various mediums.

figure in Norwegian granite, and plantings designed to attract native birds. ⊠ *253 Barcelona Rd., West Palm Beach* ☎ *561/832–5328* ⊕ *www.ansg.org* ✉ *$10* ⊘ *Closed Aug.*

FAMILY **Lion Country Safari.** Drive your own vehicle along 4 miles of paved roads through a cageless zoo with free-roaming animals (chances are you'll have a giraffe nudging at your window) and then let loose in a 55-acre fun-land with camel rides, bird feedings, and a pontoon-boat cruise past islands with monkeys. A CD included with admission narrates the winding trek past white rhinos, zebras, and ostriches grouped into exhibits like Gir Forest that's modeled after a sanctuary in India and has native twisted-horned blackbuck antelope and water buffalo. (For obvious reasons, lions are fenced off, and no convertibles or pets are allowed.) Aside from dozens more up-close critter encounters after debarking, including a petting zoo, kids can go paddleboating, do a round of mini-golf, climb aboard carnival rides, or have a splash in a 4,000-square-foot aquatic playground (some extra fees apply). ⊠ *2003 Lion Country Safari Rd., at Southern Blvd. W, West Palm Beach* ☎ *561/793–1084* ⊕ *www.lioncountrysafari.com* ✉ *$35, $7 parking.*

FAMILY **Manatee Lagoon.** Once a casual spot next to the local electric plant's
Fodor'sChoice discharge waters, this center celebrating the manatee—South Florida's
★ popular winter visitors—opened in 2016 at a spot where the peaceful creatures naturally congregate. The airy, two-story facility is surrounded by wraparound decks to accommodate sea-cow spotters from fall to spring. Educational, interactive displays tell the story of this once-endangered species. A long deck along the seawall leads to picnic pavilions from where you can watch the action at nearby Peanut Island

and the Port of Palm Beach. Free admission makes it group-friendly; a live "manatee cam" shows manatee counts before you go. ⊠ *6000 N. Flagler Dr., West Palm Beach* ✛ *Entrance is on Flagler Dr., via 58th St. east of U.S. 1 and south of the Port of Palm Beach flyover* ☎ *561/626–2833* ⊕ *www.visitmanateelagoon.com* ⊠ *Free* ☾ *Closed Mon.*

Mounts Botanical Garden. The oldest public green space in the county is, unbelievably, across the road from the West Palm Beach airport; but the planes are the last thing you notice while walking around and relaxing amid the nearly 14 acres of exotic trees, rain-forest flora, and butterfly and water gardens. The gift shop contains a selection of rare gardening books on tropical climes. Frequent plant sales are held here, and numerous plant societies with international ties hold meetings open to the public in the auditorium. Experts in tropical edible and ornamental plants are on staff. ⊠ *531 N. Military Trail, West Palm Beach* ☎ *561/233–1757* ⊕ *www.mounts.org* ⊠ *$5 (suggested donation).*

Norton Museum of Art. Constructed in 1941 by steel magnate Ralph H. Norton and his wife, Elizabeth, the museum has grown to become one of the most impressive in South Florida with an extensive collection of 19th- and 20th-century American and European paintings—including works by Picasso, Monet, Matisse, Pollock, Cassatt, and O'Keeffe—plus Chinese art, earlier European art, and photography. To accommodate a growing collection, the museum is undergoing an extensive expansion to include 12,000 additional square feet of gallery space in a new west wing, event spaces, and a great hall. A garden will also be incorporated into the space. Until the opening of the expansion, which is expected in 2018, admission is free; until then, the museum is only open in the afternoon. ■ TIP→ The popular Art After Dark, Thursday from 5 to 9 pm, is a gathering spot for art lovers, with wine and music in the galleries. ⊠ *1451 S. Olive Ave., West Palm Beach* ☎ *561/832–5196* ⊕ *www.norton.org* ⊠ *Free* ☾ *Closed Mon.*

WORTH NOTING

Armory Art Center. Built by the Works Progress Administration (WPA) in 1939, this art deco facility is now a nonprofit art school hosting rotating exhibitions and art classes throughout the year. The Armory Art Center became an institution for art instruction when the Norton Museum Gallery and School of Art dropped the latter part of its name in 1986 and discontinued art-instruction classes. ⊠ *1700 Parker Ave., West Palm Beach* ☎ *561/832–1776* ⊕ *www.armoryart.org* ⊠ *Free.*

National Croquet Center. The world's largest croquet complex, the 10-acre center is also the headquarters for the U.S. Croquet Association. Vast expanses of orderly lawns are the stage for fierce competitions. There's also a clubhouse with a pro shop and the Croquet Grille, with verandas for dining and viewing (armchair enthusiasts can enjoy the games for no charge). You don't have to be a member to try your hand out on the lawns, and on Saturday morning at 10 am, there's a free group lesson with an introduction to the game, and open play; call in advance to reserve a spot. ⊠ *700 Florida Mango Rd., at Summit Blvd., West Palm Beach* ☎ *561/478–2300* ⊕ *www.croquetnational.com* ⊠ *Center free; full day of croquet $30.*

Richard and Pat Johnson Palm Beach County History Museum. A beautifully restored 1916 courthouse in downtown opened its doors in 2008 as the permanent home of the Historical Society of Palm Beach County's collection of artifacts and records dating back before the town's start—a highlight is furniture and decorative objects from Mizner Industries (a real treat since many of his mansions are not open to the public). ✉ *300 N. Dixie Hwy., West Palm Beach* ☎ *561/832–4164* ⊕ *www.historicalsocietypbc.org* 🗺 *Free* ☉ *Closed Sun.*

FAMILY **South Florida Science Center and Aquarium.** Both fresh- and saltwater aquariums greet the curious at this interactive, family-friendly science museum. Permanent exhibits of moon and Mars rocks and meteorites, a giant sphere with global animation projection for Earth sciences, and Everglades conservation exhibit teach while entertaining. A planetarium with daily themed shows and a conservation 9-hole mini-golf course designed by Gary Fazio and Jim Niklaus are popular with all ages and carry separate admission charges. ✉ *4801 Dreher Trail N, West Palm Beach* ☎ *561/832–1988* ⊕ *www.sfsciencecenter.org* 🗺 *$16.95; planetarium $5; mini-golf $7.*

LAKE WORTH

For years, tourists looked here mainly for inexpensive lodging and easy access to Palm Beach, since a bridge leads from the mainland to a barrier island with Lake Worth's beach. Now Lake Worth has grown into an arts community, with several blocks of restaurants, nightclubs, shops, and galleries, making this a worthy destination on its own.

TOP ATTRACTIONS

Museum of Polo and Hall of Fame. The history of the sport of kings is displayed in a time line here, with other exhibits focusing on polo ponies, star players, trophies, and a look at how mallets are made. It provides a great introduction to the surprisingly exciting, hoof-pounding sport that is played live on Sundays from January to April in nearby Wellington. ✉ *9011 Lake Worth Rd., Lake Worth* ☎ *561/969–3210* ⊕ *www.polomuseum.com* 🗺 *Free (donations accepted)* ☉ *Closed Sun. Closed Sat. May–Dec.*

LANTANA

Lantana—just a bit farther south from Palm Beach than Lake Worth—has inexpensive lodging and a bridge connecting the town to its own beach on a barrier island. Tucked between Lantana and Boynton Beach is **Manalapan,** a tiny but posh residential community.

BOYNTON BEACH

In 1884, when fewer than 50 settlers lived in the area, Nathan Boynton, a Civil War veteran from Michigan, paid $25 for 500 acres with a mile-long stretch of beachfront thrown in. How things have changed, with today's population at about 118,000 and property values still on an upswing. Far enough from Palm Beach to remain low-key, Boynton Beach has two parts, the mainland and the barrier island—the town of Ocean Ridge—connected by two bridges.

The posh Palm Beach area has its share of luxury villas on the water; many are Mediterranean in style.

TOP ATTRACTIONS

FAMILY **Arthur R. Marshall Loxahatchee National Wildlife Refuge.** The most robust part of the northern Everglades, this 221-square-mile refuge is one of two huge water-retention areas accounting for much of the "River of Grass" outside the national park near Miami. Start at the visitor center, which has fantastic interactive exhibits and videos like "Night Sounds of the Everglades" and an airboat simulator. From there, you can take a marsh trail to a 20-foot-high observation tower, or stroll a ½-mile boardwalk lined with educational signage through a dense cypress swamp. There are also guided nature walks (including some specifically for bird-watching), and there's great bass fishing (bring your own poles and bait) and a 5½-mile canoe and kayak trail loop (both can be rented from a kiosk by the fishing pier). ⊠ *10216 Lee Rd., off U.S. 441 between Rte. 804 and Rte. 806, Boynton Beach* ☎ *561/732–3684* ⊕ *www.fws.gov/refuge/arm_loxahatchee/* ⊇ *$5 per vehicle; $1 per pedestrian or bicyclist.*

BEACHES

PALM BEACH

Phipps Ocean Park. About 2 miles south of "Billionaire's Row" on Ocean Boulevard sits this public ocean-side park, with two metered parking lots separated by a fire station. There are four entry points to the beach, but the north side is better for beachgoers. At the southern entrance, there is a six-court tennis facility. The beach is narrow and has natural rock formations dotting the shoreline, making it ideal for snorkelers. There are picnic tables and grills on-site, as well as the Little Red

Schoolhouse, an 1886 landmark that hosts educational workshops for local kids. If a long walk floats your boat, venture north to see the mega-mansions, but don't go too far inland, because private property starts at the high-tide line. Parking is metered, and time limits strictly enforced. There's a two-hour time limit for free parking—but read the meter carefully: it's valid only during certain hours at some spots. **Amenities:** parking (no fee); toilets; showers; lifeguards. **Best for:** walking; solitude. ⊠ *2201 S. Ocean Blvd.* ☎ *561/838–5400 Ext. 8, 561/227–6450 tennis reservations* ▣ *Free.*

Town of Palm Beach Municipal Beach. You know you're here if you see Palm Beach's younger generation frolicking on the sands and locals setting up chairs as the sun reflects off their gleaming white veneers. The Worth Avenue clock tower is within sight, but the gateways to the sand are actually on Chilean Avenue, Brazilian Avenue, and Gulfstream Road. It's definitely the most central and longest lifeguarded strip open to everyone and a popular choice for hotel guests from the Colony, Chesterfield, and Brazilian Court. Lifeguards are present from Brazilian Avenue down to Chilean Avenue. It's also BYOC (bring your own chair). You'll find no water-sport or food vendors here; however, casual eateries are a quick walk away. Metered spots line A1A. **Amenities:** lifeguards; showers. **Best for:** swimming; sunset. ⊠ *S. Ocean Blvd. from Brazilian Ave. to Gulfstream Rd.* ☎ *561/838–5483 beach patrol.*

LAKE WORTH

FAMILY   **Lake Worth Beach.** This public beach bustles with beachgoers of all ages thanks to the prolific family offerings. The waterfront retail promenade—the old-fashioned nongambling Lake Worth "casino"—has a Mulligan's Beach House Bar & Grill, a T-shirt store, a pizzeria, and a Kilwin's ice-cream shop. The beach also has a municipal Olympic-sized public swimming pool, a playground, a fishing pier—not to mention the pier's wildly popular daytime eatery, Benny's on the Beach (open for dinner weekends in season). Tideline Ocean Resort and Four Seasons guests are steps away from the action; Eau Palm Beach guests are a short bike ride away. **Amenities:** food and drink; lifeguards; parking (fee); showers; toilets; water sports. **Best for:** sunset; swimming. ⊠ *10 S. Ocean Blvd., at A1A and Lake Ave., Lake Worth* ⊕ *www.lakeworth. org* ▣ *$1 to enter pier, $3 to enter and fish, $2 per hr for parking.*

LANTANA

Town of Lantana Public Beach. Ideal for quiet ambles, this sandy stretch is also noteworthy for a casual restaurant, the no-frills breezy Dune Deck Café, which is perched above the waterline and offers great views for an oceanfront breakfast or lunch. The beach's huge parking lot is directly adjacent to the Eau Palm Beach (meters take credit cards), and diagonally across the street is a sizable strip mall with all sorts of conveniences, including boutiques and more eateries. Note: the beach is very narrow and large rocks loom in the water. However, these are some of the clearest waters along the Florida coastline, and they make an idyllic background for long walks and great photos. **Amenities:** food and drink; lifeguards; parking (fee); showers; toilets. **Best for:** walking. ⊠ *100 E. Ocean Ave., Lantana* ▣ *$1.50 per hr for parking.*

WHERE TO EAT

PALM BEACH

$$$$
ITALIAN
✗**Bice Ristorante.** The bougainvillea-laden trellises set the scene at the main entrance on Peruvian Way, off posh Worth Avenue. Even though it's a chain, this is a favorite of Palm Beach society, and both the restaurant and the bar become packed and noisy during high season. **Known for:** seafood risotto; homemade pizzaccia bread made with basil, chives, and oregano; outdoor dining where you can watch the scene on Worth Avenue. $ *Average main: $35* ✉ *313½ Worth Ave.* ✛ *Entrance is on Peruvian Ave.* ☎ *561/835–1600* ⊕ *www.palmbeach.bicegroup.com.*

$$$$
FRENCH
✗**Bistro Chez Jean-Pierre.** With walls adorned by avant-garde contemporary art, this family-run bistro is where the Palm Beach old guard likes to let down its hair, all the while partaking of sumptuous northern French cuisine along with an impressive wine selection. Forget calorie or cholesterol concerns, and indulge in scrambled eggs with caviar or house-made foie gras, or the best-selling Dover sole. **Known for:** Dover sole; foie gras prepared in-house; dessert soufflés. $ *Average main: $39* ✉ *132 N. County Rd.* ☎ *561/833–1171* ⊕ *www.chezjean-pierre.com* ☽ *Closed mid-July–Aug. and Sun. No lunch.*

$$$$
ECLECTIC
Fodor's Choice
★
✗**bûccan.** Young blue bloods rocking D&G jeans slip into tightly packed copper-topped tables alongside groups of silver-haired oil scions with the kitchen in view. It's island casual in its trendiest, most boisterous, yet still refined incarnation, with a regional American menu to match. **Known for:** small sharing plates; hot dog panini; short rib empanadas. $ *Average main: $32* ✉ *350 S. County Rd.* ☎ *561/833–3450* ⊕ *www.buccanpalmbeach.com* ☽ *No lunch.*

$$$$
FRENCH
Fodor's Choice
★
✗**Café Boulud.** Palm Beach socialites just can't get enough of this prized restaurant by celebrated chef Daniel Boulud. This posh, French-American venue in the Brazilian Court hotel, which was renovated in 2016 and added a new contemporary bar with its own menu, is casual yet elegant. **Known for:** house-cured charcuterie; seared duck breast with cherry duck jus; an extensive wine list. $ *Average main: $38* ✉ *The Brazilian Court Hotel & Beach Club, 301 Australian Ave.* ☎ *561/655–6060* ⊕ *www.cafeboulud.com.*

$$$$
INTERNATIONAL
✗**Café L'Europe.** Since 1980, the favorite spot of society's movers and shakers—and a few celebs—has remained a regular stop on foodie itineraries. Service and consistency are big reasons for its longevity. **Known for:** veal chops; romantic setting; Champagne and caviar bar with extensive selections. $ *Average main: $47* ✉ *331 S. County Rd.* ☎ *561/655–4020* ⊕ *www.cafeleurope.com* ☽ *Closed Mon. June–Nov.*

$$$
ASIAN
✗**Echo.** Palm Beach's window on Asia has a sleek sushi bar and floor-to-ceiling glass doors separating the interior from the popular terrace dining area. Chinese, Japanese, Thai, and Vietnamese selections are neatly categorized: Wind (small plates starting your journey), Water (seafood mains), Fire (open-flame wok creations), Earth (meat dishes), and Flavor (desserts, sweets). **Known for:** sushi and specialty rolls; fresh seafood; cocktails in the Dragonfly Lounge. $ *Average main: $30* ✉ *230-A Sunrise Ave.* ☎ *561/802–4222* ⊕ *www.echopalmbeach.com* ☽ *Closed Mon. No lunch.*

6

Where to Eat and Stay in Palm Beach and West Palm Beach

Restaurants ▼

Avocado Grill **8**

Belle and Maxwell's **17**

Bice Ristorante **12**

Bistro Chez Jean-Pierre **3**

büccan **6**

Café Boulud **9**

Café L'Europe ..**11**

Echo **1**

Grato **16**

Howley's **18**

Marcello's La Sirena **19**

Mediterranean Market & Deli **5**

PB Catch **2**

Pistache French Bistro **7**

Pizza Al Fresco **14**

The Regional Kitchen & Public House **15**

Renato's **13**

Rhythm Cafe ...**10**

Testa's Palm Beach **4**

Hotels ▼

The Brazilian Court Hotel **2**

The Breakers Palm Beach **1**

Casa Grandview West Palm Beach **6**

The Chesterfield Palm Beach **3**

The Colony **4**

Four Seasons Resort Palm Beach **11**

Grandview Gardens Bed & Breakfast **7**

Hampton Inn & Suites Wellington **9**

Hilton West Palm Beach **5**

Hotel Biba **8**

The Tideline Resort & Spa ...**10**

KEY

❶ *Restaurants*

① *Hotels*

$$$$ ✕ **PB Catch.** As the name implies, it's all about fins and shells here,
SEAFOOD including the live ones that entertain diners in their tanks in the modern dining room. The menu includes a raw bar with a good selection of raw (or grilled) oysters, clams, and the chef's "seacuterie" platter, a build-your-own sampler of such choices as salmon pastrami, citrus-cured fluke, cured sea bass, or octopus torchon. **Known for:** in-house cured fish; shellfish tower from the raw bar; craft cocktails. $ *Average main: $35* ✉ *251 Sunrise Blvd.* ☎ *561/655–5558* ⊕ *www.pbcatch.com* ⊘ *Closed Sun.*

$$ ✕ **Pizza Al Fresco.** The hidden-garden setting is the secret to the success of
PIZZA this European-style pizzeria, where you can dine under a canopy of century-old banyans in an intimate courtyard. Specialties are 12-inch hand-tossed brick-oven pizzas with such interesting toppings as prosciutto, arugula, and caviar. **Known for:** caviar-and-smoked-salmon pizza; fresh salads; garden setting. $ *Average main: $19* ✉ *14 Via Mizner, at Worth Ave.* ✥ *Tucked in a courtyard off Worth Ave.* ☎ *561/832–0032* ⊕ *www. pizzaalfresco.com.*

$$$$ ✕ **Renato's.** Here, at one of the most romantic restaurants in Palm Beach,
ITALIAN guests can dine Italiano. Sit in the beautiful courtyard, with stars above and twinkling lights on the bougainvillea, or in the intimate, low-lighted dining room flickering with candles and enhanced with fresh flowers and quiet classical music. **Known for:** fresh pasta dishes; house-made soups; romantic setting. $ *Average main: $37* ✉ *87 Via Mizner* ☎ *561/655–9752* ⊕ *www.renatospalmbeach.com* ⊘ *No lunch Sun.*

$$$ ✕ **Testa's Palm Beach.** Attracting a loyal clientele since 1921 (Howdy
AMERICAN Doody is listed among its "celebs"), this restaurant is still owned by the
FAMILY Testa family. Dine inside in an intimate pine-paneled room with cozy bar, out back in a gazebo-style room for large groups, or outside—popular at breakfast—at sidewalk tables that are pet-friendly. **Known for:** shrimp-and-artichoke scampi; blueberry pancakes for breakfast; signature strawberry pie. $ *Average main: $27* ✉ *221 Royal Poinciana Way* ☎ *561/832–0992* ⊕ *www.testasrestaurants.com.*

WEST PALM BEACH

$$ ✕ **Avocado Grill.** In downtown West Palm Beach's waterfront district,
ECLECTIC this hot spot is an alternative to the bar food, tacos, and burgers more common in the area. "Green" cuisine seasonal salads, vegetarian dishes, and sustainably produced meats and seafood is making waves at the avocado-themed restaurant. **Known for:** everything avocado, including wonderful guacamole; mushroom fricassee with cheddar grits; kale and duck salad. $ *Average main: $19* ✉ *125 Datura St., West Palm Beach* ☎ *561/623–0822* ⊕ *www.avocadogrillwpb.com.*

$$ ✕ **Belle and Maxwell's.** Palm Beach ladies who lunch leave the island for
AMERICAN an afternoon at Belle and Maxwell's, while young professionals loosen up after work at the wine bar, part of the bistro's expanded dining area. Tucked along Antique Row, it looks like a storybook tea party at lunch, with eclectic furnishings and decor, and charming garden. **Known for:** classic chicken marsala; extensive list of lunch salads; house-made desserts. $ *Average main: $18* ✉ *3700 S. Dixie Hwy., West Palm Beach* ☎ *561/832–4449* ⊕ *www.belleandmaxwells.com* ⊘ *Closed Sun. No dinner Mon.*

$$$

TUSCAN

✕**Grato.** At this boisterous, trendy sibling to bûccan, pizzas and pastas are served up to neighborhood and Palm Beach island diners in a chic, open space. An open kitchen also hosts a small bar to accommodate viewing the chef in action. **Known for:** wood-fired-oven pizzas; fresh pastas; busy bar scene. ⑤ *Average main: $24* ⊠ *1901 Dixie Hwy., West Palm Beach* ☎ *561/404–1334* ⊕ *www.gratowpb.com.*

$

AMERICAN

✕**Howley's.** Since 1950, this diner's eat-in counter and "cooked in sight, it must be right" motto have made it a congenial setting for meeting old friends and making new ones. Nowadays, Howley's prides itself on its kitsch factor and old-school eats like turkey potpie and a traditional Thanksgiving feast, as well as its retro-redux dishes like potato-and-brisket burrito. **Known for:** kitschy setting; retro diner specialties; late-night dining. ⑤ *Average main: $13* ⊠ *4700 S. Dixie Hwy., West Palm Beach* ☎ *561/833–5691* ⊕ *www.sub-culture.org/howleys/.*

$$$$

ITALIAN

✕**Marcello's La Sirena.** A longtime favorite of locals, this sophisticated Italian restaurant is in an unexpected, nondescript location on Dixie Highway away from downtown and central hubs. But warm hospitality from a husband-and-wife team, along with smart service and delectable traditional dishes, await. **Known for:** fresh pasta dishes; award-winning wine list; great desserts. ⑤ *Average main: $31* ⊠ *6316 S. Dixie Hwy., West Palm Beach* ☎ *561/585–3128* ⊕ *www.lasirenaonline.com* ⊙ *Closed Sun.*

$

MIDDLE EASTERN

Fodor'sChoice

★

✕**Mediterranean Market & Deli.** This hole-in-the-wall Middle Eastern bakery, deli, and market is packed at lunchtime with regulars who are on a first-name basis with the gang behind the counter. From the nondescript parking lot the place doesn't look like much, but inside, delicious hot and cold Mediterranean treats await the take-out crowd. **Known for:** lamb salad; gyros; freshly baked pita bread. ⑤ *Average main: $10* ⊠ *327 5th St., West Palm Beach* ☎ *561/659–7322* ⊕ *www. mediterraneanmarketanddeli.com* ⊙ *Closed Sun.*

$$$

FRENCH

✕**Pistache French Bistro.** Although "the island" is no doubt a bastion of French cuisine, this cozy bistro across the bridge on the Clematis Street waterfront entices a lively crowd looking for an unpretentious good meal. The outdoor terrace can't be beat, and the fabulous modern French menu with twists such as roasted sliced duck with truffled polenta is a delight. **Known for:** fresh seafood; cheese and charcuterie; great desserts. ⑤ *Average main: $27* ⊠ *101 N. Clematis St., West Palm Beach* ☎ *561/833–5090* ⊕ *www.pistachewpb.com.*

$$$

SOUTHERN

✕**The Regional Kitchen & Public House.** *Top Chef* Lindsay Autry debuted her own Southern-inspired American cuisine in CityPlace to the acclaim of local critics. The menu of updated comfort food includes tea-brined fried chicken, creamy tomato pie, pimento cheese done table-side, and shrimp and grits. **Known for:** reinvented Southern classics; table-side pimento cheese; weekend brunch. ⑤ *Average main: $24* ⊠ *CityPlace, 651 Okeechobee Blvd., West Palm Beach* ✛ *Directly across from the Convention Center* ☎ *561/557–6460* ⊕ *www.eatregional.com.*

$$$

MODERN AMERICAN

✕**Rhythm Cafe.** West Palm Beach's Rhythm Cafe is anything but Palm Beach formal (the decor includes a feathered pink flamingo perched on the terrazzo floor). Fun, funky, cheesy, campy, and cool all at once, the former 1950s-era drugstore-cum-restaurant on West Palm Beach's

Antique Row features an ever-changing creative menu of house-made items with Italian, Greek, American, and Creole influences. **Known for:** "tapas-tizer" small plates; fresh fish; graham-cracker-crusted key lime chicken. ⑤ *Average main: $24 ⊠ 3800 S. Dixie Hwy., West Palm Beach* ☎ *561/833–3406* ⊕ *www.rhythmcafe.com* ⊘ *No lunch.*

LAKE WORTH

$ ✕**Benny's on the Beach.** Perched on the Lake Worth Pier, Benny's has

AMERICAN a walk-up bar, a take-out window, and a full-service beach-themed restaurant serving casual fare at bargain prices. "Beach Bread" is a take on a waffle sandwich; the fresh seafood is from Florida waters. **Known for:** Florida seafood; beach brunch; afternoon drinks. ⑤ *Average main: $12 ⊠ Lake Worth Beach, 10 S. Ocean Blvd., Lake Worth* ⊹ *On Lake Worth Pier* ☎ *561/582–9001* ⊕ *www.bennysonthebeach. com* ⊘ *No dinner May–early Dec.*

LANTANA

$$ ✕**Old Key Lime House.** An informal seafood spot—serving crab cakes,

SEAFOOD fish sandwiches, and fillets—and a favorite of locals and tourists, is perched on the Intracoastal Waterway with spectacular views. Observation decks with separate bars wrap around the back where boats can dock; indoors is more family-oriented. **Known for:** unpretentious, casual atmosphere; fried and grilled fish; great key lime pie. ⑤ *Average main: $20 ⊠ 300 E. Ocean Ave., Lantana* ☎ *561/582–1889* ⊕ *www. oldkeylimehouse.com.*

WHERE TO STAY

PALM BEACH

$$$$ ⊡ **The Brazilian Court Hotel.** This posh boutique hotel, stomping ground

HOTEL of Florida's well-heeled, is full of historic touches and creature com-

Fodor'sChoice forts—from its yellow facade with dramatic white-draped entry, to

★ modern draws like the renowned spa and Daniel Boulud restaurant. **Pros:** stylish and hip local crowd; charming courtyard; free beach shuttle. **Cons:** small fitness center; nondescript pool; 10-minute ride to ocean and suggested 24-hour advance reservation for shuttle. ⑤ *Rooms from: $609 ⊠ 301 Australian Ave.* ☎ *561/655–7740* ⊕ *www.thebraziliancourt.com* ⇆ *80 rooms* ⦿| *No meals.*

$$$$ ⊡ **The Breakers Palm Beach.** More than an opulent hotel, The Breakers

RESORT is a legendary 140-acre self-contained jewel of a resort built in a Medi-

FAMILY terranean style and loaded with amenities, from a 20,000-square-foot

Fodor'sChoice luxury spa and grandiose beach club with four pools and a half-mile

★ private beach, to 10 tennis courts, croquet courts, and two 18-hole golf courses. **Pros:** impeccable attention to detail; fantastic service; beautiful room views; extensive activities for families. **Cons:** big price tag; short drive to reach off-property attractions. ⑤ *Rooms from: $699 ⊠ 1 S. County Rd.* ☎ *561/655–6611, 888/273–2537* ⊕ *www.thebreakers.com* ⇆ *540 rooms* ⦿| *No meals.*

$$$$ ⊡ **The Chesterfield Palm Beach.** A distinctly upper-crust northern Euro-

HOTEL pean feel pervades the peach stucco walls and elegant rooms here; the hotel sits just north of the western end of Worth Avenue, and high tea, a cigar parlor, and daily turndown service recall a bygone, more refined era. **Pros:** gracious, attentive staff; Leopard Lounge entertainment; free valet parking. **Cons:** long walk to beach; only one elevator; to some, can come off as a bit stuffy. $ *Rooms from: $495* ✉ *363 Cocoanut Row* ☎ *561/659–5800, 800/243–7871* ⊕ *www.chesterfieldpb.com* ⤸ *52 rooms* ⦿ *No meals.*

$$$$
HOTEL
⛉ **The Colony.** In 2014, nearly $10 million was spent to redecorate and refurbish every room at the island's legendary British-colonial-style hotel. **Pros:** unbeatable location; famous bar at Polo Steakhouse; pillow-top mattresses; full English breakfast included. **Cons:** lobby is small; elevators are tight. $ *Rooms from: $600* ✉ *155 Hammon Ave.* ☎ *561/655–5430, 800/521–5525* ⊕ *www.thecolonypalmbeach.com* ⤸ *90 rooms* ⦿ *Breakfast.*

$$$$
RESORT
FAMILY
Fodor's Choice
★
⛉ **Four Seasons Resort Palm Beach.** Couples and families seeking relaxed seaside elegance in a luxe yet understated setting will love this mani-cured 6-acre oceanfront escape at the south end of Palm Beach, with serene, bright, airy rooms in a cream-colored palette and spacious mar-ble-lined baths. **Pros:** accommodating service; all rooms have balconies; outstanding complimentary kids' program. **Cons:** 10-minute drive to downtown Palm Beach (but can walk to Lake Worth); pricey. $ *Rooms from: $739* ✉ *2800 S. Ocean Blvd.* ☎ *561/582–2800, 800/432–2335* ⊕ *www.fourseasons.com/palmbeach* ⤸ *210 rooms* ⦿ *No meals.*

$$$
RESORT
⛉ **The Tideline Resort & Spa.** This Zenlike boutique hotel, a member of the Kimpton group, has a loyal following of young, hip travelers, who appreciate the guest rooms that were updated in 2016 and the full-service spa. **Pros:** most rooms have beautiful views of the private beach; ultracontemporary vibe; luxury setting. **Cons:** a hike from shopping and nightlife; the infinity pool is across the driveway. $ *Rooms from: $340* ✉ *2842 S. Ocean Blvd.* ☎ *561/540–6440, 888/344–4321* ⊕ *www.tidelineresort.com* ⤸ *144 rooms* ⦿ *No meals.*

WEST PALM BEACH

$$
B&B/INN
⛉ **Casa Grandview West Palm Beach.** In West Palm's charming Grandview Heights historic district—and just minutes away from both downtown and the beach—this warm and personalized B&B offers a wonderful respite from South Florida's big-hotel norm. **Pros:** daily dry cleaning of all linens; complimentary soft drinks, coffee, and snacks (and lots of them) in lobby; simple keyless entry (number code lock system). **Cons:** cottages and suites have seven-day minimum; free breakfast in B&B rooms only; art deco suites don't have air-conditioning. $ *Rooms from: $289* ✉ *1410 Georgia Ave., West Palm Beach* ☎ *561/655–8932* ⊕ *www.casagrandview.com* ⤸ *17 rooms* ⦿ *Breakfast.*

$$
B&B/INN
⛉ **Grandview Gardens Bed & Breakfast.** Defining the Florida B&B experi-ence, this 1925 Mediterranean-revival home overlooks a serene court-yard pool and oozes loads of charm and personality, while the fabulous owners provide heavy doses of bespoke service. **Pros:** multilingual own-ers; outside private entrances to rooms; free bicycle use; innkeepers offer historic city tours. **Cons:** not close to the beach; in a residential area; rental car needed. $ *Rooms from: $225* ✉ *1608 Lake Ave., West Palm Beach* ☎ *561/833–9023* ⊕ *www.grandview-gardens.com* ⤸ *5 rooms, 2 cottages* ⦿ *Breakfast.*

$$ ⊞ **Hampton Inn & Suites Wellington.** The only hotel near the polo fields
HOTEL in the equestrian mecca of Wellington—10 miles west of downtown
Palm Beach—feels a bit like a tony clubhouse, with rich wood paneling,
hunt prints, and elegant chandeliers; but inside the rooms are standard
Hampton Inn fare. **Pros:** complimentary hot breakfast; free Wi-Fi; out-
door swimming pool; close to a large shopping center; near the county
fairgrounds. **Cons:** no restaurant; Intracoastal Waterway is a 30-minute
drive, and beach is farther. $ *Rooms from: $250* ⊠ *2155 Wellington*
Green Dr., West Palm Beach ☎ *561/472–9696* ⊕ *hamptoninn3.hilton.*
com ⇆ *122 rooms, 32 suites* ⦿ *Breakfast.*

$$ ⊞ **Hilton West Palm Beach.** In downtown, the contemporary business
HOTEL hotel situated next door to the county convention center has a pool with
FAMILY cabanas many resorts would envy. **Pros:** walking distance to convention
center, CityPlace, Kravis Center; resort-style pool; amenities geared toward
business travelers. **Cons:** long ride to the beach; noise from downtown
construction and trains. $ *Rooms from: $279* ⊠ *600 Okeechobee Blvd.,*
West Palm Beach ✛ *Adjacent to the Palm Beach County Convention*
Center ☎ *561/231–6000* ⊕ *www3.hilton.com* ⇆ *400 rooms* ⦿ *No meals.*

$ ⊞ **Hotel Biba.** In the El Cid historic district, this 1940s-era motel has got-
HOTEL ten a fun, stylish revamp from designer Barbara Hulanicki: each room
has a vibrant mélange of colors, along with handcrafted mirrors, mosaic
bathroom floors, and custom mahogany furnishings. **Pros:** cool, punchy
design and luxe fixtures; popular wine bar; free Continental breakfast
with Cuban pastries. **Cons:** water pressure is weak; bathrooms are tiny;
noisy when the bar is open late and trains run nearby; not all rooms
have central air-conditioning. $ *Rooms from: $160* ⊠ *320 Belvedere*
Rd., West Palm Beach ☎ *561/832–0094* ⊕ *www.hotelbiba.com* ⇆ *43*
rooms ⦿ *Breakfast.*

LAKE WORTH

$ ⊞ **Sabal Palm House.** Built in 1936, this romantic, two-story B&B is
B&B/INN a short walk from Lake Worth's downtown shops, eateries, and the
Intracoastal Waterway, and each room is decorated with antiques and
inspired by a different artist, including Renoir, Dalí, Norman Rockwell,
and Chagall. **Pros:** on quiet street; hands-on owners; chairs and totes
with towels provided for use at nearby beach. **Cons:** no pool; peak times
require a two-night minimum stay; no parking lot. $ *Rooms from:*
$159 ⊠ *109 N. Golfview Rd., Lake Worth* ☎ *561/582–1090, 888/722–*
2572 ⊕ *www.sabalpalmhouse.com* ⇆ *5 rooms, 2 suites* ⦿ *Breakfast.*

SOUTH PALM BEACH AND MANALAPAN

$$$$ ⊞ **Eau Palm Beach.** In the coastal town of Manalapan (just south of
RESORT Palm Beach), this sublime, glamorous destination resort (formerly the
FAMILY Ritz-Carlton) showcases a newer, younger face of luxury, including a
Fodor'sChoice 3,000-square-foot oceanfront terrace, two sleek pools, a huge fitness
★ center, and a deluxe spa. **Pros:** magnificent aesthetic details throughout;
indulgent pampering services; excellent on-site dining; kids love the cool
cyber-lounge just for them. **Cons:** golf course is off property; 15-min-
ute drive to Palm Beach. $ *Rooms from: $560* ⊠ *100 S. Ocean Blvd.,*
Manalapan ☎ *561/533–6000, 800/241–3333* ⊕ *www.eaupalmbeach.*
com ⇆ *309 rooms* ⦿ *No meals.*

6

NIGHTLIFE AND PERFORMING ARTS

PALM BEACH

NIGHTLIFE

Palm Beach is teeming with restaurants that turn into late-night hot spots, plus hotel lobby bars perfect for tête-à-têtes.

Fodor's Choice ★ **bûccan.** At this hip Hamptons-esque scene, society darlings crowd the lounge, throwing back killer cocktails like the Basil Rathbone (gin, orange juice, mint, basil, strawberry) and Buccan T (vodka, black tea, cranberry, citrus, basil, and agave nectar). ⊠ *350 S. County Rd.* ☎ *561/833–3450* ⊕ *www.buccanpalmbeach.com.*

Café Boulud. A sleek, redesigned dining room bar with bar bites from a special menu plus an extended happy hour draws locals and visitors alike. ■ **TIP→ Dress to impress.** ⊠ *301 Australian Ave.* ☎ *561/655–6060* ⊕ *www.cafeboulud.com/palmbeach.*

Cucina Dell' Arte. Though this spot is popular for lunch and dinner, it's even more popular later in the night. The younger, trendier set comes late to party, mingle, and dance into the wee hours. ⊠ *257 Royal Poinciana Way* ☎ *561/655–0770* ⊕ *www.cucinadellarte.com.*

The Leopard Lounge. In the Chesterfield hotel, this enclave feels like an exclusive club. The trademark ceiling and spotted floors of the renovated lounge are a nod to this hotel's historic roots, but the rest of the decor is new age Palm Beach glam. Though it starts each evening as a restaurant, as the night progresses the Leopard is transformed into an old-fashioned club with live music for Palm Beach's old guard. The bartenders know how to pour a cocktail here. ⊠ *The Chesterfield Palm Beach, 363 Cocoanut Row* ☎ *561/659–5800* ⊕ *www.chesterfieldpb.com.*

WEST PALM BEACH

NIGHTLIFE

West Palm is known for its exuberant nightlife—Clematis Street and CityPlace are the prime party destinations. In fact, downtown rocks every Thursday from 6 pm on with Clematis by Night (⊕ *www.wpb. org/clematis-by-night*), a celebration of music, dance, art, and food at Centennial Square.

Blue Martini. The CityPlace outpost of this South Florida hot spot for thirty-, forty-, and fiftysomething adults gone wild has a menu filled with tons of innovative martini creations (42 to be exact), tasty tapas, and lots of cougars on the prowl, searching for a first, second, or even third husband. And the guys aren't complaining! The drinks are great and the scene is fun for everyone, even those who aren't single and looking to mingle. Expect DJs some nights, live music others. ⊠ *CityPlace, 550 S. Rosemary Ave., #244, West Palm Beach* ☎ *561/835–8601* ⊕ *www.bluemartinilounge.com.*

ER Bradley's Saloon. People of all ages congregate to hang out and socialize at this kitschy open-air restaurant and bar to gaze at the Intracoastal Waterway; the mechanical bull is a hit on Saturdays. Live music's on tap five to seven nights a week. ⊠ *104 Clematis St., West Palm Beach* ☎ *561/833–3520* ⊕ *www.erbradleys.com.*

Fodor's Choice
★

Rocco's Tacos and Tequila Bar. In the last few years, Rocco's has taken root in numerous South Florida downtowns and become synonymous with wild nights of chips 'n' guac, margaritas, and intoxicating fun. This is more of a scene than just a restaurant, and when Rocco's in the house and pouring shots, get ready to party hearty. With pitchers of margaritas continuously flowing, the middle-age crowd is boisterous and fun, recounting (and reliving) the days of spring break debauchery from their pre-professional years. Get your party started here with more than 220 choices of tequila. There's another branch at 5250 Town Center Circle in Boca Raton; at 110 Atlantic Avenue in Delray Beach; and in Palm Beach Gardens in PGA Commons at 5090 PGA Boulevard. ✉ *224 Clematis St., West Palm Beach* ☎ *561/650–1001* ⊕ *www. roccostacos.com.*

PERFORMING ARTS

Palm Beach Dramaworks (pbd). Housed in an intimate venue with only 218 seats in downtown West Palm Beach, the modus operandi is "theater to think about," with plays by Pulitzer Prize winners on rotation. ✉ *201 Clematis St., West Palm Beach* ☎ *561/514–4042* ⊕ *www.palmbeach-dramaworks.org.*

Palm Beach Opera. The organization celebrates its 55th anniversary with the 2017 season. Three main-stage productions are offered during the season from January through April at the Kravis Center with English-language supertitles. There's an annual Children's Performance where all tickets are $5, plus a free outdoor concert at the Meyer Amphitheatre in downtown West Palm Beach. Tickets start at $25. ✉ *1800 S. Australian Ave., Suite 301, administrative office, West Palm Beach* ☎ *561/833–7888* ⊕ *www.pbopera.org.*

Fodor's Choice
★

Raymond F. Kravis Center for the Performing Arts. This is the crown jewel amid a treasury of local arts attractions, and its marquee star is the 2,195-seat Dreyfoos Hall, a glass, copper, and marble showcase just steps from the restaurants and shops of CityPlace. The center also boasts the 289-seat Rinker Playhouse, 170-seat Persson Hall, and the Gosman Amphitheatre, which holds 1,400 total in seats and on the lawn. A packed year-round schedule features a blockbuster lineup of Broadway's biggest touring productions, concerts, dance, dramas, and musicals; the Miami City Ballet, Palm Beach Opera, and the Palm Beach Pops perform here. ✉ *701 Okeechobee Blvd., West Palm Beach* ☎ *561/832–7469 box office* ⊕ *www.kravis.org.*

6

SHOPPING

As is the case throughout South Florida, many of the smaller boutiques in Palm Beach close in the summer, and most stores are closed on Sunday. Consignment stores in Palm Beach are definitely worth a look; you'll often find high-end designer clothing in impeccable condition.

PALM BEACH

SHOPPING AREAS

Royal Poinciana Way. Cute shops dot the north side of Royal Poinciana Way between Bradley Place and North County Road. Wind through the courtyards past upscale consignment stores to Sunset Avenue, then

Worth Avenue is the place in Palm Beach for high-end shopping, from international boutiques to independent jewelers.

stroll down Sunrise Avenue: this is the place for specialty items like out-of-town newspapers, health foods, and rare books. ⊠ *Royal Poinciana Way, between Bradley Pl. and N. County Rd.*

Fodor's Choice
★

Worth Avenue. One of the world's premier showcases for high-quality shopping runs half a mile from east to west across Palm Beach, from the beach to Lake Worth. The street has more than 200 shops (more than 40 of them sell jewelry), and many upscale chain stores (Gucci, Hermès, Saks Fifth Avenue, Neiman Marcus, Louis Vuitton, Chanel, Cartier, Tiffany & Co., and Tourneau) are represented—their merchandise appealing to the discerning tastes of the Palm Beach clientele. Don't miss walking around the vias, little courtyards lined with smaller boutiques; historic tours are available each month during "season" from the Worth Avenue Association. ■TIP➔ **For those looking to go a little lighter on the pocket book, just north of Worth Avenue, the six blocks of South County Road have interesting and somewhat less expensive stores.** ⊠ *Worth Ave., between Cocoanut Row and S. Ocean Blvd.* ⊕ *www.worth-avenue.com.*

WEST PALM BEACH

SHOPPING AREAS

Fodor's Choice
★

Antique Row. West Palm's U.S. 1, "South Dixie Highway," is the destination for those who are interested in interesting home decor. From thrift shops to the most exclusive stores, it is all here within 40 stores—museum-quality furniture, lighting, art, junk, fabric, frames, tile, and rugs. So if you're looking for an art deco, French-provincial, or Mizner pièce de résistance, big or small, schedule a few hours for an Antique Row stroll. You'll find bargains during the off-season (May to November).

Antique Row runs north–south from Belvedere Road to Forest Hill Boulevard, although most stores are bunched between Belvedere Road and Southern Boulevard. ⊠ *U.S. 1, between Belvedere Rd. and Forest Hill Blvd., West Palm Beach* ⊕ *www.westpalmbeachantiques.com.*

CityPlace. The 72-acre, four-block-by-four-block commercial and residential complex centered on Rosemary Avenue attracts people of all ages to with restaurants like Italian-inspired Il Bellagio, bars like Blue Martini, a 20-screen Muvico and IMAX theater, Revolutions—a bowling alley and sports bar, the Harriet Himmel Theater, and the Improv Comedy Club. In the courtyard, a 36,000-gallon water fountain and light show entertains, along with live bands on weekends. The dining, shopping, and entertainment are all family-friendly; at night, however, a lively crowd likes to hit the outdoor bars. Among CityPlace's stores are such popular national retailers as H&M, Tommy Bahama, and Restoration Hardware. Anushka Spa and Salon draws locals and visitors. ⊠ *700 S. Rosemary Ave., West Palm Beach* ☎ 561/366–1000 ⊕ *www.cityplace.com.*

FAMILY **Clematis Street.** If lunching is just as important as window-shopping, the renewed downtown West Palm around Clematis Street that runs west to east from South Rosemary Avenue to Flagler Drive is the spot for you. Centennial Park by the waterfront has an attractive design—and fountains where kids can cool off—which adds to the pleasure of browsing and resting at one of the many outdoor cafés. Hip national retailers such as Design Within Reach mix with local boutiques like third-generation Pioneer Linens, and both blend in with restaurants and bars. ⊠ *Clematis St., between S. Rosemary Ave. and Flagler Dr., West Palm Beach* ⊕ *www.westpalmbeach.com/clematis.*

Palm Beach Outlets. An outlet mall worthy of Palm Beach finally opened in 2014 in West Palm Beach. It features more than 130 retailers, with big names among the usual suspects. Off Fifth (Saks Fifth Avenue's store), Nordstrom Rack, White House | Black Market, Brooks Brothers, DKNY, and Calvin Klein are interspersed with stores selling shoes, discounted home decor, sports gear, kids fashions, and more. The mall has several restaurants as well as coffee shops and a food court. And it continues to expand, so check the website for an updated list of shops. ■TIP→ The wine bar in Whole Foods Market is the "see and be seen" scene at this outdoor mall. ⊠ *1751 Palm Beach Lakes Blvd., West Palm Beach* ☎ 561/515–4400 ⊕ *www.palmbeachoutlets.com.*

SPORTS AND THE OUTDOORS

PALM BEACH

Palm Beach Island has two good golf courses—The Breakers and the Palm Beach Par 3 Golf Course, but only the latter is open to the public. Not to worry, there are more on the mainland, as well as myriad other outdoor sports opportunities, including a new spring-training baseball stadium where two teams will play.

BIKING

Bicycling is a great way to get a closer look at Palm Beach. Only 14 miles long, half a mile wide, flat as the top of a billiard table, and just as green, it's a perfect biking place.

FAMILY   **Lake Trail.** This palm-fringed trail, about 4 miles long, skirts the backyards of mansions and the edge of Lake Worth. The start ("south trail" section) is just up from Royal Palm Way behind the Society of the Four Arts; follow the signs and you can't miss it. As you head north, the trail gets a little choppy around the Flagler Museum, so most people just enter where the "north trail" section begins at the very west end of Sunset Avenue. The path stops just short of the tip of the island, but people follow the quiet residential streets until they hit North Ocean Boulevard and the dock there with lovely views of Peanut Island and Singer Island, and then follow North Ocean Boulevard the 4 miles back for a change of scenery. ⊠ *Parallel to Lake Way* ✛ *Behind Society of the Four Arts.*

Fodor'sChoice   **Palm Beach Bicycle Trail Shop.** Open daily year-round, the shop rents bikes
★   by the hour or day, and it's about a block from the north Lake Trail entrance. The shop has maps to help you navigate your way around the island, or you can download the main map from the shop's website. They are experts on the nearby, palm-fringed, 4-mile Lake Trail. ⊠ *223 Sunrise Ave.* ☎ *561/659–4583* ⊕ *www.palmbeachbicycle.com.*

GOLF

Fodor'sChoice   **Palm Beach Par 3 Golf Course.** This course has been named the best par-3
★   golf course in the United States by *Golf Digest* magazine. The 18-hole course—originally designed by Dick Wilson and Joe Lee in 1961—was redesigned in 2009 by Hall of Famer Raymond Floyd. The par-3 course includes six holes directly on the Atlantic Ocean, with some holes over 200 yards. The grounds are exquisitely landscaped, as one would expect in Palm Beach. A lavish clubhouse houses Al Fresco, an Italian restaurant. A cart is an extra $15, but walking is encouraged. Summer rates are greatly discounted. ⊠ *2345 S. Ocean Blvd.* ☎ *561/547–0598* ⊕ *www.golfontheocean.com* ◫ *$50 for 18 holes* ⚑ *18 holes, 2458 yards, par 58.*

WEST PALM BEACH
BASEBALL

FAMILY   **Ballpark of the Palm Beaches.** There's a lot to root for at the new-in-2017 state-of-the-art baseball stadium. It plays host to spring training for the Houston Astros and the Washington Nationals, along with farm team play and numerous tournaments in the summer on its many fields. Seating includes lawn, bleacher, field boxes, and suites, with full food service in the latter two. A full bar overlooks left field. With free (and plenty) parking—as well as reasonably priced tickets—it's a value day out. Check the website to see the other teams coming to play in Florida's "Grapefruit League" against the home teams. The stadium complements Roger Dean Stadium in Jupiter, which hosts the spring games for the Miami Marlins and St. Louis Cardinals. Fields for lacrosse, football, and soccer are part of the massive complex and expected to draw those games; other community events are staged here. ⊠ *5444 Haverhill Rd., West Palm Beach* ✛ *Best exit off I–95 is 45th St.; off Florida's Tpke. is Okeechobee Blvd.* ☎ *844/676–2017* ⊕ *www.ballparkpalmbeaches. com* ◫ *From $17.*

POLO

Fodor's Choice
★

International Polo Club Palm Beach. Attend matches and rub elbows with celebrities who make the pilgrimage out to Palm Beach polo country (the western suburb of Wellington) during the January–April season. The competition is not just among polo players. High society dresses in their best polo couture week after week, each outfit more fabulous than the next; they tailgate out of their Bentleys and Rollses. An annual highlight at the polo club is the U.S. Open Polo Championship at the end of season. ■TIP→ **One of the best ways to experience the polo scene is by enjoying a gourmet brunch on the veranda of the International Polo Club Pavilion; it'll cost you from $100–$120 per person depending on the month, but it's well worth it.** ⊠ *3667 120th Ave. S* ☎ *561/204–5687* ⊕ *www.internationalpoloclub.com.*

LAKE WORTH

GOLF

Palm Beach National Golf and Country Club. Despite the name, this classic 18-hole course resides in Lake Worth, not in Palm Beach. It is, however, in Palm Beach County and prides itself on being "the most fun and friendly golf course" in Palm Beach County. The championship layout was designed by Joe Lee in the 1970s and is famous for its 3rd and 18th holes. The 3rd: a par-3 island hole with a sand bunker. The 18th: a short par 4 of 358 yards sandwiched between a wildlife preserve and water. Due to the challenging nature of the course, it's more popular with seasoned golfers. The Steve Haggerty Golf Academy is also based here. Summer rates are significantly discounted. ⊠ *7500 St. Andrews Rd., Lake Worth* ☎ *561/965–0044* ⊕ *www.palmbeachnational.com* ⬛ *$94 for 18 holes* ⚐ *18 holes, 6734 yards, par 72.*

DELRAY BEACH

15 miles south of West Palm Beach.

A onetime artists' retreat with a small settlement of Japanese farmers, Delray has grown into a sophisticated beach town. Delray's current popularity is caused in large part by the fact that it has the feel of an organic city rather than a planned development or subdivision—and it's completely walkable. Atlantic Avenue, which fell from a tony downtown to a dilapidated main drag, has been reinvented into a mile-plus-long stretch of palm-dotted sidewalks lined with stores, art galleries, and restaurants. Running east–west and ending at the beach, it's a happening place for a stroll, day or night. Another active pedestrian area, the Pineapple Grove Arts District, begins at Atlantic and stretches northward on Northeast 2nd Avenue about half a mile, and yet another active pedestrian way begins at the eastern edge of Atlantic Avenue and runs along the big, broad swimming beach that extends north to George Bush Boulevard and south to Casuarina Road. Renovations and buildings in progress in adjoining areas both south and north of the avenue will offer more shops and restaurants, as well as condos.

Morikami Museum and Japanese Gardens gives a taste of the Orient through its exhibits and tea ceremonies.

GETTING HERE AND AROUND
To reach Delray Beach from Boynton Beach, drive 2 miles south on Interstate 95, U.S. 1, or Route A1A.

ESSENTIALS
VISITOR INFORMATION
Contacts Discover the Palm Beaches. ✉ *1555 Palm Beach Lakes Blvd., Suite 800, West Palm Beach* ☎ *561/233–3000* ⊕ *www.palmbeachfl.com.*

EXPLORING

Colony Hotel. The chief landmark along Atlantic Avenue since 1926 is this sunny Mediterranean-revival-style building, which is a member of the National Trust's Historic Hotels of America. Walk through the lobby to the parking lot where original garages still stand—relics of the days when hotel guests would arrive via chauffeured cars and stay there the whole season. The bar is a locals' gathering spot. ✉ *525 E. Atlantic Ave.* ☎ *561/276–4123* ⊕ *www.thecolonyhotel.com.*

FAMILY **Delray Beach Center for the Arts at Old School Square.** Instrumental in the revitalization of Delray Beach circa 1995, this cluster of galleries and event spaces were established in restored school buildings dating from 1913 and 1925. The **Cornell Museum of Art & American Culture** offers ever-changing exhibits on fine arts, crafts, and pop culture, plus a hands-on children's gallery. From November to April, the 323-seat **Crest Theatre** showcases national-touring Broadway musicals, cabaret concerts, dance performances, and lectures. ✉ *51 N. Swinton Ave.* ☎ *561/243–7922* ⊕ *www.oldschool.org* 🎟 *$10 for museum* ☽ *Closed Mon.*

FAMILY
Fodor's Choice
★

Morikami Museum and Japanese Gardens. The boonies west of Delray Beach seems an odd place to encounter one of the region's most important cultural centers, but this is exactly where you can find a 200-acre cultural and recreational facility heralding the Yamato Colony of Japanese farmers that settled here in the early 20th century. A permanent exhibit details their history, and all together the museum's collection has more than 7,000 artifacts and works of art on rotating display. Traditional tea ceremonies are conducted monthly from October to June, along with educational classes on topics like calligraphy and sushi making (these require advance registration and come with a fee). The six main gardens are inspired by famous historic periods in Japanese garden design and have South Florida accents (think tropical bonsai), and the on-site Cornell Café serves light Asian fare at affordable prices and was recognized by the Food Network as being one of the country's best museum eateries. ⊠ *4000 Morikami Park Rd.* ☎ *561/495–0233* ⊕ *www.morikami.org* ⊇ *$15* ⊘ *Closed Mon.*

BEACHES

Fodor's Choice
★

Delray Municipal Beach. If you're looking for a place to see and be seen, head for this wide expanse of sand, the heart of which is where Atlantic Avenue meets A1A, close to restaurants, bars, and quick-serve eateries. Singles, families, and water-sports enthusiasts alike love it here. Lounge chairs and umbrellas can be rented every day, and lifeguards man stations half a mile out in each direction. The most popular section of beach is south of Atlantic Avenue on A1A, where the street parking is found. There are also two metered lots with restrooms across from A1A at Sandoway Park and Anchor Park (bring quarters if parking here). On the beach by Anchor Park, north of Casuarina Road, are six volleyball nets and a kiosk that offers Hobie Wave rentals, surfing lessons, and snorkeling excursions to the 1903 SS *Inchulva* shipwreck half a mile offshore. The beach itself is open 24 hours, if you're at a nearby hotel and fancy a moonlight stroll. **Amenities:** water sports; food and drink; lifeguards; parking (fee); toilets; showers. **Best for:** windsurfing; partiers; swimming. ⊠ *Rte. A1A and E. Atlantic Ave.* ⊇ *$1.50 per 1 hr parking.*

WHERE TO EAT

$$
BRITISH

Blue Anchor. Yes, this pub was actually shipped from England, where it had stood for 150 years in London's historic Chancery Lane. There it was a watering hole for famed Englishmen, including Winston Churchill; here you may hear stories of lingering ghosts told over some suds. **Known for:** fish-and-chips; beer selection; late-night food spot. ⑤ *Average main: $18* ⊠ *804 E. Atlantic Ave.* ☎ *561/272–7272* ⊕ *www. theblueanchor.com.*

$$$
SEAFOOD
Fodor's Choice
★

City Oyster & Sushi Bar. This trendy restaurant mingles the personalities and flavors of a New England oyster bar, a modern sushi eatery, an eclectic seafood grill, and an award-winning dessert bakery to create a can't-miss foodie haven in the heart of Delray's bustling Atlantic Avenue. Dishes like the oyster bisque, New Orleans–style shrimp and crab gumbo, tuna crudo, and lobster fried rice are simply sublime. **Known for:** large selection of oysters; excellent desserts; loud and busy, especially in high season. ⑤ *Average main: $26* ✉ *213 E. Atlantic Ave.* ☎ *561/272–0220* ⊕ *www.cityoysterdelray.com.*

$$$
MODERN
AMERICAN
Fodor's Choice
★

✕ **Max's Harvest.** A few blocks off Atlantic Avenue in the artsy Pineapple Grove neighborhood, a tree-shaded, fenced-in courtyard welcomes foodies eager to dig into its "farm-to-fork" offerings. The menu encourages people to experiment with "to share," "start small," and "think big" plates. **Known for:** menu aimed at sharing; cocktails made from artisanal spirits; Sunday brunch. ⑤ *Average main: $27* ✉ *169 N.E. 2nd Ave.* ☎ *561/381–9970* ⊕ *www.maxsharvest.com* ☾ *No lunch Mon.–Sat.*

$$$
AMERICAN
Fodor's Choice
★

✕ **The Office.** Scenesters line the massive indoor-outdoor bar from noon 'til the wee hours at this cooler-than-thou retro library restaurant, but it's worth your time to stop here for the best burger in town. There's a whole selection, but the Prime CEO steals the show: Maytag bleu cheese and Gruyère with tomato-onion confit, arugula, and bacon. **Known for:** upscale comfort food; weekend brunch; alcoholic shakes. ⑤ *Average main: $24* ✉ *201 E. Atlantic Ave.* ☎ *561/276–3600* ⊕ *www. theofficedelray.com.*

$$$$
AMERICAN
Fodor's Choice
★

✕ **32 East.** Although restaurants come and go every year on Atlantic Avenue, 32 East remains one of the best—if not the best—in Delray Beach. An ever-changing daily menu defines modern American cuisine. **Known for:** local seafood; extensive wine list; busy bar. ⑤ *Average main: $36* ✉ *32 E. Atlantic Ave.* ☎ *561/276–7868* ⊕ *www.32east.com* ☾ *No lunch.*

WHERE TO STAY

$
HOTEL

🏨 **Colony Hotel & Cabaña Club.** Not to be confused with the luxurious Colony in Palm Beach, this charming hotel in the heart of downtown Delray dates back to 1926; and although it's landlocked, it does have a cabana club 2 miles away for hotel guests only. **Pros:** pet-friendly; full breakfast buffet included with rooms; free use of cabanas, umbrellas, and hammocks. **Cons:** no pool at main hotel building; must walk to public beach for water-sport rentals. ⑤ *Rooms from: $195* ✉ *525 E. Atlantic Ave.* ☎ *561/276–4123, 800/552–2363* ⊕ *www.thecolonyhotel. com* ⟿ *70 rooms* �‖ *Breakfast.*

$$$
HOTEL

🏨 **Crane's Beach House Boutique Hotel & Luxury Villas.** A tropical oasis, this boutique hotel is a hidden jungle of lush exotic and tropical plants, only a block from the beach. **Pros:** private location within the city setting; short walk to the beach; free parking; property is smoke-free. **Cons:** pricey; no restaurants on-site; no fitness or spa facilities. ⑤ *Rooms from: $349* ✉ *82 Gleason St.* ☎ *866/372–7263, 561/278–1700* ⊕ *www. cranesbeachhouse.com* ⟿ *28 rooms, 4 villas* ❜❍❘ *No meals.*

$$$$
HOTEL
FAMILY

🏨 **Delray Beach Marriott.** By far the largest hotel in Delray Beach, the Marriott has two towers on a stellar plot of land at the east end of Atlantic Avenue—it's the only hotel that directly overlooks the water, yet it is still within walking distance of restaurants, shopping, and nightlife. **Pros:** fantastic ocean views; pampering spa; two pools. **Cons:** chain-hotel feel; charge for parking; must rent beach chairs. ⑤ *Rooms from: $499* ✉ *10 N. Ocean Blvd.* ☎ *561/274–3200* ⊕ *www.delraybeachmarriott.com* ⟿ *269 rooms* ❜❍❘ *No meals.*

$$$$
RESORT
FAMILY
Fodor's Choice
★

The Seagate Hotel & Spa. Those who crave 21st-century luxury in its full glory (ultraswank tile work and fixtures, marble vanities, seamless shower doors) will love this LEED-certified hotel that offers a subtle Zen-coastal motif throughout. **Pros:** two swimming pools; fabulous beach club; exceptionally knowledgeable concierge team. **Cons:** main building not directly on beach; daily resort fee; separate charge for parking. $ *Rooms from: $489* ⊠ *1000 E. Atlantic Ave.* ☎ *561/665–4800, 877/577–3242* ⊕ *www.theseagatehotel.com* ↪ *154 rooms* ⚍ *No meals.*

$$
B&B/INN
Fodor's Choice
★

Sundy House. Just about everything in this bungalow-style B&B is executed to perfection—especially its tropical, verdant grounds, which are actually a nonprofit botanical garden (something anyone can check out during free weekday tours) with a natural, freshwater swimming pool where your feet glide along limestone rocks and mingle with fish. **Pros:** charming eclectic decor; each room is unique; renowned restaurant with popular indoor-outdoor bar and free breakfast; in quiet area off Atlantic Avenue. **Cons:** need to walk through garden to reach rooms (i.e., no covered walkways); beach shuttle requires roughly half-hour advance notice; no private beach facilities. $ *Rooms from: $299* ⊠ *106 Swinton Ave.* ☎ *561/272–5678, 877/434–9601* ⊕ *www.sundyhouse. com* ↪ *11 rooms* ⚍ *Breakfast.*

$$$
HOTEL
FAMILY

Wright by the Sea. Here's a 1950s throwback to beachfront hotels in Florida—down to the venetian blinds and tropical-beachy decor in the rooms, which were last remodeled in fall 2014. **Pros:** directly on the beach; free laundry; free beach cabanas; free parking. **Cons:** dated decor in some rooms; no elevators; no restaurant. $ *Rooms from: $314* ⊠ *1901 S. Ocean Blvd.* ☎ *561/257–0885* ⊕ *www.wbtsea.com* ↪ *29 rooms* ⚍ *No meals.*

NIGHTLIFE

Boston's on the Beach. You'll find beer flowing and the ocean breeze blowing at this beach bar and eatery, a local watering hole since 1983. The walls are laden with paraphernalia from the Boston Bruins, New England Patriots, and Boston Red Sox, including a shrine to Ted Williams. Boston's can get loud and rowdy (or lively, depending on your taste) later at night. Groove to reggae on Monday, live blues bands on Tuesday, and other live music from rock to country on Friday, Saturday, and Sunday. ⊠ *40 S. Ocean Blvd.* ☎ *561/278–3364* ⊕ *www.bostonsonthebeach.com.*

Dada. Bands play in the living room of this historic house, though much of the action is outdoors on the lawn in fair weather, where huge trees and lanterns make it a fun stop for drinks or a group night out. It's a place where those who don't drink will also feel comfortable, however, and excellent gourmet nibbles are a huge bonus (a full dinner menu is available, too). A bohemian, younger crowd gathers later into the night. ⊠ *52 N. Swinton Ave.* ☎ *561/330–3232* ⊕ *www.sub-culture.org/dada.*

Jellies Bar at the Atlantic Grille. Within the Seagate Hotel, the fun and fabulous bar at the Atlantic Grille is known locally as Jellies Bar. The over-thirty set consistently floats over to this stunning bar to shimmy to live music Tuesday to Saturday; the namesake jellyfish tank never fails to entertain as well. ⊠ *The Seagate Hotel & Spa, 1000 E. Atlantic Ave.* ☎ *561/665–4900* ⊕ *www.theatlanticgrille.com.*

6

SHOPPING

Atlantic Avenue and Pineapple Grove, both charming neighborhoods for shoppers, have maintained Delray Beach's small-town integrity. Atlantic Avenue is the main street, with art galleries, boutiques, restaurants, and bars lining it from just west of Swinton Avenue all the way east to the ocean. The now established Pineapple Grove Arts District is centered on the half-mile strip of Northeast 2nd Avenue that goes north from Atlantic; these areas are broadening as the downtown area expands south and east.

Furst. This studio-shop gives you the chance to watch designer Flavie Furst or her pupils at work—and then purchase their fine, handcrafted gold, gold-filled, and silver jewelry. The other half of this space is the Ronald Furst bespoke handbag store, selling unique bags, purses, and sacks. ✉ *123 N.E. 2nd Ave.* ☎ *561/272–6422* ⊕ *www.flaviefurst.com.*

Snappy Turtle. Jack Rogers sandals and Trina Turk dresses mingle with other fun resort fashions and beachy gifts for the home and family at this family-run store. ✉ *1100 E. Atlantic Ave.* ☎ *888/762–7798* ⊕ *www. snappy-turtle.com.*

SPORTS AND THE OUTDOORS

BIKING

There's a bicycle path in Barwick Park, but the most popular place to ride is up and down the special oceanfront bike lane along Route A1A. The city also has an illustrated and annotated map on key downtown sights available through the Palm Beach Convention and Visitors Bureau.

Richwagen's Bike & Sport. Rent bikes by the hour, day, or week (they come with locks, baskets, and helmets); Richwagen's also has copies of city maps on hand. A seven-speed cruiser rents for $60 per week, or $30 a day. They also rent bike trailers, child seats, and electric carts. The shop is closed Sunday. ✉ *298 N.E. 6th Ave.* ☎ *561/276–4234* ⊕ *www. delraybeachbicycles.com.*

TENNIS

Delray Beach Tennis Center. Each year this complex hosts simultaneous professional tournaments where current stars like Ivo Karlovic and Marin Cilic along with legends like Andy Roddick, Ivan Lendl, and Michael Chang duke it out. Florida's own Chris Evert hosts the Pro-Celebrity Tennis Classic charity event here. The rest of the time, you can practice or learn on 14 clay courts and seven hard courts; private lessons and clinics are available, and it's open from 7:30 am to 9 pm weekdays and until 6 pm weekends. Since most hotels in the area do not have courts, tennis players visiting Delray Beach often come here to play. ✉ *201 W. Atlantic Ave.* ☎ *561/243–7360* ⊕ *www.delraytennis.com.*

BOCA RATON

6 miles south of Delray Beach.

Less than an hour south of Palm Beach and anchoring the county's south end, upscale Boca Raton has much in common with its fabled cousin. Both reflect the unmistakable architectural influence of Addison Mizner, their principal developer in the mid-1920s. The meaning of the name Boca Raton (pronounced boca rah-*tone*) often arouses curiosity, with many folks mistakenly assuming it means "rat's mouth." Historians say the probable origin is Boca Ratones, an ancient Spanish geographical term for an inlet filled with jagged rocks or coral. Miami's Biscayne Bay had such an inlet, and in 1823 a mapmaker copying Miami terrain confused the more northern inlet, thus mistakenly labeling this area Boca Ratones. No matter what, you'll know you've arrived in the heart of downtown when you spot the historic town hall's gold dome on the main street, Federal Highway. Much of the Boca landscape was heavily planned, and many of the bigger sights are clustered in the area around town hall and Lake Boca, a wide stretch of the Intracoastal Waterway between Palmetto Park Road and Camino Real (two main east–west streets at the southern end of town).

GETTING HERE AND AROUND

To get to Boca Raton from Delray Beach, drive south 6 miles on Interstate 95, Federal Highway (U.S. 1), or Route A1A.

ESSENTIALS

VISITOR INFORMATION

Contacts Discover the Palm Beaches. ✉ *1555 Palm Beach Lakes Blvd., Suite 800, West Palm Beach* ☎ *561/233–3000* ⊕ *www.palmbeachfl.com.*

EXPLORING

FAMILY **Boca Raton Museum of Art.** Changing-exhibition galleries on the first floor showcase internationally known artists—both past and present—at this museum in a spectacular building that's part of the Mizner Park shopping center; the permanent collection upstairs includes works by Picasso, Degas, Matisse, Klee, Modigliani, and Warhol, as well as notable African and pre-Columbian art. Daily tours are included with admission. In addition to the treasure hunts and sketchbooks you can pick up from the front desk, there's a roster of special programs that cater to kids, including studio workshops and gallery walks. Another fun feature is the cell phone audio guide—certain pieces of art have a corresponding number you dial to hear a detailed narration. ✉ *501 Plaza Real, Mizner Park* ☎ *561/392–2500* ⊕ *www.bocamuseum.org* ☞ *$12* ⊙ *Closed Mon.*

FAMILY **Gumbo Limbo Nature Center.** A big draw for kids, this stellar spot has four huge saltwater tanks brimming with sea life, from coral to stingrays to spiny lobsters, touch tanks, plus a sea turtle rehabilitation center. Nocturnal walks in spring and early summer, when staffers lead a quest to find nesting female turtles coming ashore to lay eggs, are popular; so are the hatching releases in August and September. (Call to purchase tickets in advance as there are very limited spaces.) This is one of only a handful of centers that offer this. There is also a nature trail and butterfly garden, a ¼-mile boardwalk, and a 40-foot observation tower, where you're likely to see brown pelicans and osprey. ⊠ *1801 N. Ocean Blvd.* ☎ *561/544–8605* ⊕ *www.gumbolimbo.org* ⧉ *Free ($5 suggested donation); turtle walks $15.*

Old Floresta. This residential area was developed by Addison Mizner starting in 1925 and is beautifully landscaped with palms and cycads. Its houses are mainly Mediterranean in style, many with balconies supported by exposed wood columns. Explore by driving northward on Paloma Avenue (Northwest 8th Avenue) from Palmetto Park Road, then weave in and out of the side streets. ⊠ *Paloma Ave., north of W. Palmetto Park Rd.*

BEACHES

Boca's three city beaches (South Beach, Red Reef Park, and Spanish River Park, south to north, respectively) are beautiful and hugely popular; but unless you're a resident or enter via bicycle, parking can be very expensive. Save your receipt if you care to go in and out, or park hop—most guards at the front gate will honor a same-day ticket from another location if you ask nicely. Another option is the county-run South Inlet Park that's walking distance from the Boca Raton Bridge Hotel at the southern end of Lake Boca; it has a metered lot for a fraction of the cost, but not quite the same charm as the others.

FAMILY **Red Reef Park.** The ocean with its namesake reef that you can wade up to is just one draw: a fishing zone on the Intracoastal Waterway across the street, a 9-hole golf course next door, and the Gumbo Limbo Environmental Education Center at the northern end of the park can easily make a day at the beach into so much more. But if pure old-fashioned fun in the sun is your focus, there are tons of picnic tables and grills, and two separate playgrounds. Pack snorkels and explore the reef at high tide when fish are most abundant. Swimmers, be warned: once lifeguards leave at 5, anglers flock to the shores and stay well past dark. **Amenities:** lifeguards; parking (fee); showers; toilets. **Best for:** snorkeling; swimming; walking. ⊠ *1400 N. Rte. A1A* ☎ *561/393–7974, 561/393–7989 for beach conditions* ⊕ *www.ci.boca-raton.fl.us/rec/parks/redreef.shtm* ⧉ *$16 parking (weekdays), $18 parking (weekends).*

South Beach Park. Perched high up on a dune, a large open-air pavilion at the east end of Palmetto Park Road offers a panoramic view of what's in store below on the sand that stretches up the coast. Serious beachgoers need to pull into the main lot ¼ mile north on the east side of A1A, but if a short-but-sweet visit is what you're after, the 15 or so one-hour spots with meters in the circle driveway will do (and not cost you the normal $15 parking fee). During the day, pretty young things blanket the shore, and windsurfers practice tricks in the waves. Quiet quarters are farther north. **Amenities:** lifeguards; parking (fee); toilets; showers. **Best for:** sunset; windsurfing; walking; swimming. ⊠ *400 N. Rte A1A* ⊕ *www.ci.boca-raton.fl.us/rec/parks/southbeach.shtm* ⧉ *$15 parking (weekdays), $17 parking (weekends).*

Spanish River Park. At 76 acres and including extensive nature trails, this is by far one of the largest ocean parks in the southern half of Palm Beach County and a great pick for people who want more space and fewer crowds. Big groups, including family reunions, favor it because of the number of covered picnic areas for rent, but anyone can snag a free table (there are plenty) under the thick canopy of banyan trees. Even though the vast majority of the park is separated from the surf, you never actually have to cross A1A to reach the beach, because tunnels run under it at several locations. **Amenities:** lifeguards; parking (fee); showers; toilets. **Best for:** swimming; walking; solitude. ✉ *3001 N. Rte. A1A* ☎ *561/393–7815* ⊕ *www.ci.boca-raton.fl.us/rec/parks/ spanishriver.shtm* ⛱ *$16 parking (weekdays), $18 parking (weekends).*

WHERE TO EAT

$$$$
TUSCAN
Fodor's Choice
★

✕ **Casa D'Angelo Ristorante.** The lines are deservedly long at chef Angelo Elia's upscale Tuscan restaurant in tony Boca Raton. The outpost of his renowned Casa D'Angelo in Broward impresses with an outstanding selection of antipasti, carpaccios, pastas, and specialties from the wood-burning oven. **Known for:** wide range of antipasti; veal osso buco and scaloppine; extensive wine list. ⑤ *Average main: $38* ✉ *171 E. Palmetto Park Rd.* ☎ *561/996–1234* ⊕ *www.casa-d-angelo.com* ☾ *No lunch.*

$$$
MODERN
AMERICAN

✕ **Farmer's Table.** Taking up the local-food mantle, the menu here includes inventive dishes following the seasons using locally sourced meats, seafood, and vegetables. Whenever possible, the foods are organic or sustainable. **Known for:** Buddha bowl with stir-fried vegetables and udon; good wine, cocktails, and beer; some vegan options. ⑤ *Average main: $22* ✉ *Wyndham Boca Raton, 1901 N. Military Trail* ☎ *561/417–5836* ⊕ *www.farmerstableboca.com.*

$$$
AMERICAN

✕ **Racks Downtown Eatery & Tavern.** Whimsical indoor–outdoor decor and comfort food with a twist help define this popular eatery in tony Mizner Park. Instead of dinner rolls, pretzel bread and mustard get things started. **Known for:** menu made for sharing; raw bar; popular happy hour. ⑤ *Average main: $23* ✉ *402 Plaza Real, Mizner Park* ☎ *561/395–1662* ⊕ *www.racksboca.com.*

$$$$
SEAFOOD
Fodor's Choice
★

✕ **Truluck's.** This popular Florida and Texas seafood chain is so serious about its fruits of the sea that it supports its own fleet of 16 fishing boats. Stone crabs are the signature dish, and you can have all you can eat on Monday night from October to May. **Known for:** fresh seafood; large portions; gluten-free menu. ⑤ *Average main: $35* ✉ *351 Plaza Real, Mizner Park* ☎ *561/391–0755* ⊕ *www.trulucks.com.*

$$$
CHINESE

✕ **Uncle Tai's.** The draw at this longtime upscale eatery offers up some of the best Hunan cuisine on Florida's east coast. Specialties include sliced duck with snow peas and water chestnuts in a tangy plum sauce, and orange beef delight—flank steak stir-fried until crispy and then sautéed with pepper sauce, garlic, and orange peel. **Known for:** spicy cuisine that can be toned down on request; General Tso's chicken; sunset dinner specials. ⑤ *Average main: $21* ✉ *5250 Town Center Circle* ☎ *561/368–8806* ⊕ *www.uncletais.com.*

6

WHERE TO STAY

$$$$
RESORT
FAMILY
Fodor'sChoice
★

🏨 **Boca Beach Club.** Dotted with turquoise lounge chairs, ruffled umbrellas, and white-sand beaches, this newly reconceived and rebranded hotel is now part of the Waldorf-Astoria collection and looks as if it was carefully replicated from a retro-chic postcard. **Pros:** great location on the beach; kids' activity center. **Cons:** pricey; shuttle ride away from the main building; resort fee. $ *Rooms from: $542* ⊠ *900 S. Ocean Blvd.* ☎ *888/564–1312* ⊕ *www.bocabeachclub.com* ⊲ *212 rooms* ⦿ *No meals.*

$$$
RESORT
FAMILY
Fodor'sChoice
★

🏨 **Boca Raton Resort & Club.** Addison Mizner built this Mediterranean-style hotel in 1926, and additions over time have created a sprawling, sparkling resort, one of the most luxurious in all of South Florida and part of the Waldorf-Astoria collection. **Pros:** superexclusive—grounds are closed to the public; decor strikes the right balance between historic roots and modern comforts; plenty of activities. **Cons:** daily resort charge; conventions often crowd common areas. $ *Rooms from: $309* ⊠ *501 E. Camino Real* ☎ *561/447–3000, 888/543–1277* ⊕ *www.bocaresort.com* ⊲ *635 rooms* ⦿ *No meals.*

$$
HOTEL

🏨 **Waterstone Resort & Marina.** The former Bridge Hotel was transformed into a sleek, modern resort with a $20 million restoration in 2014. **Pros:** short walk to beach; pet-friendly; waterfront views throughout. **Cons:** parking fee; no quiet common space; some rooms noisy from nearby bridge traffic. $ *Rooms from: $289* ⊠ *999 E. Camino Real* ☎ *561/368–9500* ⊕ *www.waterstoneboca.com* ⊲ *139 rooms* ⦿ *No meals.*

SHOPPING

Mizner Park. This distinctive 30-acre shopping center off Federal Highway, one block north of Palmetto Park Road, intersperses apartments and town houses among its gardenlike commercial areas. Some three dozen retailers—including Lord and Taylor, which moved in as the only national department store east of Interstate 95 in Boca—line the central axis. It's peppered with fountains and green space, restaurants, galleries, a jazz club, a movie theater, the Boca Raton Museum of Art, and an amphitheater that hosts major concerts as well as community events. ⊠ *327 Plaza Real* ☎ *561/362–0606* ⊕ *www.miznerpark.com.*

Royal Palm Place. The retail enclave of Royal Palm is filled with independent boutiques selling fine jewelry and apparel. By day, stroll the walkable streets and have your pick of sidewalk cafés for a bite alongside Boca's ladies who lunch. Royal Palm Place assumes a different personality come nightfall, as its numerous restaurants and lounges attract throngs of patrons for great dining and fabulous libations. Parking here is free. ⊠ *101 Plaza Real S* ☎ *561/392–8920* ⊕ *www.royalpalmplace.com.*

Town Center at Boca Raton. Over on the west side of the interstate in Boca, this indoor megamall has over 220 stores, with anchor stores including Saks and Neiman Marcus and just about every major high-end designer, including Kate Spade and Anne Fontaine. But not every shop here requires deep pockets. The Town Center at Boca Raton is also firmly rooted with a variety of more affordable national brands like Gap and Guess. ⊠ *6000 Glades Rd.* ☎ *561/368–6000* ⊕ *www.simon.com/mall/town-center-at-boca-raton.*

SPORTS AND THE OUTDOORS

GOLF

Red Reef Park Executive Golf Course. This executive golf course offers 9 holes with varying views of the Intracoastal and the Atlantic Ocean. The Joe Palloka– and Charles Ankrom–designed course dates back to 1957. It was refreshed in 2001 through a multimillion-dollar renovation. The scenic holes are between 54 and 227 yards each—great for a quick round. Carts are available, but the short course begs to be walked. Park in the lot across the street from the main beach entrance, and put the greens fees receipt on the dash; that covers parking. ⊠ *1221 N. Ocean Blvd.* ☎ *561/391–5014* ⊕ *www.bocacitygolf.com* ⊠ *$17 to to walk; $27 to ride* ⚘. *9 holes, 1357 yards, par 32.*

SCUBA AND SNORKELING

Force-E. This company, in business since the late 1970s, rents, sells, and repairs scuba and snorkeling equipment—and organizes about 80 dive trips a week from the Palm Beach Inlet to Port Everglades in Broward County. The PADI–affiliated five-star center has instruction for all levels and offers private charters, too. They have two other outposts besides this Boca Raton location—one north in Riviera Beach and one south in Pompano Beach. ⊠ *2181 N. Federal Hwy.* ☎ *561/368–0555, 561/368–0555* ⊕ *www.force-e.com.*

NORTH COUNTY

Just over the bridge at the Port of Palm Beach are the more laid-back towns of North County, where families and golf pros, not to mention the celebs on Jupiter Island, call home. On **Singer Island**, visible from Palm Beach across the Palm Beach Inlet, and a mere 20 minutes by land, are the towns of **Palm Beach Shores** and **Riviera Beach.** With good beach access and waterfront parks, surf- and sun-seekers have several options, including the nearby Peanut Island. On the mainland north and west, suburban **Palm Beach Gardens** is the golf capital of the county, with PGA courses and country club greens making for greenspace throughout, along with a shoppers' paradise (malls abound). The tiny seaside **Juno Beach,** with turtle-rich beaches, melds quickly into Jupiter, where the beach is the star—for both two- and four-legged sun worshippers—with parks and public pavilions providing gathering sites for groups.

PALM BEACH GARDENS

13½ miles north of West Palm Beach.

About 15 minutes northwest of Palm Beach is this relaxed, upscale residential community known for its high-profile golf complex, the **PGA National Resort & Spa.** Although not on the beach, the town is less than a 15-minute drive from the ocean. Malls and dining are centered on the main street, PGA Boulevard, running east from the resort to U.S. 1.

WHERE TO EAT

$$$$
AMERICAN

✕ **Café Chardonnay.** A longtime local favorite, Café Chardonnay is charming, romantic, and has some of the most refined food in the suburban town of Palm Beach Gardens. Soft lighting, warm woods, white tablecloths, and cozy banquettes set the scene for a quiet lunch or romantic dinner. **Known for:** outstanding wine list; innovative specials; many locally sourced ingredients. ⑤ *Average main: $34* ⊠ *The Gardens Square Shoppes, 4533 PGA Blvd.* ☎ *561/627–2662* ⊕ *www. cafechardonnay.com* ⊘ *No lunch weekends.*

$$$
AMERICAN

✕ **Coolinary Cafe.** It's tucked away in a strip mall and has only 50 seats inside (counting the bar) and a handful out on the sidewalk, but everything down to the condiments is made in-house here. Rabbit sausage and noodles or lamb meatball risotto are examples on the seasonal one-page menus the chef puts together daily. **Known for:** small, focused regular menu; fresh fish specials; long waits for dinner in season. ⑤ *Average main: $22* ⊠ *Donald Ross Village Plaza, 4650 Donald Ross Rd., Suite 110* ☎ *561/249–6760* ⊕ *www.coolinarycafe. com* ⊘ *Closed Sun.*

$$$
AMERICAN

✕ **The Cooper.** With a contemporary farm-to-table menu, and spacious dining rooms and bars, this spot in PGA Commons has plenty of local fans. Happy-hour crowds fill the patio bar-lounge area to sip the craft cocktails and nibble from a cheese or salumi board. **Known for:** wide-ranging American menu; extensive wine list; gluten-free options. ⑤ *Average main: $23* ⊠ *PGA Commons, 4610 PGA Blvd.* ☎ *561/622–0032* ⊕ *www.thecooperrestaurant.com.*

$$$$
STEAKHOUSE

✕ **Ironwood Steak & Seafood.** Located in the PGA National Resort & Spa, this eatery draws guests, locals, and tourists alike eager for a taste of its fired-up Vulcan-cooked steaks (Vulcan to meat eaters is like Titleist to golfers—the best equipment around). Wagyu and Angus beef cuts are featured. **Known for:** wide range of steaks; raw bar; extensive wine list. ⑤ *Average main: $38* ⊠ *PGA National Resort & Spa, 400 Ave. of the Champions* ☎ *561/627–4852* ⊕ *www.pgaresort.com/restaurants/ ironwood-grille.*

$$$
SEAFOOD

✕ **Spoto's Oyster Bar.** If you love oysters and other raw bar nibbles, head here, where black-and-white photographs of oyster fisherman adorn the walls. The polished tables give the eatery a clubby look. **Known for:** wide range of oysters and clams; fresh seafood; live music in the Blue Point Lounge. ⑤ *Average main: $26* ⊠ *PGA Commons, 4560 PGA Blvd.* ☎ *561/776–9448* ⊕ *www.spotosoys- terbar.com.*

WHERE TO STAY

$$
HOTEL

⊡ **Hilton Garden Inn Palm Beach Gardens.** A hidden find in Palm Beach Gardens, this hotel sits on a small lake next to a residential area, but near two shopping malls and close to PGA golf courses. **Pros:** 24-hour free business center; walk to two different malls with shops, restaurants, and movie theaters. **Cons:** outdoor self-parking; no bell service; pool closes at dusk; 15 minutes from the beach. ⑤ *Rooms from: $209* ⊠ *3505 Kyoto Gardens Dr.* ☎ *561/694–5833, 561/694–5829* ⊕ *hilton- gardeninn3.hilton.com* ⊷ *180 rooms* ⊙ *No meals.*

$$$
RESORT
Fodor's Choice
★

⬚ **PGA National Resort & Spa.** This golfer's paradise (five championship courses and the site of the yearly Honda Classic pro-tour tournament) is a sleek modern playground with a gorgeous zero-entry lagoon pool, seven different places to eat, and a full-service spa with unique mineral-salt therapy pools. **Pros:** dream golf facilities; affordable rates for top-notch amenities; close to shopping malls. **Cons:** no beach shuttle; difficult to get around if you don't have a car; long drive to Palm Beach proper. ⑤ *Rooms from: $348 ⊠ 400 Ave. of the Champions ☎ 561/627–2000, 800/633–9150 ⊕ www.pgaresort.com ⇴ 339 rooms* ⑩ *No meals.*

SHOPPING

FAMILY
Downtown at The Gardens. This open-air pavilion down the street from The Gardens Mall has boutiques, chain stores, a grocery store, day spas, a 16-screen movie theater, and a lively restaurant and nighttime bar scene that includes the Dirty Martini and the Yard House, both of which stay open late. A carousel, children's barbershop, boutiques, and Cool Beans (an indoor playground), make this a family-friendly mall. ⊠ *11701 Lake Victoria Gardens Ave.* ☎ *561/340–1600* ⊕ *www. downtownatthegardens.com.*

Fodor's Choice
★
The Gardens Mall. One of the most refined big shopping malls in America, the 160-store Gardens Mall in northern Palm Beach County has stores like Chanel, Gucci, Louis Vuitton, and David Yurman, along with Saks Fifth Avenue and Nordstrom. There are also plenty of reasonably priced national retailers like H&M and Abercrombie & Fitch, Bloomingdale's, and Macy's. This beautiful mall has prolific seating pavilions, making it a great place to spend a humid summer afternoon. ⊠ *3101 PGA Blvd.* ☎ *561/775–7750* ⊕ *www.thegardensmall.com.*

6

SPORTS AND THE OUTDOORS

Spring-training fans travel to the area to see the Cardinals and Marlins tune up for their seasons at Roger Dean Stadium in Palm Beach Gardens, and to watch their AAA feeder teams in summer. Port St. Lucie and Vero Beach stadiums and more teams are only a short drive up Interstate 95.

GOLF

Fodor's Choice
★
PGA National Resort & Spa. If you're the kind of traveler who takes along a set of clubs, you'll achieve nirvana on the greens of PGA National Resort & Spa. The five championship courses are open only to hotel guests and club members, which means you'll have to stay to play, but packages that include a room and a round of golf are reasonably priced. The Champion Course, redesigned by Jack Nicklaus and famous for its Bear Trap holes, is the site of the yearly Honda Classic pro tournament. The four other challenging courses are also legends in the golfing world: the Palmer, named for its architect, the legendary Arnold Palmer; the Fazio (formerly the "Haig," the resort's first course reopened in November 2012 after a major renovation) and the Squire, both from Tom and George Fazio; and the Karl Litten–designed Estates, the sole course not on the property (it is located 5 miles west of the PGA resort). Lessons are available at the David Leadbetter Golf Academy, and they also run a summertime kids' golf camp. ⊠ *PGA National Resort & Spa, 1000*

Ave. of the Champions ☎ *561/627–1800* ⊕ *www.pgaresort.com/golf/ pga-national-golf* ▧ *$409 for 18 holes for Champion Course, Fazio Course, and Squire Course. $250 for 18 holes for Palmer Course and Estates Course.* ⚐ *Champion Course: 18 holes, 7048 yards, par 72. Palmer Course: 18 holes, 7079 yards, par 72. Fazio Course: 18 holes, 6806 yards, par 72. Squire Course: 18 holes, 6465 yards, par 72. Estates Course: 18 holes, 6694 yards, par 72.*

SINGER ISLAND

6 miles north of West Palm Beach.

Across the inlet from the northern end of Palm Beach is Singer Island, which is actually a peninsula that's big enough to pass for a barrier island, rimmed with mom-and-pop motels and high-rises. Palm Beach Shores occupies its southern tip (where tiny Peanut Island is a stone's throw away); farther north are Riviera Beach and North Palm Beach, which also straddle the inlet and continue on the mainland.

EXPLORING

Palm Beach Maritime Museum. Though the main building of the Palm Beach Maritime Museum is found in Currie Park in West Palm Beach, its main treasure—the restored "Kennedy Bunker," a bomb shelter built for President John F. Kennedy, and a historic Coast Guard station—is located on Peanut Island. You can take a guided tour of the bunker through the museum's Peanut Island outpost. The museum also has a nice little gift shop, an outdoor deck on the water, and a lawn where you can play games including horseshoes. To get there, catch a water taxi from Riviera Beach Municipal Marina, but be aware that the boats won't run in choppy waters. ⊠ *Peanut Island, Riviera Beach* ☎ *561/848–2960* ⊕ *www.pbmm.info* ▧ *$17 (not including water transportation)* ⊘ *Closed Mon.–Wed.*

BEACHES

FAMILY
Fodor'sChoice
★

John D. MacArthur Beach State Park. If getting far from rowdy crowds is your goal, this spot on the north end of Singer Island is a good choice. Encompassing 2 miles of beach and a lush subtropical coastal habitat, inside you'll find a great place for kayaking, snorkeling at natural reefs, bird-watching, fishing, and hiking. You might even get to see a few manatees. A 4,000-square-foot nature center has aquariums and displays on local flora and fauna, and there's a long roster of monthly activities, such as surfing clinics, art lessons, and live bluegrass music. Guided sea turtle walks are available at night in season, and daily nature walks depart at 10 am. Check the website for times and costs of activities. **Amenities:** water sports; parking (fee); toilets; showers. **Best for:** swimming; walking; solitude; surfing. ⊠ *10900 Jack Nicklaus Dr., North Palm Beach* ☎ *561/624–6950* ⊕ *www.macarthurbeach.org* ▧ *Parking $5, bicyclists and pedestrians $2.*

Peanut Island Park. Partiers, families, and overnight campers all have a place to go on the 79 acres here. The island, in a wide section of the Intracoastal between Palm Beach Island and Singer Island with an open channel to the sea, is accessible only by private boat or water taxi, two of which set sail regularly from the Riviera Beach Municipal Marina (⊕ *peanutislandferry.com*) and the Sailfish Marina (⊕ *www.sailfishmarina.com/water_taxi*). Fun-loving seafarers looking for an afternoon of Jimmy Buffett and picnics aboard pull up to the day docks or the huge sandbar on the north—float around in an inner tube, and it's spring break déjà vu. Walk along the 20-foot-wide paver-lined path encircling the island, and you'll hit a 170-foot fishing pier, a campground, the lifeguarded section to the south that is particularly popular with families because of its artificial reef, and last, but not least, the Palm Beach Maritime Museum's "Kennedy Bunker" (a bomb shelter prepared for President John F. Kennedy that was restored and opened to the public in 1999). There are picnic tables and grills, but no concessions. A new ordinance means alcohol possession and consumption is restricted to permit areas. **Amenities:** lifeguards (summer only); toilets; showers. **Best for:** partiers; walking; swimming; sunrise. ⊠ *6500 Peanut Island Rd., Riviera Beach* ☎ *561/845–4445* ⊕ *www.pbcgov.com/parks/peanutisland* ⇨ *Beach free; water taxi $10; park stay $17.*

WHERE TO STAY

$$$$
RESORT
FAMILY
⚏ **Palm Beach Marriott Singer Island Beach Resort & Spa.** Families with a yen for the cosmopolitan but requiring the square footage and comforts of home revel in these one- and two-bedroom suites with spacious, marble-tiled, granite-topped kitchens. **Pros:** wide beach; genuinely warm service; plenty of kids' activities; sleek spa. **Cons:** no upscale dining nearby; unspectacular room views for an ocean-side hotel. $ *Rooms from: $509* ⊠ *3800 N. Ocean Dr., Singer Island, Riviera Beach* ☎ *561/340–1700, 877/239–5610* ⊕ *www.marriott.com* ⇨ *202 suites* ⦿ *No meals.*

$
HOTEL
⚏ **Sailfish Marina Resort.** A marina with deepwater slips—and prime location at the mouth to the Atlantic Ocean on the Intracoastal Waterway across from Peanut Island—lures boaters and anglers here to these rather basic rooms, studios, and efficiencies. **Pros:** inexpensive rates; great waterfront restaurant; has a water taxi; pretty grounds. **Cons:** no real lobby; not directly on beach; area attracts a party crowd and can be noisy; dated decor. $ *Rooms from: $150* ⊠ *98 Lake Dr., Palm Beach Shores* ☎ *561/844–1724* ⊕ *www.sailfishmarina.com* ⇨ *30 units* ⦿ *No meals.*

SPORTS AND THE OUTDOORS
FISHING
Sailfish Marina. Book a full or half day of deep-sea fishing for up to six people with the seasoned captains and large fleet of 28- to 65-foot boats. A ship's store and restaurant are also on-site. ⊠ *Sailfish Marina Resort, 98 Lake Dr., Palm Beach Shores* ☎ *561/844–1724* ⊕ *www.sailfishmarina.com.*

JUNO BEACH

12 miles north of West Palm Beach.

This small town east of Palm Beach Gardens has 2 miles of shoreline that becomes home to thousands of sea turtle hatchlings each year, making it one of the world's densest nesting sites. A 990-foot-long pier lures fishermen and beachgoers seeking a spectacular sunrise.

EXPLORING

FAMILY

Fodor'sChoice
★

Loggerhead Park Marine Life Center of Juno Beach. Located in a certified green building in Loggerhead Park—and established by Eleanor N. Fletcher, the "turtle lady of Juno Beach"—the center focuses on the conservation of sea turtles, using education, research, and rehabilitation. The education center houses displays of coastal natural history, detailing Florida's marine ecosystems and the life and plight of the various species of sea turtles found on Florida's shores. You can visit recovering turtles in their outdoor hospital tanks; volunteers are happy to tell you the turtles' heroic tales of survival. The center has regularly scheduled activities, such as Kid's Story Time and Junior Vet Lab, and most are free of charge. During peak nesting season, the center hosts night walks to experience turtle nesting in action. Given that the adjacent beach is part of the second biggest nesting ground for loggerhead turtles in the world, your chances of seeing this natural phenomenon are pretty high (over 15,000 loggerheads nested here in 2016). ✉ *14200 U.S. 1* ☎ *561/627–8280* ⊕ *www.marinelife.org* ☞ *Free.*

BEACHES

FAMILY

Juno Beach Ocean Park. An angler's dream, this beach has a 990-foot pier that's open daily, like the beach, from sunrise to sunset—but from November through February, pier gates open at 6 am and don't close until 10 pm on weeknights and midnight on weekends, making it an awesome place to catch a full sunrise and sunset (that is, if you don't mind paying the small admission fee). A concession stand on the pier sells fish food as well as such human favorites as burgers, sandwiches, and ice cream. Rods and tackle are rented here. Families adore this shoreline because of the amenities and vibrant atmosphere. There are plenty of kids building castles but also plenty of teens having socials and hanging out along the beach. Pets are not allowed here, but they are allowed on Jupiter Beach. **Amenities:** lifeguards; food and drink; parking (no fee); showers; toilets. **Best for:** sunrise; sunset; swimming. ✉ *14775 U.S. 1* ☎ *561/799–0185 for pier* ⊕ *www.pbcgov.com/parks/locations/junobeach.htm* ☞ *$4 to fish, $1 to enter pier; beach free.*

JUPITER AND VICINITY

12 miles north of West Palm Beach.

Jupiter is one of the few towns in the region not fronted by an island but still quite close to the fantastic hotels, shopping, and dining of the Palm Beach area. The beaches here are on the mainland, and Route A1A runs for almost 4 miles along the beachfront dunes and beautiful homes.

Northeast across the Jupiter Inlet from Jupiter is the southern tip of Jupiter Island, which stretches about 15 miles to the St. Lucie Inlet. Here expansive and expensive estates often retreat from the road behind screens of vegetation, and the population dwindles the farther north you go. At the very north end, which adjoins tiny Hobe Sound in Martin County on the mainland, sea turtles come to nest.

GETTING HERE AND AROUND

If you're coming from the airport in West Palm Beach, take Interstate 95 to Route 706. Otherwise, Federal Highway (U.S. 1) and Route A1A are usually more convenient.

Contacts Discover the Palm Beaches. ✉ *1555 Palm Beach Lakes Blvd., Suite 800, West Palm Beach* ☎ *561/233-3000* ⊕ *www.palmbeachfl.com.*

EXPLORING

FAMILY
Fodor's Choice
★

Blowing Rocks Preserve. Managed by the Nature Conservancy, this protected area on Jupiter Island is headlined by an almost otherworldly looking limestone shelf that fringes South Florida's most turquoise waters. Also protected within its 73 acres are plants native to beach-front dunes, coastal strand (the landward side of the dunes), mangrove swamps, and tropical hardwood forests. There are two short walking trails on the Intracoastal side of the preserve, as well as an education center and a butterfly garden. The best time to come and see the "blowing rocks" is when a storm is brewing: if high tides and strong offshore winds coincide, the sea blows spectacularly through the holes in the eroded outcropping. During a calm summer day, you can swim in crystal-clear waters on the mile-long beach and climb around the rock formations at low tide. Park in one of the two lots because police ticket cars on the road. ✉ *574 S. Beach Rd., CR 707, Hobe Sound* ☎ *561/744-6668* ⊕ *www.nature.org/blowingrocks* ✆ *$2.*

FAMILY
Fodor's Choice
★

Hobe Sound Nature Center. Though located in the Hobe Sound National Wildlife Refuge, this nature center is an independent organization. The exhibit hall houses live baby alligators, crocodiles, a scary-looking tarantula, and more—and is a child's delight. Just off the center's entrance is a mile-long nature trail loop that snakes through three different kinds of habitats: coastal hammock, estuary beach, and sand pine scrub, which is one of Florida's most unusual and endangered plant communities and what composes much of the refuge's nearly 250 acres. ■TIP→ **Among the center's more popular events are the annual nighttime sea turtle walks, held between May and June; reservations are accepted as early as April 1.** ✉ *13640 S.E. U.S. 1, Hobe Sound* ☎ *772/546-2067* ⊕ *www.hobesoundnaturecenter.com* ✆ *Free (donation requested)* ☉ *Closed Sun.*

FAMILY
Fodor's Choice
★

Jonathan Dickinson State Park. This serene state park provides a glimpse of predevelopment "real" Florida. A beautiful showcase of Florida inland habitat, the park teems with endangered gopher tortoises and manatees. From Hobe Mountain, an ancient dune topped with a tower, you are treated to a panoramic view of this park's more than 11,000 acres of varied terrain and the Intracoastal Waterway. The Loxahatchee River, named a National Wild and Scenic River, cuts through the park, and is home to plenty of charismatic manatees in winter and alligators year-round. Two-hour boat tours of the river depart daily. Kayak rentals are available, as is horseback riding (it was reintroduced after a 30-year absence). Among the amenities are a dozen newly redone cabins for rent, tent sites, bicycle and hiking trails, two established campgrounds and some primitive campgrounds, and a snack bar. Palmettos on the Loxahatchee is a new food-and-beverage garden with wine, beer, and

Away from developed shorelines, Blowing Rocks Preserve on Jupiter Island lets you wander the dunes.

local foods featured. Don't skip the Elsa Kimbell Environmental Education and Research Center, which has interactive displays, exhibits, and a short film on the natural history of the area. The park is also a fantastic birding location, with about 150 species to spot. ⊠ *16450 S.E. U.S. 1, Hobe Sound* ☎ *772/546–2771* ⊕ *www.floridastateparks. org/jonathandickinson* ⊠ *Vehicles $6, bicyclists and pedestrians $2.*

FAMILY
Fodor'sChoice
★ **Jupiter Inlet Lighthouse & Museum.** Designed by Civil War hero Lieutenant George Gordon Meade, this working brick lighthouse has been under the Coast Guard's purview since 1860. Tours of the 108-foot-tall landmark are held approximately every half hour and are included with admission. (Children must be at least 4 feet tall to go to the top.) The museum tells about efforts to restore this graceful spire to the way it looked from 1860 to 1918; its galleries and outdoor structures, including a pioneer home, also showcase local history dating back 5,000 years. ⊠ *Lighthouse Park, 500 Capt. Armour's Way, Jupiter* ☎ *561/747–8380* ⊕ *www.jupiterlighthouse.org* ⊠ *$12* ☉ *Closed Mon. May–Dec.*

BEACHES

Carlin Park. About ½ mile south of the Jupiter Beach Resort and Indiantown Road, the quiet beach here is just one draw; otherwise, the manicured park, which straddles A1A, is chock-full of activities and amenities, and it has the most free parking of any beach park in the area. Several picnic pavilions, including a few beachside, two bocce ball courts, six lighted tennis courts, a baseball diamond, a wood-chip-lined running path, and an amphitheater that hosts free concerts and Shakespeare productions are just some of the highlights. Locals also swear by the Lazy Loggerhead Café that's right off the seaside parking lot for a great casual breakfast and lunch. **Amenities:** lifeguards; food and drink; parking (no fee); toilets; showers. **Best for:** swimming; walking. ⊠ *400 S. Rte. A1A, Jupiter* ⊕ *www.pbcgov.com/parks/locations/carlin.htm.*

Hobe Sound National Wildlife Refuge. Nature lovers seeking to get as far as possible from the madding crowds will feel at peace at this refuge managed by the U.S. Fish & Wildlife service. It's a haven for people who want some quiet while they walk around and photograph the gorgeous coastal sand dunes, where turtles nest and shells often wash ashore. The beach has been severely eroded by high tides and strong winds (surprisingly, surfing is allowed and many do partake). You can't actually venture within most of the 735 protected acres, so if hiking piques your interest, head to the refuge's main entrance a few miles away on Hobe Sound (⊠ *13640 S.E. U.S. 1 in Hobe Sound*) for a mile-long trek close to the nature center, or to nearby Jonathan Dickinson State Park (⊠ *16450 S.E. U.S. 1 in Hobe Sound*). **Amenities:** parking (fee); toilets. **Best for:** solitude; surfing; walking. ⊠ *198 N. Beach Rd., at end of N. Beach Rd., Jupiter Island* ☎ *772/546–6141* ⊕ *www.fws. gov/hobesound* 🖃 *$5.*

Fodor's Choice
★

Jupiter Beach. Famous throughout all of Florida for a unique pooch-loving stance, the town of Jupiter's beach welcomes Yorkies, Labs, pugs—you name it—along its 2½-mile oceanfront. Dogs can frolic unleashed (once they're on the beach) or join you for a dip. Free parking spots line A1A in front of the sandy stretch, and there are multiple access points and continuously refilled dog-bag boxes (29 to be exact). The dog beach starts on Marcinski Road (Beach Marker #25) and continues north until Beach Marker #59. Before going, read through the guidelines posted on the Friends of Jupiter Beach website; the biggest things to note are be sure to clean up after your dog and steer clear of lifeguarded areas to the north and south. ■ TIP→ **Dogs fare best early morning and late afternoon, when the sand isn't too hot for their paws.** **Amenities:** toilets; showers. **Best for:** walking. ⊠ *2188 Marcinski Rd., across the street from the parking lot, Jupiter* ☎ *561/748–8140* ⊕ *www. friendsofjupiterbeach.com.*

WHERE TO EAT

$$
SEAFOOD

✕ **Guanabanas.** Expect a wait for dinner, which is not necessarily a bad thing at this island paradise of a waterfront restaurant and bar. Take the wait time to explore the bridges and trails of the open-air tropical oasis, or grab a chair by the river to watch the sunset, listen to the live band, or nibble on some conch fritters at the large tiki bar until your table is ready. **Known for:** water views from the outdoor dining area; live music; weekend breakfast. ⑤ *Average main: $18* ⊠ *960 N. Rte. A1A, Jupiter* ☎ *561/747–8878* ⊕ *www.guanabanas.com.*

$$
SEAFOOD

✕ **Little Moir's Food Shack.** This local favorite is not much to look at and a bit tricky to find, but well worth the search. The fried-food standards you might expect at such a casual, small place that uses plastic utensils are not found on the menu; instead there are fried tuna rolls with basil, and panko-crusted fried oysters with spicy fruit salad. **Known for:** fresh fish; good beer selection; long lines during the season. ⑤ *Average main: $17* ⊠ *103 S. U.S. 1, Jupiter* ☎ *561/741–3626* ⊕ *www.littlemoirs.com/ food-shack* ⊗ *Closed Sun.*

6

$$$$ ✕ **Sinclair's Ocean Grill.** This upscale restaurant at the Jupiter Beach Resort
SEAFOOD & Spa has a slick, contemporary look and is a favorite of locals in the
know. The menu has a daily selection of fresh fish, such as Atlantic black
grouper over lemon crab salad, sesame-seared tuna, and mahimahi with
fruit salsa. **Known for:** fresh fish; weekend brunch; drinks in Sinclair's
Lounge. $ *Average main: $31* ✉ *Jupiter Beach Resort, 5 N. Rte. A1A,
Jupiter* ☎ *561/746–2511* ⊕ *www.jupiterbeachresort.com.*

$$ ✕ **Taste Casual Dining.** Located in the center of historic Hobe Sound, this
AMERICAN cozy dining spot with a pleasant, screened-in patio offers piano dinner
music on Fridays. Locals like to hang out at the old, English-style wine
bar; however, the food itself is the biggest draw here. **Known for:** fresh
fish specials; slow-cooked prime rib; signature Gorgonzola salad. $ *Average main: $18* ✉ *11750 S.E. Dixie Hwy., Hobe Sound* ☎ *772/546–1129* ⊕ *www.tastehobesound.com* ⊗ *May–Oct., closed Sun.*

WHERE TO STAY

$$$ ⊞ **Jupiter Beach Resort & Spa.** Families love this nine-story hotel filled
RESORT with rich Caribbean-style rooms containing mahogany sleigh beds and
FAMILY armoires; all rooms have balconies, and many have stunning views of
Fodor's Choice the ocean and local landmarks like the Jupiter Lighthouse and Juno
★ Pier. **Pros:** fantastic beachside pool area with hammocks and a fire
pit; marble showers; great restaurant. **Cons:** $25 nightly resort fee; no
covered parking; bathtubs only in suites. $ *Rooms from: $360* ✉ *5
N. Rte. A1A, Jupiter* ☎ *561/746–2511, 800/228–8810* ⊕ *www.jupiterbeachresort.com* ⊅ *168 rooms* ⊗ *No meals.*

$$$ ⊞ **Wyndham Grand Jupiter at Harbourside Place.** This luxury waterfront
HOTEL hotel is in an upscale complex of business and retail development just
minutes from the beach. **Pros:** convenient to plaza shops and restaurants; only minutes from the beach; boat docks and fitness center available. **Cons:** no covered walkway to restaurant; no green spaces; pricey.
$ *Rooms from: $309* ✉ *Harbourside Place, 122 Soundings Ave., Jupiter* ☎ *561/273–6600* ⊕ *www.wyndhamgrandjupiter.com* ⊅ *179 rooms*
⊗ *No meals.*

SPORTS AND THE OUTDOORS

BASEBALL

Roger Dean Stadium. It's a spring-training doubleheader: both the St.
Louis Cardinals and the Miami Marlins call this 6,600-seat facility
home base from February to April. The rest of the year two minor-
league teams (Jupiter Hammerheads and Palm Beach Cardinals) share
its turf. In the Abacoa area of Jupiter, the grounds are surrounded by
a mix of restaurants and sports bars for pre- and postgame action.
✉ *4751 Main St., Jupiter* ☎ *561/775–1818* ⊕ *www.rogerdeanstadium.com* ⊠ *From $12.*

BOATING AND CANOEING

Fodor's Choice **Canoe Outfitters of Florida.** See animals, from otters to eagles, along 8
★ miles of the Loxahatchee River in Riverbend County Park daily except
Tuesday and Wednesday. Canoe and two-person kayaks are available
for rent. Bike rentals are available, too. ✉ *Riverbend County Park, 9060
W. Indiantown Rd., Jupiter* ☎ *561/746–7053* ⊕ *www.canoeoutfittersofflorida.com* ⊠ *From $35 for 4 hrs for kayak rentals.*

FAMILY
Fodor's Choice
★

Jonathan Dickinson State Park River Tours. Boat tours of the Loxahatchee River and guided horseback rides, along with canoe, kayak, bicycle, and boat rentals, are offered daily. The popular Wilderness Guided Boat Tour leaves four times daily at 9 and 11 am and 1 and 3 pm (for best wildlife photos take the 11 or 1 tour). The pontoon cruises for 90 minutes up the Loxahatchee in search of manatees, herons, osprey, alligators, and more. The skipper details the region's natural and cultural history; and from Thursday to Monday the boat also stops at the Trapper Nelson Interpretive Site for a tour of the home of a local legend, the so-called Wildman of the Loxahatchee. ⊠ *Jonathan Dickinson State Park, 16450 S.E. U.S. 1, Hobe Sound* ☎ *561/746–1466* ⊕ *www.floridaparktours.com* ⊠ *$6 park admission; boat tours $20.*

GOLF

Abacoa Golf Club. Built in 1999, the tagline for this Joe Lee–designed 18-hole course in Jupiter is "public golf at its finest." Most of the courses in this golfing community are private, but the range at Abacoa is on par with them and membership (nor deep pockets) *isn't* required. Since 2013, $1 million has been spent to renovate the facilities throughout the course and clubhouse. One of the course's more interesting features includes the several elevation changes throughout, which is a rarity in flat Florida. The course caters to golfers at all skill levels. The greens fee ranges from $45 to $110 (including cart), depending on time of year, time of day, and weekday versus weekend. ⊠ *105 Barbados Dr., Jupiter* ☎ *561/622–0036* ⊕ *www.abacoagolfclub.com* ⊠ *$100 for 18 holes* ⚑ *18 holes, 7200 yards, par 72.*

Golf Club of Jupiter. Locally owned and operated since 1981, this Lamar Smith–designed golf club features a public, championship golf course—the "Jupiter" course—with 18 holes of varying difficulty. It has a course rating of 69.9 and a slope rating of 117 on Bermuda grass. There's a full-time golf pro on staff and an on-site bar and restaurant. ⊠ *1800 S. Central Blvd., Jupiter* ☎ *561/747–6262* ⊕ *www.golfclubofjupiter.com* ⊠ *$59 for 18 holes* ⚑ *18 holes, 6275 yards, par 70.*

OFF THE
BEATEN
PATH

Forty miles west of West Palm Beach, amid the farms and cattle pastures rimming the western edges of Palm Beach and Martin counties, is **Lake Okeechobee,** the second-largest freshwater lake completely within the United States. It's girdled by 120 miles of road yet remains shielded from sight for almost its entire circumference. (The best place to view it is in Port Mayaca on the north side—where you can get great sunset shots—and the Okeechobee docks on the northwest.) Lake Okeechobee—the Seminole's "Big Water" and the gateway of the great Everglades watershed—measures 730 square miles, at its longest roughly 33 miles north–south and 30 miles east–west, with an average natural depth of only 10 feet (flood control brings the figure up to 12 feet and deeper). Six major lock systems and 32 separate water-control structures manage the water and allow boaters to cross the state through its channels from the Atlantic Ocean to the Gulf of Mexico. Encircling the lake is a 34-foot-high grassy levee that locals call "the dike," and atop it, the Lake Okeechobee Scenic Trail, a segment of the Florida National Scenic Trail that's an easy, flat ride for bikers. Anglers have a field day here as well, with great bass and perch catches. ■TIP➔ There's no shade, so wear a hat, sunscreen, and bug repellent (a must). Be sure to bring lots of bottled water, too, because restaurants and stores are few and far between.

TREASURE COAST

In contrast to the glitzy, überplanned Gold Coast that includes Greater Palm Beach and Boca Raton, the more bucolic Treasure Coast stretches from south Martin County into St. Lucie and Indian River counties. Along the east are barrier islands all the way to Sebastian and beyond, starting with Jupiter Island, then Hutchinson Island, and finally Orchid Island—and reefs, too. Those reefs are responsible for the region's nickname: they've caused ships carrying riches dating back as far as 1715 to fall asunder and cast their treasures ashore. The Intracoastal Waterway here is called the Indian River starting at the St. Lucie Inlet in Stuart and morphs into a broad tidal lagoon with tiny uninhabited islands and wildlife galore. Inland, there's cattle ranching and tracts of pine and palmetto scrub, along with sugar and citrus production.

Despite a growing number of malls and beachfront condominiums, much of the Treasure Coast remains untouched, something not lost on ecotourists, game fishers, and people who want a break from the oversaturated digital age. Consequently, there are fewer lodging options in this region of Florida, but if 30 minutes in the car sounds like a breeze, culture vultures can live in the lap of luxury in Vero Beach and detour south to Fort Pierce's galleries and botanical gardens. Likewise, families will revel in every amenity imaginable at the Hutchinson Island Marriott and be able to swing northwest to hit up the Mets spring-training stadium in Port St. Lucie or down to Jupiter for the Cardinals and the Marlins.

STUART AND JENSEN BEACH

10 miles north of Hobe Sound.

The compact town of Stuart lies on a peninsula that juts out into the St. Lucie River off the Indian River and has a remarkable amount of shoreline for its size. It scores huge points for its charming historic district and is the self-described "Sailfish Capital of the World." On the southern end, you'll find Port Salerno and its waterfront area, the Manatee Pocket, which are a skip away from the St. Lucie Inlet.

Immediately north of Stuart is down-to-earth Jensen Beach. Both Stuart and Jensen Beach straddle the Indian River and occupy Hutchinson Island, the barrier island that continues into the town of Fort Pierce. Between late April and August, hundreds, even thousands, of turtles come here to nest along the Atlantic beaches. Residents have taken pains to curb the runaway development that has created commercial crowding to the north and south, although some high-rises have popped up along the shore.

GETTING HERE AND AROUND

To get to Stuart and Jensen Beach from Jupiter and Hobe Sound, drive north on Federal Highway (U.S. 1). Route A1A crosses through downtown Stuart and is the sole main road throughout Hutchinson Island. Route 707 runs parallel on the mainland directly across the tidal lagoon.

EXPLORING

Strict architectural and zoning standards guide civic-renewal projects in the heart of Stuart. Antiques stores, restaurants, and more than 50 specialty shops are rooted within the two-block area of Flagler Avenue and Osceola Street north of where A1A cuts across the peninsula (visit ⊕ *www.stuartmainstreet.org* for more information). A self-guided walking-tour pamphlet is available at assorted locations to clue you in on this once-small fishing village's early days.

FAMILY **Elliott Museum.** Opened in March 2013, the museum's glittering, green-certified, 48,000-square-foot facility is double its previous size and houses a permanent collection along with traveling exhibits. The museum was founded in 1961 in honor of Sterling Elliott, an inventor of an early automated-addressing machine, the egg crate, and a four-wheel bicycle, and it celebrates history, art, and technology, much of it viewed through the lens of the automobile's effect on American society. There's an impressive array of antique cars, plus paintings, historic artifacts, and nostalgic goods like vintage baseball cards and toys. ⊠ *825 N.E. Ocean Blvd., Jensen Beach* ☎ *772/225–1961* ⊕ *elliottmuseum.org* ▢ *$14.*

FAMILY **Florida Oceanographic Coastal Center.** This hydroland is the place to go for an interactive marine experience and live the center's mission "to inspire environmental stewardship of Florida's coastal ecosystems through education and research." Petting and feeding stingrays can be done at various times; in the morning, a sea turtle program introduces you to three full-time residents. Make sure to catch the "feeding frenzy" when keepers toss food into the 750,000-gallon lagoon tank and sharks, tarpon, and snook swarm the surface. Join a 1-mile guided walk through the coastal hardwood hammock and mangrove swamp habitats, or explore the trails on your own—you may see a dolphin or manatee swim by. ⊠ *890 N.E. Ocean Blvd., Stuart* ☎ *772/225–0505* ⊕ *www.floridaocean.org* ▢ *$12.*

Gilbert's Bar House of Refuge Museum. Built in 1875 on Hutchinson Island, this is the only remaining example of 10 such structures that were erected by the U.S. Life-Saving Service (a predecessor of the Coast Guard) to aid stranded sailors. The displays here include antique lifesaving equipment, maps, artifacts from nearby wrecks, and boatbuilding tools. The museum is affiliated with the nearby Elliott Museum; package tickets are available. ⊠ *301 S.E. MacArthur Blvd., Jensen Beach* ☎ *772/225–1875* ⊕ *www.houseofrefugefl. org* ▢ *$8.*

CLOSE UP

Florida's Sea Turtles: The Nesting Season

From May to October, turtles nest all along the Florida coast. Female loggerhead, Kemp's ridley, and other species living in the Atlantic Ocean or Gulf of Mexico swim as much as 2,000 miles to the Florida shore. By night they drag their 100- to 400-pound bodies onto the beach to the dune line. Then each digs a hole with her flippers, drops in 100 or so eggs, covers them up, and returns to sea.

The babies hatch about 60 days later. Once they burst out of the sand, the hatchlings must get to sea rapidly or risk becoming dehydrated from the sun or being caught by crabs, birds, or other predators.

Instinctively, baby turtles head toward bright light, probably because for millions of years starlight or moonlight reflected on the waves was the brightest light around, serving to guide hatchlings to water. Many coastal towns enforce light restrictions during nesting months. Florida homeowners are asked to dim their lights on behalf of baby sea turtles.

At night, volunteers walk the beaches, searching for signs of turtle nests. Upon finding telltale scratches in the sand, they cordon off the sites, so beachgoers will leave the spots undisturbed. (It is illegal to disturb turtle nests.) Volunteers also keep watch over nests when babies are about to hatch, and assist disoriented hatchlings.

Several local organizations offer nightly turtle walks during nesting season. Most are in June and July, starting around 8 pm and sometimes lasting until midnight. Expect a $10 to $15 fee. Call in advance to confirm times and to reserve a spot—places usually take reservations as early as April. If you're in southern Palm Beach County, contact Boca Raton's **Gumbo Limbo Nature Center** (☎ 561/338–1473 ⊕ www.gumbolimbo.org). The **John D. MacArthur Beach State Park** (☎ 561/624–6952 ⊕ www. macarthurbeach.org) is convenient for Palm Beach–area visitors at the northern end of Singer Island. **Hobe Sound Nature Center** (☎ 772/546–2067 ⊕ www.hobesoundnaturecenter.com) is farther up. Treasure Coasters in or near Vero Beach can go to **Sebastian Inlet State Park** (☎ 321/984–4852 ⊕ www.floridastateparks.org/ sebastianinlet).

6

BEACHES

FAMILY **Bathtub Reef Beach.** Rough tides are often the norm in this stretch of the Atlantic Ocean, and frequently take away the beach, but a charming enclave at the southern end of Hutchinson Island—after the Marriott's beach and right by the Indian River Plantation luxury development—provides a perfect escape for families with young children and anyone who likes to snorkel. The waters are shallow and usually calm, and youngsters can walk up to the reef and see a dazzling assortment of fish. The parking lot is small, so get there early. Erosion is a problem, and sometimes lifeguards can't pull their hefty chairs out, leaving the beach unguarded (but it shouldn't deter you, because the sea isn't rough). **Amenities:** toilets; parking (no fee); lifeguards. **Best for:** swimming; snorkeling. ✉ *1585 S.E. MacArthur Blvd., Stuart.*

FAMILY **Stuart Beach.** When the waves robustly roll in, the surfers are rolling in, too. Beginning surfers are especially keen on Stuart Beach because of its ever-vigilant lifeguards, and pros to the sport like the challenges that the choppy waters here bring. But the beach is equally popular with surf fishers. Families enjoy the snack bar known for its chicken fingers, the basketball courts, the large canopy-covered playground, and the three walkways interspersed throughout the area for easy ocean access. **Amenities:** lifeguards; food and drink; parking (no fee); showers; toilets. **Best for:** surfing; swimming. ⊠ *889 N.E. Ocean Blvd., Stuart.*

WHERE TO EAT

$$$ ✕**Conchy Joe's.** Like a hermit crab sliding into a new shell, Conchy
SEAFOOD Joe's moved up from West Palm Beach in 1983 to its current home, a 1920s rustic stilt house on the Indian River. It's full of antique fish mounts, gator hides, and snakeskins, and is a popular tourist spot—but the waterfront location, very casual vibe, and delicious seafood lures locals, too. **Known for:** conch chowder; grouper marsala; live reggae Thursday–Sunday. ⑤ *Average main: $27* ⊠ *3945 N.E. Indian River Dr., Jensen Beach* ☎ *772/334–1130* ⊕ *www.conchyjoes.com.*

$$$ ✕**Courtine's.** A husband-and-wife team oversees this quiet and hos-
FRENCH pitable restaurant under the Roosevelt Bridge. French and American influences are clear in the Swiss chef's dishes, from rack of lamb with Dijon mustard to grilled filet mignon stuffed with Roquefort and fresh spinach. **Known for:** refined Continental cuisine; elegant atmosphere; more casual bar menu. ⑤ *Average main: $25* ⊠ *514 N. Dixie Hwy., Stuart* ☎ *772/692–3662* ⊕ *www.courtines.com* ⊘ *Closed Sun. and Mon. No lunch.*

$$$ ✕**District Table and Bar.** Farm-fresh foods with a Southern accent are
SOUTHERN served up at this chef-owned restaurant with a theater kitchen, where comfort foods are taken to new levels. (Slow Foods, a group that celebrates local foods and artisans, has given the restaurant a "Snail of Approval.") **Known for:** farm-to-table menu; lively bar scene; everything house made, including condiments and jams. ⑤ *Average main: $23* ⊠ *900 S.E. Indian St., Stuart* ☎ *772/324–8357* ⊕ *www.district-tableandbar.com* ⊘ *Closed Mon.*

$$$$ ✕**11 Maple Street.** This cozy spot is as good as it gets on the Treasure
ECLECTIC Coast. Soft music and a friendly staff set the mood in the antiques-filled dining room of this old house, which holds only 21 tables. **Known for:** nice selection of wines; good desserts; Old Florida setting in vintage house. ⑤ *Average main: $42* ⊠ *3224 N.E. Maple Ave., Jensen Beach* ☎ *772/334–7714* ⊕ *www.elevenmaple.com* ⊘ *Closed Sun. and Mon. No lunch.*

$$$ ✕**Ian's Tropical Grill.** Tucked inside a small plaza, the restaurant has a
SEAFOOD small, cozy dining room and covered alfresco patio. The menu changes often, depending on what's fresh in the markets and from local farms, which are named. **Known for:** fresh Florida seafood; primarily locally sourced ingredients; inventive cocktails. ⑤ *Average main: $25* ⊠ *2875 S.E. Ocean Blvd., Stuart* ☎ *772/334–4563* ⊘ *Closed Sun.*

WHERE TO STAY

$$
RESORT
FAMILY

Hutchinson Island Marriott Beach Resort & Marina. With a 77-slip marina, a full water-sports program, a golf course, two pools, tons of tennis courts, and children's activities, this self-contained resort is excellent for families, most of whom prefer to stay in the tower directly on the ocean. **Pros:** attentive, warm staff; rooms are comfortable and casually chic; all rooms have balconies. **Cons:** only one sit-down indoor restaurant; common areas are a bit dated; no spa; daily resort fee. $ *Rooms from: $230 ⊠ 555 N.E. Ocean Blvd., Stuart ☎ 772/225–3700, 800/775–5936 ⊕ www.marriott.com/pbiir ⇨ 274 rooms ❄ No meals.*

$
RESORT

Pirate's Cove Resort & Marina. This cozy enclave on the banks of the Manatee Pocket with ocean access at the southern end of Stuart is the perfect place to set forth on a day at sea or wind down after one—it's relaxing and casual, and has amenities like a swimming-pool courtyard, restaurant, and fitness center. **Pros:** spacious tropical-themed rooms; great for boaters, with a 50-slip, full-service, deepwater marina; each room has a balcony overlooking the water; free Wi-Fi and parking. **Cons:** lounge gets noisy at night; decor and furnishings are pretty but not luxurious; pool is on the small side. $ *Rooms from: $150 ⊠ 4307 S.E. Bayview St., Port Salerno ☎ 772/287–2500 ⊕ www.piratescoveresort.com ⇨ 50 rooms ❄ No meals.*

SHOPPING

More than 60 restaurants and shops with antiques, art, and fashion draw visitors downtown along Osceola Street.

B&A Flea Market. A short drive from downtown and operating for more than two decades, the oldest and largest weekend-only flea market on the Treasure Coast has a street-bazaar feel, with shoppers happily scouting the 500 vendors for the practical and unusual. A produce market carries local tropical fruits and vegetables. If you have an open mind and love to shop garage sales, you'll do just fine here. ⊠ *2885 S.E. U.S. 1, Stuart ☎ 772/288–4915 ⊕ www.bafleamarket.com ⌂ Free.*

SPORTS AND THE OUTDOORS

BOAT TOURS

Island Princess **Cruises.** Cruise the Indian River and St. Lucie River as well as Jupiter Sound aboard the *Island Princess,* an 82-footer that docks at the Sailfish Marina in Stuart. In season, there are nature cruises and cruises that go through the St. Lucie River locks. Have lunch during their Jupiter Island cruise, embarking Tuesday and weekends year-round. The schedule, which changes often, is posted on the company's website. All ages are welcome, and advance reservations are required. ⊠ *Sailfish Marina, 3585 S.E. St. Lucie Blvd., Stuart ☎ 772/225–2100 ⊕ www.islandprincesscruises.com ⌂ Cruises from $25.*

FISHING

Sailfish Marina of Stuart. Nab a deep-sea charter here to land a sailfish, a popular sport fish that is prolific off the St. Lucie Inlet. This is the closest public marina to the St. Lucie Inlet. Recently expanded, it is home to *Island Princess* Cruises, which takes visitors to Vero Beach or Jupiter via the Intracoastal Waterway. ⊠ *3565 S.E. St. Lucie Blvd., Stuart ☎ 772/283–1122 ⊕ www.sailfishmarinastuart.com.*

FORT PIERCE AND PORT ST. LUCIE

11 miles north of Jensen Beach.

About an hour north of Palm Beach, Fort Pierce has a distinctive rural feel—but it has a surprising number of worthwhile attractions for a town of its size, including those easily seen while following Route 707 on the mainland (A1A on Hutchinson Island). The downtown is expanding, and sports new theater revivals, restaurants, and shops. A big draw is an inlet that offers fabulous fishing and excellent surfing. Nearby Port St. Lucie is largely landlocked southwest of Fort Pierce and is almost equidistant from there and Jensen Beach. It's not a big tourist area except for two sports facilities near Interstate 95: the St. Lucie Mets' training grounds, Tradition Field, and the PGA Village. If you want a hotel directly on the sand or crave more than simple, motel-like accommodations, stay elsewhere and drive up for the day.

GETTING HERE AND AROUND

You can reach Fort Pierce from Jensen Beach by driving 11 miles north on Federal Highway (U.S. 1), Route 707, or Route A1A. To get to Port St. Lucie, continue north on U.S. 1 and take Prima Vista Boulevard west. From Fort Pierce, Route 709 goes diagonally southwest to Port St. Lucie, and Interstate 95 is another choice.

ESSENTIALS

Visitor Information St. Lucie County Tourist Development Council. ⊠ *2300 Virginia Ave., Fort Pierce* 🕾 *800/344–8443* ⊕ *www.visitstluciefla.com.*

EXPLORING

Heathcote Botanical Gardens. Stroll through this 3½-acre green space, which includes a palm walk, a Japanese garden, and a collection of 100 bonsai trees. There is also a gift shop with whimsical and botanical knickknacks. Guided tours are available by appointment for an extra fee. ⊠ *210 Savannah Rd., Fort Pierce* 🕾 *772/464–0323* ⊕ *www. heathcotebotanicalgardens.org* 🎫 *$6* ⊘ *Closed Mon.*

FAMILY **National Navy UDT-SEAL Museum.** Commemorating the more than 3,000 troops who trained on these shores during World War II when this elite military unit got its start, there are weapons, vehicles, and equipment on view. Exhibits honor all frogmen and underwater demolition teams and depict their history. The museum houses the lifeboat from which SEALs saved the *Maersk Alabama* captain from Somali pirates in 2009. Kids get a thrill out of the helicopters and aircraft on the grounds. ⊠ *3300 N. Rte. A1A, Fort Pierce* 🕾 *772/595–5845* ⊕ *www.navysealmuseum. com* 🎫 *$10* ⊘ *Closed Mon.*

FAMILY **Savannas Recreation Area.** Once a reservoir, the 550 acres have been returned to their natural wetlands state. Today the wilderness area has campgrounds, interpretive trails, and a boat ramp, and the recreation area is open year-round. Canoe and kayak rentals are available Thursday through Monday. A dog park (open daily) is also on-site. Amenities include showers, toilets, and free Wi-Fi for campers. ⊠ *1400 E. Midway Rd., Fort Pierce* 🕾 *772/464–7855* ⊕ *www.stlucieco.gov/parks/savannas.htm* 🎫 *Free; $25.25 for campers (full service).*

BEACHES

Fort Pierce Inlet State Park. Across the inlet at the northern side of Hutchinson Island, a fishing oasis lures beachgoers who can't wait to reel in snook, flounder, and bluefish, among others. The park is also known as a prime wave-riding locale, thanks to a reef that lies just outside the jetty. Summer is the busiest season by a long shot, but don't be fooled: it's a laid-back place to sun and surf. There are covered picnic tables but no concessions; however, from where anglers perch, a bunch of casual restaurants can be spotted on the other side of the inlet that are a quick drive away. Note that the area of Jack Island Preserve has been closed indefinitely. **Amenities:** toilets; showers; parking (fee); lifeguards (summer only). **Best for:** surfing; walking; solitude. ✉ *905 Shorewinds Dr., Fort Pierce* ☎ *772/468–3985* ⊕ *www.floridastateparks.org/fortpierceinlet* 💳 *Vehicle $6, bicyclists and pedestrians $2.*

WHERE TO STAY

$
HOTEL

Dockside Inn. This hotel is the best of the lodgings lining the scenic Fort Pierce Inlet on Seaway Drive (and that's not saying much); it's a practical base for fishing enthusiasts with nice touches like two pools and a waterfront restaurant. **Pros:** good value; overnight boat docking available; reasonable rates at marina; parking included. **Cons:** basic decor; some steps to climb; grounds are nothing too fancy but have great views. ⑤ *Rooms from: $125* ✉ *1160 Seaway Dr., Fort Pierce* ☎ *772/468–3555, 800/286–1745* ⊕ *www.docksideinn.com* 🛏 *36 rooms* ◎ *No meals.*

SPORTS AND THE OUTDOORS

BASEBALL

Tradition Field. Out west by Interstate 95, this Port St. Lucie baseball stadium, formerly known as Digital Domain Park as well as Thomas J. White Stadium, is where the New York Mets train; it's also the home of the St. Lucie Mets minor-league team. ✉ *525 N.W. Peacock Blvd., Port St. Lucie* ☎ *772/871–2115* ⊕ *www.stluciemets.com.*

GOLF

PGA Village. Owned and operated by the PGA of America, the national association of teaching pros, PGA Village is the winter home to many Northern instructors, along with permanent staff. The facility is a little off the beaten path and the clubhouse is basic, but serious golfers will appreciate the three championship courses by Pete Dye and Tom Fazio and the chance to sharpen their skills at the 35-acre PGA Center for Golf Learning and Performance, which has nine practice bunkers mimicking sands and slopes from around the globe. Between the Fazio-designed Wanamaker Course, the Ryder Course, and the Dye-designed Dye Course, there are 54 holes of championship golf at PGA Village. Also affiliated is the nearby St. Lucie Trail Golf Club, another Fazio design. Beginners can start out on the lesser known (and easier) 6-hole PGA Short Course. Holes are 35 to 60 yards each, and course play is free. ✉ *1916 Perfect Dr., Port St. Lucie* ☎ *772/467–1300, 800/800–4653* ⊕ *www.pgavillage.com* 💳 *Wanamaker Course $131; Ryder Course $131; Dye Course $131; St. Lucie Trail Golf Club $89*

🏌 *Wanamaker Course: 18 holes, 7123 yards, par 72; Ryder Course: 18 holes, 7037 yards, par 72; Dye Course: 18 holes, 7279 yards, par 72; St. Lucie Golf Club Trail Course: 18 holes, 6901 yards, par 72.*

SCUBA DIVING

The region's premier dive site is actually on the National Register of Historic Places. The *Urca de Lima* was part of the storied treasure fleet bound for Spain that was destroyed by a hurricane in 1715. It's now part of an underwater archaeological preserve about 200 yards from shore, just north of the National Navy UDT-SEAL Museum and under 10 to 15 feet of water. The remains contain a flat-bottom, round-bellied ship and cannons that can be visited on an organized dive trip.

Dive Odyssea. This full-service dive shop offers kayak rentals, tank rentals, and scuba lessons. The shop can arrange a scuba charter in Jupiter or Palm Beach (two-tank dive trips typically start at $65), but Dive Odyssea no longer offers dive trips of its own. ⊠ *Fort Pierce Inlet, 621 N. 2nd St., Fort Pierce* ☎ *772/460–1771* ⊕ *www.diveodyssea.com.*

VERO BEACH

12 miles north of Fort Pierce.

Tranquil and picturesque, this upscale Indian River County town has a strong commitment to the environment and culture, and it's also home to eclectic galleries and trendy restaurants. Downtown Vero is centered on the historic district on 14th Avenue, but much of the fun takes place across the Indian River (aka the Intracoastal Waterway) around Orchid Island's beaches. It was once home to the Dodgers Spring Training base, and there's still a strong affinity for baseball here, and it's kid-friendly, with the former Dodgertown Stadium hosting LIttle League tournaments, and plenty of parks around. Its western edges still are home to cattlemen and citrus growers, so there is a juxtaposition of country and gentry.

GETTING HERE AND AROUND

To get here, you have two basic options: Route A1A along the coast (not to be confused with Ocean Drive, an offshoot on Orchid Island), or either U.S. 1 or Route 605 (also called Old Dixie Highway) on the mainland. As you approach Vero on the latter, you pass through an ungussied-up landscape of small farms and residential areas. On the beach route, part of the drive bisects an unusually undeveloped section of the Florida coast. If flying in, consider Orlando International Airport, which is larger and a smidge closer than Palm Beach International Airport.

VISITOR INFORMATION

Contacts Indian River County Chamber of Commerce. ⊠ *1216 21st St.* ☎ *772/567–3491* ⊕ *www.indianriverchamber.com.*

EXPLORING

Environmental Learning Center. Off Wabasso Beach Road, the 64 acres here are almost completely surrounded by water. In addition to a 600-foot boardwalk through the mangrove shoreline and a 1-mile canoe trail, there are aquariums filled with Indian River creatures. Boat and kayak trips to see the historic Pelican Island rookery are on offer along with guided nature walks and touch-tank encounters. Call or check the center's website for times. ✉ *255 Live Oak Dr.* ☎ *772/589–5050* ⊕ *www. discoverelc.org* 💲*$5* ⊙ *Closed Mon.*

McKee Botanical Garden. On the National Register of Historic Places, the 18-acre plot is a tropical jungle garden—one of the most lush and serene around. This is *the* place to see spectacular water lilies, and the property's original 1932 Hall of Giants, a rustic wooden structure that has stained-glass and bronze bells, contains what is claimed to be the world's largest single-plank mahogany table at 35 feet long. There's a Seminole bamboo pavilion, a gift shop, and café (open for lunch Tuesday through Saturday—and Sunday in season), which serves especially tasty snacks and sandwiches. ✉ *350 U.S. 1* ☎ *772/794–0601* ⊕ *www. mckeegarden.org* 💲*$12* ⊙ *Closed Mon.*

Pelican Island National Wildlife Refuge. Founded in 1903 by President Theodore Roosevelt as the country's first national wildlife refuge, the park encompasses the historic Pelican Island rookery itself—a small island in the Indian River lagoon and important nesting place for 16 species of birds such as endangered wood storks and, of course, brown pelicans—and the land surrounding it overlooking Sebastian. The rookery is a closed wilderness area, so there's no roaming alongside animal kingdom friends; however, there is an 18-foot observation tower across from it with direct views and more than 6 miles of nature trails in the refuge. Another way to explore is via guided kayak tours from the Florida Outdoor Center. Make sure to bring a camera—it's a photographer's dream. ✉ *Rte. A1A, 1 mile north of Treasure Shores Park* ✛ *Take A1A and turn on Historic Jungle Trail* ☎ *772/581–5557* ⊕ *www.fws. gov/pelicanisland* 💲*Free.*

6

BEACHES

Most of the hotels in the Vero Beach area are clustered around South Beach Park or line Ocean Drive around Beachland Boulevard just north of Humiston Park. Both parks have lifeguards daily. South Beach, at the end of East Causeway Boulevard, is one of the widest, quietest shores on the island, and has plenty of hammock shade before the dunes to picnic in, plus volleyball nets on the beach. Humiston Park is smack-dab in the main commercial zone with restaurants galore, including the lauded Citrus Grillhouse at its southern tip.

Humiston Park. Just south of the Driftwood Resort on Ocean Drive sits Humiston Park, one of the best beaches in town. Parking is free and plentiful, as there's a large lot on Easter Lily Lane and there are spots all over the surrounding business district. The shore is somewhat narrow and there isn't much shade, but the vibrant scene and other amenities make it a great choice for people who crave lots of activity. With lifeguards on call daily, there's a children's playground, plus a ton of hotels, restaurants, bars, and shops within walking distance. **Amenities:** lifeguards; food and drink; toilets; showers. **Best for:** swimming; partiers; sunsets; walking. ✉ *3000 Ocean Dr., at Easter Lily La.* ☎ *772/231–5790.*

FAMILY
Fodor's Choice
★

Sebastian Inlet State Park. The 1,000-acre park, which runs from the tip of Orchid Island across the passage to the barrier island just north, is one of the Florida park system's biggest draws, especially because of the inlet's highly productive fishing waters. Views from either side of the tall bridge are spectacular, and a unique hallmark is that the gates never close—an amazing feature for die-hard anglers who know snook bite better at night. Two jetties are usually packed with fishers and spectators alike. The park has two entrances, the entrance in Vero Beach and the main entrance in Melbourne (⌧ 9700 Rte. A1A). Within its grounds, you'll discover a wonderful two-story restaurant that overlooks the ocean, a fish and surfing shop (by the way, this place has some of the best waves in the state, but there are also calmer zones for relaxing swims), two museums, guided sea turtle walks in season, 51 campsites with water and electricity, and a marina with powerboat, kayak, and canoe rentals. **Amenities:** food and drink; parking (fee); showers; toilets; water sports. **Best for:** surfing; sunrise; sunset; walking. ⌧ 14251 N. Rte. A1A ☎ 321/984–4852 ⊕ www.floridastateparks. org/sebastianinlet ⌧ $8 vehicles with up to 8 people, $4 single drivers, $2 bicyclists and pedestrians.

FAMILY

Wabasso Beach Park. A favorite for local surfboarding teens and the families at the nearby Disney's Vero Beach Resort, the park is nestled in a residential area at the end of Wabasso Road, about 8 miles up from the action on Ocean Drive and 8 miles below the Sebastian Inlet. Aside from regular amenities like picnic tables, restrooms, and a dedicated parking lot (which really is the "park" here—there's not much green space—and it's quite small, so arrive early), the Disney crowd walks there for its lifeguards (the strip directly in front of the hotel is unguarded) and the local crowd appreciates its conveniences, like a pizzeria and a store that sells sundries, snacks, and beach supplies. **Amenities:** food and drink; lifeguards; parking (no fee); toilets; showers. **Best for:** swimming; surfing. ⌧ 1820 Wabasso Rd.

WHERE TO EAT

$$$
MODERN
AMERICAN
Fodor's Choice
★

✕ **Citrus Grillhouse.** There are rooms with a view, and then there's this view: uninterrupted sea from a wraparound veranda at the southern end of Humiston Park. Even better, the food here is a straightforward, delicious celebration of fresh and fabulous. **Known for:** fresh Florida seafood, especially snapper; some gluten-free options; bargain prix fixe Monday–Wednesday 5–6. ⑤ Average main: $24 ⌧ Humiston Park, 1050 Easter Lily La. ☎ 772/234–4114 ⊕ www.citrusgrillhouse.com ⊘ No lunch Sun.

$
DINER
FAMILY

✕ **The Lemon Tree.** If Italy had old-school luncheonettes, this is what they'd look like: a storefront of yellow walls, dark-green booths, white linoleum tables, and cascading sconces of faux ivy leaves and hand-painted Tuscan serving pieces for artwork. It's self-described by the husband-and-wife owners (who are always at the front) as an "upscale diner," and locals swear by it for breakfast (served all day) and lunch. **Known for:** shrimp scampi; treats on the house; waits during the high season. ⑤ Average main: $11 ⌧ 3125 Ocean Dr. ⊕ www.lemontreevero. com ⊘ No lunch or dinner Sun. No dinner June–Sept.

$$$
SEAFOOD

✕**Ocean Grill.** Opened in 1941, this family-owned Old Florida–style restaurant combines its ocean view with Tiffany-style lamps, wrought-iron chandeliers, and paintings of pirates. Count on at least three kinds of seafood any day on the menu, along with steaks, pork chops, soups, and salads. **Known for:** just OK food; great drinks; the Pusser's Painkiller. ⑤ *Average main: $28* ✉ *1050 Beachland Blvd.* ☎ *772/231–5409* ⊕ *www.ocean-grill.com* ⊙ *Closed 2 wks around Labor Day. No lunch Sun.*

$$$
ECLECTIC
Fodor'sChoice
★

✕**The Tides.** A charming cottage restaurant west of Ocean Drive prepares some of the best food around—not just in Vero Beach, but all of South Florida. The chefs, classically trained, give a nod to international fare with disparate dishes such as tuna tataki, Asian-inspired carpaccio with satay, penne *quattro formaggi,* and classic lobster bisque. **Known for:** fresh Florida fish; jumbo crab cakes with corn-and-pepper sauce; chef's table with wine pairings. ⑤ *Average main: $29* ✉ *3103 Cardinal Dr.* ☎ *772/234–3966* ⊕ *www.tidesofvero.com* ⊙ *No lunch.*

WHERE TO STAY

$
RESORT
Fodor'sChoice
★

▦ **Costa d'Este Beach Resort.** This stylish, contemporary boutique hotel in the heart of Vero's bustling Ocean Drive area has a gorgeous infinity pool overlooking the ocean and a distinctly Miami Beach vibe—just like its famous owners, singer Gloria Estefan and producer Emilio Estefan, who bought the property in 2004. **Pros:** all rooms have balconies or secluded patios; huge Italian marble showers; complimentary signature mojitos on arrival. **Cons:** spa is on small side; rooms have only blackout shades; daily resort fee. ⑤ *Rooms from: $139* ✉ *3244 Ocean Dr.* ☎ *772/562–9919* ⊕ *www.costadeste.com* ⇨ *94 rooms* ❝❞*No meals.*

$$$
RESORT
FAMILY

▦ **Disney's Vero Beach Resort.** This oceanfront, family-oriented retreat tucked away in a residential stretch of Orchid Island has a retro Old Florida design and not too much Mickey Mouse, which is a welcome surprise for adults. **Pros:** a great pool with waterslide and kiddie splash pool; campfire circle; several dining options on property. **Cons:** far from shopping and dining options; minimal Disney-themed decor. ⑤ *Rooms from: $365* ✉ *9250 Island Grove Terr.* ☎ *772/234–2000, 407/939–7540* ⊕ *www.disneybeachresorts.com/vero-beach-resort/* ⇨ *181 rooms* ❝❞*No meals.*

$
RESORT
FAMILY

▦ **The Driftwood Resort.** On the National Register of Historic Places, the two original buildings of this 1935 inn were built entirely from ocean-washed timbers with no blueprints; over time more buildings were added, and all are now decorated with such artifacts as ship's bells, Spanish tiles, a cannon from a 16th-century Spanish galleon, and plenty of wrought iron, which create a quirky, utterly charming landscape. **Pros:** central location and right on the beach; free Wi-Fi; laundry facilities; weekly treasure hunt is a blast. **Cons:** older property; rooms can be musty; no-frills furnishings. ⑤ *Rooms from: $150* ✉ *3150 Ocean Dr.* ☎ *772/231–0550* ⊕ *www.verobeachdriftwood.com* ⇨ *100 rooms* ❝❞*No meals.*

$$
RESORT
FAMILY
Fodor's Choice
★

☐ **Vero Beach Hotel & Spa.** With a sophisticated, relaxed British West Indies feel, this luxurious five-story beachfront hotel at the north end of Ocean Drive is an inviting getaway and, arguably, the best on the Treasure Coast. **Pros:** beautiful pool; complimentary daily wine hour with hors d'oeuvres. **Cons:** separate charge for valet parking; some rooms overlook parking lot. $ *Rooms from: $299* ☒ *3500 Ocean Dr.* ☎ *772/231–5666* ⊕ *www.verobeachhotelandspa.com* ⇆ *102 rooms* ❍ *No meals.*

SHOPPING

The place to go when in Vero Beach is **Ocean Drive.** Crossing over to Orchid Island from the mainland, the Merrill P. Barber Bridge turns into Beachland Boulevard; its intersection with Ocean Drive is the heart of a commercial zone with a lively mix of upscale clothing stores, specialty shops, restaurants, and art galleries.

Just under 3 miles north of that roughly eight-block stretch on A1A is a charming outdoor plaza, the **Village Shops.** It's a delight to stroll between the brightly painted cottages that have more unique, high-end offerings.

Back on the mainland, take 21st Street westward and you'll come across a small, modern shopping plaza with some independent shops and national chains. Keep going west on 21st Street, and then park around 14th Avenue to explore a collection of art galleries and eateries in the historic downtown.

RECOMMENDED STORES

Maison Beach. Formerly called Christine, the owner changed the name of this cute shop and moved to Pelican Plaza. It still is *the* place to find gorgeous hostess and dining entertainment gifts like Mariposa napkin holders, Julia Knight bowls, and Michael Aram picture frames, along with trendy Mudpie household ware. ☒ *Pelican Plaza, 4895 Hwy. A1A* ☎ *772/492–0383* ⊕ *www.christineshop.com.*

Sassy Boutique. One of the chicest spots in town sells bright, punchy, and pretty women's designer fashions such as Calypso St. Barth, Tory Burch, Kate Spade New York, Kenneth Jay Lane, Stacia, and Nanette Lepore. ☒ *3375 Ocean Dr.* ☎ *772/234–3998* ⊕ *www.sassyboutique.com.*

Shells & Things. Stop here for lovely handcrafted goods inspired by the sea, many by local artisans. Choose from jewelry, candles, gifts for kids, home decor items, and artwork. ☒ *3119 Ocean Dr.* ☎ *772/234–4790* ⊕ *www.shellsandthings.com.*

SHOPPING CENTERS AND MALLS

Vero Beach Outlets. Need some retail therapy? Just west of Interstate 95 off Route 60 is a discount shopping destination with 50 high-end brand-name stores, including Ann Taylor, Calvin Klein, Christopher & Banks, Dooney & Bourke, Polo Ralph Lauren, Restoration Hardware, and White House/Black Market. ☒ *1824 94th Dr.* ✛ *On Rte. 60, west of I–95 at Exit 147* ☎ *772/770–6097* ⊕ *www.verobeachoutlets.com.*

6

SPORTS AND THE OUTDOORS
GOLF

Sandridge Golf Club. The Sandridge Golf Club features two public 18-hole courses designed by Ron Garl: the Dunes course, with 6 holes located on a sand ridge; and the Lakes course, named for—you guessed it—the ubiquitous lakes around the course. The Dunes course, opened in 1987, follows a history-steeped pathway once used during mining operations. The Lakes course, opened in 1992, is renowned for the very challenging, par-4 14th hole with an island green. There's a pro shop on-site offering lessons and clinics. Florida and Indian River County residents can get membership cards to book tee times eight days out—and get discounts for play. ⊠ *5300 73rd St.* ☎ *772/770–5000* ⊕ *www.sandridgegc.com* ⊠ *$50 for 18 holes with cart* ⅃. *Dunes course: 18 holes, 6817 yards, par 72; Lakes course: 18 holes, 6181 yards, par 72.*

TRAVEL SMART
SOUTH FLORIDA

GETTING HERE AND AROUND

▌AIR TRAVEL

Average flying time to Florida's international airports is 3 hours from New York, 4 hours from Chicago, 2¾ hours from Dallas, 4½–5½ hours from Los Angeles, and 8–8½ hours from London.

AIRPORTS

South Florida has three major airports; the busiest are Miami International Airport (MIA) and Fort Lauderdale–Hollywood International Airport (FLL). Flying to alternative airports can save you both time and money. Fort Lauderdale is close to Miami, Palm Beach International (PBI) is close to Fort Lauderdale. FLL is a 30-minute drive from MIA.

▐TIP➔ **Flying to secondary airports can save you money, so price things out before booking. Sometimes one-way car rentals in Florida can be more cost-effective than shared van shuttles.**

Airport Information Fort Lauderdale–Hollywood International Airport (FLL). ⊠ 100 Terminal Dr., Fort Lauderdale ☎ 866/435–9355 ⊕ www.broward.org/airport. **Key West International Airport** (EYW). ⊠ 3491 S. Roosevelt Blvd., Key West ☎ 305/809–5200, 305/296–5439 ⊕ www.eywairport.com. **Miami International Airport** (MIA). ⊠ N.E. 20th St. and LeJeune Rd., Miami ☎ 305/876–7000 ⊕ www.miami-airport.com. **Palm Beach International Airport** (PBI). ⊠ 1000 Palm Beach International Airport, West Palm Beach ☎ 561/471–7420 ⊕ www.pbia.org.

GROUND TRANSPORTATION

SuperShuttle service operates from several Florida airports: Fort Lauderdale, Miami, and the Palm Beaches. That said, most airports offer some type of shuttle or bus service.

If you book a shuttle from your hotel to the airport, allow at least 24 hours, and expect to be picked up at least 2½ hours before your scheduled departure.

Cab fares from Florida's larger airports into town can be high, and there can be a departure fee from an airport. (In Fort Lauderdale, that airport departure fee is $3.) Note that in some cities airport cab fares are a single flat rate; in others, flat-rate fares vary by zone; and in others still, the fare is determined by the meter. Private car service fares are usually higher than taxi fares.

Shuttle Service SuperShuttle. ☎ 800/258–3826 ⊕ www.supershuttle.com.

FLIGHTS

American Airlines. Flies to Daytona Beach, Fort Lauderdale, Fort Myers, Fort Walton Beach, Gainesville, Jacksonville, Key West, Melbourne, Miami, Orlando, Pensacola, Sarasota, Tallahassee, Tampa, and the Palm Beaches ☎ 800/433–7300 ⊕ www.aa.com.

Delta. Flies to Daytona Beach, Fort Lauderdale, Fort Myers, Fort Walton Beach, Gainesville, Jacksonville, Key West, Melbourne, Miami, Orlando, Panama City, Pensacola, Sarasota, Tallahassee, Tampa, and the Palm Beaches. ☎ 800/221–1212 for U.S. reservations, 800/241–4141 for international reservations ⊕ www.delta.com.

Frontier. Flies to Fort Lauderdale, Fort Myers, Jacksonville, Orlando, and Tampa. ☎ 800/432–1359 ⊕ www.frontierairlines.com.

JetBlue. Flies to Fort Lauderdale, Fort Myers, Jacksonville, Key West, Sarasota, Tampa, and the Palm Beaches. ☎ 800/538–2583 ⊕ www.jetblue.com.

Southwest. Flies to Fort Lauderdale, Fort Myers, Jacksonville, Key West, Orlando, Panama City, Pensacola, Tampa, and the Palm Beaches. ☎ 800/435–9792 ⊕ www.southwest.com.

Spirit Airlines. Flies to Fort Lauderdale, Fort Myers, Orlando, Tampa, and the Palm Beaches. ☎ 801/401–2200 ⊕ www.spirit.com.

United. Flies to Daytona, Fort Lauderdale, Fort Myers, Fort Walton Beach, Gainesville, Jacksonville, Key West, Miami, Orlando, Panama City, Pensacola, Sarasota Bradenton, Tallahassee, Tampa, and the Palm Beaches. ☎ 800/864–8331 for U.S. reservations, 800/538–2929 for international reservations ⊕ www.united.com.

FROM–TO	MILES	HOURS +/–
Fort Lauderdale–Miami	30	0:45
Miami–Naples	125	2:15
Miami–Key Largo	65	1
Miami–Palm Beach	70	1:45
Key Largo–Key West	100	2

■ CAR TRAVEL

Three major interstates lead to Florida. Interstate 95 begins in Maine, runs south through the Mid-Atlantic states, and enters Florida just north of Jacksonville. It continues south past Daytona Beach, the Space Coast, Vero Beach, Palm Beach, and Fort Lauderdale, ending just south of Miami.

Interstate 75 begins in Michigan at the Canadian border and runs south through Ohio, Kentucky, Tennessee, and Georgia, then moves south through the center of the state before veering west into Tampa. It follows the west coast south to Naples, then crosses the state through the northern section of the Everglades, and ends in Miami. Despite its interstate status, the Interstate 75 stretch between Naples and just west of Fort Lauderdale levies a toll each way per car, with higher tolls for motor homes, boat carriers, and such.

California and most Southern and Southwestern states are connected to Florida by Interstate 10, which moves east from Los Angeles through Arizona, New Mexico, Texas, Louisiana, Mississippi, and Alabama. It enters Florida at Pensacola and runs straight across the northern part of the state, ending in Jacksonville.

SUNPASS

To save time and money while on the road, you may want to purchase a SunPass for your personal or rental vehicle. It provides a discount on most tolls, and you'll be able to sail past collection booths without stopping. You also can use SunPass to pay for parking at Palm Beach, Miami, and Fort Lauderdale airports. (SunPass now interfaces with North Carolina's Quick Pass and Georgia's Peach Pass.) With SunPass—transponders can be purchased for $4.99 to $25, at drugstores, supermarkets, or tourism welcome centers—you can charge up with a credit card and reload as needed. For more info, check out ⊕ www.sunpass.com.

RENTAL CARS

Unless you're going to plant yourself at a beach or theme-park resort, you really need a vehicle to get around in Florida. Rental rates, which are loaded with taxes, fees, and other costs, sometimes can start around $35 a day/$160 a week, plus the aforementioned add-ons. In Florida you must be 21 to rent a car, must have a credit card, and need to know rates are higher if you're under 25.

ROAD CONDITIONS

Downtown areas of major cities can be extremely congested during rush hours, usually 7–9 am and 3:30–6:30 pm or later on weekdays. ■TIP➔ Florida has a website (www.fl511.com) with real-time traffic information for six regional zones.

RULES OF THE ROAD

Speed limits are generally 60 mph on state highways, 30 mph within city limits and residential areas, and 70 mph on interstates, some Orlando-area toll roads, and Florida's Turnpike. Supervising adults must ensure that children under age seven are positioned in federally approved child car seats. Infants up to 20 pounds must be secured in rear-facing carriers in the backseat. Children younger than four years old must be strapped into a separate carrier or child seat; children four through five

CAR RENTAL RESOURCES

Local Agencies

Gold Coast Car Rental (Fort Lauderdale)	800/421–8752 or 954/522–0665	www.gold-coastcruise-andflyparking.com
Sunshine Rent A Car (Fort Lauderdale)	888/786–7446 or 954/467–8100	www.sunshi-nerentacar.com

Major Agencies

Alamo	877/222–9075	www.alamo.com
Avis	800/331–1212	www.avis.com
Budget	800/218–7992	www.budget.com
Hertz	800/654–3131	www.hertz.com
National Car Rental	800/227–7368	www.nation-alcar.com

can be secured in a separate carrier, an integrated child seat, or by a seat belt. The driver will be held responsible for passengers under the age of 18 who aren't wearing seat belts, and all front-seat passengers are required to wear seat belts.

Florida's Alcohol/Controlled Substance DUI Law is one of the toughest in the United States. A blood-alcohol level of 0.08 or higher can have serious repercussions even for a first-time offender.

▮ FERRY TRAVEL

If you would like to avoid road traffic to the Keys and make the trip a watery adventure, Key West Express ferries people from Fort Myers Beach on a daily basis (and Marco Island in season) to Key West's historic seaport. The trip, just under four hours, is cheaper than airfare, and doesn't require months-in-advance booking.

Contact Key West Express. ✉ *1200 Main St., Fort Myers* ☎ *888/539–2628* ⊕ *www.keywest-express.us.*

ESSENTIALS

■ ACCOMMODATIONS

In general, peak seasons are during Christmas/New Year's holidays and late January through Easter. Holiday weekends at any point during the year are packed; if you're considering home or condo rentals, minimum-stay requirements are longer during these periods, too. Fall is the slowest season, with only a few exceptions (Key West is jam-packed for the 10-day Fantasy Fest at Halloween). Rates are low and availability is high, but this is also prime time for hurricanes.

Children are generally welcome throughout Florida, except for some Key West B&Bs and inns; however, the buck stops at spring breakers. While many hotels allow them—and some even cater to them—most rental agencies won't lease units to anyone under 25 without a guardian present.

Pets, although allowed at many hotels (one upscale chain, Kimpton, with properties in Miami and Palm Beach, celebrates its pet friendliness with treats in the lobby and doggie beds for rooms), often carry an extra flat-rate fee for cleaning and de-allergen treatments, and are not a sure thing. Inquire ahead if Fido is coming with you.

APARTMENT AND HOUSE RENTALS

The state's allure for visiting snowbirds (Northerners "flocking" to Florida in winter) has caused private home and condo rentals to boom in popularity, at times affording better options for vacationers, particularly families who want to have some extra space and cooking facilities. In some destinations, home and condo rentals are more readily available than hotels. Fort Myers, for example, doesn't have many luxury hotel properties downtown. Everything aside from beach towels is provided during a stay, but some things to consider are that sizable down

payments must be made at booking (15% to 50%), and the full balance is often due before arrival. Check for any cleaning fees (usually not more than $150). If being on the beach is of utmost importance, carefully screen properties that tout "water views," because they might actually be of bays, canals, or lakes rather than of the Gulf of Mexico or the Atlantic.

Finding a great rental agency can help you weed out the junk. Target offices that specialize in the area you want to visit, and have a personal conversation with a representative as soon as possible. Be honest about your budget and expectations. For example, let the rental agent know if having the living room couch pull double-duty as a bed is not OK. Although websites listing rentals directly from homeowners are growing in popularity, there's a higher chance of coming across Pinocchios advertising "gourmet" kitchens that have one or two nice gadgets but fixtures or appliances from 1982. To protect yourself, talk extensively with owners in advance, see if there's a system in place for accountability should something go wrong, and make sure there's a 24-hour phone number for emergencies.

Contacts Endless Vacation Rentals.
☎ 877/782–9387 ⊕ www.evrentals.com.
Florida Keys Rental Store. ✉ MM 82, 81800 Overseas Hwy., Upper Matecumbe Key ☎ 800/585–0584, 305/451–3879 ⊕ www. floridakeysrentalstore.com. **Freewheeler Vacations.** ✉ MM 98.5, 85992 Overseas Hwy., Key Largo ☎ 866/664–2075, 305/664–2075 ⊕ www.freewheeler-realty.com. **Interhome.** ☎ 954/791–8282, 800/882–6864 ⊕ www. interhomeusa.com. **Villas International.** ☎ 415/499–9490, 800/221–2260 ⊕ www. villasintl.com.

BED-AND-BREAKFASTS

Small inns and guesthouses in Florida range from modest, cozy places with home-style breakfasts and owners who treat you like family, to elegantly furnished

Victorian houses with four-course breakfasts and rates to match. Since most B&Bs are small, they rely on various agencies and organizations to get the word out and coordinate reservations.

Reservation Services Bed & Breakfast Inns Online. ☏ 800/215-7365 ⊕ www.bbonline. com. **BedandBreakfast.com.** ☏ 512/322–2710, 800/462-2632 ⊕ www.bedandbreakfast.com. **Florida Bed & Breakfast Inns.** ☏ 561/223-9550 ⊕ www.florida-inns.com.

HOTELS AND RESORTS

Wherever you look in Florida you'll find lots of plain, inexpensive motels and luxurious resorts, independents alongside national chains, and an ever-growing number of modern properties as well as quite a few classics. All hotels listed have a private bath unless otherwise noted.

Hotel reviews have been shortened. For full reviews, visit Fodors.com.

■ EATING OUT

Smoking is banned statewide in most enclosed indoor workplaces, including restaurants. Exemptions are permitted for stand-alone bars where food takes a backseat to libations.

One caution: raw oysters pose a potential danger for people with chronic illness of the liver, stomach, or blood, or who have immune disorders. All Florida restaurants that serve raw oysters must post a notice in plain view warning of the risks associated with their consumption.

MEALS AND MEALTIMES

Unless otherwise noted, you can assume that the restaurants we recommend are open daily for lunch and dinner.

RESERVATIONS AND DRESS

We discuss reservations only when they're essential (there's no other way you'll ever get a table) or when they're not accepted. It's always smart to make reservations when you can, particularly if your party is large or if it's high season. It's critical to do so at popular restaurants (book as

---

FLORIDA'S SCENIC TRAILS

Florida has some 8,000 miles of land-based routes (plus another 4,000 miles for paddling!). About 1,400 miles of these connect to create the Florida Trail, one of only 11 National Scenic Trails in the United States. Info on top segments is available at ⊕ www.floridatrail.org, and you can find a searchable list of all trails at ⊕ www. visitflorida.com/trails.

far ahead as possible, often 30 days, and reconfirm on arrival).

We mention dress only when men are required to wear a jacket or a jacket and tie. Expect places with dress codes to truly adhere to them.

Restaurant reviews have been shortened. For full reviews, visit Fodors.com.

Contacts OpenTable. ⊕ www.opentable.com.

■ HEALTH

Sunburn and heat prostration are concerns, even in winter. So hit the beach or play tennis, golf, or another outdoor sport before 10 am or after 3 pm. If you must be out at midday, limit exercise, drink plenty of nonalcoholic liquids, and wear both sunscreen and a hat. If you feel faint, get out of the sun and sip water slowly.

Even on overcast days, ultraviolet rays shine through the haze, so use a sunscreen with an SPF of at least 15, and have children wear a waterproof SPF 30 or higher.

While you're frolicking on the beach, steer clear of what look like blue bubbles on the sand. These are Portuguese men-of-war, and their tentacles can cause an allergic reaction. Also be careful of other large jellyfish, some of which can sting.

If you walk across a grassy area on the way to the beach, you'll probably encounter the tiny, light-brown, incredibly prickly sand spurs. If you get stuck with one, just pull it out.

■ HOURS OF OPERATION

Many museums are closed Monday but have late hours on another weekday and are usually open on weekends. Some museums have days when admission is free. Popular attractions are usually open every day but Thanksgiving and Christmas Day. Watch out for seasonal closures at smaller venues; we list opening hours for all sights we recommend, but these can change on short notice. If you're visiting during a transitional month (for example, May in the southern part of the state), it's always best to call before showing up.

■ MONEY

Prices here are given for adults. Substantially reduced fees are almost always available for children, students, and senior citizens.

CREDIT CARDS

We cite information about credit cards only if they aren't accepted at a restaurant or a hotel. Otherwise, assume that most major credit cards are acceptable.

It's good to inform your credit-card company before you travel to prevent it from putting a hold on your card owing to unusual activity—not a good thing halfway through your trip. Record all your credit-card numbers—as well as the phone numbers to call if your cards are lost or stolen—in a safe place, so you're prepared should something go wrong.

Both MasterCard and Visa have general numbers you can call if your card is lost, but you're better off calling the number of your issuing bank, since MasterCard and Visa usually just transfer you to your bank; your bank's number is usually printed on your card.

Reporting Lost Cards American Express. ☎ 800/528-4800 ⊕ www.americanexpress. com. **Diners Club.** ☎ 800/234-6377 ⊕ www. dinersclub.com. **Discover.** ☎ 800/347-2683 ⊕ www.discovercard.com. **MasterCard.** ☎ 800/622-7747 ⊕ www.mastercard.com. **Visa.** ☎ 800/847-2911 ⊕ www.visa.com.

■ PACKING

Northern Florida is much cooler in winter than southern Florida, so pack a heavy sweater or more. Even in summer, ocean breezes can be cool, so it's good to have a lightweight sweater or jacket.

Aside from an occasional winter cold spell (when the mercury drops to, say, 50), Miami and the Naples–Fort Myers areas are usually warm year-round and extremely humid in summer. Be prepared for sudden storms all over in summer, and note that plastic raincoats are uncomfortable in the high humidity. Often, storms are quick, often in the afternoons, and the sun comes back in no time. (This also means that it's best to get in your beach time earlier in the day; if it's nice in the morning in August, go to the beach. Don't wait.)

Dress is casual throughout the state—sundresses, sandals, or walking shorts are appropriate. Palm Beach is more polos and pearls, Miami is designer jeans, and elsewhere the Tommy Bahama–esque look dominates. Even beach gear is OK at a lot of places, but just make sure you've got a proper outfit on (shirt, shorts, and shoes). A very small number of restaurants request that men wear jackets and ties, but most don't. Where there are dress codes, they tend to be fully adhered to. Take note that the strictest places are golf and tennis clubs. Many ask that you wear whites or at least special sport shoes and attire. Be prepared for air-conditioning working in overdrive anywhere you go.

You can generally swim year-round in peninsular Florida from about New Smyrna Beach south on the Atlantic coast and from Tarpon Springs south on the Gulf Coast. Bring a sun hat and sunscreen.

∎ SAFETY

Stepped-up policing against thieves preying on tourists in rental cars has helped address what was a serious issue in the mid-1990s. Still, visitors should be wary when driving in unfamiliar neighborhoods and leaving the airport, especially near Miami. Don't leave valuables unattended—and that can include food and drink—while you walk the beach or go for a dip. And never leave handbags, cameras, etc., in your vehicle. Visitors have reported theft of belongings while stopped for meals as they travel to or from the airport. Don't blatantly stow valuables in your car trunk just before walking away, either, since thieves can be adept at popping lids. And don't assume that valuables are safe in your hotel room; use in-room safes or the hotel's safety-deposit boxes. Try to use ATMs only during the day or in brightly lighted, well-traveled locales.

If you're visiting Florida during the June through November hurricane season and a hurricane is imminent, be sure to follow safety orders and evacuation instructions from local authorities.

∎ TAXES

Florida has no state personal income tax, instead heavily relying on tourism revenues. The state sales tax in Florida is 6% (with the exception of most groceries and medicine); when combined with local taxes, the total sales tax rate is between 6% and 7.5%. Hotel taxes, often called "bed taxes," "resort taxes," or "transient rental taxes," vary. In Central Florida, including Orlando, for example, taxes on purchases range from 6.5% to 7%. A 6%

resort tax is imposed on all hotel rooms in addition to the sales tax.

Palm Beach County has raised its bed tax to 6%, for a combined total of 12% with state sales tax. In Greater Fort Lauderdale, the bed tax is 5%, for a combined total of 11%.

∎ TIME

South Florida is in the Eastern time zone.

∎ TIPPING

Tip airport valets or hotel bellhops $1 to $3 per bag (there typically is also a charge to check bags outside the terminal, but this isn't a tip). Maids often get $1 to $2 per night per guest, more at high-end resorts or if you require special services, ideally left each morning since the person servicing your room or suite could change from day to day during your stay. Room service waiters still hope to receive a 15% tip despite hefty room-service charges and service fees, which often don't go to the waiters. A door attendant or parking valet hopes to get $1 to $3. Waiters generally count on 15% to 20% (on the before-tax amount) or more, depending on your demands for special service. Bartenders get $1 or $2 per round of drinks. Golf caddies get 15% of the greens fee.

∎ VISITOR INFORMATION

Contact Visit Florida. ✉ *Visit Florida, 2540 W. Executive Center Circle, Tallahassee* ☎ *850/488–5607, 877/435–2872* ⊕ *www.visitflorida.com.*

INDEX

PHOTO CREDITS

Front cover: Stelios Michael / Alamy [Description: Art Deco Hotels on Ocean Drive, South Beach, Miami, Florida]. 1, Visit Florida. 2-3, Fotoluminate I Dreamstime.com. 5, FloridaStock/Shutterstock. **Chapter 1: Experience South Florida:** 8-9, S.Borisov/Shutterstock. 13, fun- inthetub, Fodors.com member. 14 and 15, Jeff Greenberg/age fotostock. 16 (left), Visit Florida. 16 (right), JeffGreenberg/ Alamy. 17 (top right), RIEGER Bertrand/ age fotostock. 17 (left), Lisa5201/iStockphoto. 17 (bottom right), Jloveland/Shutterstock. **Chapter 2: Miami and Miami Beach:** 21, iStockphoto. 22, Stuart Westmorland/age fotostock. 23, Jeff Greenberg/age fotostock. 24, Roxana Gonzalez/Shutterstock. 25(top), JUPITERIMAGES/ Brand X / Alamy. 25 (bottom), Alena Haurylik / Shutterstock. 26, Ivan Cholakov/ Shutterstock. 40, Garth Aikens/Miami Beach Convention Center. 46, Robert Harding Picture Library Ltd / Alamy. 71 (left), dk/Alamy. 71 (right), Nicholas Pitt/Alamy. 73 (top), Nicholas Pitt/Alamy. 73 (second from top), Ryan Forbes / AVABLU. 73 (3rd from top), Ian Patrick Alamy. 73 (4th from top), Laura Paresky. 73 (bottom), Tinamou I Dreamstime.com. 74 (top), INTERFOTO Pressebildagentur/ Alamy. 74 (bottom left), Ian Patrick/Alamy. 74 (bottom right), culliganphoto/Alamy. 81, John Tunney I Dreamstime.com. **Chapter 3: The Everglades:** 103, David Lyons / Alamy. 104, Visit Florida. 105, FloridaStock/Shutterstock. 106-07, tbkmedia.de/Alamy. 110 (left), inga spence/Alamy. 110 (top center), FloridaStock/Shutterstock. 110 (bottom center), Andrewtappert/wikipedia. org. 110 (top right), wikipedia.org. 110 (bottom right), David R. Frazier Photolibrary, Inc./Alamy. 111 (top left), Larsek/Shutterstock. 111 (bottom left), Caleb Foster/Shutterstock. 111 (bottom center), mlorenz/ Shutterstock. 111 (top right), umar faruq/Shutterstock. 111 (bottom right), Peter Arnold, Inc./Alamy. 112 (left), John A. Anderson/Shutterstock. 112 (top right), FloridaStock/Shutterstock. 112 (bottom center), Norman Bateman/Shutterstock. 112 (bottom right), FloridaStock/Shutterstock. 113 (top left), David Drake & Deborah Jaffe. 113 (bottom left), Krzysztof Slusarczyk/Shutterstock. 113 (bottom center), Norman Bateman/Shutterstock. 113 (right), Jerry Zitterman/Shutterstock. 115, Larsek/Shutterstock. 123, Steven Widoff / Alamy. 128, Marc Muench / Alamy. 133, jimfeng/iStockphoto. 138, Visit Florida. **Chapter 4: The Florida Keys:** 143, f11photo / Shutterstock. 144, Pawel Lipiec/iStockphoto. 145, Sheri Armstrong/Shutterstock. 146, Gregory Wrona / Alamy. 147 (top), Claudio Lovo/ Shutterstock. 147 (bottom), Michael Ventura/Alamy. 148, Meinzahn I Dreamstime.com. 156, Stephen Frink/ Florida Keys News Bureau. 165, flasporty/flickr. 171, Korzeniewski I Dreamstime.com. 172, PBorowka/Shutterstock. 175, Melissa Schalke/iStockphoto. 184, Henryk Sadura / Alamy. 196, CedarBendDrive/Flickr. 199, Visit Florida. 201, John P Franzis. 212, Starwood Hotels & Resorts. 216, Daniel Korzeniewski / Shutterstock. **Chapter 5: Fort Lauderdale:** 225, James Schwabel / age fotostock. 227 (top), Dean Bergmann/iStockphoto. 227 (bottom), Jeff Greenberg / Alamy. 228, Jorg Hackemann/Shutterstock. 237, Nicholas Pitt /Alamy. 246, Eric Gevaert/Shutterstock. 251, Lago Mar Resort & Club. 259, Terrance Klassen / age fotostock. **Chapter 6: Palm Beach and the Treasure Coast:** 263, RIEGER Bertrand/age fotostock. 265, Perry Correll/Shutterstock. 266, FloridaStock/Shutterstock. 271, Sargent Photography. 276, mrk_photo/flickr. 279, FloridaStock/Shutterstock. 290, Andre Jenny / Alamy. 294, Morikami Museum and Japanese Gardens. 310 and 324, Visit Florida. **Back cover:** (from left to right), Chuck Wagner/Shutterstock; Tap10/Shutterstock; ShaneKato/iStockphoto. **Spine:** Michael Phillips/iStockphoto.

About Our Writers: All photos are courtesy of the writers except for the following: Lynne Helm, courtesy of John Rude.

NOTES

NOTES

NOTES

NOTES

NOTES

NOTES

NOTES

ABOUT OUR WRITERS

After being hired sight unseen by a South Florida newspaper, Fort Lauderdale–based freelance travel writer and editor Lynne Helm arrived from the Midwest anticipating a few years of palm-fringed fun. More than a quarter century later (after covering the state for several newspapers, consumer magazines, and trade publications), she's still enamored of Florida's sun-drenched charms. Lynne updated the Everglades chapter.

Updating the Florida Keys and much of the Lower Gulf Coast is Miami native, Jill Martin. As a freelance writer, she has blogged more than 1,000 articles for the state's tourism website, Visit Florida, and also writes for various travel sites and print magazines. She has appeared on numerous TV and radio shows as a Florida travel expert and is the creator of Sunshine Brain Games, a trivia card game all about Florida. She resides full time in the Redland and part time on Sanibel.

Galena Mosovich, who updated Fort Lauderdale, is known for covering cutting-edge developments and personalities in cocktail culture, gastronomy, travel, and visual art for top publications. In 2015, she spent time in Europe and Japan, bringing her back to South Florida with endless inspiration. She's considered an international expert on cocktails and was selected to judge the 2014 Spirited Awards at Tales of the Cocktail as well as the World's 50 Best Bars competition for Drinks International (2014–2016). Galena was raised in Coral Springs, in the northwest corner of Broward County, and she now lives in Miramar with her two dogs.

Paul Rubio's quest to discover the world has taken him to 107 countries and counting. Paul graduated from Harvard in 2002 with master's degrees in both Public Administration and Economics, but in 2008 he gave into his passion and became a full-time travel writer. He's won over a dozen national awards for his articles and guidebooks. The prolific writer is the travel editor of *Palm Beach Illustrated, Naples Illustrated,* and *Weddings Illustrated* and regularly contributes to *Ultratravel US, Robb Report, Private Clubs,* and the full family of Modern Luxury publications.